Ensuring America's Health

Ensuring America's Health explains why the U.S. health care system offers world-class medical services to some patients but is also exceedingly costly, with fragmented care, poor distribution, and increasingly bureaucratized processes. Based on exhaustive historical research, this work traces how public and private power merged to favor a distinctive economic model that places insurance companies at the center of the system, where they both finance and oversee medical care. Although the insurance company model was created during the 1930s, it continues to drive health care cost and quality problems today. This wide-ranging work not only evaluates the overarching political and economic framework of the medical system but also provides rich narrative detail, examining the political dramas, corporate maneuverings, and forceful personalities that created American health care as we know it. This book breaks new ground in the fields of health care history, organizational studies, and American political economy.

Christy Ford Chapin is an assistant professor in the department of history at the University of Maryland, Baltimore County. Her areas of research include political, economic, and business history as well as the history of capitalism. A key question driving her research is how the blending of public and private power has created a distinctive form of capitalism – American capitalism. Chapin has won numerous awards to support her work, including the John E. Rovensky Fellowship in American Business and Economic History and a Miller Center for Public Affairs Fellowship. Her work has been published in *Studies in American Political Development*, the *Journal of Policy History*, *Enterprise and Society*, and the *Business History Review*.

Ensuring America's Health

The Public Creation of the Corporate Health Care System

CHRISTY FORD CHAPIN

University of Maryland, Baltimore County

CAMBRIDGE
UNIVERSITY PRESS

CAMBRIDGE
UNIVERSITY PRESS

University Printing House, Cambridge CB2 8BS, United Kingdom

One Liberty Plaza, 20th Floor, New York, NY 10006, USA

477 Williamstown Road, Port Melbourne, VIC 3207, Australia

4843/24, 2nd Floor, Ansari Road, Daryaganj, Delhi - 110002, India

79 Anson Road, #06-04/06, Singapore 079906

Cambridge University Press is part of the University of Cambridge.

It furthers the University's mission by disseminating knowledge in the pursuit of education, learning and research at the highest international levels of excellence.

www.cambridge.org
Information on this title: www.cambridge.org/9781107622876

© Christy Ford Chapin 2015

This publication is in copyright. Subject to statutory exception and to the provisions of relevant collective licensing agreements, no reproduction of any part may take place without the written permission of Cambridge University Press.

First published 2015
First paperback edition 2017

A catalogue record for this publication is available from the British Library

Library of Congress Cataloging in Publication data
Chapin, Christy Ford, author.
Ensuring America's health : the public creation of the corporate health care system / Christy Ford Chapin.
p. ; cm.
ISBN 978-1-107-04488-3 (Hardback)
I. Title.
[DNLM: 1. Delivery of Health Care–United States. 2. Health Care Reform–United States. 3. History, 20th Century–United States. 4. Insurance, Health–United States. 5. Professional Corporations–United States. W 84 AA1]
RA410.53 362.10973–dc23
2014036381

ISBN 978-1-107-04488-3 Hardback
ISBN 978-1-107-62287-6 Paperback

In memory of my father and for "the kids"

Contents

Acknowledgments

The very first person I wish to thank is my adviser, Brian Balogh. Brian is the model of what an adviser should be – both patient and brilliant. As I worked on the dissertation, Brian's incisive, penetrating insights helped me expand the boundaries of my investigation and improve the work's clarity and analysis.

I am indebted to Lou Galambos, who has tutored me on everything from political economy to developing "rhinoceros-thick skin" (a phrase that Galambos students everywhere will recognize).

At the University of Virginia, I received a good deal of assistance and kindness from Bernie Carlson. I also wish to thank Olivier Zunz, Eric Patashnik, Stephen Schuker, Sid Milkis, Mel Leffler, Herman Schwartz, and Guian McKee. I was fortunate to have as peers and friends Laura Phillips Sawyer, Emily Charnock, Andrew McGee, Logan Sawyer, Amy Rebecca Jacobs, Julian Hayter, and Allison Elias.

Larry D. Brown generously shared his vast store of health care expertise; he read the entire manuscript and provided me with invaluable feedback. For advising me either on the manuscript or academia while offering encouragement to aid me through the long endeavor of researching and writing a book, I wish to thank Julia Ott, Deborah Stone, Sharon Murphy Forziati, Mark Rose, Walter Friedman, Pamela Laird, David Sicilia, Ken Lipartito, Richard John, David Freund, Roger Horowitz, Nancy Robertson, Donald Critchlow, Rosemary Stevens, and Ed Berkowitz.

I have been privileged to be teaching in a collegial and supportive history department at the University of Maryland, Baltimore County (UMBC). I am especially grateful to Amy Froide, Marjoleine Kars, Dan

Ritschel, Michelle Scott, and Meredith Oyen. I appreciate the support of our dean, Scott Casper. Kate Brown's guidance has made me a better historian and storyteller.

As I traveled the country doing archival work, I received help from numerous people. Going above and beyond the call of duty were Jane Selph at the Medical Society of Virginia; Sarita Oertling at the History of Medicine Collections, University of Texas Medical Branch; and Brian Hobbs at the Archives and Special Collections of the University of Nebraska–Lincoln Libraries. I am greatly obliged to Robert Cunningham III for allowing me to invade his basement and shed to access his father's Blue Cross and Blue Shield papers. Jim Ashton's and David Anderson's editing assistance were very useful.

At Cambridge University Press, I received sage advice and assistance from Lew Bateman and his assistant Shaun Vigil. Joseph Gautham Ramou, the Project Manager, was quick, accommodating, and courteous.

This manuscript was completed with support from the Miller Center of Public Affairs; a John E. Rovensky Fellowship from the Business History Conference; an American Historical Association Albert J. Beveridge Grant; a UMBC Summer Faculty Fellowship; and several awards from the University of Virginia, including the Bankard Fund for Political Economy Fellowship, a Dissertation Acceleration Fellowship, and an Award for Excellence in Scholarship in the Humanities and Social Sciences.

Finally, I wish to acknowledge my family. I appreciate the kindness and support of Angie, Corin, Mike, and Janet. Mercedes Barreda Ford, my dear abuelita and Oma, thank you. I am grateful to my son Brandt whose overflowing, joyful spirit continually reminded me to get over myself and live fully present in each moment. This book is dedicated to the memory of my father, Douglas "Kiko" Ford, who sacrificed his life to raise six children by himself. He nurtured "the kids" with loving care, intelligence, and wisdom, training us to seek larger truths by connecting every situation and detail, no matter how seemingly mundane, to broader ideas of philosophy, economics, politics, and religion. Finally, to my brothers and sisters – Matthew, Scott, Tesha, Nicole, and Mark – thank you for teaching me and loving me. Perhaps one day I will write our story.

Abbreviations

AALL	American Association for Labor Legislation
ACA	Patient Protection and Affordable Care Act
AFL	American Federation of Labor
AFL-CIO	American Federation of Labor and Congress of Industrial Organizations
AHA	American Hospital Association
AHIP	America's Health Insurance Plans
ALC	American Life Convention
AMA	American Medical Association
AMCP	Associated Medical Care Plans
AMPAC	American Medical Political Action Committee
BCA	Blue Cross Association
BCBSA	Blue Cross and Blue Shield Association
Bureau	Bureau of Accident and Health Underwriters
CCMC	Committee on the Costs of Medical Care
CES	Committee on Economic Security
CHAMPUS	Civilian Health and Medical Program of the Uniformed Services
CHIP	Comprehensive Health Insurance Program
CIO	Congress of Industrial Organizations
Conference	Health and Accident Underwriters Conference
COPE	Committee on Political Education
CPS	California Physicians Service
DRG	Diagnosis-Related Group
FEHBP	Federal Employees Health Benefits Program
FTC	Federal Trade Commission
GHA	Group Health Association
HEW	Department of Health, Education, and Welfare
HIAA	Health Insurance Association of America (known today as AHIP)

HIC	Health Insurance Council
HMO	Health Maintenance Organization
HSA	Health Systems Agency
HSI	Health Services Incorporated
IESA	Insurance Economics Society of America
IRS	Internal Revenue Service
JAMA	*Journal of the American Medical Association*
LIAA	Life Insurance Association of America
MIA	Medical Indemnity of America
NABSP	National Association of Blue Shield Plans
NHI	National Health Insurance
NPC	National Physicians' Committee for the Extension of Medical Service
PSRO	Professional Standards Review Organization
RVS	Relative Value Scale
SAMA	Student American Medical Association
SSA	Social Security Administration
TNEC	Temporary National Economic Committee
UAW	United Automobile Workers
UCR	usual, customary, and reasonable (physician reimbursements)
UMW	United Mine Workers
UR	utilization review

Introduction

The U.S. health care system boasts outstanding care. From all across the globe, the wealthy travel to the United States to receive innovative treatments from accomplished physicians practicing in renowned medical centers. Yet the American medical system has glaring imperfections that have long puzzled observers.

Why is health care so expensive? Accounting for almost 18 percent of the nation's gross domestic product (GDP), the cost of American medical care is exorbitant. A yawning gap separates the United States from the second most expensive systems of Germany, France, and the Netherlands, which spend between 11 and 12 percent of GDP on medical services.[1] In the United States, high-priced health insurance has traditionally placed coverage out of the reach of many consumers who lack either employer subsidies or some form of government provision.

Furthermore, why is U.S. health care delivery fragmented? Rather than providing patients with integrated medical care in one location, physicians generally practice either individually or in single-specialty groups. This structure forces elderly, chronically ill, and difficult-to-diagnose patients to navigate arduous and lengthy care routes in an attempt to obtain services from various specialists. Because no single physician or group of physicians is responsible for the patient's complete care, doctors lack incentive to scrutinize the extensive prescription lists of elderly patients or ensure that difficult cases obtain proper diagnoses. In theory, general practitioners fill these roles. However, once a general practitioner has referred a patient to a specialist, only rarely do both physicians find space in their busy schedules to consult with each other, whether via phone or computer, about that patient. Moreover, general practitioners are not rewarded financially for taking time to sort through complex cases; they are usually paid flat annual per-patient fees or fixed reimbursements for office visits and certain services and procedures. They can consequently spend only so much time on activities that are not, to use a favorite term of lawyers, "billable."

This problem leads us to a related series of conundrums. What has happened to the "art" of medicine? Why do many physicians practice with one eye directed at the patient while the other eye is fixated on insurance company reimbursements and standardized treatment parameters?

The answer to these questions can be found in the distinctive economic arrangements that order health care financing and delivery – what I will refer to throughout this study as the "insurance company model." Insurance companies occupy a central position in medical care. Insurers decide which services and procedures qualify for policy coverage, influence physician pay and hospital revenues by setting reimbursement fees, and shape medical practices by requiring that health care providers follow treatment blueprints to obtain compensation. Many scholars have taken this authority for granted, assuming that insurance companies are filling an intrinsic role in private medical care. Yet the insurance company model was only one option among an array of organizational possibilities that might have structured the private market.[2] And in comparison with alternative arrangements, the insurance company model has delivered medical services less efficiently and more expensively.

So how did insurance companies acquire such a dominant role in health care? Politics – not the logic of the market – positioned insurance companies at the heart of American health care.

During the late 1930s, American Medical Association (AMA) leaders decided that, among all the ways of organizing medical services, insurance-company–funded policies offered physicians the most professional security. The AMA derived authority to shape the market not only from the doctoring profession's cultural standing, but also from state licensing and medical practice laws that endowed the association with regulatory power. For AMA officials, safeguarding physician sovereignty trumped economic efficiency. They therefore created a particular insurance company model: their design required insurers to reimburse the services of individual physicians rather than medical groups; compensate practitioners for each service or procedure provided; and allow doctors to practice medicine as they saw fit, free from supervision or interference. Both physicians and insurers hoped to severely limit health insurance.

Doctors feared losing autonomy to third-party financiers. Insurers were troubled by the cost implications of funding physicians who could arbitrarily increase the price and supply of medical services. Meanwhile, the AMA opposed and suppressed all other health care prepayment plans, whether sponsored by businesses, mutual aid societies, consumer organizations, unions, or even physician groups.

Professional calculations soon merged with national politics to cement into place the centrality of insurance companies. Most policymakers and health care experts – indeed, insurers themselves – recognized that insurance company financing that complied with AMA demands would cause problems. Of particular concern was the likelihood that the payment mechanism would rapidly drive up service costs and insurance premiums, thereby limiting coverage rates among the populace. To prevent such a scenario, both Democrats and Republicans offered numerous health care reform proposals throughout the 1940s and 1950s. Paradoxically, reform initiatives further entrenched the AMA-crafted insurance company model. This development occurred when insurers and physicians decided that the best way to defeat health care reform was by rapidly and dramatically expanding insurance in order to prove that the "voluntary"* market could supply generous, comprehensive coverage for all population groups.[3]

Predictably, as the insurance company model spread, medical costs skyrocketed. So ground-level organizations – insurance companies, physician offices, medical societies, and hospitals – began evolving to regulate the relationship between financiers and service providers. As insurers attempted to contain costs, they gradually expanded their function from simply financing services to also supervising medical care and coordinating the health care system.

Once a durable institutional framework was established in the private sector, policymakers began accommodating that pattern. In 1965, they built Medicare around the insurance company model: the program incorporated the financing and cost control structures that physicians and insurers had already created. Policymakers also appointed insurance companies to act as administrators on behalf of the federal government. Thus, over the course of approximately three decades, insurers developed from system outsiders into the primary financiers of voluntary health care as well as the overseers of both private and public medical services.

---

* Throughout this work, the terms "voluntary" and "private" will be used interchangeably. This reflects contemporary usage – how many interest group leaders, health care analysts, and policymakers used these terms during the period under study.

Meanwhile, policymakers and citizens came to see their role as a "natural" feature of the health care system.[4]

EXPLAINING DISTINCTIVE FEATURES OF U.S. HEALTH CARE

Understanding the insurance company model and how it came to govern health care sheds light on three system characteristics: high costs, fragmented care, and corporate arrangements. Most narratives assert that medical costs became a significant issue after the passage of Medicare.[5] Yet recognition of the cost problems associated with third-party financing that complied with AMA specifications discouraged commercial insurance companies from entering the health care market until the late 1930s – and even then they did so reluctantly, on the most restricted basis possible. By the end of the 1940s, most insurance company policies still limited coverage to a portion of hospital costs. Nevertheless, as medical insurance gained traction among consumers during this period, health care costs rose so quickly that they began outstripping price increases in every other category of goods and services.[6]

The fundamental principle of moral hazard warned underwriters not to issue insurance products that would decrease policyholders' incentive to avoid the risks for which they were insured. Home and automobile insurance have been stable underwriting fields because, barring outright fraud, subscribers attempt to avoid house fires and car accidents. Illness, however, is difficult to define, and many patients seek out excessive services and procedures when they are paid for by a third party. Most significantly, under the insurance company model, physicians – the individuals with the requisite expertise and skills to determine when a patient truly required medical care – were financially rewarded for providing as many services as possible. To comply with AMA guidelines, insurance companies had to reimburse physicians, not with set salaries or per-patient capitation fees, but on a fee-for-service basis. Moreover, for many years after the insurance company model was introduced, insurers lacked the authority to even question, much less regulate, physician practices. These broadly understood cost problems fueled health care reform initiatives throughout the 1940s and 1950s.

Other factors – including overprovision of care driven by physician fear of malpractice suits and increased demand from government programs such as Medicare – have certainly contributed to rising costs. Nevertheless, the insurance company model and the way it has structured patient and service provider incentives remains the primary culprit.[7] This legacy constitutes one of the greatest economic challenges facing Americans today.

Fragmented care emerged as a second key feature of the insurance company model. Fearing that corporate, hierarchical organization would overtake health care, AMA leaders insisted, from the time that they endorsed insurance in the 1930s, that insurers finance only individual physicians or, at most, doctors who practiced with one or two peers from the same specialty. Insurers were prohibited from contracting with multi-specialty organizations. This directive proved critical as, during the first half of the twentieth century, doctors demonstrated a desire to provide integrated patient care by forming groups that incorporated physicians from various specialties, ranging from general practitioners to surgeons and ophthalmologists. There were sound medical reasons to establish such groups as they facilitated discussion of complex cases. Moreover, because these groups were responsible for the entire patient – for the patient's overall wellness – doctors were impelled to find proper diagnoses, even in cases that required considerable amounts of diagnostic testing and consultation. Today, if a physician encounters difficulty with a chronically ill patient or tricky-to-diagnosis individual, the simplest course of action is to refer the patient to another doctor or specialist. If the patient never receives adequate care or a proper diagnosis, no one practitioner is respon-sible for or would likely even know the patient's final health outcome.

The third aspect of U.S. health care that this narrative explains is its corporate or pseudo-corporate structure. As health care coverage expanded and costs rose, insurance companies forged overlapping institutions with doctors and hospitals, creating payment systems, channels of communication, and cost containment procedures that established and tightened the financier–provider relationship. Through these structures, insurance companies grad-ually assumed the role of managers attempting to supervise the work of employees, in this case, physicians and hospital administrators.[8] Although the process occurred incrementally and only through numerous battles with service providers, insurance companies expanded their mandate from simply underwriting the risks associated with medical services consumption to, ultimately, regulating health care. This process began during the 1950s and continues to this day. In this way, insurance companies have become intri-cately involved in the delivery of care, issuing, in the name of cost control, blueprints and parameters that guide physicians on how to practice medicine.

ORGANIZATION OF THE NARRATIVE

To fully explore the organizations, ideas, and people that helped create the insurance company model, this narrative employs a multilevel institutional approach. Trade and professional associations acted as institutional bridges that connected events in the federal political realm with developments at the ground level, in the organizations – such as doctors' offices and insurance companies – that interacted directly with patients and policyholders. Thus, the primary characters in this story are the AMA, which represented physicians; the Health Insurance Association of America (HIAA, known today as America's Health Insurance Plans or AHIP), which promoted commercial or for-profit insurance companies; and the National Association of Blue Shield Plans (NABSP), which led nonprofit medical plans that insured physician services.[9] The leaders of these associations lobbied policymakers, not only to prevent the adoption of universal, government-managed health care but also to obstruct even modest reform policies that would have altered the insurance company model. The Blue Cross Association (BCA), which represented nonprofit hospital plans, played a crucial supporting role, peeling away from other private interests to favor limited government intervention in health care while also contesting the AMA for the loyalty of NABSP leaders. In addition to conducting political operations, each of these associations translated lessons learned during federal reform debates into marching orders that directed the economic behavior of members: physicians, insurance companies, and nonprofit insurance plans. This chain of command allowed interest groups to shape the health care market in response to the criticisms that political reformers lodged against the insurance company model.

Chapter 1 surveys early forms of health care organization, evaluating how, through the first half of the twentieth century, the AMA stifled an evolving and innovative market rife with numerous financing experiments. During the 1930s and 1940s, mounting calls for federal health care reform finally forced AMA officials to compromise and allow the market to progress beyond its nineteenth-century template. They approved health insurance *but only* policies funded by insurance companies that complied with stringent criteria, including fee-for-service compensation for individually practicing doctors. AMA leaders chose the insurance company model hoping to maintain physician independence by keeping third-party financiers far removed from the delivery of medical care.

Chapter 2 considers political developments under Presidents Harry S. Truman and Dwight D. Eisenhower. In response to the innate problems of the insurance company model, both Democrats and Republicans persistently attempted to reform the health care sector in order to provide broader and more generous insurance coverage. Private interests battled these measures by attempting to develop health insurance in a manner that would allow them to declare the voluntary market superior to any scenario that entailed federal intervention. Within this setting, physicians, for-profit insurance companies, and nonprofit plans jockeyed to obtain political power and market standing. Chapters 3 through 5 assess these activities by presenting detailed examinations of the AMA, HIAA, and NABSP. Evaluating the effectiveness of their divergent political, economic, and organizational strategies elucidates the contested nature of professional and occupational standing.[10]

Chapter 6 completes the process of tracing federal political influence through trade associations, down to ground-level organizations. It explores how insurance companies, nonprofit plans, AMA medical societies, physician offices, and hospitals developed to support the rapid growth of insurance products that were designed to mitigate political critiques. The problem of rising costs profoundly shaped their activities. Although insurers initially operated in the health care field entirely dependent on the goodwill and support of doctors and hospital leaders, as they pursued cost containment, they gradually inverted that relationship to obtain authority over service providers.

Chapter 7 reviews the Medicare debates between 1957 and 1965, examining them in the light of voluntary sector developments. Although health interests had sufficiently expanded insurance to thwart previous legislative reforms, the inherent inefficiency of private arrangements combined with the higher costs of caring for aged patients hindered their success in the field of elderly coverage. However, by this point, the policymakers seeking government-funded aged health care believed it necessary to harness the institutional scaffolding that insurers and physicians had already constructed. After years of maturation, the voluntary sector had far more organizational capacity than the public sector; moreover, employing existing financing and delivery structures allowed policymakers to brand Medicare as an ideologically moderate response to the problem of elderly care. By adopting the insurance company model that had previously been so controversial, Medicare validated that very paradigm and obscured numerous alternatives.

STATE–SOCIETY RELATIONS

Ensuring America's Health displays four closely related, indeed, overlapping themes that illuminate state–society relations. Each of these themes emphasizes the symbiotic relationship between public policy and private market development. In presenting this narrative about health care, I am advancing a larger project that attempts to dismantle the imaginary wall that scholars and opinion makers often erect between government and civil society.[11]

The first key point this history demonstrates is that the U.S. health care economy was assembled through intertwining public and private authority.[12] Scholars have increasingly brought private sector development into the narrative of health care policy. I build upon this theme to emphasize how a specific economic model, generally categorized as a creation of the private sector, is in fact rooted in complex state–society relations.[13] Even as attempts to reform health care failed, calls for government intercession reverberated through the medical services market, shifting the economic strategies and actions of private interests. Through public policy debates, government officials and reformers articulated their aims for health insurance growth and the insurance product's design, including liberal coverage benefits. Trade associations hurried to accomplish these goals to forestall federal programming. Indeed, the consistent pattern of interaction between policymakers and large interest groups created a variety of corporatism, a "soft corporatism," in which the government played an informal and indirect – although pivotal – role in fashioning the "private" market's final form. Though policymakers did not wish to expand the insurance company model, they nevertheless accomplished their objectives of making medical insurance policies widely available and more generous.[14]

Second, just as one cannot understand market configuration without looking to the political sphere, one cannot fully appreciate the nature of political debates or the choices that legislators made in assembling public programs without delineating the voluntary market's architecture. The insurance company model's deficiencies animated reform debates throughout the tenures of both Truman and Eisenhower. At the same time, as the institutions supporting private health insurance matured, their very presence narrowed the range of options available to politicians seeking reform. Thus, the voluntary sector demarcated the boundaries of political debates and informed the distinctive attributes of government programming. By the mid-1960s, federal officials were ready to legitimize the insurance company model by designing Medicare to adopt its structural arrangements and by appointing insurance companies and nonprofit plans as program administrators. Since the passage of Medicare, it has been almost impossible to dislodge the insurance company model from the health care system.

The third major theme – path dependency – explains why these public–private linkages endured. Institution building creates path dependency. During the 1930s, neither the public nor private sectors were organized to meet mass consumer demand for health insurance. A critical juncture occurred when AMA leaders designated the insurance company model the only acceptable form of health care prepayment, thereby determining the particular avenue through which the public–private compact would be negotiated. The insurance company framework subsequently filtered the range of acceptable responses to political pressure, and health interests swiftly advanced the market through AMA-blessed provisions. The decision of policymakers to design Medicare around insurance company arrangements represented the zenith of this feedback process. Moreover, unlike organizations, which have defined boundaries, institutions drive broader transformations, embodying the "rules of the game in a society" or "the humanly devised constraints that shape human interaction."[15] As the insurance company model and its products expanded, the tacit assumptions and ideas supporting them became entrenched. Thus, evolving institutional norms endowed a particular economic model with cultural power and, eventually, political authority, bestowing upon it an air of naturalness and inevitability.[16]

The final theme examined in this narrative is the interrelated nature of political and economic power among private actors. Analyzing trade associations' planning and behavior reveals the extent to which professional and occupational authority is contingent upon policy developments. Not only did the AMA's battle to prevent federal intervention in health care fall short, but doctors also failed to escape corporate organization with its attendant third-party controls and regulations. Furthermore, after Medicare's passage, the reputation of the AMA as a collection of compassionate experts laboring for the public good lay in tatters.[17]

Meanwhile, insurers elevated their station in the marketplace and in the federal political arena: after Medicare's passage, they joined with public policymakers to restrict service provider sovereignty as the primary means toward reducing costs. Insurance company dictates, constructed to depress health care prices, increasingly constrained the earning potential of doctors, or at least how they earned their income, and regimented the practice of medicine. Yet for all the problems associated with the insurance company model, it has proven resilient. Indeed, the recent passage of comprehensive health care reform has only further embedded insurance companies in their position at the center of the American medical system.

Background: Physicians Choose the Insurance Company Model, Late Nineteenth Century–1940s

Throughout the twentieth century, American physicians exercised an enormous degree of cultural authority. Occupational groups possess cultural authority to the extent that they can shape the institutions, collective ideas, scripts, and patterns of behavior that order human interactions within their sphere of activity.[1]

Associations are key to securing this power. Whether medical, legal, or academic, professional associations secure cultural authority by establishing and validating member expertise to the public. Educational and credentialing requirements, even ethical codes, verify that members of a profession belong to an "exclusive, elite group" meriting broad grants of societal influence.[2] Founded in 1847, the American Medical Association (AMA) helped doctors renovate their somewhat humble occupation into an esteemed, powerful profession. However, the task of securing command over health care and then elevating the profession was filled with conflict and uncertainty – the process required AMA leaders to negotiate with, haggle among, and even bully other societal groups, ranging from competing medical practitioners to political challengers.

At the end of the nineteenth century, revolutionary scientific advances endowed physicians with valuable knowledge and skills in the most critical of subjects – human life. AMA leaders seized upon and leveraged this expertise to acquire governing power over the medical sector. They secured licensing laws that permitted them to determine who could become a physician and also deployed substantial control over the organizations most crucial to the production of health services: medical schools and hospitals.[3] Through these mechanisms, American physicians became the chief arbiters of what constitutes a legitimate disease or illness and the appropriate standards of care. If you question the importance of who defines illness, consider recent debates over whether alcoholism, post-traumatic stress disorder, and chronic fatigue syndrome are valid diagnoses. Only by obtaining conferral of disease status from organized physicians have such illness categories been able to garner significant research funding, ready access to health services, and treatment reimbursements from insurance companies and governmental programs.

American physicians have not only controlled the meaning and practice of medical care, they have also molded the economic and political arrangements that intersect with their professional realm. In an effort to protect physician dominion, AMA leaders waged war against so-called third-party influence over health care. Among their many battles, a key campaign occurred during the first half of the twentieth century when the AMA brandished its full regulatory power to weaken and destroy private efforts to make medical services more broadly accessible. At least partially in response to the ways in which organized physicians had retarded market development, policymakers began calling for federal health care reform during the 1930s. To thwart calls for government oversight, AMA officials reluctantly endorsed a method of financing that allowed third parties to enter medical care – that is, health insurance. But it was a particular, indeed peculiar, kind of insurance. Among the numerous possible ways of financing and delivering health care, AMA leaders chose an inherently inefficient and costly method: the insurance company model. As this model developed, it grew to structure the entire medical services market while also animating political debates and limiting the choices available to policymakers.

THE EARLY YEARS: PHYSICIANS FORGE A COLLECTIVE IDENTITY

During the nineteenth century, physician prestige and societal stature were determined largely on an individual basis. As a collective entity, the profession had a rather modest standing. Because many of their medical treatments were ineffective, physicians contended for patients alongside an array of healers, ranging from midwives to homeopathic practitioners. Although they founded the AMA at midcentury, physician leaders had to wait for the groundbreaking medical discoveries of the 1870s and 1880s to begin building a robust identity for their profession.[4]

Before the twentieth century, doctoring displayed the fluidity of labor specialization in health care. Particularly in the medium-sized and small towns that permeated the American landscape, physicians filled numerous roles, ranging from nurse to surgeon. They bandaged wounds, tended to the chronically ill, delivered babies, and performed "kitchen-table" surgeries. Even as doctors began writing prescriptions for patients to fill with the local druggist, they continued to dispense calomel, quinia pills, and opium from their little black bags.[5]

The portable black bag was an emblem of the physician's itinerant practice. While some doctors hung a shingle over a Main Street office or dedicated a room in their residence to medical service, many physicians made so many house calls that they chiefly practiced in patient homes. Not until the first decades of the twentieth century would the telephone begin to replace the errand boy or anxious mother calling on physicians to deliver patient care at all hours of the day and night. Owing to the peripatetic nature of their duties, doctors were among the first occupational groups to purchase automobiles. "Dr. Vehicle can salute acquaintances as his carriage or automobile meets them and ride on," counseled a physician advice book. It likewise warned that "Dr. Dustyfoot may be compelled to stop and lose valuable time in conversation with the convalescent patient, old friends, and other acquaintances."[6]

Doctors had strong social ties to their communities because they were in attendance for the most intimate family moments. During routine house calls, the physician might check on a tubercular shut-in or administer mandrake root juice for a child's ringworm. Such visits usually included friendly banter with the patient, family members, and neighbors about the yearly crop or town politics. In graver situations – following the loss of a baby due to breech presentation, a farm accident requiring limb amputation, or multiple deaths during a diphtheria outbreak – patients and their loved ones often looked to the physician for solace. For the good doctor not only tended to corporeal maladies, he (the physician would almost never be a "she") also dispensed "light and hope and comfort" to remedy emotional and spiritual wounds.[7]

While close interpersonal relationships and comparatively higher education levels bolstered the doctor's community status, each physician had to take great care to establish his reputation as a medical expert. Patients had good reason to question doctors. Through about the first half of the nineteenth century, physicians often treated patients using the theory of bodily fluids or "humors." As they attempted to balance these humors, physicians bled, purged, and blistered patients, often aggravating their illnesses and speeding their journeys to the grave. While such "heroic" measures fell out of favor after the Civil War, physicians continued to promote erroneous ideas about illness. One popular belief posited that "miasma" or "bad air" emanating from dirt and decaying matter caused disease. Indeed, because they lacked efficacious treatments for most severe illnesses, nineteenth-century doctors practiced medicine in a crowded field. Physicians often vied for patients against homeopathic practitioners, midwives, Thomsonians, and the pharmacists who dispensed therapeutic advice along with their medicinal compounds. More lowly rivals came in the form of home remedy books, traveling medicine men, and the eccentric old lady on the outskirts of town who peddled a secret cure for cancer and, in so doing, professed "to know more about how to take the Eel of Science by the tail without study than those who have devoted their lives to it."[8] Yet rather than competing for patients primarily on the basis of their profession's identity and association with science, physicians established community standing individually, through medical education, social connections, and personal repute for competent and compassionate care. And because medical understanding remained rudimentary, cultivating professional authority required calculated performance: advice books counseled physicians to shun timidity and display confidence with a "concise, clear, and distinct manner" that would dispel patient mistrust and "meddling" from family members and friends inclined to question the doctor's actions.[9]

To manage the business side of medical practice, physicians used informal accounting methods, usually maintaining a master ledger – often a small notebook – to record charges accrued for each patient. Around the turn of the twentieth century, a typical office sign read "Consultations – from $1 to $10, Cash."[10] To formulate the patient's bill, doctors used a sliding fee scale, which not only took into consideration services performed but also the ability to pay. Household visits and close personal relationships allowed physicians to judge each patient's economic status. Physicians who lived in rural areas or served poor patients often had to content themselves with in-kind compensations of firewood, produce, whiskey, or manual labor. Professional ethics obliged doctors to care for all sick individuals, regardless of ability to pay, and accounting ledgers indicate that charity work was a regular activity for most practitioners. Even in urban areas – where, away from the community's watchful eye, social mores frayed – physicians found serving in charitable hospitals desirable for training students and for acquiring experience managing unusual and interesting cases. Sliding fee scales compelled wealthier patients to subsidize at least some of the physician's charitable care; however, they also encouraged the best doctors to focus on engaging a wealthy clientele.

Physician incomes varied widely and generally reflected the practitioner's socioeconomic background and educational attainment. At the top of the earning ladder were a select few doctors, often from prominent families, who studied in European medical schools and then returned home to cater to the urban upper classes. These physicians were among the first to specialize, establishing such fields as obstetrics and surgery. Doctors who served middle-class, poor, and rural patients usually either attended the second-rate medical colleges housed in the United States or, in lieu of university training, served an apprenticeship. Income estimates for early-twentieth-century practitioners place most in the middle class, but many doctors showed up at the lower end of that economic grouping. Physicians in poor rural areas and urban doctors who primarily served working-class families might barely scrape together enough money for living expenses.[11] Their financial struggles reveal the occupation's tenuous societal position through the nineteenth and into the early twentieth century.

Professional transformation was imminent, however, as scientific breakthroughs had already begun to improve the collective reputation of physicians. The discovery of germ theory during the 1870s initiated a steady stream of medical advances whereby physician services became progressively more effective and respected. Once scientists understood that microorganisms caused illness, they began creating medicines and vaccines for previously deadly diseases, including diphtheria, rabies, and yellow fever. Meanwhile, the promotion of antiseptic techniques initiated the process of converting hospitals from filthy places of disrepute, reserved for the poor, into hygienic citadels of modern medicine where patients could access the latest surgical techniques.

The AMA provided doctors the organizational purchase necessary to translate their newfound expertise into authority over the health care sector. During the last decades of the nineteenth century, constituent AMA medical societies convinced state governments to either establish or strengthen licensing laws for medical practice. Licensing laws legitimized physician skills while officially demoting the abilities of competing practitioners. Dominated by AMA member physicians, most licensing boards acted as regulatory appendages of the association.[12]

Physician leaders also supervised the evolution of medical education. Although licensing laws required doctors to attend medical school, the university system initially proved a weak standard bearer for validating professional expertise. Disreputable commercial institutions, established primarily for physicians to collect student fees, proliferated. Not until the last quarter of the nineteenth century did the medical schools attached to the most prestigious American universities begin requiring that students meet somewhat rigorous graduation requirements. Endeavoring to improve American education, nonprofit foundations funded a comprehensive examination of medical schools. Abraham Flexner's famed 1910 report ranking medical colleges spurred charitable giving to the highest-rated schools and accelerated the demise of marginal programs.[13] Crucially, Flexner's report built a platform upon which AMA leaders could stand and issue medical school guidelines. State medical boards, controlled by AMA physicians, added teeth to association directives by determining which institutions provided degrees that qualified graduates to take the licensing exam.[14] Licensing and educational standards enhanced professional quality. And by reducing the supply of doctors, they also increased medical fees and salaries.

At the same time, physicians took advantage of their increasingly valuable skills to gain oversight of hospitals. As efficacious medical treatments and Joseph Lister's standards of cleanliness helped transform hospitals into more appealing institutions of care, administrators relied on doctors, not only to continue providing charitable services but also to attract middle- and upper-class patients who could deliver much-needed revenue. Physicians used their pecuniary power to insist that hospital administrators and governing boards grant them complete sovereignty and control over medical care.[15]

Modern scientific knowledge catapulted AMA leaders to higher levels of occupational prestige. Through licensing, educational, and hospital reforms, physicians not only appropriated the governance of the medical system but also enhanced the quality of their product. Patients expressed confidence in their new and improved professional brand by beginning to favor physician services over those of alternative practitioners. Yet organized physicians refused to accommodate the increasing demand for their services – a fact that drove much of the health care narrative during the first half of the twentieth century. Physician leaders instead nurtured romantic visions of nineteenth-century medical practice, believing that to properly dispense an expert mixture of art and science, of technique and personal ministrations, the doctor had to practice alone, funded entirely from his own pocketbook.

EARLY ATTEMPTS TO ORGANIZE HEALTH CARE

While American medicine was rapidly becoming the most advanced in the world, the delivery of care was still positioned within an antiquated framework of individual physician practice. Stasis in the medical care economy was particularly conspicuous given the profound changes occurring in the broader economy during this period. Corporate mass production provided consumers with relatively inexpensive clothing, shoes, processed foods, furniture, and automobiles. Unlike factory goods, health care had to be delivered from numerous geographical sites located close to patients. But revolutionary improvements in medical care and technology without accompanying enhancements in supply or distribution increased service costs. Working- and middle-class families found it progressively more difficult to budget for medical care. While they could often save for routine illnesses, by the 1920s, an acute episode, particularly one that required a hospital stay, could easily account for 10 percent or more of a family's annual income.[16] Nevertheless, from their position as the guardians of modern medicine, AMA leaders resolved to maintain traditional health care arrangements. Thus, groups outside organized medicine often assumed the lead in developing new methods to make physician services more abundant and accessible.

One of the earliest innovations in health care provision evolved out of the nineteenth-century cooperative movement. African American and immigrant groups – Italian, Jewish, German, and Irish, among others – established mutual aid societies, often as fraternal orders or lodges. In addition to hosting social functions, these associations pooled member resources to fund a variety of services ranging from banking and lending to life insurance. Some mutual aid societies began contracting with physicians. So-called "lodge doctors" supplied members' medical care in return for a portion of the organization's dues.[17]

Businesses also experimented with a variety of medical care arrangements. During the nineteenth century, railroads began engaging physicians – often known as "railway surgeons" – to treat the workers and passengers involved in the fledgling industry's many accidents.[18] Other corporations hired physicians to evaluate applicants and employees to weed out the sick. Journalistic exposés of dangerous and dirty factory conditions motivated some business owners to employ physicians as salaried managers. These doctors oversaw the work environment and provided employee medical care at on-site clinics. By the first decade of the twentieth century, "industrial medicine" had become a recognized physician specialty. Business leaders also supplied employee health care as part of "welfare capitalism" campaigns designed to improve worker morale and deflate union organizing.[19] For example, the Endicott-Johnson Corporation furnished employees and their families with physician, hospital, and dentistry care through a network of service providers. In 1928, the company spent approximately $22 a year for each worker's medical care.[20]

One of the best-known business forays into health care originated during the 1930s. Industrialist Henry J. Kaiser contracted with a physician group to provide health care for laborers on the Grand Coulee Dam. As his payroll swelled to support ship construction during World War II, Kaiser and his son Edgar expanded the medical care plan to serve more than thirty thousand West Coast workers. Set up on a "closed panel" basis, Kaiser physicians served only plan members and drew fixed salaries rather than per-patient or per-service fees. After the war, what became the nonprofit Kaiser Foundation worked with physician-owned Permanente medical groups to enroll patients from the broader community.[21]

Consumer cooperatives created an additional form of medical organization. In 1929, with help from the local Farmers Union, Dr. Michael Shadid founded a medical cooperative in Elk City, Oklahoma. Families paid an initial fifty-dollar fee and a yearly payment of twenty-five dollars to join. Cooperative members received all-inclusive medical and hospital care. They also elected directors to oversee daily operations and monitor physician work. By 1939, the Elk City cooperative served approximately ten thousand patients. Shadid's plan also inspired New Deal programming. Officials with the Farm Security Administration helped establish rural cooperatives, which made use of federal subsidies to create health care programs. In hundreds of counties across the nation, AMA medical society leaders negotiated with federal administrators and the representatives of farmers' organizations to determine physician reimbursements and available services for program recipients.[22]

Hospitals also developed ways to finance consumer care. In 1929, a hospital administrator in Baylor, Texas, devised a plan of guaranteed hospital care for employee groups in exchange for a monthly fee. Soon afterward – first in New Orleans and then in Newark, New Jersey – hospitals began joining together in communitywide networks to sell prepaid policies.[23] With the support of the American Hospital Association (AHA), what became known as Blue Cross plans sprang up around the country. These nonprofit plans were marketed as civic initiatives because they held open enrollment periods; used uniform "community rates" to determine policy prices; and denominated benefits in terms of fully covered hospital days, without the copayments and deductibles that often accompanied other prepaid policies.[24] By 1938, Blue Cross had more than 2.8 million subscribers.[25]

Labor unions participated in early health care experiments as well. In the late nineteenth and early twentieth centuries, labor's prevailing "self-help" doctrine spawned union welfare funds, which, like mutual aid societies, operated on membership dues. Welfare funds provided a variety of benefit types: some compensated members for medical bills or lost wages while other plans negotiated available services and fees with physicians, doctor groups, or hospitals.[26] Managing welfare funds accorded labor officials considerable expertise in health care organization. For example, union leaders explored methods for supplying workers with generous benefits while containing costs. In New York, the Transport Workers Union contracted with a network of fifty-two doctors to offer members one annual physical exam and, in case of illness, office visits and any physician services delivered during a hospital stay. To prevent service overutilization and soaring costs, union representatives appointed general practitioners to act as gatekeepers who decided which patients had illnesses that merited specialist care or hospitalization. As unions gained organizing strength during the 1930s, labor leaders plied their knowledge of health care financing to establish programs that they, rather than employers, managed.[27]

Meanwhile, physicians created medical or doctor groups. At the end of his surgical career, during the 1880s, Dr. William W. Mayo began practicing out of a Rochester, Minnesota, hospital. His sons – surgeons William and Charles – soon joined him. In an effort to focus more of their time on surgery, the Mayo brothers brought a general practitioner into the group. They then hired additional physicians and specialists. The multispecialty clinic developed a reputation for pioneering medical services and, in 1919, was converted into a nonprofit. Over the following decade, the Mayo Clinic grew to house a staff of more than two hundred physicians and dentists and almost nine hundred nurses, technicians, and additional employees.[28] Though usually much smaller in size, there were at least three hundred doctor groups across the country by the early 1930s.[29]

Some doctor groups incorporated the insurance concept, allowing patients to prepay set fees in return for standing access to care. During the nineteenth century, enterprising physicians organized private clubs, which, in return for dues, furnished members with medical services. While some clubs recruited patients individually, others made agreements with mutual aid associations, businesses, or labor unions.[30] The private club concept evolved into prepaid physician groups. For example, in 1929, a group of Los Angeles municipal workers approached Drs. Donald Ross and Clifford Loos about creating a health care program for approximately two thousand employees and their families. To establish their prepaid group, the doctors hired physicians from a variety of specialties and contracted with hospitals to accommodate acutely ill patients. In exchange for a monthly fee and small deductibles at the time of service, families accessed a wide array of medical care. Even during the Great Depression, the clinic thrived. By 1935, the Ross-Loos plan employed fifty doctors and served approximately forty thousand patients. The group owned a drugstore, laboratory, staff library, and ambulatory surgery facility.[31]

Prepaid physician groups were popular because they furnished high-quality care while controlling medical costs. Group practices usually delivered integrated care – they treated all of the patient's health service needs in one location, which allowed general practitioners and specialists to consult together on difficult cases.[32] Moreover, the way groups paid physicians helped contain policy prices. Many of the health care experiments previously discussed – whether managed by businesses, cooperatives, or labor officials – compensated doctors using fixed salaries or per-patient "capitation" fees. When physicians received reimbursements for each service or procedure delivered – that is, on a fee-for-service basis – they tended to oversupply care to earn more money. Salaries and capitation fees restrained coverage costs. However, patients frequently complained that physicians went too far in the other direction: doctors sometimes withheld services reasoning, however subconsciously, that they would collect the same compensation no matter how much care they provided. Prepaid physician groups, including the Ross-Loos plan, often paid doctors a combination of salary and a percentage of the plan's annual income. This remuneration method tied the physician's monetary interests directly to the plan's financial health.[33] Since their compensation depended upon group profitability, doctors had to fully deploy their medical expertise to walk the fine line between service overutilization and patient satisfaction. Providing excessive medical care frittered away valuable resources, while withholding necessary services angered patients and harmed the group's competitive position. By effectively fusing affordability with superior medical care, prepaid groups attracted consumers and, as we will see, the attention of policymakers and health care reformers.

Numerous groups formulated methods to render health care more accessible and inexpensive than the AMA's preferred system of individually financed solo practitioners. Prepaid doctor groups offered a particularly elegant way of financing and distributing medical care. Yet, because they drew the AMA's ire and organized doctors worked fervently to destroy them, many of these models would subsequently die out or become marginal players in health care, relegated to the status of "alternative delivery" arrangements. This development raises a critical question: Why, particularly given their well-known campaigns against government-managed health care, did AMA leaders suppress the private market?

THE DOCTOR: NOT AN ORGANIZATION MAN

At the end of the nineteenth century, the country transitioned from a patchwork of disparate, "island communities" into a cohesive national society and marketplace, knit together by modern communications and transportation. Many AMA leaders and members watched uneasily as this change attenuated the interpersonal relationships upon which doctors had established their reputations and careers.[34] Behemoth corporations capable of supplying mass markets occupied the space once reserved for individual purveyors of goods and services. The notion of an overtly competitive, commercial health care market dominated by medical corporations terrified physician leaders. To avert this scenario, the AMA attacked two components crucial to the operation of early health care models: doctor groups and health insurance, which was frequently referred to as "medical prepayment" or "prepaid plans." Physician leaders contended that doctor groups and insurance would not only inaugurate corporate arrangements but also, by systematizing and organizing the health care market, invite government intrusion. Rational though these beliefs may have been, they led the AMA to ruthlessly crush doctors and health care innovators who lacked the financial resources or political connections to salvage their operations.

Since the association's founding, AMA officials had taken great care to advance professional influence by stifling competition among doctors. Previously, physicians had engaged in bitter squabbles among themselves to secure patients. AMA leaders understood that augmenting professional standing required physicians to present a unified front. When a doctor questioned a colleague's care or expertise – or even his prices – he opened the entire profession to inquiry and undermined the attempt of organized physicians to become the primary overseers of medicine. Thus, AMA medical ethics forbade physicians from speaking ill of one another in front of patients, instructing doctors that "no insincerity, rivalry, or envy should be indulged."[35]

AMA leaders also checked physician competition in order to foster a professional vision that exempted doctors from the marketplace. Association ethics, therefore, prohibited advertising. By promoting the services of one physician, advertising not only challenged other doctors, however implicitly, but also exposed the profession to crass commercialism. AMA leaders argued that, rather than peddling an ordinary product, physicians provided a sacrosanct amalgam of scientific knowledge, the "art" of healing, and personal care that went beyond the physical into emotional and even spiritual domains. They believed, of course, that physicians should be paid generously for delivering such services; however, their compensation was not to be discussed openly nor scrutinized by the lay public. To the chagrin of doctors, competitive markets laid bare such financial matters. Certainly, AMA complaints about "money doctors" and practitioners who asserted that "business is business" covered a catalog of blatantly unscrupulous behaviors, from promoting dubious cures, to charging outrageously high fees, to accepting pharmacy kickbacks for writing certain prescriptions. Yet competitive grievances – which were expressed frequently during the first several decades of the twentieth century – also emanated from older and more traditional physicians troubled by the rapidly shifting social order. One competitive threat came from young doctors who ran roughshod over their elders – the "real gentlemen of the old school" – by undercutting established fees: in other words, by refusing to uphold physician collusion to fix prices.[36]

Moreover, competitive markets appeared inevitably to yield to corporate organization. Physicians had watched corporations subsume professionals such as engineers and accountants. Even lawyers, joined together in freestanding firms, bowed to "commercial interests" when serving corporate accounts. Corporate arrangements posed a grave threat to doctors' professional conceptions. Large medical enterprises would stimulate overt competition by vying with one another for patients and by forcing physicians to contend for job openings. AMA leaders warned that once doctors were positioned under "autocratic authority," they would surrender income, autonomy, and professional standing.[37] Speaking in 1924, Ray Lyman Wilbur, President of both the AMA and Stanford University, argued that the "minute we allow a bureaucracy to step in between the physician and the patient, that will degrade our profession and will put us so that we cannot render ideal professional services."[38] AMA representatives charged that as "impersonal" entities, medical corporations would vitiate the subjective nature of medicine by enforcing "too much standardization." Physicians, they alleged, had to choose between "the coldness and automaticity of the machine" and the heroic, individual doctor who could enter into intimate family settings and ply his skills to either victoriously snatch life from the teeth of death or console the bereaved.[39]

To hold corporate formation at bay, AMA leaders opposed both insurance (prepaid plans) and group practice. AMA officials assailed prepaid plans for permitting third-party financiers, the inevitable directors of medical corporations, into health care. Furthermore, according to physician leaders, group practices – with their hierarchical structures and pooling of capital – were nascent corporations. AMA ethical guidelines proscribed both arrangements by barring physicians from engaging in "contract practice" – that is, entering into an agreement with any third party, whether a mutual aid society, business, union, or even a doctor-owned group.[40] Through the *Journal of the American Medical Association* (*JAMA*), physician leaders regularly cautioned their colleagues about the dangers of prepaid groups as, for example, in the following 1921 editorial:

What of the physicians outside the group? Some evidently are seeing the advantages and are forming other groups – perhaps in some instances forced to do so in self-defense! Will not this mean group against group? May it not be one more step toward the complete elimination of the medical practitioner – of the family adviser – of him who heretofore has reflected to the public the altruistic motives of the medical profession? Does it mean that the family physician is being replaced by a corporation?[41]

In this way, AMA leaders heaped the sins of both competition and corporate organization upon prepaid groups.

AMA antagonism toward insurance and group practice also reflected the conviction that large-scale market organization spawned government control. In Europe, the popularity of prepaid medical plans appeared to have paved the way for the continent's early adoption of government-supplied health care. In Germany, for example, workers paid dues to "friendly societies" or "sickness funds" in return for health care services. Chancellor Otto von Bismarck used these sickness funds as building blocks to construct a government-managed health care system in 1883. From the late nineteenth century through approximately the first half of the twentieth century, AMA officials repeatedly asserted that "insurance schemes in the hands of the profession at the outset, drift inevitably, as do all plans initiated by private groups, into bureaucratically administered compulsory insurance under governmental control."[42] Thus, fighting the market was part and parcel of fighting the government.

Examining the roots of AMA concerns about physician groups and health insurance explains why association leaders attempted to preserve the obsolete model of doctors practicing individually and financing their own services. It also contextualizes seemingly bizarre statements about prepaid groups leading to socialism. One such case involved the Committee on the Costs of Medical Care (CCMC). In 1927, charitable foundations disbursed grants enabling the CCMC to conduct a comprehensive study of U.S. health care. The committee brought together leading academics, public health professionals, and medical leaders, including prominent physicians. To aid the CCMC investigation, the AMA supplied data on medical care. In 1932, the CCMC issued a final report recommending that the health care system be coordinated through prepaid doctor groups, which they lauded for offering patients integrated care and plentiful services at reasonable prices.[43] AMA leaders responded by severing ties with the CCMC and labeling the report "an incitement to revolution," forged by economists with "socialistic leanings."[44] Some CCMC members did indeed envision the introduction of government funding once the market had been more effectively organized. A *JAMA* editorial titled "Americanism versus Sovietism for the American People" lambasted the CCMC proposal accordingly: "Let the big business men who would reorganize medical practice and the efficiency engineers who would make doctors the cogs of their governmental machines, give a little of their horse power brains to a realization of the fact that Americans prefer to be human beings."[45] The episode reinforced assumptions among AMA leaders that doctor groups and insurance would invariably usher in corporate domination of health care followed by government control.

AMA leaders exercised broad power to reject external recommendations and cast market developments according to their professional ideology. With a national body presiding over constituent state and county medical societies, AMA authority extended into almost every corner of the nation. Because of AMA influence over licensing boards and hospital administrators, association officials could often have a physician's medical license or hospital admitting privileges revoked if he transgressed professional guidelines.[46] Failure to gain medical society admittance hindered a doctor's ability to purchase malpractice insurance on the grounds that if a lawsuit occurred, the physician lacked a stable network of professional peers to testify on his behalf.[47] Moreover, doctors organized through local medical societies frequently colluded against "unethical" practitioners by refusing to refer patients to them. AMA leaders made explicit their intention to professionally harm any physician who failed to uphold the embargo against group practice and insurance, as, for example, in this 1934 *JAMA* editorial:

> The young physician who is tempted by the offer of some commercial agency to enter into such schemes of combinations should bear in mind that he thereby jeopardizes his entire future in the practice of medicine and sacrifices the medical birthright for which he has already paid six or seven years of his life.[48]

Although many practitioners were willing, even eager, to participate in multispecialty groups and prepaid programs, the example of doctors who lost their licenses or hospital privileges convinced most physicians to shun such plans.[49]

Nor did negative press stifle AMA retribution against errant physicians. AMA attempts to shutter two prepaid groups – the Ross-Loos and Shadid plans – were widely publicized. In 1934, the Los Angeles County Medical Association expelled Dr. Ross, a fellow of the American College of Surgeons, and Dr. Loos, a former president of the San Diego County Medical Society. According to medical society representatives, Drs. Ross and Loos had violated medical ethics against advertising by submitting articles about their plan to company newsletters. The Ross-Loos ordeal was covered in newspapers and the progressive magazine *Survey Graphic*.[50] Dr. Shadid's battle against the AMA also appeared in the national press. In 1939, *Time* magazine reported that in addition to dismissing Shadid from the local medical society, physicians were attempting to have his license revoked. The Oklahoma cooperative encountered difficulties hiring staff members because physicians feared AMA retribution. Shadid managed to maintain his license only because of political connections and support from the locally powerful Farmers Union.[51] Whereas these plans garnered national attention for their tussles with the AMA, numerous lesser-known enterprises folded under medical society pressure while would-be prepaid group organizers simply abandoned their aspirations.

As mass industrialization reordered society and economic relations, AMA leaders clung to an outmoded paradigm of the physician laboring independently, detached from any sources of outside funding except patients, who were to pay for care as needed. Littering the path of AMA economic policy were ruined physician careers, demolished prepaid plans, and medical groups significantly weakened from battling organized doctors. Yet even as AMA leaders successfully implemented their economic vision, they simultaneously, by undermining market modernization, paved the way for the very types of governmental intercession they were so keen to avoid.

THE GOVERNMENTAL RESPONSE

Given how the AMA obstructed market development, it is unsurprising that reformers increasingly looked to the federal government to effect improvements in health care financing and delivery. Although the political overtures of the 1930s and 1940s failed to produce legislative victories, they nevertheless reshaped the AMA's course of action. Faced with federal reform proposals, AMA leaders beat a hasty retreat back to the private market where they endorsed health insurance, albeit halfheartedly.

During the Roosevelt administration, the specter of federal reform persistently haunted physicians. President Franklin D. Roosevelt tasked the Committee on Economic Security (CES) with producing legislation that would hang a sturdy safety net beneath a citizenry experiencing catastrophic unemployment rates. The resulting 1935 Social Security Act established pensions for senior citizens as well as grants-in-aid for states to finance unemployment insurance, public health programs, maternal and child medical and welfare services, and assistance for the blind and families with dependent children. Fearing that medical society opposition would sink the entire legislative package, the president rejected committee suggestions to include a wide-ranging program of government-funded health care. However, to explore future reform prospects, the president created the Interdepartmental Committee to Coordinate Health and Welfare Activities. The group formed a Technical Committee that proposed federal subsidies for hospital construction, disability compensation, and expanded maternal and child health care services. The plan included a plank for state-financed, compulsory medical insurance. In 1938, the administration sponsored the National Health Conference to discuss the committee's blueprint. Leading policymakers, scholars, health care professionals, and labor leaders gathered in Washington, D.C., to consider the medical system's shortcomings and avenues for reform.[52] AMA leaders in attendance decried the "ridicule" aimed at organized physicians.[53]

The month of July 1938 presented extraordinary challenges to AMA political and economic clout. One week after the national conference,

AMA leaders, fearing that proposals for government-funded insurance were gaining ground, met with the Technical Committee to offer a compromise. AMA representatives agreed to support each of the committee's recommendations – all of which they had previously opposed – as long as policymakers dropped their advocacy of compulsory health insurance. Technical Committee members refused the deal.[54] Then, on July 31, the Department of Justice filed an antitrust suit against the AMA. Persecution of group doctors had finally caught up with them. AMA officials had collaborated with Washington, D.C. hospitals to deny admitting privileges to physicians associated with the Group Health Association (GHA). The GHA was a prepaid group established to serve federal workers. Subscribers elected the governing board, and physicians, as GHA employees, received fixed salaries. In addition to colluding with area hospitals, medical society leaders promised to excommunicate doctors who joined the plan and instructed members not to refer patients to GHA physicians.[55] In the face of a federal indictment, the AMA came out swinging. AMA leaders argued that antitrust laws did not apply to them because doctors did not engage in a "trade," but instead practiced a "learned profession."[56] "The A.M.A. has the right," stated association President Rock Sleyster, "to enforce certain membership requirements and expel members who fail to comply."[57]

Despite this defiant attitude, the political environment roused AMA leaders to the realization that, in one fashion or another, the health care system would have to advance beyond nineteenth-century arrangements. Organized physicians could not continue fighting a two-front war against both government reform and market evolution.

To focus their energies on combating federal initiatives, the AMA finally endorsed health insurance. The leadership called an emergency House of Delegates session for the winter of 1938. In 1934, primarily because of the disastrous economy and plummeting physician incomes, the AMA had begrudgingly approved insurance programs for low-income families, including the rural cooperatives sponsored by the Farm Security Administration.[58] Three years later, the association sanctioned Blue Cross hospital plans – as long as they excluded coverage for physician services. During the 1938 session, AMA delegates approved private insurance for physician care. Their acceptance of insurance sprang not from an inclination to organize health care more effectively, but rather from a desire to claim that private sector development rendered government programming redundant.[59]

The concession failed to alleviate pressure for government reform. In 1939, Senator Robert Wagner (D, NY) introduced legislation to provide states with federal funds to create compulsory health insurance programs. By the 1940s, reformers were seeking a more centralized system, to be managed at the federal level through the Social Security Administration.[60] The Wagner-Murray-Dingell bills of 1943 and 1945 proposed national health insurance financed through payroll taxes.[61] While measures for government-funded medical care hung over the AMA, the Department of Justice pursued its antitrust allegations. The first federal judge who heard the GHA case sided with the AMA and dismissed the indictment. However, the Court of Appeals overturned the decision, and a jury found the association guilty. In 1943, the Supreme Court issued a writ of certiorari upholding the AMA's conviction.[62]

As the world changed around them – through a grand transformation of science and medicine, a new economy premised on mass consumption, and a polity shifting toward more active government – organized physicians clung to anachronistic notions about the health care market. Their activities, as inspired by these beliefs, encouraged political attempts to reform medical care and provoked judicial scrutiny. Under this political pressure, AMA leaders finally made a half-hearted peace with a fundamental aspect of modern health care organization – insurance. The episode fixed the AMA's pattern of action: rather than offering their own forward-looking vision of health care arrangements, physician leaders would continue to strain their policies through the sieve of past events, always reacting to political and market developments after they occurred.

THE INSURANCE COMPANY MODEL

Throughout this study, the term "insurance company model" will refer to a specific type of health care prepayment – third-party financing that complied with AMA dictates. At a time when many options were available in the marketplace, physicians pushed health care organization toward a profoundly flawed design. When they authorized insurance in 1938, AMA delegates attached four stipulations to its provision. These stipulations ensured that commercial insurance companies and, once some exceptions were made, nonprofit plans would dominate health care financing. To comply with AMA guidelines, third parties had to finance individual physicians rather than doctor groups, send indemnity payments to subscribers rather than to physicians, calculate reimbursements on a fee-for-service basis, and permit complete doctor autonomy. These requirements created the insurance company model – an inherently inefficient structure that fragmented health care services and fueled cost increases.[63] While the following overview broadly surveys problems intrinsic to the insurance company model, Chapter 6 provides a detailed historical examination of how physicians altered their behavior in response to these financing characteristics and how insurers vainly attempted to manage rising costs.

Despite federal judicial action, AMA leaders still wielded the power to undercut aspects of the insurance market that failed to match their standards. The court's antitrust ruling restrained national leaders from publicly threatening group or prepaid group doctors. However, state and county medical societies continued rejecting applicants who participated in prepaid groups or any arrangements at variance with AMA directives. Now acting more covertly, locally organized physicians simply refused to refer patients to nonconforming doctors or convinced hospital administrators to deny them admitting privileges. Furthermore, state laws passed during the first decades of the twentieth century and certain articulations of licensing regulations prohibited "the corporate practice of medicine." After 1939, organized physicians convinced twenty-six state governments to pass additional laws regulating insurance to match AMA concepts. The laws varied. Seventeen states effectively banned prepaid groups by requiring that insurance plans allow all area doctors to participate. Sixteen states obliged insurance organizations to obtain medical society approval.[64] Using both their professional clout and state bequests of authority, AMA leaders insisted that third-party insurers follow four guidelines.

The first proviso banned prepaid groups – like the state laws for which physicians had lobbied, it required insurers to cover the services of any doctor whom the subscriber chose to see. By retarding the growth of physician groups, the "free choice of doctor" prerequisite undermined integrated patient care. Because of this historical decision, health care, outside of certain alternative arrangements, continues to be delivered in fragmented form, with patients visiting various physician offices and specialists to obtain treatments for their different illnesses.

The second condition that AMA leaders attached to medical prepayment was exclusive use of indemnity fees. Rather than establishing direct financing relationships with physicians, insurers had to send indemnity payments to subscribers. This compensation structure preserved individual physician-patient financing and allowed doctors to set their own fees. However, indemnity policies drove up service prices because they attenuated the fee-setting restraints placed on doctors when patients paid the entire bill from their own pocket. Physicians could more readily rationalize bill padding when a nameless, faceless company was supplying part of the payment. Sliding fee scales exacerbated the situation. Because doctors were accustomed to setting fees according to the patient's ability to pay, many practitioners charged insured patients higher prices than uninsured patients. Despite this obvious glitch, AMA leaders maintained that "cash (indemnity) benefits only will not disturb or alter the relations of patients, physicians and hospitals."[65]

The third AMA demand was for insurance plans to reimburse policy-holders on a fee-for-service basis. Because insurers were prohibited from directly employing physicians, fixed salaries were excluded, but so were per-patient capitation fees. Fee-for-service arrangements produced an oversupply of health care, at least among the insured.[66] Because providing additional services and procedures garnered higher revenues, physicians had incentive to cater to patient requests for unnecessary care.

Together, bill padding and service overutilization rapidly increased health care and insurance costs. Besides the conspicuous manner in which they escalated prices, inflating bills and oversupplying care raised costs in less apparent ways: they discouraged physicians from attempting to increase productivity either by identifying measures to more efficiently perform procedures or by dividing labor. (Of course, effective labor division was also hindered by the AMA injunction against physician groups.) As insurance spread during the 1940s and 1950s, the simplest way for doctors to increase revenue was not through new forms of organization, nor through innovative delivery methods, nor even necessarily through attracting many additional patients, but instead, through the provision of as many insured services as possible.[67]

AMA leaders' final insurance requirement was that physicians would retain absolute sovereignty to practice medicine as they saw fit. Organizations bankrolling health care lacked authority to regulate the supply or price of services, much less question physician performance quality. The most an insuring agency could expect was for physicians to fill out forms indicating the patient's diagnosis and delivered procedures. The policyholder then mailed the forms to the insurance company and, in return, received set payments for each insured service. These indemnity payments might, but often would not, cover the entire doctor's bill. Indeed, because insurance companies lacked the ability to set physician fees, indemnity policies could never promise consumers "complete coverage" for any health care service.

Despite all the strictures that physician leaders affixed to insurance, they continued to display hostility toward medical prepayment. In 1941, for example, national leaders asserted in *JAMA* that although medical societies had recently approved more than two hundred insurance plans, the public "was not particularly enthusiastic about prepayment for medical service."[68] This was a bit of wishful thinking. Nevertheless, and as we will see in subsequent chapters, until the late 1940s and the battle over President Truman's health care plan, AMA leaders would provide little aid or comfort for the insuring organizations that did manage to comply with their myriad rules.

The AMA's preferred insurance arrangements might well have languished under such burdensome requirements. However, four factors drove insurance sales over AMA roadblocks. First, consumers were eager to purchase products granting them access to modern health care. Second, the success of Blue Cross – which experienced soaring growth, from 4.4 million policyholders in 1940 to 15.7 million subscribers in 1945 – convinced hesitant commercial insurance executives that they might be able to profitably underwrite and sell medical insurance.[69] Third, business-labor relations interacted with tax policy to support insurance sales. In the spirit of welfare capitalism and attempting to thwart union power, employers supplied workers with health care – even though such benefits were now based on the insurance company model rather than earlier experiments with industrial medicine and prepaid groups. Tax policy helped businesses wrest control of health care provision away from unions by indirectly subsidizing employer-purchased insurance. Long-standing Internal Revenue Service (IRS) rules permitted businesses to count employee fringe benefits as tax write-offs. Thus, when the War Labor Board issued a wage freeze during World War II, employers could simultaneously decrease their tax burden and attract scarce labor by furnishing health insurance.[70] Finally, medical prepayment spread because both insurance executives and their business clients viewed the expansion of worker coverage as a means to obstruct nationalized health care.[71]

Amid pent-up demand for prepaid health services, AMA leaders attached not strings but heavy chains to insurance. As they crafted the insurance company model – requiring individual practice, indemnity payments, fee-for-service compensation, and complete doctor autonomy – physician leaders laid the foundation for a fragmented, expensive health care system. Moreover, AMA stipulations whittled down the number of viable sponsoring agencies, leaving only commercial insurance companies, as well as Blue Cross and their soon-to-be-born sibling, Blue Shield, to take control of health care financing.

COMMERCIAL INSURERS: DRAGGED INTO HEALTH CARE

While businesses, unions, consumer groups, and physicians established prepayment plans during the first decades of the twentieth century, insurance companies largely eschewed the health care field because of profitability concerns. Insurance executives also recognized the financial perils of sponsoring medical coverage that met AMA specifications. Actuarial science augured grave financial difficulties for companies that sponsored health insurance without the ability to regulate either policyholder demand for care or physician service supply. However, AMA directives cleared the market, leaving only insurance companies and nonprofit Blue Cross plans eligible to support medical prepayment. During the 1930s and 1940s, insurance companies were reluctantly, incrementally drawn into health care coverage by businesses requesting employee group policies. Furthermore, to block health care reform and the prospect that nationalized medicine might set a precedent for intensified federal interference across the economy, insurers wished to mount a political argument about the strength of voluntary insurance. Therefore, despite their aversion, commercial insurers had to develop a presence in health care financing.

At the end of the nineteenth century, commercial insurers made a tentative, ultimately unsuccessful entrance into medical financing. During the 1860s, a group of businessmen in Hartford, Connecticut, organized Travelers insurance company to provide railroad passengers with remunerative policies in case of accident or death during their journey. These policies evolved into accident coverage for a wider range of misfortunes, including those incurred in the course of daily living. Accident policies became quite popular. From this foundation, insurance companies began experimenting with "accident and sickness" policies. To avoid financial ties with health care providers, insurance companies supplied subscribers with lump sum payments according to diagnosis. Policyholders used these disbursements as they saw fit, whether to cover medical bills or lost wages. However, the policies were highly susceptible to fraud. Because companies had to charge substantial premium prices and restrict coverage to a very limited number of qualifying illnesses, accident and sickness policies failed to take hold among consumers. The experience helped convince underwriters that health insurance was impractical.[72]

One reason that insurance executives wished to avoid health care underwriting was moral hazard. Moral hazard occurred when insurance lessened the motivation of policyholders to protect themselves against the liabilities for which they were insured. Rather than attempting to avoid medical care, insured patients more readily sought health services because they were not responsible, or only partially responsible, for the bill.[73] Under alternative prepayment models, third-party financiers either supervised physician practices or incentivized them to limit service supply, for example, by paying them per-capita fees. Unwilling to become so intricately involved in health care, insurance executives were content to leave medical prepayment to other organizations. Exemplifying this outlook, the chief actuary of Metropolitan Life Insurance Company scoffed at the idea of underwriting health services. In 1931 he told an interviewer, "I don't think insurance companies are about to get into the medical care business."[74]

Nonetheless, during the 1930s, persistent requests from firms seeking employee medical coverage pulled insurers into health care. Because they supplied life insurance, disability coverage, and pension products for employee groups, insurance companies had established relationships with businesses. The executives of these businesses, often in an attempt to quell union organizing, began asking insurers to also provide medical care policies. Although insurers initially refused these petitions, they began to gradually modify their stance. Insurers moved extremely cautiously by first adding "blanket medical expense riders" to accident and disability coverage. Now accident policies not only provided lump sum payments, they also delivered compensation specifically for medical care. Medical expense riders became so popular that by the end of the decade they were included in almost half of disability contracts.[75]

At the same time, the rapid growth of Blue Cross convinced insurers to begin experimenting with hospitalization policies. In 1930, representatives of the Union Switch and Signal company approached Equitable Life Assurance Society about the possibility of purchasing employee hospital coverage. Equitable's chief actuary counseled executives to deny the request, stating that he was "not enthusiastic about opening up this field of hospital benefits."[76] In 1934, following five years of Blue Cross success, Equitable leaders decided to compromise with clients by adding hospital coverage to disability policies. The coverage still tied medical insurance to a serious accident. However, one year later, Metropolitan Life began offering employee groups a per-diem hospitalization policy. The coverage created an enormous crack in the wall that industry leaders had erected to protect themselves from health insurance – now companies were underwriting stand-alone policies explicitly for health care services.

Business-labor conflict kept the ball rolling through the commercial insurance industry. For example, in response to union organizing at local plants, executives with DuPont corporation solicited Equitable to provide employees with both hospital and surgical coverage, which financed the services of physician-surgeons. Equitable executives assented to the request in 1936. Still fearful about the financial hazards of underwriting health care, commercial insurers told themselves that they would not become any further involved in medical insurance.[77]

Soon, however, commercial insurance firms, along with nonprofit Blues plans, were the only enterprises qualified to sell prepaid policies that adhered to AMA principles. AMA requirements for fee-for-service compensation and physician autonomy only aggravated moral hazard problems by encouraging doctors to accommodate patient requests for unnecessary care. Moreover, unlike most early prepayment programs, insurance company coverage entailed a wide geographical and institutional gulf between payers, situated in a specific firm, and service providers located around the country. Requests to constrain costs on behalf of a distant insurance company could never offset physician inclinations to earn additional income. Nevertheless, insurance companies, by virtue of their ability to support AMA-blessed arrangements, inherited the task of protecting the private health care sector from government intrusion.

During the 1940s, even as they expressed uneasiness about health insurance, industry executives discussed the "social desirability" of growing employee group coverage to counter "social planners" seeking government-funded care.[78] So they continued slowly expanding their medical insurance offerings. In 1945, Continental Casualty broadened the medical expense riders in disability policies so that they not only covered health care costs for accidents but also for serious illnesses. In reaction to the success of "polio contracts," insurers began selling policies that covered medical expenses for groups of diseases. A typical policy, for example, might partially cover health care costs associated with leukemia, smallpox, scarlet fever, meningitis, rabies, and polio. These policies developed into the commercial industry's most popular form of coverage – major medical.[79]

Insurers believed that major medical policies, also referred to as catastrophic coverage, presented the ideal solution for spreading health insurance while avoiding some of the problems associated with AMA-sanctioned arrangements. Major medical policies covered most health care events and illnesses but only after the policyholder paid a hefty deductible. Subscribers had to budget for routine care – their insurance became

active only with a serious accident or illness. Liberty Mutual Insurance
Company is widely credited with introducing the first major medical
contract in 1949. The policy required an annual deductible of $300 – a
considerable sum for the period – and coinsurance of 25 percent up to
a maximum of $1,500 in medical coverage.[80] Equitable, Prudential,
and New York Life soon followed with their own versions of major
medical.[81]

Despite such restricted coverage, many insurers continued to worry
about the profitability of health care policies. They sternly warned their
peers against any additional coverage expansion.[82] Some insurers went
further, arguing that the industry should abandon medical care underwriting altogether. In 1953, for example, one industry executive declared
the entire health insurance field an "unnecessary evil" because companies
had no control over the quantity of services that they financed.[83] Insurance executives considered the sale of major medical policies a bold and
courageous move – designed to fulfill business requests for employee
coverage while aiding the fight against national health care. They certainly never intended to extend their underwriting activities beyond this
limited coverage.

MEDICAL SOCIETIES LAUNCH BLUE SHIELD

At the end of the 1930s, AMA medical societies began establishing
prepayment plans for physician services. They became known as "Blue
Shield" plans – the organizational corollary to hospitals issuing insurance
policies through Blue Cross plans. Blue Shield allowed physicians to
retain influence over the expanding insurance mechanism while offering
them political protection. At the national level, AMA leaders were uneasy
about medical societies developing prepayment programs, particularly on
a nonprofit basis and in league with Blue Cross. Nevertheless, medical
society plans pushed AMA leaders to expand their concept of the insurance company model to include nonprofit organization and service
benefits.

During the 1920s and 1930s, medical societies in Washington and
Oregon began selling health insurance. National AMA leaders tolerated
these programs because they were created to compete with medical
corporations known as "hospital associations." Mining and timber companies engaged hospital associations to provide health services for their
geographically isolated workers. Often launched by a budding entrepre-
neur or lay promoter, hospital associations contracted with physicians

and hospitals to create health care packages for employee groups. Medical society officials resented that hospital associations regulated physician practices and sometimes remunerated doctors with salaries or per-patient fees. They therefore sponsored competing plans that safeguarded physician autonomy and exclusively used fee-for-service compensation.[84]

The next generation of medical society programs would follow the Blue Cross framework. In 1939, the California Medical Association was locked in an intense battle to defeat a state-led proposal for compulsory health insurance.[85] As part of their strategy to defeat the measure, physicians created the first statewide medical-society–sponsored insurance program. California Physicians Service (CPS) mimicked Blue Cross arrangements by organizing as a nonprofit. Nonprofit designation allowed CPS to skirt state laws banning medical corporations and exempted the plan from paying taxes or following insurance regulations. In their bid to convince policymakers that the program merited nonprofit status, California doctors agreed to follow the Blue Cross example of selling service benefits, which provided subscribers with fully paid units of care, rather than partial indemnity payments.[86] CPS, nevertheless, limited the sale of service benefit policies to families under certain income ceilings. The system acknowledged physician preferences for setting their own fees by allowing doctors to "balance bill" higher-income earners for additional compensation above the plan's fixed payments.[87]

At the national level, AMA leaders questioned the wisdom of medical societies sponsoring insurance, especially according to nonprofit standards. Morris Fishbein, the nationally known editor of the *JAMA*, dispatched staff members to the West Coast to convince California Medical Association delegates to vote against the CPS plan. However, the threat of state-financed insurance persuaded California physicians to break with the national leadership.[88] Around the country, events on the ground quickly outran national AMA leaders' disdain for nonprofit plans.

Within a few years of CPS's founding, medical societies in Michigan, Pennsylvania, and New York also started nonprofit plans; all of these programs would eventually march under the banner of Blue Shield. Medical societies partnered with local Blue Cross programs to obtain nonprofit designation, to tap into existing administrative capabilities, and because the logic of the AHA supervising Blue Cross paralleled that of AMA societies overseeing Blue Shield. Blue Shield grew spectacularly. In 1940, medical nonprofits provided approximately 400,000 members with surgical coverage. By 1950, most states had at least one medical society plan and surgical policies covered more than twenty million subscribers across the country.[89]

Blue Shield's rapid growth compelled the AMA to modify what qualified as "ethical" insurance. In 1942, four years after declaring indemnity payments the only permissible form of insurance reimbursement, the House of Delegates changed course. Delegates authorized service benefits, which compelled physicians to accept fixed fees for each service, but this approval extended only to plans supervised by medical societies. Moreover, AMA leaders urged Blue Cross and Blue Shield to reserve service benefits for low-income subscribers and charity cases.[90] Because officers and staff in the association's Chicago headquarters remained wary of health insurance, and in particular nonprofit plans, the relationship between the AMA and Blue Shield would subsequently develop under tension and fraught with misgivings.

CONCLUSION

The rules and regulations that AMA leaders attached to medical prepayment produced a costly and inefficient insurance company model. Although there existed many possible ways of configuring health care financing and delivery, AMA heads settled on a faulty model because they believed it offered doctors the best prospects for safeguarding professional power. Thus, as insurance began spreading during the 1940s, it was funneled through a narrow conduit, with only commercial insurance companies and Blue Cross and Blue Shield capable of complying with AMA standards.

It was an arrangement with which few seemed pleased. Physicians feared third-party financing would ultimately diminish physician sovereignty and pay. Commercial insurers worried that the AMA's preferred prepayment structure would increase medical costs and insurance policy prices beyond sustainability. Nor were national AMA leaders happy with the bastard child – Blue Shield – birthed from a contemptible alliance between medical societies and Blue Cross. As organized physicians and third-party financiers prepared to battle Truman's proposal for universal health insurance, they eyed each other warily.

2

Federal Reform Politics: Implanting the Insurance Company Model, 1945–1960

Scholars have traditionally depicted the history of health care reform as episodic skirmishes that pit progressive Democrats against Republicans. In these accounts, private health interests, aligned with Republicans, triumphantly battled Truman's proposal for universal insurance and then retired to enjoy political tranquility under President Eisenhower. This oft-told narrative holds much truth. However, slightly adjusting the analytical lens reveals underlying bipartisan accord in midcentury Washington – many policymakers were unhappy with the developmental direction of voluntary health insurance. Among both Democrats and Republicans, a broad consensus existed about the need to either displace or modify the emerging insurance company model.

Although most politicians agreed that the health care sector required reform, they clashed among themselves over the necessary degree of government intervention. Advocates of Truman's plan argued that nationalizing health insurance would allow officials to streamline a fragmented system and cover all citizens with more benefits at lower costs than voluntary provision. After Truman's initiative failed, Eisenhower as well as moderate Republicans and Democrats in Congress sponsored a variety of legislative measures to generate widespread, liberal insurance coverage through existing private channels. These reforms called for milder applications of government authority than did Truman's program; nevertheless, they proposed restructuring the market in ways that threatened private interests, particularly organized physicians and commercial insurers.

Repeated legislative attempts to dislodge the insurance company model produced a variant of corporatism – what I will refer to as "soft corporatism" – that profoundly shaped the health care sector. Under the formal corporatism seen in countries like Germany and Italy, the government arbitrates among interests, such as workers and businesses, that are organized into representative associations. In the case of U.S. health care politics, an institutionalized pattern of interaction developed between large associations and the state, and state–society relations began to follow a fixed regularity uncharacteristic of purely pluralistic arrangements. Through political debates and lobbying, health care associations – representing physicians, commercial insurers, and nonprofit plans – as well as labor groups, put forth divergent visions of the medical economy. Although policymakers did not explicitly mediate among these competing conceptions, they did guide trade and professional associations toward the overriding objective of providing more widely accessible, liberal health insurance coverage.[1] Policymakers used both informal and formal governmental authority to apply this direction.

Federal officials exercised informal power through a constant succession of reform proposals that, by their very presence, deemed the existing health insurance sector inadequate. Legislative initiatives and accompanying debates allowed politicians to outline the appropriate product features of health insurance. By premising reform on the need for insurance to cover all population groups and pay most medical costs, policymakers defined a "consumer ideal" that focused the actions of private interests. Organized physicians and insurers attempted to obstruct federal reform by promoting their ability to fulfill the consumer ideal that policymakers had delineated. Through their representative associations, physicians and insurers – once mistrustful of one another and unhappy with the very notion of health care prepayment – now joined together to intensively develop insurance for broader coverage and more generous benefits.

Policymakers also employed formal authority, in the shape of federal regulations and programs, to influence private sector actions. The inherent inefficiencies of the insurance company model drove up health care costs, making coverage expansion difficult. Federal tax guidelines helped private interests overcome this impediment. The tax code granted write-offs to businesses that provided worker fringe benefits, including health insurance.[2] Additionally, lawmakers created the country's largest employer-supplied insurance account with the Federal Employees Health Benefits Program (FEHBP). These policies concealed swiftly increasing premium prices: by indirectly subsidizing employer-purchased insurance through tax write-offs and by encouraging employers to contribute to worker coverage, federal programs hid high insurance costs from most consumers.

Through the framework of soft corporatism, policymakers were able to achieve some of their health insurance aims, in particular, rapid and far-reaching coverage growth. But because private interests stymied their ability to more directly mold the health care sector, policymakers failed to achieve their initial, primary goal of restructuring institutional arrangements. Instead, public and private power coalesced to entrench the very insurance company model that reformers hoped to replace.

THE IDEOLOGICAL SETTING OF SOFT CORPORATISM

As the Cold War contracted the nation's political framing, ideological encampments on the left and right repositioned toward the center. Liberal policymakers abandoned New Deal ambitions to fundamentally restructure the capitalist economy. In its hollowed-out form, liberalism attempted to wring social justice from markets by intensifying business regulation and expanding the welfare state.[3] Politicians not only defined themselves in opposition to communism, but also strove to avoid the heated political contests that had only recently set Europe ablaze. Thus, the most influential Republican leaders endorsed limited government intervention in the economy. Reflecting this belief, Eisenhower refused to roll back what remained of the New Deal state and also presided over broad expansions to the Social Security program. Although libertarians and conservative Republicans denounced what they viewed as "creeping socialism," they found themselves outside the policymaking mainstream.[4]

Officials and pundits occupying the ideological center pictured a dignified, depoliticized federal setting in which the government would act as a "helpful partner" to the private economy. Illustrative of ideologically moderate Democrats and Republicans, President Eisenhower conceived of the marketplace not as a self-regulating sector but as a collection of chaotic arrangements that, without supervision, would deepen societal inequality and spawn abuses from "the unbearable selfishness of vested interests."[5] Eisenhower envisioned policymakers using small doses of federal authority to compel disparate and competing groups to act in socially beneficial ways, thereby effecting class harmony and building support for the American brand of capitalism.[6]

Keynesian economics offered an attractive solution to policymakers occupying "the vital center."[7] It was, however, a superficial Keynesianism. Whether or not policymakers believed the British economist's theories explained the business cycle or called forth appropriate investment policies, his concern for aggregate demand to sustain employment and maintain economic growth provided justification for politicians who wished to tinker with capitalism at the margins.[8] Where the competitive market left gaps in the social structure, policymakers applied a plaster that blended Keynesian spending with programs designed to boost consumption.

One way policymakers could stimulate purchasing power was by surveying market sectors to identify and promote the manufacture of products to fit a consumer ideal – that is, products that were easy and cheap to acquire and that, by their availability to the mass public, fully displayed the prosperity and vitality of the U.S. economy. For example, politicians determined that most citizens should be able to purchase a home. They defined a healthy housing market as one that generated inexpensive and abundant home mortgages with low interest rates, minimal down payments, and long repayment periods. To comply with this objective, bankers accepted strict government regulation of mortgage products in exchange for federal underwriting to cover potential losses.[9]

By paying homage to King Keynes and his royal court of consumers, policymakers sought to strengthen the economy and, more broadly, the "American system." Families that purchased suburban homes with manicured lawns and one – perhaps even two – automobiles for commuting to work and visiting the new shopping mall would be immune to appeals from demagogues fomenting revolution. In the international public relations war against the Soviets, American leaders could point to not only homes and cars but also movie theaters, clothing, TVs, and well-stocked supermarkets to prove capitalism's superiority over communism. Never mind that government policies promoted cheap credit to enable such purchases and supplied the agricultural subsidies and highway construction grants that kept grocery stores bursting at the seams.[10]

Against this backdrop, private health care interests staunchly resisted government intermediation on behalf of consumers. Since the early twentieth century, organized physicians and business interests had obstructed both state and federal proposals to make health services more widely available. Furthermore, although the American Medical Association (AMA) finally approved health insurance at the end of the 1930s, the association's decades-long suppression of physician groups and medical prepayment had weakened the private sector. By 1945, only about a quarter of the population had health insurance.[11] Because employers purchased most insurance policies, white males in professional or union positions were far more likely to have coverage than African Americans or women. The elderly and chronically ill, who were generally unable to obtain insurance because of their employment status and the financial risks of covering them, relied on family resources or charity for medical care. Moreover, even insured individuals could amass large medical bills. Commercial insurance policies usually covered only a portion of catastrophic costs. Blue Cross provided more generous service benefits; however, the nonprofit's focus on first-dollar costs meant that seriously ill subscribers ran up considerable debt after their allocation of covered hospital days expired. Indeed, most commercial and nonprofit policies restricted coverage to hospital care; even insurance for physician bills slighted services rendered outside the hospital.[12]

Highlighting the underdeveloped state of health care financing and delivery was society's captivation with modern medicine. Media accounts heralded the "revolution in U.S. medicine" – penicillin, radiation therapies, advanced antibiotics, and pioneering surgeries made health care services more valuable than ever to patients.[13] Newly prosperous Americans desired ready access to these innovations, through both the family physician as well as specialists and modern hospitals.

Policymakers concluded that the prevailing insurance company model was incapable of satisfying this consumer demand – it certainly appeared far too flawed to deliver a consumer ideal of widely available, low-cost insurance with ample benefits. The health care system thus dangled low-hanging fruit before politicians seeking to enhance the economy. Anemic private sector organization even encouraged liberal policymakers to recommend nationalizing health care. However, to honor ideological trends that shunned broad exertions of governmental power, officials advanced their proposal using market concepts of product value and price.

TRUMAN'S PRAGMATIC REFORM

In 1945, President Truman inaugurated postwar reform debates by calling on Congress to nationalize health care. The proposal gained firm footing when, upsetting expert political projections, Truman won reelection in 1948, in part by campaigning on the issue of health care. To circumvent accusations of "communism," Truman and his allies promoted the program using nonideological, pragmatic arguments that emphasized the high costs, scanty benefits, and narrow coverage base of voluntary insurance. Reformers argued that federal supervision would impose order on health care arrangements, restructuring them to manufacture not only universal coverage but also inexpensive, generous insurance products with more consumer appeal.

The Truman plan, packaged legislatively as a revision of the Wagner-Murray-Dingell bill, proposed a comprehensive overhaul of the health care sector. To build up system infrastructure, the program would have poured federal funds into hospitals, medical schools, public health initiatives, and scientific research. The legislation contained state grants-in-aid to augment programming for both indigent and maternal and child health services. Additionally, the measure would have provided Social Security payments to workers for wages lost due to illness and disability. The most controversial platform called for expanding Social Security to establish universal health insurance.

Through federal administration and financing, reformers intended to supplant the insurance company model. However, to allay the concerns of voters and health care interests, administration officials underscored continuity between existing arrangements and the proposed framework. Citizens, promised reformers, would be able to choose their general practitioner. Doctors could decide whether or not to join the program. Policymakers pledged, moreover, that hospitals and participating physicians could safeguard their interests by nominating organizations in each geographical district to negotiate service requirements and compensation with federal representatives.[14] Despite these assurances, administration officials planned to gradually build up prepaid doctor groups while simultaneously weakening the individual physician practices and fee-for-service compensation associated with the insurance company model. Indeed, the legislation stipulated that only "qualified groups or medical organizations" could "furnish services" in return for federal payments.[15]

Reformers viewed prepaid groups as the best medium for making quality medical services widely accessible while also limiting the costs of social insurance. As discussed in Chapter 1, multispecialty doctor groups integrated medical care while constraining costs by remunerating physicians with fixed fees or a portion of revenues. They also provoked the ire of AMA leaders. However, Social Security Administration (SSA) officials had long been aligned with the prepaid group movement.[16] The principal authors of Truman's reform legislation – Isidore S. Falk and Wilbur Cohen – admired the economic model. Falk was director of the SSA's Bureau of Research and Statistics. Before holding that position, Falk had served as associate director for the Committee on the Costs of Medical Care (CCMC), where he had helped shape the well-known 1932 report recommending that the health care system be structured around prepaid groups. Wilbur Cohen served as the SSA's legislative liaison and chief assistant to Commissioner Arthur Altmeyer. Cohen began his government career during the 1930s as a research assistant for the Committee on Economic Security. There he worked with reformers, such as Falk, who came from the CCMC well versed in the advantages of prepaid groups. Moreover, labor leaders, who were important administration collaborators on health care reform, had long supported prepaid groups. Social Security officials displayed their allegiance to the organizational form by joining the Washington, D.C.–based Group Health Association (GHA) at the same time it was involved in an antitrust suit against the AMA.[17] Among GHA subscribers were Cohen, Altmeyer, and Nelson Cruikshank, an American Federation of Labor lobbyist and honorary member of the "social security 'family.'"[18]

Nevertheless, to avoid further provoking antagonists of national health care, particularly the AMA, reformers refrained from openly promoting new arrangements. Officials repeatedly claimed that doctors would be allowed to practice individually, although the frequency with which they made the assertion suggested one who "doth protest too much," thereby fostering physician suspicions.[19] When addressing an audience of doctors, Altmeyer sidestepped the issue, saying it "would be hazardous for a layman to undertake to discuss with physicians the pros and cons of individual practice versus group practice."[20] For all these reasons, it appears that policymakers intended to use prevailing organizational conventions, such as individual practice and fee-for-service payments, during the initial stages of nationalization and then progressively phase out features considered uneconomical.[21]

In another tactic designed to deflate political opposition, reformers couched their advocacy in pragmatic instead of ideological terms. When detractors charged that Truman's measure would "socialize medicine," supporters countered that the government would not own hospitals or directly employ physicians.[22] "I repeat," stated the president in his 1945 congressional message, "what I am recommending is not socialized medicine." He continued: "The American people want no such system. No such system is here proposed."[23] To skirt accusations of collectivism, reformers rarely employed broader political arguments about social justice or equity but instead used statistics and utilitarian descriptions to establish that voluntary arrangements were "expensive and burdensome."[24] Oscar Ewing, Secretary of the Federal Security Agency, forecast that the high costs of voluntary coverage would prevent insurers from ever covering more than half of citizens.[25] One oft-cited figure highlighted the poor health of World War II recruits: authorities classified 30 percent of draftees – almost five million men – as "unfit for military service."

Many of these men, contended reformers, had remediable health problems but lacked access to care.²⁶ Additionally, Social Security reports
catalogued the high price of insurance in exchange for paltry benefits.
One report showed that, on average, policies covered only 13 percent of
subscribers' annual medical costs. Recognizing that such data-driven
analysis represented their best means of swaying public opinion, SSA
officials included pharmaceutical, dental, and personal item expenses to
produce the dramatic statistic.²⁷

Reformers also furthered their cause by using the market-oriented
language of consumer preferences. Truman and his allies argued that
for a small investment, through increased payroll taxes and a portion of
general revenues, all citizens could access abundant medical care. The
Committee for the Nation's Health, a reform advocacy group founded
in 1946, published pamphlets and newspaper editorials to make this case:

American families right now are spending enough money for health care to
provide themselves with comprehensive services for all types of illness in and
out of the hospital including preventative care that would keep them well. The
only reason we don't have this type of comprehensive care is because we spend our
money the wrong way.²⁸

In this manner, reformers emphasized how "inefficient and wasteful"
the insurance company model was compared to the "efficiency and economy" of their program.²⁹

The way reformers framed the political debate helped transform the
attitudes of health care leaders who opposed Truman's plan. Organized
physicians, commercial insurers, and Blue Shield administrators – many
of whom had only recently and very reluctantly accepted health
insurance – now began championing medical prepayment. They more
aggressively nurtured the growth of insurance, maintaining that their
progress proved that the voluntary sector could adequately supply health
care without government interference. Blue Cross leaders, who favored
limited federal funding for insurance, nevertheless, opposed Truman's
far-reaching reforms; they therefore joined with other private interests
to support and publicize the vitality of voluntary coverage.

Republicans and business leaders also encouraged insurance market
expansion to aid the political position against nationalized health care.
Senator Arthur Vandenberg, a Michigan Republican, corresponded with
Blue Cross, Blue Shield, and physician leaders in his state, asking them
to swiftly grow coverage to present politicians with an "alternative ...
to give Congress a chance to register its preference for this voluntary

system."[30] Similarly, National Association of Manufacturers and Chamber of Commerce leaders urged member firms to supply health insurance for employees as a means of frustrating welfare state gains.[31]

The Truman bill failed for several reasons but primarily because, despite reformer efforts, debates ended up pitting socialism against "free enterprise." The AMA forcefully pounded the message of "socialized medicine" through newspapers, radio ads, allied civic groups, and the family doctor. Conservative lawmakers and business associations reiterated this message. A Chamber of Commerce brochure warned citizens that up to 10 percent of their salary would be diverted to fund health services similar to "socialized" services in England where "it's four minutes a patient."[32] Furthermore, a series of postwar strikes turned public opinion against unions, thereby weakening the image of key administration allies. Finally, because conservatives dominated the strategically crucial House Ways and Means and Senate Finance Committees, the proposal faced an arduous legislative route.

Nevertheless, Truman's initiative profoundly influenced health care by securely fastening the system to soft corporatist arrangements. The explicit comparisons made between voluntary coverage and government-managed insurance during legislative debates convinced private interests to more eagerly develop health care prepayment in order to, at least partially, meet product specifications laid out in the political realm. The legislation also created a template for future reform proposals. Although subsequent propositions sought more limited applications of government power, they also attempted to improve the health insurance product available to consumers.

TOWARD THE CONSUMER IDEAL IN HEALTH CARE

Many politicians who opposed Truman's plan nevertheless conceded that the insurance company model was inefficient and inequitable. They therefore offered their own legislative initiatives to remake the market so that it produced generous, all-inclusive health insurance for most Americans. Recurrent reform proposals, offered throughout the Eisenhower administration, intensified soft corporatist conditions by guiding private interests not only toward multiplying the number of insurance subscribers, but also toward fulfilling a consumer ideal for comprehensive insurance that covered most costs associated with medical care. To understand this process, we must examine how various interest groups hoped to steer the marketplace immediately following the defeat of Truman's plan.

Private interests divided over whether liberalizing insurance coverage was a laudable goal. The view of each group – labor unions, nonprofit plans, organized physicians, and commercial insurers – depended on the economic objectives of members. Thus, understanding how each group sought to augment members' market status clarifies the divergent political positions among private interests.

The Truman reform proposal prompted physicians, insurers, and employers to more fully embrace and expand medical coverage; nevertheless, health insurance remained expensive and limited. Just as underwriters had forecast, insurance company arrangements caused medical service costs and, concomitantly, policy premiums to escalate swiftly. During the late 1940s, right as health insurance gained firm footing among the populace, medical care cost surges began outpacing price increases in all other goods categories in the Consumer Price Index.[33] Although almost half the population had medical coverage by 1950, cost concerns persuaded insurers to continue restricting policy benefits.[34] On average, subscribers had approximately 70 percent of their hospital bill paid if they had an illness severe enough to warrant hospital admission. Routine illnesses generally failed to activate insurance: fewer than 15 percent of citizens had coverage for services delivered outside the hospital.[35]

Union leaders argued that only policies that fully covered health care costs could adequately maintain worker security. This concept reinforced an ideological commitment to the common laborer arrayed against powerful interests. In political debates, activism on behalf of generous, government-funded insurance set unions in opposition to insurance companies, the AMA, and employers in the form of the National Association of Manufacturers and the Chamber of Commerce. Unions confronted members of many of these same groups when they negotiated over privately supplied worker benefits.[36] According to A. J. Hayes, President of the International Association of Machinists, workers desired all-inclusive insurance, which would provide "greater access to the kind of health care which prevents illness or nips it in the bud." He warned that without such coverage, "we must, and I predict we will, turn to some system of national health insurance."[37] Through such advocacy, unions captured a more expansive role than simply representing members – they informally acted on behalf of the broader consuming public.

Labor officials often attacked the insurance company model for failing to furnish comprehensive coverage. They also questioned the connection between health care and for-profit insurance companies, particularly since commercial insurers had a long history of cooperating with businesses to unilaterally introduce employee benefits as a way to obstruct union organizing. Like many of their political allies, labor leaders preferred to see health care develop around prepaid groups. Prepaid groups offered generous benefits, in part by checking physician autonomy to set individual fees. Moreover, by constraining provider sovereignty, prepaid groups would potentially give unions more influence over the health care system. Within the insurance company model, union representatives favored Blue Cross because nonprofit administrators claimed to privilege community goals above revenue concerns. Nonprofit service benefits – which covered the full cost of each policy provision – came much closer to fulfilling union aims for worker coverage than did the indemnity benefits and partial payments of commercial insurers.[38]

Like unions, Blue Cross leaders furthered the notion among consumers that health insurance should cover most medical bills. To demonstrate their fealty to social welfare, the administrators who ran nonprofit hospital plans offered policies with service benefits and community rating, or uniform prices for all subscribers within each age group. And plan administrators continually sought ways to liberalize this coverage. One early nonprofit leader explained that when commercial companies moved in on Blue Cross territory, entering the health insurance market during the late 1930s, the "competitive pressure" only "sharpened the plans['] desire to broaden their benefits, to jockey for a higher percent of coverage and do a better job."[39] Blue Cross, for example, pioneered maternity coverage during the 1940s.[40] Following the defeat of Truman's plan, Frank Van Dyk, an administrator with the New York City Blue Cross Plan and a recognized leader in the national movement, urged nonprofit plans to continue enlarging policy benefits. Striking a very different chord than his cautious brethren in the for-profit industry, Van Dyk declared there was "a clear indication that the public seeks a full measure of protection."[41] However, Blue Cross sold only hospital insurance, and Blue Shield, which covered physician services, did not share this outlook. Because of Blue Shield's close association with physicians, nonprofit medical plan leaders, particularly during the 1940s and early 1950s, held much narrower conceptions of insurance coverage. Blue Cross administrators thus charged ahead of commercial companies and Blue Shield, content to fulfill the consumer ideal policymakers advanced during reform debates.

However, Blue Cross leaders recognized that offering generous benefits at uniform prices to all population groups required government funding. Providing liberal coverage in a competitive market had created serious financial difficulties for nonprofit plans. On one hand, service benefits appealed to consumers. On the other hand, because insurance companies sold indemnity benefits, which usually covered only a portion of each service or procedure, they could undercut nonprofits with lower-priced policies. Additionally, commercial insurers used experience rating instead of community rating to offer less expensive coverage to relatively healthy employee groups. As insurance companies ate into Blue Cross market share and hospital plans expanded coverage for increasingly expensive care, nonprofits struggled to right their balance sheets. Federal aid presented a simple remedy. Blue Cross leaders therefore joined with their American Hospital Association (AHA) partners to lobby for federal subsidies to state programs to purchase insurance for the poor, elderly, and unemployed.

The connection between Blue Cross devotion to liberal benefits and support for federal health care funding was not lost on AMA leaders. AMA President Walter Martin criticized policies "with the provision that the recipient pays no part of the cost." Martin warned that with such coverage, "a situation will evolve whereby the taxing authority will be the only agency that can finance such an operation."[42] A strengthened Blue Cross, which received federal assistance and joined with politicians to pursue social goals, posed a considerable threat to physician power and autonomy.

Thus, even as they advertised spectacular insurance expansion to prove the voluntary sector's superiority over government programming, physicians complained that labor officials and nonprofit leaders were persuading consumers to expect an economically unrealistic product. Physicians shuddered at the thought of attaching third-party financing to every aspect of medicine. They feared that as generous coverage drove up health care prices, insurers would attempt to constrain costs by regulating doctors.[43] AMA leaders therefore condemned the "insistence of certain labor groups on comprehensive coverage" and emphasized the "pitfalls" of the "Blue Cross service concept."[44] "The man on the street," groused AMA official Frank Dickinson, "has been lulled into believing that he is being robbed if he does not get at least one claim check from his health insurance plan almost every year." Dickinson, who served as director of the AMA's Bureau of Medical Economic Research, observed that "most car owners deem their collision insurance 'comprehensive,' even though they must pay the first $50 of a collision claim."[45]

Commercial insurers also worried about unreasonable public expectations. Underpinning this concern were the inherent flaws of insurance company arrangements – insurers lacked the ability to restrain consumer demand for excessive health services or prevent physicians from providing such care. Companies thus limited the amount of care they would insure, generally restricting policies to cover a portion of costs incurred during catastrophic health care events. Insurance firms also expended considerable resources to educate subscribers to view health insurance as a "limited mechanism."[46] Industry trade associations dispatched speakers to civic organizations, women's groups, and businesses to lecture policyholders on the merits of catastrophic or major medical coverage. Covering small claims, contended industry representatives, produced a system of "trading dollars" that only drove up premium prices. Pamphlets distributed to consumers argued that the purpose of insurance was to protect against large, unforeseeable financial risks, such as those posed by serious accidents or grave diseases.[47] Equitable explained to customers that only "through our type of Major Medical Expense policy is it possible to hedge against such misfortune at reasonable cost."[48] Notwithstanding such publicity and marketing campaigns, for-profit insurers failed to curb consumer appetites for all-inclusive coverage. An industry leader commented on how nonprofit benefits were altering the evolution of commercial insurance:

[T]he public has become accustomed to forms of protection which provide payment for small bills. . . . The development of public acceptance [for such coverage] will affect labor union bargaining. It will affect the attitude of employers in the purchase of group insurance. It will affect the attitude of public leaders, of those in public office, and of public opinion generally.[49]

Insurers began to understand that, despite their best efforts, their perception of the insurance product's form and function was failing to win adherents in either the marketplace or the political arena.

Indeed, throughout the 1950s, media exposés spotlighted meager insurance benefits, including policies that left subscribers who assumed they were protected with large medical bills. *Reader's Digest* counseled consumers to exercise caution when purchasing coverage: "At its shabby worst, it [health insurance] can amount to a legalized confidence game that involves brow beating the sick, the maimed and the bereaved."[50] While sick patients who battled profiteering insurance companies made good copy, the muckraking campaign also helped popularize the idea that policy benefits should be liberalized. According to a 1956 survey, the leading complaint among the insured was that policies failed to adequately cover medical bills. The majority of respondents reported willingness to pay higher premiums in exchange for more complete coverage.[51]

We can imagine a health insurance market, similar to the automobile insurance market, in which consumers purchased coverage for unusually large bills related to acute medical events. To the disappointment of physician leaders and for-profit insurers, this market paradigm would not be realized. Instead, through political and public discussions, policymakers, labor officials, and Blue Cross leaders forwarded the idea that health insurance should cover almost all costs associated with medical care. Each of these groups sought varying degrees of government subsidization to support their vision of an expansive health insurance market.

INFORMAL AUTHORITY: HEALTH CARE REFORM UNDER EISENHOWER

Under Eisenhower, unremitting political pressure compelled private interests, even those preferring limited insurance, to work vigorously to enlarge both the depth and breadth of health care coverage. Although Truman's plan had been decisively defeated, many policymakers viewed the insurance company model as fragile and therefore vulnerable to subsequent calls for nationalization. In 1953, Oveta Culp Hobby, Eisenhower's Health, Education, and Welfare (HEW) secretary, declared that the medical insurance sector required "expanding and perfecting."[52] Eisenhower insisted that "[b]etter health insurance protection for more people can be provided."[53] Throughout the 1950s, ideologically moderate politicians – often described as "liberal Republicans" or "conservative Democrats" – proposed tempered forms of federal intervention to create a market worthy of being proclaimed a triumph of "free enterprise." These legislative measures varied: some sought to empower prepaid groups, others attempted to strengthen nonprofit plans, and the president proposed federal subsidies or "reinsurance" for insuring agencies that incurred losses when broadening coverage in a socially desirable manner.

These "compromise" reforms were modest compared to Truman's legislation; however, they had the potential to reorganize the marketplace in ways that imperiled private interests, particularly physicians and commercial insurers. Health interests therefore attempted to defeat the initiatives by fulfilling the consumer ideal for widely available, comprehensive coverage. Consequently, moderate reform proposals, though unsuccessful in the legislative realm, wrought extensive informal authority. Indeed, the federal direction accompanying soft corporatism intensified after 1950 because reform bills were continually presented, over the space of almost a decade, and because the measures came from the political bedfellows of private health interests.

Prepaid Groups

As we have seen, prepaid doctor groups had long appealed to liberal policymakers, health care reformers, and labor leaders. However, by Eisenhower's term, their allure had faded somewhat. Because of decades of AMA hostility toward group physicians, prepaid groups had difficulty establishing themselves: by the 1950s, they provided less than 10 percent of health insurance.[54] Nevertheless, the efficiency of prepaid groups, coupled with their reputation for quality care, continued to entice politicians seeking ways to reform health care.

After losing the fight for universal insurance, Truman created the President's Commission on the Health Needs of the Nation. In 1952, the bipartisan commission delivered a remarkably prescient report with recommendations that closely paralleled the reforms that policymakers would pass over the following two decades. The report advocated increased federal funding for hospitals, medical research, and medical schools; it also called for a new Social Security program to provide health insurance for the elderly.[55] One of the few suggestions that failed to gain passage was a proposal to cultivate prepaid doctor groups through federal subsidization.[56]

The 1955 Wolverton-Kasier bill also attempted to bolster prepaid groups. The legislation would have supplied prepaid groups with federally insured loans to purchase or construct medical facilities. The initiative attracted bipartisan interest – Representative Charles A. Wolverton, a New Jersey Republican, received union support, albeit tepid given the proposal's limited nature. Wolverton found a more enthusiastic advocate in Henry J. Kaiser, the West Coast industrialist who had founded prepaid groups to deliver health care to his workers and the broader community.[57]

These reform efforts fell easily before the united disapproval of organized physicians, commercial insurers, and nonprofit insurance leaders. After decades of fighting "corporate medicine" as incompatible with doctor autonomy and a foundation for government-managed health care, the AMA vigorously contested initiatives to strengthen prepaid groups. The *Journal of the American Medical Association* labeled the Health Needs of the Nation report "creeping socialism by commission."[58] Worried about the Wolverton-Kaiser bill's potential to subvert insurance company arrangements, AMA leaders urged members to write their congressmen by explaining the legislation as follows:

Labor unions, industries and others who could qualify would build hospitals and clinics and hire physicians on a salary basis to staff them. Thus the private practitioner who practices on a fee [-for-service] basis would find himself involved in strong competition with the federally subsidized physician.[59]

Commercial and nonprofit insurers objected to any federal plan that would aid their prepaid group competitors. Particularly in western states where prepaid groups were more prevalent, some medical societies had founded Blue Shield plans specifically to thwart their expansion. In a delightful mingling of metaphors, one Blue Shield leader branded prepaid groups "supermarket medicine," where doctors offered "cold, impersonal service rendered with the same interest as a postal clerk dispensing stamps."[60]

Proposals to strengthen prepaid group policies failed, and they remained a small market niche. Yet the mere existence of prepaid groups – which commonly provided more generous coverage at lower costs than insurance companies – highlighted inefficiencies in the broader market. Indeed, during the 1970s, policymakers would return to the prepaid group idea under the refurbished label of "Health Maintenance Organizations."

Nonprofit Service Benefits

Nonprofit plans appealed to politicians desiring to expand insurance organizations governed in "the public interest." With their uniform community pricing and generous service benefits, nonprofit plans put a kinder, gentler face on health insurance. Some policymakers advanced initiatives explicitly intended to boost Blue Cross and Blue Shield while other politicians advocated proposals that would have effectively privileged nonprofit policies over commercial insurance, even if not specifically designed to do so.

During the Truman debates, many legislators who wished to impede comprehensive reform backed scaled-down, alternative measures. The 1946 Taft-Smith-Ball bill, which carried the sponsorship of conservative lion Senator Robert Taft (R, OH), proposed federal funding for states that purchased health insurance for the poor. The legislation required means testing for beneficiaries but otherwise granted local authorities broad flexibility.[61] Using the template of federal grants-in-aid for state programming, legislators put forth additional substitutes for Truman's plan. During the Eisenhower administration, these initiatives reemerged as alternatives, this time to the Republican president's suggested reforms.

Flanders-Ives legislation would have organized the health care market exclusively around nonprofit insurance. Under the proposal, state governments, aided by federal funding, would purchase nonprofit policies and then resell those policies with prices adjusted to reflect each subscriber's income. The poor would receive coverage for free. Prominent Republicans – Senators Ralph Flanders (VT) and Irving Ives (NY) as well as Representative Richard Nixon (CA) – formulated the measure in 1949.[62] Because the legislation provided universal coverage, Arthur Altmeyer later lamented that Democrats had missed a critical opportunity for reform by declining to negotiate over the plan.[63] Senators Flanders and Ives reintroduced the bill in 1953 and 1955, touting their measure as superior to Eisenhower's health care recommendations.[64]

Another bill advancing nonprofit insurance also surfaced during the Truman administration. The AHA helped Senators George Aiken (R, VT) and Lister Hill (D, AL) draft legislation providing federal aid to states that purchased insurance for low-income citizens.[65] Although the bill did not require administrators to purchase nonprofit insurance, AHA leaders and their Blue Cross counterparts recognized that state officials would tend to favor nonprofit over commercial coverage. Nonprofit, community values would appeal to local policymakers. Moreover, nonprofit service benefits would reduce out-of-pocket expenses for program recipients. The Hill-Aiken bill gained considerable support among Southern Democrats, but advocates of universal insurance criticized the legislation as a lavish sop to voluntary interests.

The Hill-Aiken approach became the cornerstone of subsequent Blue Cross petitions for federal aid.[66] Blue Cross administrators favored Hill-Aiken over Flanders-Ives legislation because it provided government funding with minimal oversight. The executive director of Philadelphia Blue Cross, E. A. Van Steenwyk, promoted Hill-Aiken arrangements in his 1952 testimony before the President's Commission on the Health Needs of the Nation. Van Steenwyk emphasized that because program recipients would be able to use the same Blue Cross cards as regular subscribers, "the indignity of a means test imposed at the time of requiring service would be avoided."[67] The commission's final report endorsed the Hill-Aiken model and praised nonprofit service benefits for permitting subscribers to receive preventative care.[68] In 1954, Senator Hill asked

AHA and Blue Cross leaders to provide his office with cost estimates for government-provided elderly insurance. In response, the two associations established a joint committee that, using the Hill-Aiken bill as a blueprint, drafted legislation directing federal aid to states to purchase coverage for the elderly, poor, and unemployed.[69] Throughout Eisenhower's tenure, Blue Cross representatives lobbied administration officials and Congress for a Hill-Aiken–type program to buttress their faltering market position.

Initiatives that directed federal funding toward nonprofits foundered because they failed to attract sufficient support among politicians on either side of the aisle. The Eisenhower administration and many congressional Republicans refused to privilege nonprofit coverage over other forms of voluntary insurance.[70] Policymakers on the left supported another approach. After the defeat of Truman's proposal, reformers began pursuing health insurance for the elderly through Social Security. Because the program would be administered at the federal level, liberal politicians believed it held considerable promise as a foundation for universal coverage. Furthermore, although labor leaders and reformers had traditionally favored nonprofits over commercial insurance companies, that inclination began to wane during the 1950s. Blue Cross and Blue Shield had evolved into significant components of the insurance company model. Not only were nonprofit policy prices rising rapidly but also, to avoid bankruptcy, nonprofit plans began to desert community rating. These developments caused long-time nonprofit allies to reevaluate their loyalties.

Moreover, outside of Blue Cross, private health interests opposed grants-in-aid measures. At the end of the 1940s, AMA representatives had consulted with Senator Taft on his grants-in-aid legislation and were friendly to the cause; however, the association's Board of Trustees ultimately declined to endorse the plan.[71] Organized physicians resisted any federal funding for health care on the grounds that all such "fringe bills," no matter how moderate, would eventually produce complete governmental control. And they ardently opposed proposals that would endow ideologically unreliable Blue Cross leaders with federal subsidies. Although Blue Shield would have also received a financial boost from the Hill-Aiken approach, medical plan leaders had to fall in line behind the AMA and the medical societies that supervised them.[72] Moreover, commercial insurers lobbied heavily against federal programs that would strengthen their nonprofit competitors. In 1956, industry leaders extracted assurances from Eisenhower's second HEW secretary, Marion Folsom, that the Republican administration would not back legislation that privileged nonprofit plans.[73]

Legislation that supported nonprofit benefits would have preserved the insurance company model and accompanying cost problems. However, sponsors believed that federal funding would ameliorate nonprofit financial difficulties while undermining the health care system's commercial elements and achieving the consumer ideal through generous service benefits. Although fragmented political support hindered legislative success, the proposals caused alarm among physicians and commercial insurers who perceived that policymakers were determined – in one way or another – to not only increase insurance coverage rates but also liberalize benefits.

Reinsurance

In January 1954, Eisenhower sent a special message to Congress proposing a reinsurance plan as a means of "rejecting the socialization of medicine." Citing rising health care costs, the president offered financial assistance to help voluntary interests fulfill the consumer ideal. The proposal, explained Eisenhower, was calculated "to encourage private and nonprofit health insurance organizations to offer broader health protection to more families."[74]

The Eisenhower administration introduced legislation for federal reinsurance in 1954 and again in 1955 with increased funding. The measure called for $100 million to establish the Health Services Corporation, a federal agency that would subsequently be funded through a tax on insurance premiums. Similar to federal underwriting programs for home mortgages, the plan would cover up to 75 percent of losses that insurance agencies incurred when liberalizing benefits or extending policies to "marginal actuarial risks," such as the elderly and chronically ill. Officials in the Health Services Corporation would decide which companies qualified for the subsidies by behaving "responsibly" and issuing policies that "showed promise of enlarging the scope of voluntary health insurance coverage or improving the benefits it provides."[75]

Some commercial insurance leaders considered supporting the plan, both to head off comprehensive reform and to lend the Republican administration support. However, a conservative faction of insurers carried the day, arguing that federal reinsurance threatened for-profit firms and, more broadly, private health care. To participate in the program, insurers would have to open their accounting books to federal bureaucrats. And, argued conservative insurers, officials in the Health Services Corporation would have the discretion to favor nonprofits and prepaid groups with subsidies if they deemed them more "responsible" than commercial companies. Opponents also worried that policymakers would exploit the program to gain control over the insurance market by incrementally extending their purview to begin regulating policy prices and benefits as well as physician and hospital fees.[76]

The Eisenhower administration pulled out all the stops to coax support out of the AMA. HEW officials arranged a meeting between the AMA's top brass and insurance executives who backed federal reinsurance. The administration also dispatched political allies, such as Republican Senator H. Alexander Smith (NJ), to lobby AMA heads. HEW Secretary Hobby appeared before the AMA's House of Delegates, arguing that the reform package offered physicians their only hope of preventing socialized medicine.[77] Nevertheless, conservative insurers had little difficulty persuading AMA officials to contest reinsurance legislation on the grounds that it would inevitably evolve into government-managed medicine.[78]

Nonprofit leaders split over the measure. As was their wont, Blue Shield administrators sided with the AMA. "I am convinced," argued a Blue Shield spokesman, "that a Government reinsurance program is quite as likely to bring Government control of the medical economy as any of the other devices that have been proposed in the past."[79] Blue Cross representatives, though lacking enthusiasm, testified before Congress on behalf of the administration's reform. Blue Cross leaders backed reinsurance legislation, but only to earn goodwill among the officials whom they were lobbying for state grants-in-aid and because they wanted to influence the final bill in case it did pass.[80]

Like other moderate reform proposals, the reinsurance initiative failed to attract sufficient political backing. Conservative congressmen were reluctant to incur the wrath of organized physicians. Moderate legislators split over which health reform package to support, with some preferring the Flanders-Ives or Hill-Aiken proposals. Republican congressional leaders had difficulty rounding up affirmative votes, and even congressmen who carried the administration's water during hearings displayed halfhearted support.[81] On the left, politicians criticized the legislation as a "diversionary effort."[82]

Defeating Reform Proposals with the Insurance Company Model

Organized physicians and their allies among insurers emerged triumphant from each political skirmish. However, to achieve their victories they had to undertake activities beyond debates and lobbying, outside the political realm. Reinsurance, along with alternative reform proposals, served notice to private interests that they had not yet reached the consumer ideal – put forth by policymakers in league with groups such as labor unions – for increased policyholder numbers and more generous insurance.

Governmental action, reformers contended, was necessary to produce health insurance that conformed to political ideas about a robust economy that was both sustained by and also solicitous of purchasing power. Secretary Hobby explained that Eisenhower's conservative, pro-business administration sought reform because health care presented an exceptional case "where the resources of only the Federal Government" were "sufficient to assure economical and effective action."[83] Similarly, the president argued for reinsurance legislation, asserting that "the Federal government should perform an essential task only when it cannot otherwise be adequately performed."[84] Thus, doctors and insurers understood that a significant portion of their political combat would involve sculpting and shaping the insurance company model to prove it could fulfill the politically endorsed consumer ideal.

Federal officials carried the message about consumers directly to private interests, warning them that the government would enter health care if they failed to substantially expand coverage. Democratic Congressman Oren Harris (AR) delivered the following missive to the AMA's House of Delegates:

If the American people should feel that large segments of the population, as, for example, the aged or the chronically ill, are unable to secure adequate medical care because the cost of such medical care is beyond their ability to pay, then they will call upon the Congress to meet these needs. . . . I hope that some of the serious health needs to which I have referred can be met by your profession with the aid of private "third parties." If they are not met in this manner, public pressure will be growing steadily about enlarging the area in which the federal government should participate as a "third party in medicine."[85]

Similarly, at their annual industry meeting, HEW Secretary Folsom encouraged commercial insurers to broaden health coverage, reminding them that "as you in private enterprise meet the needs of the people, then the people will not find it necessary to resort to broad Government action."[86]

This political atmosphere explains why organized physicians and insurers altered their market behavior and, despite their initial wishes to the contrary, dramatically enlarged subscriber numbers and policy benefits. The only way to defeat proposed reforms was by accomplishing the very objectives that many politicians had identified as too difficult for the voluntary sector. AMA, Blue Shield, and commercial insurance leaders who had only grudgingly supported health care prepayment evolved into its most fervent supporters. During the 1950s, almost every meeting or publication of private medical groups featured speeches and articles calling on doctors and insurers to prevent federal interference in health care by expanding coverage. An insurance executive summed up the degree to which political purposes had shaped the goals of private interests:

[S]omehow and in some way the base of insurance coverage for protection against disease must be broadened. The Utopia is, of course, that we may evolve a system of total and comprehensive medical care ... we should make every effort to achieve this goal by voluntary means instead of by compulsion.[87]

To thwart legislative initiatives, not only did voluntary interests have to cover more citizens, they also had to reconceptualize the function of insurance. Stripped-down policies that covered only a portion of hospital costs were no longer feasible – nothing less than all-inclusive benefits would satisfy the objectives laid out by policymakers.

Whenever doctors and insurers challenged health care legislation – whether in congressional testimony, public statements, advertisements, or newspaper editorials – they grounded their opposition in the significant increase and liberalization of voluntary insurance. Examining the testimony of physicians and insurers in only one instance, the 1954 House hearings on reinsurance legislation, demonstrates broad "acceptance of the thesis that if private enterprise over a reasonable period of time does not meet public demands, the people turn to the government."[88] In their testimony against the initiative, AMA leaders lauded "the tremendous strides" of voluntary insurance and the "improvement in benefits provided to meet the desire of the public for more adequate protection." They also apprised committee members of medical society efforts to fill in coverage gaps by establishing programs for indigent care.[89] A Blue Shield representative boasted that in the previous ten years, nonprofit medical plans had enrolled over 29 million subscribers, were adding about 20,000 members a day, and were experimenting with coverage "on a more liberal basis," including the "removal of certain types of exclusions, and the extension of benefits into previously uncovered areas of medical and surgical care."[90] A commercial insurance executive explained how the industry had expanded policies far beyond what actuaries initially thought feasible:

[W]e are doing things today that 30 years ago any health underwriter could have proved were impossible. One by one we have issued a little bit of this and it has worked, and so we have issued some more. Hospital insurance was impossible and surgical insurance was impossible and major medical insurance was certainly impossible. We learned by trying and, lo and behold, they do not work out as bad as we thought they would.[91]

More than simply a recitation of facts and figures, congressional testimonies – occurring throughout the 1950s around a variety of reform measures – acted as periodic progress reports, allowing physicians and insurers to reveal what they had achieved in designing the insurance product to meet political expectations.

Through such interactions, health insurance evolved from a marketplace-based, commercial product into a product forged, at least partly, in the realm of politics. To continually beat back reform initiatives, physicians and insurers had to prove that they were making headway toward fulfilling the publicly negotiated consumer ideal. This demonstration required them to develop health insurance far beyond what had seemed conceivable only a decade earlier. Private interests attempted to cover an overwhelming majority of the population as well as transform insurance into a means for covering most health care bills. However, given the insurance company model's imperfections, voluntary interests could broaden coverage only so far without help from the government.

FORMAL AUTHORITY: EMPLOYER-PROVIDED INSURANCE

In addition to informally directing insurance development by laying out consumer standards in legislative proposals and political debates, policymakers applied formal governmental authority to foster market maturation. Tax guidelines that encouraged businesses to purchase insurance for workers and a massive health benefits program for federal workers yoked the insurance company model to employer provision. Scholars have demonstrated how employer-provided insurance spurred voluntary coverage growth and, in so doing, undermined the possibility of comprehensive health care reform.[92]

These policies had the added effect of entrenching soft corporatist arrangements, that is, the pattern of negotiations among interest groups and the state over what form the insurance product would assume. Because union leaders had a significant voice in brokering worker benefits, employer provision empowered them to influence the insurance market by demanding generous coverage, which, in turn, created a benchmark that affected the expectations of policymakers and consumers. Moreover, during congressional hearings on the FEHBP, the competing market perspectives of nonprofit and commercial insurers became matters of public debate. Most crucially, employer-provided benefits assisted health interests as they expanded coverage and broadened benefits. Rapidly rising premium prices, caused by inefficiencies inherent to the insurance company model, may well have sunk the voluntary sector campaign to spread insurance as an antidote to government reform. However, indirect federal subsidization in the form of business tax write-offs stimulated employer contributions to worker benefits, thereby hiding the full cost of insurance from most policyholders. In sum, federal policies both fueled the consumer ideal for liberal benefits and also made it possible.

Internal Revenue Code of 1954

Since the founding of the Internal Revenue Service (IRS) in 1913, the agency had permitted businesses to deduct contributions to employee fringe benefits from total taxable income. What was initially a minor tax regulation developed into a policy with significant repercussions. By subsidizing the purchase of employee health insurance, the tax loophole served several business objectives, including frustrating union organizing, aiding workers, and impeding federal health care reform. By the 1950s, labor leaders were making the system work on their behalf. Unions had lost the fight to move the health care economy away from the insurance company model; nevertheless, employer-provided benefits granted them substantial influence over product features within that model.

As employer-provided benefits spread at the end of the 1940s, some policymakers began questioning the government's annual forfeiture of millions of dollars in corporate tax revenues. Moreover, a series of court cases and IRS rulings created uncertainty about what types of benefits qualified for the write-off. The Eisenhower administration wanted to preserve the write-off to support the growth of "privately" supplied pensions as well as life and health insurance.[93] Accordingly, Treasury officials convinced Congress to codify the provision in the Internal Revenue Act of 1954. Administration representatives worked with corporate leaders, including two insurance executives, to fashion a tax exemption without any regulatory strings.[94]

Labor leaders' astute understanding of how the tax code would affect the insurance sector underscored their critical role in guiding market

developments. Union representatives lobbied Treasury officials to preserve tax guidelines that rewarded businesses for purchasing employee
benefits and that allowed workers to receive insurance tax free, unham-
pered by regulations that might treat policies as earned income. Caught
between their preference for government-supplied universal insurance
and the impossibility of obtaining that aim under a Republican administration, labor leaders adopted a pragmatic stance – they embraced their
position at the negotiating table to shape the insurance product.[95]
Tailoring their political appeal to attract administration officials, Congress of Industrial Organizations (CIO) representatives contended that
the tax break would propel "the continued growth of voluntary prepayment plans and their development as a mechanism for providing comprehensive health services."[96]

As they bargained with employers over fringe benefits, union leaders
cast the insurance company product to fit their vision of worker security.
Nor did they hesitate to position their full weight behind this objective.
Marie Gottschalk found that during the first half of the 1950s, approximately 70 percent of strikes involved health and welfare issues.[97] In
response to union pressure on employers, both nonprofit and commercial
insurers customized their products to fit labor preferences. By the second
half of the 1950s, unions were crafting a new gold standard in health
insurance: they convinced employers to purchase last-dollar, commercial
major medical policies to layer atop first-dollar, nonprofit service plans.
This market trend, in conjunction with the political environment, persuaded commercial insurers to begin selling comprehensive policies that
covered everything from lab and diagnostic tests to physician visits.
"Labor has been a prime mover in creating the health insurance market,"
reported a union official in the 1960s. He continued, adding with satisfaction: "it has drawn the commercial insurance business deep into what
the carriers regard as the insecure ground of service plans that include a
wide range of contingencies and many small medical bills."[98]

Employer-supplied insurance emboldened demands for liberal benefits
in another way: business contributions to worker premiums obscured
the full costs of coverage from policyholders. Insurance executives and
physician leaders had long argued that workers should pay a significant
portion of policy premiums, thus compelling them to consider the advantage of less coverage for lower prices. However, federal tax breaks encouraged management to assume a growing percentage of insurance costs.
Because businesses could purchase insurance with untaxed dollars and
because medical care prices were rising more rapidly than other goods

and services, labor representatives often preferred increased employer contributions to health coverage over higher wages.[99] According to one estimate, in 1950, only 12 percent of all Blue Cross subscribers enjoyed employer contributions toward their coverage.[100] By 1954, employers paid the full cost of health insurance, whether nonprofit or commercial, for 62 percent of union members.[101] Generous benefits for organized workers rippled through the employment sector, affecting nonunion provision as well: by 1962, businesses shouldered 65–70 percent of the average employee's health insurance premium.[102] Since workers directly paid for only a fraction of their health insurance, they often sought comprehensive coverage.[103]

Liberal insurance benefits drove up premium prices, deepening disparities between employee group subscribers and citizens who purchased policies individually, without the aid of employer contributions. Because group benefits were linked to employment, women were less likely to have coverage. Only one-third of women worked for wages during the 1950s and of those, two-thirds worked part-time or seasonally. Although employers increasingly offered workers coverage for dependents, the practice linked women's health care access to a male breadwinner. Additionally, as benefits were related to one's position in the corporate hierarchy, African Americans, the working poor, and rural laborers often lacked insurance.[104] A 1955 survey found that although 80 percent of families with annual incomes over $5,000 had insurance, only 40 percent of families with earnings below $3,000 and 45 percent of rural residents owned medical coverage.[105]

Tax breaks for businesses that purchased employee benefits helped private interests spread and liberalize insurance despite swiftly increasing costs. Employer provision also furnished an avenue for channeling union conceptions of coverage into the developing insurance system. Labor leaders helped reshape the boundaries of the insurance company model so that all consumers, not just union members, began to view the insurance product as nothing less than a means for covering most health care costs. Nevertheless, groups with weak ties to the labor force were often left out of the consumer pact.

Federal Employees Health Benefits Program

The second policy through which officials exercised formal authority was the Federal Employees Health Benefits Program (FEHBP). Politicians recognized that in covering almost two million federal workers, the program would support health interests as they expanded insurance while also setting a norm for private sector benefits. Nonprofit and commercial leaders competed with one another to secure a dominant place in the FEHBP – in order to legitimize their benefits as superior, acquire a lucrative government account, and create a precedent for future federal programming. The resulting plan, which allowed workers to choose among commercial and nonprofit coverage options, ratified the process of strengthening the insurance company model by enshrining and subsidizing liberal coverage as standard.

Blue Cross officials spent much of the 1950s petitioning policymakers to create a health insurance fund for government workers. By the late 1950s, about half of federal employees had Blue Cross coverage. However, without a formal benefits program, workers lacked employer contributions, and nonprofit administrators had to collect premium payments either individually or through unions.[106]

Commercial insurers worried about nonprofits controlling health insurance for federal workers. They not only loathed the idea of losing such a large account to nonprofits but also feared that Blue Cross and Blue Shield benefits for federal employees would create a pattern for subsequent government programs – whether for veterans, the elderly, or indigent.[107] Thus, for-profit leaders went on the offensive by leveraging their position as life insurance providers for the federal government. The 1954 legislation that created life insurance benefits for federal employees required participating companies to establish a contingency reserve. The reserve grew so large that, two years later, industry leaders proposed offering program participants major medical policies at no additional cost.[108] The Eisenhower administration supported the bid as a cost-effective way to provide government workers with health insurance. Blue Cross leaders were furious at the attempt of commercial insurers to steal the federal account out from under them.[109]

In congressional hearings, private health interests replayed long-standing arguments about coverage generosity and what form insurance should take. Blue Cross representative James Stuart blasted commercial coverage. Because large annual deductibles required major medical subscribers to pay for routine health care, Stuart compared the coverage to "building a house from the roof down." Nonprofit service benefits, argued Stuart, were "the keystone in the arch of family protection against the cost of illness."[110] Commercial insurers responded by playing upon policymaker concerns about program costs. One industry lobbyist counseled congressmen that "available insurance dollars are best used when they are concentrated on benefits which are available in the time of desperate need when costs of illness have reached a catastrophic point." He continued: "Where a choice is to be made, it should be made in favor of the last dollar and not the first dollar of protection."[111] In the end, the desire of union officials to exact a more generous program and one that offered an array of choices sank the commercial industry's major medical proposal.[112]

Blue Cross representatives worked with HEW and Civil Service Commission officials to help write the final 1959 bill. Under a system that largely replicated the existing voluntary market, employees could choose either a high or low option among three categories of coverage: nonprofit service benefits, commercial indemnity coverage, and prepaid doctor groups. At both levels, Blue Cross and Blue Shield benefits cost more than commercial and prepaid group policies.[113]

Even within the context of high and low options, the legislation stipulated generous benefits. All plans had to provide maternity benefits and immediate coverage despite age or preexisting conditions. Moreover, federal employees made choices that reflected consumer demand for liberal coverage. Fifty-four percent of workers chose Blue Cross and Blue Shield policies, whereas 27 percent chose commercial coverage. Eighteen percent of subscribers selected a prepaid group plan. Among all three categories, 82 percent of subscribers chose to pay more for the top tier of coverage. As in the private market, the cost of lavish insurance was partially hidden by employer funding, which in the case of federal workers initially amounted to about 40 percent of premiums.[114]

Like federal tax policy, the FEHBP greased the wheels of private interests as they raced to expand insurance and meet consumer expectations for comprehensive coverage. Over a decade of debates about the purpose of health insurance culminated with union members and federal employees purchasing policies that covered most medical care costs. What a decade earlier had been an exotic if not an eccentric wish was now a standard expectation for millions.

CONCLUSION

During debates over Truman's health care plan, the way policymakers framed the need for government oversight moored the politics of reform to market development. Over the next two decades, health care would advance through a contest that set the government's capabilities in the medical care system – or at least its promised capabilities, according to proposed legislation – against the organizational facilities of voluntary insurers. This competition revolved around which sector could more cheaply and efficiently manufacture the insurance product with a host of bells and whistles, including coverage provision for services ranging from doctor's office visits to laboratory tests and annual checkups. Private interests won the race by radically broadening voluntary coverage and thereby implanting the insurance company model into the health care system. This outcome was a grand irony considering that policymakers of every ideological stripe had attempted to either replace or fundamentally modify the insurance company paradigm.

Even as private health interests – organized physicians, commercial insurers, and nonprofit plans – joined together to expand insurance, each group designed its specific political stance to reflect how proposed reforms would influence the market position of members. Physicians opposed all reform initiatives fearing that they would either gradually develop into government-managed medicine or strengthen alternative health care arrangements that imperiled doctor sovereignty. Insurance company representatives fought reform proposals because each of them seemed intent on weakening or even eliminating commercial coverage. In the shadow of their physician patrons, Blue Shield administrators either joined the AMA's bandwagon or remained quiet. Meanwhile, Blue Cross leaders supported policies that offered them subsidies with minimal federal oversight.

However, to fully understand how developments in the public and private sectors intimately informed one another, we must examine, in detail, trade associations – the institutional linkages that connected federal debates and programs to on-the-ground market evolution. As we will see, each association – the AMA, Health Insurance Association of America, National Association of Blue Shield Plans, and Blue Cross Association – adopted distinct organizational characteristics to express their members' interwoven political and market strategies.

3

Sclerotic Institution: The Declining Power of Organized Physicians and the AMA

During the postwar era, the doctoring profession reached the commanding heights of reputation and cultural authority. A jubilant cultural celebration hailed the feats of modern medicine. Press accounts chronicled the discovery and production of penicillin, children saved from polio, and coronary artery bypass surgeries. But the public not only admired the likes of Alexander Fleming, Jonas Salk, and Michael DeBakey, they also revered the ordinary physicians who, in the course of everyday practice, skillfully manipulated modern science and technology to save lives.

The association that aided physicians as they amassed and leveraged this esteem – the American Medical Association (AMA) – had four attributes that further bolstered the standing of organized doctors. First, as we have seen, AMA leaders regulated the health care sector through licensing and credentialing activities. Physician leaders used this power to bend the entire medical services market to fit their professional conceptions, insisting that the insurance company model dominate health care financing. Second, the AMA's influential role in occupational development generated impressive membership rates, which, by the early 1950s, reached approximately three-quarters of practicing physicians. AMA membership accorded physicians easier access to hospital admitting privileges, malpractice insurance, and patient referrals. Membership also conveyed a subscription to the internationally renowned scientific publication the *Journal of the American Medical Association (JAMA)*.[1] The association's size and prestige led to its third advantage – money. Proceeds from *JAMA* advertisements funded a large staff capable of pursuing numerous objectives. National membership dues, instituted in 1949, further enhanced AMA wealth.[2] The fourth key feature undergirding AMA power was a federated structure, which paralleled U.S. governing arrangements by positioning a national association over state and county medical societies. AMA leaders derived a great deal of organizational capacity and political strength from constituent societies that directly lobbied congressional representatives and launched campaigns to sway local voter opinion.[3]

Nevertheless, focusing on these assets has prevented scholars from painting a complete picture of the AMA. Narratives of U.S. health care frequently cite the power of organized physicians as a primary reason that government reform measures failed.[4] Yet AMA leaders, at least at the national level, hesitated to fully engage in politics before the 1940s. Once they formally undertook federal lobbying, organized physicians decisively defeated Truman's plan for nationalized medicine. Thereafter, the AMA's political power began to wane. Indeed, organized physicians resoundingly lost the 1965 Medicare battle. This chapter strips away the AMA's polished exterior to expose the political machinery, organizational gears, and market mechanisms that undermined the influence of organized physicians.

After World War II, an unyielding, ideologically conservative faction steered the AMA into a new political phase of fervent federal activity. Behind the veneer of shrewd postwar political operations lay a chaotic, conflict-ridden organization. AMA leaders, to the chagrin of many members, publicly trumpeted their positions on myriad legislative proposals, ranging from Social Security benefits to international treaties. Through these battles, physician leaders frittered away political authority with inflexible arguments that often failed to advance beyond red-baiting.

Many of the AMA's difficulties, including its inability to formulate an effective long-term political strategy, were rooted in organizational characteristics. The leadership was drawn from an elite group of physicians who were largely detached from the concerns of rank-and-file doctors. Moreover, two governing bodies shared and thus bickered over responsibility for association policies. When the leadership did find consensus on an issue, that decision was then ground through a sprawling bureaucracy that chipped away at the original objective until only a withered fragment remained. In combination with the association's political tactics, the organizational structure undermined member cohesion. Numerous political fights aggravated members with differing ideological opinions, while the association's decentralized, democratic structure bred conflict.

Further complicating matters, organized physicians failed to craft realistic responses to the growing pressure for mass-produced, cost-effective

health insurance. AMA leaders wielded enormous influence to designate
the insurance company model as the primary means for financing health
care. They then assumed a passive stance while their preferred arrangements fueled skyrocketing costs, thereby provoking additional calls for
federal reform.

Instead of unifying members behind positive political and market
strategies calculated to benefit professional authority over the long term,
the AMA reacted defensively, responding to legislation initiated by
others and bemoaning the rapidly changing health care market. When
the challenge assumed the shape of single-payer health care financing –
"socialized medicine" – the AMA could mount a powerful campaign. But
as the cost of medical services rose and the demand for federal financing
through compromise measures grew, the common interests of the profession splintered and the organizational vitality located in the association's
federated structure attenuated. As a result, the AMA failed to preserve
physician autonomy and economic control through subsequent decades.

CRAFTING A NATIONAL POLITICAL VOICE

To understand the AMA's postwar political image and how physician
leaders developed their ideas about effective governmental strategies,
we must examine the association's earlier history. When support for
federally funded health care began bubbling up during the 1930s and
1940s, organized doctors were uncertain of how to represent themselves
on the national political stage. Certainly, organized physicians had
already won a great deal of political authority – state licensing laws
effectively endowed the AMA with regulatory control over the medical
economy. However, the activities sustaining that power – the political
meet-and-greets, fundraisers, country club luncheons, and, yes, even
the shared backroom cigars – naturally occurred among elite social
groups at the state and community levels. Politicking at the national
level posed a different set of problems. To participate directly in federal
contests, physicians would have to work through the national organization, thus invoking the full name brand of the "AMA." Collectively
enunciating public policy stands, particularly controversial positions,
could incite political reprisals, stir up patient resentment, provoke
conflict among members, and sully the cultural image of doctors as
objective scientific experts. Fearing the muck and the mud of national
politicking, AMA leaders shunned an overt federal political role until
the late 1940s.

Before the 1940s, AMA leaders exerted federal political influence remotely. At the national level, "lobbying" generally amounted to announcing the AMA's position in association publications and, occasionally, in congressional testimony. The amount of political weight these declarations carried depended on whether rank-and-file physicians decided to advocate them by lobbying their congressional representatives. In 1905, the national AMA stood atop more than forty state medical societies and almost eighteen hundred county medical societies.[5] The physicians who composed these societies generally saved their political energy for issues that affected their medical practices. So, for example, through *JAMA* editorials and policy votes during meetings, national leaders repeatedly called on Congress to create a federal department of health. However, this policy recommendation was largely ignored because the leadership failed to muster support among grassroots members who were content to leave the issue to public health associations.[6] In another instance, the AMA unsuccessfully opposed the 1921 Sheppard-Towner Act, which provided federal funding for state maternal and infant health care programs. The AMA convinced Congress to allow the legislation to expire in 1929, but only after rank-and-file doctors had observed local Sheppard-Towner programs and determined that they were a competitive threat. Only then did members organize through state and local medical societies to pressure congressmen to vote against the act's renewal.[7]

The AMA also exercised national political power informally, through individual relationships. When Roosevelt's Committee on Economic Security (CES) was considering government-funded health care, the nationally prominent physician Dr. Harvey Cushing lobbied the administration through his personal network. As a medical advisor for the CES, Cushing petitioned the chair, Labor Secretary Frances Perkins, to bury the measure. The neurosurgeon also appealed to the president through his daughter Betsy, who had married Roosevelt's oldest son, James.[8] AMA President Charles Gordon Heyd and *JAMA* editor Morris Fishbein met with Eleanor Roosevelt; however, after explaining that they could not make any deals without approval from the association's House of Delegates, they were dropped from further administration meetings.[9] The national AMA's official lobbying efforts were so tepid that members besieged Chicago headquarters with telegrams and letters, pleading with association leaders to actively combat the proposal.[10] AMA leaders called a special session of the House of Delegates in February 1935, but delegates simply voted to record the association's opposition to "all forms of compulsory sickness insurance."[11] When Roosevelt decided not to pursue health care reform within the Social Security bill, he stated that his administration "can't go up against the State Medical Societies."[12] Even the president understood that the association's political clout would emanate from the state, not the federal, level.

During Roosevelt's tenure physicians argued over whether the AMA, as organized at the national level, should become explicitly involved in federal politics. In 1937, the House of Delegates rejected a proposal to create a public relations department capable of orchestrating federal political activities.[13] Members worried that such a move would undercut the AMA's standing as an internationally preeminent scientific association. Moreover, during this same period, the Internal Revenue Service (IRS) ruled that the AMA was subject to income taxes. Although the courts eventually overturned the ruling, association leaders feared that blatant political activity would jeopardize their tax-exempt status. When Roosevelt won reelection in 1944, AMA officials finally decided to open an office in Washington, D.C. National leaders defended the decision to members, promising that the office would only act "as a listening post and as a means for distributing information about medicine and the medical profession."[14] On the other hand, some doctors expressed dissatisfaction with the AMA's indirect political approach. Officials with the Medical Society of the District of Columbia asserted that what the profession needed "above anything else" was political "leadership which inspires confidence – able, constructive leadership."[15]

Although AMA heads eschewed formal lobbying, they refused to entirely sit out contests over government-funded health care. During the 1930s and through much of the 1940s, physicians deployed two political attack dogs – the National Physicians' Committee for the Extension of Medical Service (NPC) and Dr. Morris Fishbein. Doctors founded the NPC in 1938 to fight federal health reform by supporting Republican candidates and encouraging businesses to purchase medical insurance for workers. The NPC assumed a brash demeanor that at times offended voters as, for example, when their political cartoons painted the Wagner-Murray-Dingell bills as communist plots.[16] One NPC-sponsored newsletter that addressed "Christian Americans" and likened government-funded health care to the "monster of Anti-Christ" conveyed an anti-Semitic tone. Although such incendiary messaging threatened to tarnish the reputation of physicians, AMA leaders proclaimed innocence because the NPC was financed by pharmaceutical firms and individual doctors and thus officially independent of the association.[17] Yet several

AMA leaders were also at the helm of the NPC. Furthermore, AMA delegates passed a resolution in 1942 praising the NPC "for the efforts they have made to enlighten the general public."[18]

Supplementing and in full support of NPC activities was Morris Fishbein, who used his position as *JAMA* editor to politick on behalf of physicians.[19] Though merely a journal editor, the "small, hunchy man with the bald head, big ears, waving hands and cheerful insolence" was a celebrity.[20] Indeed, his visage bedecked a 1937 cover of *Time* magazine. Fishbein published numerous popular books on medicine; by the mid-1940s, he had authored or edited eighteen works, including the *Modern Home Medical Adviser*. He wrote a syndicated newspaper column on health matters. And over the issue of government-funded health insurance, the physician debated liberal luminaries including Congressman John Dingell (D, MI), Senator Claude Pepper (D, FL), and American Federation of Labor leader Nelson Cruikshank.[21] The *JAMA* editor delivered so many speeches that he had to hire an agent. Because his name appeared ubiquitously in press accounts covering medical topics that ranged from tuberculosis and hay fever to health care economics, Fishbein became known as "Dr. A.M.A."[22]

Fishbein was born in 1889 to Austrian Americans, Fanny and Benjamin. Fishbein was the second eldest of eight children, though his almost five-hundred-page autobiography rarely mentions his siblings. Morris met his future wife, assistant, and traveling companion – Anna Mantel – as a child. The Mantels, like the Fishbeins, belonged to Indianapolis's tight-knit Jewish community. Fishbein's father was a devout man who spent a good deal of time in synagogue. As the proprietor of a glass store, Benjamin gradually worked his family out of the lower-middle class and into prosperity. The additional income allowed the elder Fishbein to send young Morris to the University of Chicago and then to Rush Medical College. Few people in Fishbein's hometown would have imagined that the awkward, bookish child who bruised easily would grow up to lead such an exciting life that he would regularly chronicle his social exploits – replete with name dropping and witty badinage – under the *JAMA* column "Doctor Pepys' Diary." His autobiography reads like *Who's Who* volumes spanning decades of American culture, with Fishbein making small talk at a 1920s Hollywood cocktail party with Charlie Chaplin, Lilyan Tashman, and Kay Francis; lunching with Senator Robert Taft during the 1940s; regularly communicating with the famous physician brothers Mayo; palling around with H. L. Menken; befriending publishers Richard "Dick" Simon and Lincoln

"Max" Schuster; and even, according to his account, giving Sinclair Lewis the idea to write *Arrowsmith*. Fishbein was sure of himself. He wore loud ties. He was smart, funny, and despite his boasting, displayed remarkable equanimity when personally attacked.[23]

Upon assuming the post of *JAMA's* assistant editor in 1912, Fishbein made his name chasing medical quacks and charlatans. After becoming the journal's editor during the 1920s, he acquired the title of "the best-known and least-liked doctor in the United States" by stridently fighting social reformers.[24] Fishbein took to the pages of the association's renowned scientific journal to print heated editorials that accused compulsory health insurance advocates of being "communists" fomenting "revolution."[25] Fishbein's role reveals the ambiguity of the AMA's political approach, because he did not hold an elected office in the association nor did his editorials necessarily accord with official policy. Yet, outside of congressional testimony and the formal policy opinions voted on by the House of Delegates and printed in *JAMA*, Fishbein's rhetorical firebombs provided the mainstay of the AMA's national political "relations."

Although some AMA members agreed with Fishbein's sentiments and admired his tireless efforts on behalf of the profession, others worried that the editor's attacks cast all physicians as reactionary and undermined the association's credibility.[26] Most problematically, Fishbein not only condemned health care reform legislation but also continued criticizing voluntary insurance after the AMA officially accepted medical prepayment in 1938. As late as 1945, the *JAMA* editor was publicly dragging his feet, questioning the "various detrimental influences" inherent in third-party-financed health care.[27] Meanwhile, representatives of the California Medical Association, many of whom were still angry about Fishbein's attempt to quash their Blue Shield plan, began sponsoring House of Delegates resolutions to strip the editor of his duties. Although these resolutions were defeated, the turmoil convinced leaders to hire a consulting firm to evaluate the association's public relations strategy.[28]

The 1946 report of Raymond Rich Associates urged the AMA's leadership to explicitly undertake political activities and remove both the NPC and Fishbein as the primary mouthpieces of organized doctors. The consulting firm contended that "gross inaccuracies" and "inappropriate content" in NPC materials had "injured the American Medical Association's public relations."[29] The Rich report suggested that Fishbein's political rants be reserved for one of the AMA's lesser publications, such as its consumer magazine, *Hygeia*. Rich consultants also assured AMA officials that IRS rulings permitted them to participate, without fear of losing their tax-exempt status, in legislative activities.[30] In response to the report, physician leaders created a public relations department and tasked Rich representatives with hiring an experienced executive to manage the AMA's image and political publicity.

The Rich evaluation rankled some AMA leaders, and controversy erupted when the Board of Trustees attempted to withhold the full report from the House of Delegates. Some members charged that Fishbein was behind the action – giving voice to growing dissent, a Colorado delegate accused the editor of being a "spoiled child."[31] Delegates finally received the Rich report, and a committee was appointed to review its suggestions. The committee, which included one NPC founder, repudiated the Rich findings. Following intense debate, AMA delegates voted to approve the committee's conclusions and endorse NPC activities, although some of their statements "might not have been dignified or appropriate had they emanated from a scientific body such as the AMA."[32] The vote was far from unanimous: a participant commented that the "'Ayes' were loud and dutiful. The 'Noes' were tense and disgusted."[33] The AMA hastily dumped Raymond Rich Associates, withdrew the resources originally pledged to the public relations department, and allowed the newly hired executive to resign.[34]

Despite maintaining the leadership's support through several rocky episodes, the NPC and Fishbein failed to survive the AMA's official entry into federal politics. After Truman surprised the punditry by winning the 1948 election, AMA leaders hired the political consulting firm of Whitaker and Baxter to aid their battle against the president's plan for government-sponsored health insurance. To accommodate the AMA's new political posture, the NPC disbanded operations. After years of proposed resolutions against the *JAMA* editor, the House of Delegates finally ousted Fishbein in 1949 amid a storm of media attention.[35] "Dr. Fishbein was the repudiated symbol of our old reactionary leadership," observed one physician: "Whitaker and Baxter are symbols of the new."[36]

The Whitaker and Baxter campaign's central message was that the Truman plan was "socialized medicine." The husband-and-wife team of Clem Whitaker and Leone Baxter were seasoned public relations specialists who had primarily served Republican candidates in California, although the state's medical association had hired them to spearhead a drive against Republican Governor Earl Warren's attempt to create state-funded compulsory insurance. Campaign experience had taught the consultants the effectiveness of charging one's opponent with having a philosophy that was either "German-inspired" or "communist," depending on which way the political winds were blowing.[37] Such harsh rhetoric had potential to harm the AMA's image. However, before an audience of public relations specialists, Whitaker explained that "[w]e can't beat State Socialism in this country by running away from controversy." He continued: "You should never wear your best trousers when you go out to fight for freedom and truth!"[38]

The political operation cemented into place the AMA's long-term strategy of promoting "voluntary" insurance as preferable to "socialist" programming. Following the Whitaker and Baxter dictum that "you can't beat something with nothing," AMA leaders, at least officially, adopted a more positive attitude toward health insurance.[39] AMA pamphlets boasted that private policies were growing by a million subscribers a month. Such progress, they argued, precluded the need for "radical" health care measures.[40]

To publicize this message, Whitaker and Baxter launched the "National Education Campaign," which was probably the largest political offensive ever waged against a single piece of legislation in U.S. history. With the objective of reaching every citizen, the campaign distributed over 55 million leaflets and pamphlets containing arguments against Truman's plan. Whitaker and Baxter hired a firm to write canned editorials, which they mailed to newspapers, magazines, and radio programs. The operation distributed about twenty million stickers declaring opposition to government-funded medical insurance and five million copies of a *Reader's Digest* article that disparaged the United Kingdom's nationalized health care system.[41] Additionally, the consultants dispatched speakers to make medicine's case before hundreds of groups: the AMA received support from the Farm Bureau, the U.S. Chamber of Commerce, and many locally organized Kiwanis, Rotary, YMCA, and women's clubs.[42]

Whitaker and Baxter directed medical societies to ally with local dentists and pharmacists to establish "Healing Arts" or "Medical Arts" political committees.[43] These committees ran advertisements in local newspapers against political contestants who supported Truman's plan and purchased radio spots that quoted Lenin as saying "The Keystone in the arch of the socialized state is Socialized Medicine."[44] Doctors affixed political stickers to patient bills and wrote prescriptions to cure "socialized medicine" with the name of their preferred congressional candidate. Sir Luke Fildes's painting of a doctor thoughtfully tending to a child in his home was stamped with the slogan "Keep Politics Out of This Picture" and hung in thousands of physician offices across the country.[45]

Expert publicity and intensive campaigning came with a large price tag. The AMA spent over $2.25 million – a stunning amount for the time – on Whitaker and Baxter activities.[46] Previously, the national association had relied on *JAMA* advertisements to fund operations; members paid dues only to their county and state societies. To finance the Whitaker and Baxter offensive, the AMA began assessing members an additional twenty-five dollars annually. National dues aggravated doctors who opposed either the AMA's political position or its participation in nonscientific activities. Seventy-seven percent of eligible members elected to pay the new charge, but a dissatisfied minority withheld their dues.[47]

Though an expensive, one-time stopgap, the Whitaker and Baxter drive aided AMA officials as they broadcast the message of "voluntary insurance" versus "socialized medicine" into every region of the country, from small town to urban center, helping turn a majority of voters against nationalized health care.[48] Yet this very message indicated how Truman's legislative initiative generated profound change within the AMA. Physicians who had once opposed medical prepayment were converted into health insurance boosters hawking the product's accomplishments and rapid advance. The Truman debates also inspired physicians to alter their political approach. Once AMA leaders overcame their uncertainty about direct involvement in federal politics, they undertook their new role with enthusiasm.

POLITICS: STYLE AND METHODS

The Whitaker and Baxter crusade inspired a false sense of confidence among AMA officials, leading them to believe that stridently broadcasting resistance to federal measures would sustain political power over the long term. This conceit convinced AMA leaders to dramatically enlarge their political footprint. They assumed an ultra-conservative stance, not only opposing all medical system reforms no matter how moderate, but also expounding rigid positions on a spectacular array of supplementary legislation. While national leaders adopted an attention-grabbing, truculent political style, AMA representatives in the nation's capital bungled lobbying efforts as they attempted to keep track of confusing directions from headquarters while struggling to learn the inner workings of federal policymaking.

Having tasted political victory, AMA leaders forgot their previous restraint and eagerly dug into a menu of federal legislative activities. The D.C. office evolved to reflect this change. In 1950, *Medical*

Economics congratulated AMA lobbyists for enunciating detailed positions on proposed legislation rather than employing their traditional tack of "'reserving judgment' or 'approving the spirit of the bill' (gobble-dygook for 'we can't make up our minds')."[49] Soon thereafter, AMA officials began proactively issuing news releases rather than simply responding to requests for information from policymakers and journalists.[50] From that point, the legislative workload increased rapidly. In 1955 alone the AMA's Committee on Legislation reported that it had analyzed and recommended action on 50 percent more federal bills than the previous year.[51] Chapter 2 examined how the AMA contested all initiatives to reform the health insurance market. Yet those undertakings constituted only a portion of their political tasks. Organized doctors adopted vocal positions on vaccine distribution, veterans' health benefits, medical education, water pollution, prescription-writing rules, flood control, and tax provisions. They even weighed in on the Bricker Amendment to restrict international treaties! Although this assortment of political activities partially reflected the federal government's increasing size, it also revealed the new penchant of organized physicians for mounting their ideological soapbox. AMA strategists argued that such a broad political approach was necessary because "medical freedom cannot long endure as an island in a sea of collectivism."[52] Physician leaders thus took it upon themselves to shape the entire political system. According to an internal report, the AMA had "a wonderful opportunity to take the lead in a restatement of the fundamentals underlying our private competitive enterprise system."[53]

Yet occupying the helm of this massive political operation was muddled leadership. The AMA's Chicago headquarters deployed multiple lines of authority over the D.C. office, thus creating confusion. Federal lobbyists reported to both the Board of Trustees and the Committee on Legislation.[54] Moreover, while waiting for trustees or committee members to make policy decisions, D.C. lobbyists often conferred with the association's general manager. This unclear chain of command caused the AMA to send conflicting signals to lawmakers. In 1954, for example, Congress was putting finishing touches on Social Security amendments to bring additional workers into the program and create a "disability freeze," which would permit individuals who left the labor force because of illness or injury to continue accruing pension benefits as if they had maintained employment. After consulting with the general manager in Chicago, AMA lobbyists resolved to protest only the disability freeze, alleging it was a liberal ruse to incrementally introduce "socialized medicine."[55] D.C. staffers decided not to make any additional requests, fearing that if legislators reopened other portions of the bill, then doctors might be forced into the Social Security pension program for the first time. Meanwhile, the AMA's Committee on Legislation instructed rank-and-file members to write Senate Finance Committee members requesting that they reopen the legislation to add the Jenkins-Keogh Amendment, which would have allowed physicians to fund private pensions with pretax dollars. The conflicting requests confused and irritated AMA allies in the Senate. Washington lobbyists reported back to Chicago that in the middle of the association's fierce battle to prevent the expansion of Social Security, the AMA was "treading on very thin ice" before the crucially important Senate Finance Committee.[56]

Compounding difficulties that sprang from the association's reporting hierarchy, AMA representatives seemed unaware of how to exert influence from within the nation's capital. Not until the mid-1950s did association lobbyists begin to grasp the necessity of doing more than publicizing their positions before the press and Congress. In 1956, an AMA official lamented that association representatives had consistently neglected to acquire copies of proposed legislation to dissect for details that might aid their political arguments and lobbying efforts. After the Social Security disability freeze had already passed both congressional houses, an AMA staffer found legislative language that defined citizens applying for the benefit as wards of the state. Chicago officials believed they had missed a critical opportunity to convince voters and some congressional members that a seemingly harmless safety net actually threatened individual freedom. To obtain copies of pending legislation and air AMA views, D.C. lobbyists began hosting conferences, lunches, and phone calls with congressmen and their staffers.[57] They also discovered that lobbying involved more than just pressuring Congress. In 1956, AMA representatives related that they had just learned the importance of forging connections with the administration officials who translated laws into specific guidelines:

[I]t has become apparent that there is an opportunity that may not have been taken advantage of sufficiently in the past. Once bills are enacted, the original intent of Congress may be modified one way or the other in the process of writing the regulations to implement the law.[58]

By the end of the decade, D.C. lobbyists finally understood that the federal political game required more than issuing proclamations from on high.

Even with these insights, the AMA's ability to influence policymakers
was limited by their intransigent positions. Eisenhower, along with each
of his Health, Education, and Welfare (HEW) Secretaries, believed that
the best means of preventing nationalized health care was by passing a
scaled-down, tempered reform measure to strengthen the voluntary
market. Yet AMA leaders refused to assist with this strategy. Although
HEW Secretary Marion Folsom regularly met and dined with AMA
representatives, he failed to convince them to support any course of
reform.[59] In an interview, HEW administrator Roswell Perkins described
his department's relationship with the AMA:

> [W]e did make an extraordinary effort to go through the elementary fundamental
> processes of consultation ... [but] their approach to government at this time
> was that you've got to stand firm, you've got to buck and you've got to fight with
> all-out efforts in any showdown.[60]

AMA leaders thus alienated some of their original supporters. Indeed,
after losing one of the battles for his reinsurance proposal, President
Eisenhower angrily blamed physicians, warning that the "American
people are going to get the medical care to which they are entitled, in
some form or other."[61]

The AMA's inability to build federal alliances took its toll. Organized
physicians lost one of their most important political drives during the
1950s – to prevent significant expansion of Social Security. The original
1935 act sent federal funding to state programs that provided maternal
and child welfare, assistance to the blind, and means-tested aid for the
elderly. In 1950, Congress amended the legislation to supply state welfare
officials with resources to directly pay medical vendors, in other words,
doctors, hospitals, and insurance companies. The financing relationships
that evolved out of these programs created the institutional underpinnings
for future Medicaid plans. AMA leaders vigorously contested federally
subsidized health care, even for the poor. They argued that government
charity should be completely financed and managed at the local or – at
most – the state level. Nevertheless, between 1956 and 1958, Congress
repeatedly increased funding for charitable medical services through
Social Security amendments that modified state grants-in-aid formulas.[62]

The AMA also lost a bitter fight to obstruct Social Security benefits
for the permanently disabled. Policymakers established Social Security
Disability Insurance in 1956. Before its creation, AMA officials charged
that the program would provide reformers with a building block for
universal health insurance, particularly since it would be managed by,

according to their view, the most dangerous federal agency. Physicians testified that the Social Security Commissioner's proposed responsibilities under the program would make him "a menace to the private practice of medicine."[63] AMA leaders also worried that Disability Insurance would make physicians conducting medical examinations to determine who qualified for benefits agents of federal power, thereby alienating patients.[64] Policymakers attempted to alleviate these concerns by amending the legislation to lodge more authority within state governments. Physician leaders, nevertheless, continued to assail the program. In the end, the creation of federal insurance for the disabled signaled that organized doctors lacked the influence to defeat every piece of legislation that threatened their professional power.[65]

In addition to harming their reputation on Capitol Hill, the AMA's political strategies tainted the image of organized physicians among citizens and the press. Physician resistance to the Social Security disability program garnered a great deal of negative publicity, such as the *New York Times* headline announcing "A.M.A. Attacks Aid to Disabled."[66] A *Life* editorial titled "Watch it, Doc" denounced the AMA for opposing federally funded indigent care.[67] According to *Consumer Reports*, organized physicians were inoculated with "the virus of total oppositionism. . . . [E]very important health measure . . . has been fought by the AMA."[68] In one episode, AMA delegates passed a resolution contesting government-funded care for veterans' non-service-related illnesses. The action initiated a war of words between the AMA and the American Legion. Although physician leaders feared federal administrators would use the program to expand government-managed care to other groups, to the public, it appeared that the AMA simply wished to deny benefits to "deserving" veterans.[69] Furthermore, AMA insinuations that even ideologically moderate programs and policymakers had socialist tendencies increasingly goaded voters (particularly after the 1954 televised spectacle of Senator Joseph McCarthy aggressively questioning Army officials over alleged subversive activities). A 1950s *Yale Law Journal* article accused the AMA of attempting to drive up physician incomes by blocking reform legislation, limiting the supply of doctors, and dominating hospitals. Newspapers and magazines widely publicized the critique, and scholars began citing the work to advance similar conclusions.[70]

AMA leaders' ultra-conservative approach and inclination to weigh in on a multitude of legislative issues repelled political allies and attracted negative publicity. As physicians condemned compromise health care reforms and numerous additional proposals that seemed remote to medicine, labels of "socialism" increasingly missed their mark. The moral authority of organized physicians deteriorated, and the AMA began to lose political clout. Physician leaders could have taken steps to reclaim their power by revising the AMA's political methods. However, formulating effective, cohesive policies was becoming increasingly difficult for the elected officials and staff members who attempted to navigate the association's organizational labyrinth.

ORGANIZATION IN DISARRAY

As physicians tried to hold the medical realm tightly within their grip, to shape every part of society that influenced or was influenced by health care – ranging from politics and economics to science – the AMA's organizational apparatus struggled to keep pace. To grapple with the rapidly changing world around them, AMA leaders needed to identify a limited number of well-defined goals and energetically pursue them. But the AMA's ability to unify members around clear long-term strategies was hobbled by an aloof leadership, divided policymaking authority, copious associational objectives, and an unmanageable bureaucracy.

The AMA was organized around democratic, federated arrangements. To gain an AMA membership, physicians had to win acceptance through their local medical society. County and city medical societies sent representatives to the state medical society, which elected members to the national House of Delegates.[71] AMA bylaws designated the House of Delegates as the association's primary policymaking body. Delegates also elected the president and Board of Trustees. The president nominated Judicial Council members, and the House voted whether to approve them. The Judicial Council acted as the association's Supreme Court: members evaluated constitutional and ethical issues and reviewed the disciplinary actions of state medical societies. Trustees served as operational directors, supervising association staff, overseeing committees, and making interim decisions between House of Delegates sessions.

Critics charged that, contrary to these supposedly democratic processes, a powerful oligarchy ruled the association.[72] Indeed, the AMA's configuration encouraged the development of an elite leadership that was generally disconnected from rank-and-file concerns. In his work on interest groups, David B. Truman found that, particularly in associations with large memberships and numerous goals, an "active minority" often exercises disproportional influence.[73] Because AMA service required a great deal of time, national leaders tended to be wealthy urban specialists with the resources to devote to association activities. A 1950s survey of the officeholders in constituent medical societies – the physician members most likely to ascend to national positions – estimated that to perform their duties, doctors spent, on average, approximately sixteen hours a week and $120 a month in out-of-pocket expenses and lost earnings.[74] Most rural and general practitioners either worked among populations that depended on their uninterrupted services or faced competitive situations that afforded little free time. For these reasons, fewer than 10 percent of national AMA delegates were ordinary family doctors.[75] Complaining about the "big-shot specialists" who issued "communiqués from the Chicago Citadel," one member observed that "[n]o one knows better what the common people need and desire, what local handicaps to health services there are, than the little family medic – who is never asked to express his opinion."[76] Grassroots sentiments seldom found a hearing before national leaders because years of moving up the ranks through county, state, and then national office required physicians to impress already-established officials. Consequently, the AMA's leadership seemed inflexible and aged. With an average age of fifty-nine, most delegates were nearing retirement.[77]

Power concentrated among an elite group might have enabled the leadership to construct clear long-term strategies. However, policymaking authority was split between the House of Delegates and the Board of Trustees. Although the House of Delegates was the official policymaking organ, in reality, the board had the most governing influence. Four characteristics empowered the board. First, the board controlled association finances, thus allowing trustees to channel resources into the projects they favored.[78] Second, the board wielded interim authority between biannual House of Delegates sessions. Third, trustees directed operational activities: they oversaw the Chicago staff and nominated members to important positions on committees, bureaus, journals, and councils. Finally, the board constrained the House's policymaking capabilities by dominating the Reference Committee. Delegates elected their speaker from among ex officio board members. Because the speaker managed Reference Committee nominations, he could choose members who would reliably protect trustee preferences. The Reference Committee was particularly important because it reviewed all proposed resolutions, determined which ones to put before delegates, and recommended how delegates should vote.[79]

The division of authority between the board and delegates fostered disputes and hindered the leadership's ability to formulate a clear vision for the association. At times, the board's controlling position triggered a backlash, such as when members grew increasingly disgruntled with Fishbein as the AMA's unelected spokesman. The board protected the *JAMA* editor for years while a vocal faction of state society representatives attempted to convince Reference Committee members to put resolutions regarding his role before the House of Delegates. Every now and then, delegates attempted to undermine the board's assumption of authority. In 1955, for example, a resolution was introduced that would have required committees to submit reports to delegates at least one month prior to meetings. The rule would have granted delegates sufficient time to study each issue and review policy preferences with their state associations rather than just blindly accepting board preferences. The Reference Committee suppressed the measure, explaining that the "Board of Trustees believes the intent of this resolution is sound but that its implementation is impractical."[80] Despite intermittent protests, the association's massive workload convinced most delegates to accept their secondary role and settle for "buck-passing to the Board of Trustees."[81] Two four-day meetings a year simply did not afford delegates adequate time to consider the numerous issues facing the AMA. Every year the agenda became more crowded, and committee and council meetings were rushed. Usually by the fourth day of meetings, delegates had difficulty holding together a quorum as members left town, having "done their bit," having "had enough," and leaving "the most complex issues for the frequently heard action, 'Referred to the Board of Trustees.'"[82]

Exacerbating these problems, the association had grown too unwieldy for effective management. To handle the burgeoning load of scientific, political, and socioeconomic activities, AMA leaders continually established new committees. By 1957, Chicago officials attempted to supervise more than sixty-four committees, twelve councils, and approximately eight hundred employees spread across twenty departments.[83] Operational expenses increased almost threefold over the decade, from $5.5 million at the beginning of the 1950s to $15.3 million by 1959.[84] A small sampling of association undertakings reveals how far-flung and diverse AMA objectives had become: a Bureau of Investigation acted as medicine's FBI by uncovering fraudulent therapeutic schemes, the State Journal Advertising Bureau ensured that medical society publications followed official guidelines, and a magazine called *Today's Health* educated the public on medical matters. Committee assignments often overlapped, some committees worked toward conflicting purposes, and officeholders and staff squabbled over turf. According to AMA chronicler

Frank D. Campion, there was "jealousy, a testiness about prerogatives, a wasteful maneuvering for position."[85] The secretary-general manager overseeing the staff, the aptly named George F. Lull, was an amiable gentleman; but he was also a passive supervisor who, rather than exerting his authority, permitted officials to argue over assigned tasks and spheres of influence.[86]

The disarray persuaded AMA leaders to consider an organizational overhaul. Responding to the belief that "the A.M.A. was riding off in too many directions at once, without enough top-level coordination," the board voted in 1957 to bring in consultants for a comprehensive review of the association's structure and goals.[87] The respected firm of Robert Heller and Associates issued a report critical of the AMA's ambiguous direction, overstaffing and replication of duties, squandered resources, and general disorganization. Heller consultants recommended that AMA leaders locate all long-range planning within one body and then reevaluate and purge some of the association's numerous objectives. To reclaim its leadership among proliferating medical groups and specialties, Heller representatives suggested that the AMA reemphasize its scientific mission. The consultants also called for a massive cutback in legislative pursuits so that AMA leaders could focus their political efforts on public health matters and the promotion of a preferred economic model for medical care.[88]

The Heller report fell victim to the very problems it sought to remedy. By pressing and straining Heller proposals through several delegations and committees, officials were able to discard any advice that threatened their pet positions or personal clout.[89] Indeed, to acquire the patina of reform, officials ended up expanding association activities. For example, to comply with the suggestion that the AMA concentrate on reassuming national scientific leadership, officials established a committee to reevaluate the association's scholarly pursuits and appointed liaisons to correspond with other medical organizations.[90]

The most significant change the Heller report effected was a reorganization of the AMA's Chicago headquarters. Over the years, trustees had become bogged down in numerous administrative details, from reviewing the costs of paper to individually approving hundreds of employee raises. Following Heller guidance, AMA leaders placed all staff supervision duties under a chief executive officer who was to report directly to the board. The position of general manager was elevated to an executive vice president and charged with overseeing all departments, which included communications, field service, scientific publications, business, law, socioeconomic activities, and scientific affairs.[91]

The reorganization endowed the general manager with enormous authority, if he was willing to seize and utilize it. The trustees guaranteed just such a development when they replaced the easy-going Lull with Francis James Levi Blasingame. Known as "Bing" to friends and colleagues, Blasingame had the strong, forceful personality necessary not only to bring the staff under his control but also to shape the AMA's political direction. In this role, Blasingame became one of the most influential physician leaders of the postwar era. The staunchly conservative physician had long advised colleagues to resist the "Fabian tactics" behind moderate reform proposals, arguing that policymakers would use seemingly innocuous legislation to construct a programmatic perch from which they would incrementally nationalize medicine.[92]

A well-dressed, towering man, Blasingame was otherwise plain in appearance – graying and balding by his forties, with black Shurset spectacles that adorned a protuberant nose. While sufficiently educated and traveled to exude a diplomatic air, the surgeon reveled in his image as a tough, self-reliant Texan. In crafting his personal narrative, Blasingame wove in details that highlighted his family's pioneering experience. The physician commonly introduced his biography with the story of his grandfather, who was killed by lightning while herding cattle in Galveston. The accident left his widowed grandmother to open a boarding house for medical students who moved to the island to attend the University of Texas Medical Branch. Because she had befriended so many medical students as a child, Blasingame's mother would later encourage her son to become a doctor. Blasingame was born in Arkansas in 1907; his family moved to the town of Hempstead, Texas, when he was two. Also known as "Six Shooter Junction," Hempstead had fewer than two thousand residents. When he was older, Blasingame returned to the island where his grandfather had died tragically. There, he fulfilled his mother's dream by graduating from medical school with honors in 1932. After completing a surgical internship at Henry Ford Hospital in Detroit, Blasingame returned to his alma mater to serve as an anatomy professor. Wishing to earn more money, the surgeon left academia and moved to Wharton, where he co-founded the Rugeley-Blasingame Clinic in 1937. As he grew prosperous, Blasingame undertook numerous civic and professional activities, including various posts with the local medical society. The Texas physician dutifully worked his way through the AMA power structure, serving as president of the state medical association; a national delegate; and in 1949, one of the youngest ever AMA trustees.[93]

Although rigid in his conservative political beliefs, Blasingame avoided the flamboyant public style of the exiled *JAMA* editor Fishbein. Blasingame understood how to exercise power from behind the throne, without calling undue attention to himself. For example, during the early 1950s, fellow Texas doctor Ernest E. Anthony wrote to congratulate Blasingame on a *JAMA* article he had written to spotlight weaknesses in Social Security. Anthony then chastised his friend for implying that pension provision was "a legitimate function of government." Anthony believed Blasingame should have "made the statement that 'Social Security' as we have it, as Karl Marx advocated it ... is nothing more than a vicious fraud." Blasingame responded that he wholeheartedly agreed with Anthony but wanted to avoid offending politically moderate trustees. "I am about as far to the right as are you," confided Blasingame. He continued, explaining, "I am amazed at the number of people that disagrees [*sic*] with this point of view."[94]

Upon assuming the position of general manager, Blasingame leveraged his long-standing relationships with association leaders and his regular attendance at board meetings to argue that the AMA should maintain and, where necessary, shore up ultra-conservative political policies. Indeed, Blasingame's penumbra appeared over the board's abrupt decision to dismiss most Committee on Legislation members, appoint replacements, and elevate the committee to a council with broader responsibilities.[95] Because Blasingame was tasked with implementing Council on Legislation programs, he gained control over the association's D.C. activities. The general manager restructured the reporting ladder so that all Washington representatives answered directly to him. He then fired most of the lobbying corp. Although the AMA had already developed a reputation for political obstinacy, Blasingame sought representatives who would work even more energetically and unapologetically to prevent federal encroachment in medicine. Scorning the social mores of Washington, Blasingame derided the type of lobbyist who acted as an "appeaser or back slapper." He looked for representatives "who would much rather lose many times than back down" on their "principles once."[96] The task proved difficult: Blasingame went through several D.C. directors before finally appointing fellow Texan Roy T. Lester – "someone who had no Potomac fever and who would have a high immunity to it."[97]

By setting in motion reforms that led to Blasingame's promotion, the Heller Report inadvertently encouraged the very type of political approach that consultants had warned was harming the AMA's public standing. The Heller Report did help the AMA streamline administrative functions at Chicago headquarters. Nevertheless, the association's bureaucracy had already assumed a life of its own. It continually sprouted novel objectives and new fiefdoms of power for various officials while sapping vigor from the association's central purpose – to defend the professional position of doctors. Physician leaders would soon discover that their detachment from the everyday realities of practicing medicine was generating widespread restlessness in the ranks.

GRASSROOTS DISCONTENT

More so than any other time in the association's history, national leaders looked to constituent state and local societies to carry out crucial tasks, such as managing political operations and negotiating insurance company relations. However, the national leadership's political and organizational policies provoked member dissension, which, in turn, undermined the power that the AMA had traditionally derived from grassroots activities. Although some physicians expressed displeasure with the AMA's decision to enter politics and battle the Truman reform plan, the danger that the legislation posed to professional independence had united the vast majority of doctors. Once the threat of a centralized, federally managed program passed, member political cohesion fractured. By staking out positions on numerous legislative issues, association leaders inevitably transgressed the beliefs of doctors who placed their ideological identity as conservative, moderate, or liberal above their identity as an AMA member. Furthermore, the association's decentralized, democratic arrangements permitted members to air their displeasure.[98]

Notwithstanding the AMA's reputation for conservative political positions, a militant group of physicians attacked association policies from the right. These members, who frequently hailed from southern states, alleged that the leadership had failed to adequately educate doctors and the public about "deceitful" attempts to socialize medicine through moderate reform proposals.[99] They chafed whenever the AMA strayed from total resistance to any federal interference in health care. For example, conservative physicians protested when the AMA endorsed President Eisenhower's creation of the Department of HEW. For much of the twentieth century, the AMA had called for a department of health with cabinet-level status. However, physician leaders opposed combining health and welfare policy under the same umbrella. They feared that an alliance between health policy and welfare officials would encourage calls for federally funded medical care. Despite this long-held position, AMA leaders wanted to demonstrate support for the newly elected Republican president – Eisenhower had not only campaigned against "socialized medicine" but had also roused the ire of liberal policymakers by proposing a department that, in its very name, elevated health above welfare and Social Security programming.[100] In 1952, the House of Delegates convened a rare special session to consider the matter. After President Eisenhower addressed the delegates, they unanimously voted to support legislation establishing HEW.[101] In a *JAMA* article defending the decision, President Louis H. Bauer implied that association leaders would exercise considerable control over HEW through the appointment of a special assistant to the secretary.[102] Nonetheless, a faction of conservative doctors complained that association officials had misrepresented the issue and predicted that the federal department would "prove to be the dragon that" will "devour us." The dispute became so heated that, during the following meeting, Bauer took to the floor of the House of Delegates to defend himself against critical resolutions.[103] Doctors soon felt betrayed by the administration when HEW Secretary Oveta Culp Hobby not only refused to meet with the AMA's policy advisory group but also appointed a "liberal" doctor to the position of special assistant.[104] When HEW began promoting Eisenhower's reinsurance legislation, conservative physicians groused that their warnings about the department had been vindicated.

Conservative members kicked up another row in 1956 when the Board of Trustees, which generally opposed government support for medical education, endorsed federal grants for medical school construction. Texas doctors introduced a resolution condemning the association's political compromise. Lamenting that the decision was "nothing in the world but a hauling down of our flag," one delegate predicted that "once subsidies have begun, the next step is to increase those subsidies until finally all freedom is gone."[105] Trustees countered that delegates had already accepted the political precept when they voted to support the 1946 Hill-Burton Act to federally finance the construction and renovation of hospital facilities.[106] AMA President John Cline reminded delegates that even Republicans favored minor governmental interventions to bolster the private economy: "I do not believe it is the proper function of the organization representing American medicine to make an effort to revise the whole economic system of this country."[107] With Blasingame's ascendancy to the position of general manager and the strengthening of ultra-conservative forces within the AMA, such advice was soon discarded.

Of course, association policies also frustrated members who wanted to alter the AMA's conservative, regressive reputation. For example, the Physician's Forum, which was founded in 1939, represented a small bloc of doctors who advocated government-managed universal health care. More common, however, were calls to support moderate reforms that proposed federally funded health benefits for the poor and difficult-to-insure. In 1949, a group of approximately two hundred prominent physicians called upon the AMA to back one of the initiatives offered as a compromise to Truman's plan, such as Hill-Aiken or Flanders-Ives legislation:

[T]he obvious direct way to avoid an all inclusive compulsory health insurance and to make secure the valuable features of our present system is for the Association to develop a program that will be manifestly so considerate of the ends of the people and at the same time so eminently fair to the interests of the physicians that it will command general approbation.[108]

The Medical Society of New Jersey expressed a similar sentiment when it passed a resolution stating, "we must particularize, specify, and spell out in detail precisely how we propose to solve the problem of providing medical care."[109] Also dismaying doctors who believed the association was out of step with mainstream politics was the AMA's hostility toward Social Security, which included resisting grants-in-aid for state indigent health services, opposing the extension of pension benefits to include physicians, and fighting the creation of federal disability insurance. Many AMA members failed to understand why their leadership branded such programs threatening when they were widely favored by citizens; indeed, both Democratic and Republican policymakers acted to expand the Social Security system throughout the 1950s.[110]

Conservative and moderate physicians generally sought to influence AMA policy as members, from within the association. Nonmember doctors who contested association policies undercut the assertion that the AMA was the legitimate representative of physician professional concerns. A 1953 *Medical Economics* survey attempted to determine why approximately seventy thousand physicians did not belong to the AMA.[111] About half of nonmembers were in a stage of their career where membership dues were too burdensome, either because they were in training or retired. The other half of nonmembers either expressed indifference, refused to apply because they disagreed with AMA policies, or had been denied participation by the local medical society. Medical societies had rejected at least seven thousand membership applications. Particularly in the South, black physicians were refused admission to the

AMA; indeed, most of them would not have bothered to apply. The national association had officially declared that membership "should not be denied to any person solely on the basis of race." However, local society autonomy over membership affairs was an important component of AMA policy because it allowed national leaders to deny complicity in systematic discrimination against certain types of physicians.[112] In addition to African Americans, excluded doctors generally fell into one of the following categories: "leftists," group practice members, and any providers out of step with the prevailing practices of local physicians. AMA critics had long maintained that the association failed to represent the political and economic views of many doctors. One survey participant echoed this claim: "Organized medicine, from the local level on up, is run by and for a small clique of older specialists who oppose any changes in the status quo." Another doctor employed harsher terms: "The AMA is a medieval, anti-social, highbrow, impotent, reactionary organization."[113]

Amplifying AMA troubles with physician discontent, medical associations proliferated during the postwar era. As a growing number of doctors specialized, they joined medical groups tailored to their practice, whether surgery or neurology. By vying for physician membership and participation, specialty societies weakened the AMA's position as the primary representative of American doctors.[114] The AMA reached the peak of its membership rates at the opening of the 1950s, when about 75 percent of practicing doctors belonged to the association.[115] By the end of the decade, with membership down to about 65 percent of physicians, an internal AMA report was asking, "is medicine organized or disorganized?"[116] Thereafter, membership rates progressively deteriorated.

Perhaps most dangerous to AMA power was membership apathy. "The AMA," observed Texas medical society leaders, "needs to be resold to its own members."[117] Many doctors only affiliated with the association to qualify for malpractice insurance or to obtain hospital admitting privileges. During the 1950s, AMA officials regularly took to the pages of *JAMA* to warn members about the "danger from within," cautioning that failure to vigorously support medical society activities threatened to undermine association authority and, by extension, professional power.[118]

Yet at the same time that rank-and-file dissension and indifference were becoming grave problems, Chicago officials dramatically increased member workload by assigning numerous additional tasks to constituent societies. The Whitaker and Baxter campaign had demonstrated that AMA political success relied on grassroots activities. After the intense organizing that had accompanied the Truman battle subsided, leaders

returned to their traditional practice of issuing member political instructions through *JAMA*. However, repeatedly calling on members to contact
their congressional representatives steadily drained enthusiasm from the
ranks. The leadership, for example, had difficulty mobilizing members
to oppose the Social Security disability program:

Now that the chips are down we are calling on our individual members realizing
that what scant success we have had has been due to the efforts of the rank and
file. In the past too little effort has been made to inform the rank and file so that
they could be worth something when called upon.[119]

After the 1956 legislative defeat, officials instituted reforms to strengthen
ground-level political efforts. In collaboration with the Council on
Legislation, Blasingame increased funding and resources for the Field Service
Division and appointed a new director – another Texan, the politically savvy
and well-connected Aubrey Gates.[120] Under the revamped field service
arrangements, state medical societies elected a liaison or "key man" who was
paired with a Council on Legislation member. When AMA representatives
in Washington believed that they required the supplementary influence of
physicians personally lobbying their congressmen, they communicated
with council members who then funneled their directives through key men.
Key men contacted state society members and county society leaders to
instruct them on legislative issues and effective means of communication.[121]

To build political energy among members, national officials began
working more closely with constituent societies to strengthen loyalty to
both the AMA and conservative ideology. Field service representatives
visited medical societies to sell members on the "tremendous constructive
influence the American Medical Association has on all phases of American
life."[122] To rouse member devotion, they detailed the role of organized
doctors in school health programs, civil defense planning, and polio
campaigns. They also helped medical societies develop political organizing
programs, particularly in states where important congressional members
lived. Gates arranged regional conferences to instruct physicians on AMA
policy stances. During these meetings, officials explained how seemingly
inoffensive government programs could develop into federally managed
medicine.[123] To maintain continuous member education, *JAMA* editors
made space for a "Legislative Roundup" section, and Chicago staffers
began sending the *AMA News* to all medical society leaders.[124] In sum,
rather than backing away from some of the political positions that had
caused member disharmony, the leadership assigned medical societies new
responsibilities and prodded physicians to fall in line.

National leaders also leaned on medical societies to boost the association's deteriorating public image. They began sending a bimonthly newsletter, the "PR Doctor," to local leaders, instructing them on how to improve the public face of physicians in their area.[125] To elevate the AMA's standing in newsrooms, doctors were directed to nurture connections with local reporters and newspaper editors.[126] Physicians were also encouraged to host radio shows on topics of public interest, such as cutting-edge cancer treatments or the medical society's emergency call program.[127] Through both newsletters and regional conferences, physician leaders discussed how medical societies could "mend PR fences" by working with local and state authorities to provide health services to the uninsured and poor. Where government programs did not exist, physicians were advised to create and finance their own indigent care plans.[128]

Medical societies also assumed a host of new obligations to manage the spread of health insurance. State societies had the enormous task of supervising Blue Shield plans. Physician representatives also consulted with commercial insurance companies to help them create and revise indemnity fee schedules. As insurance expanded and health care costs became an ever-growing concern, medical society committees began to handle patient and insurance company complaints about physicians who overbilled or provided unnecessary procedures. Some societies implemented regular utilization review processes. These undertakings will be discussed more fully in Chapter 6.

Without a motivated membership, local societies had difficulty shouldering these numerous, onerous endeavors. Physicians who had grown unhappy with the association's political positions or who failed to tie AMA success to their personal careers, preferred to spend their time practicing medicine or in other activities. Throughout this period, AMA leaders futilely pleaded – through speeches, newsletters, and *JAMA* articles – for more grassroots participation, continually reminding members that with "the general public, an impersonal, national organization does not have the influence that the trusted family physician has."[129] Yet AMA leaders were never able to fully recapture what had been essential to their associational strength – enthusiastic doctor participation.

THE AMA AND THE HEALTH INSURANCE MARKET

As we have seen, organized doctors responded to political pressure by selecting and elevating the insurance company model above an assortment of health care financing and delivery arrangements. Calling this model "voluntary insurance" – as if the competitive marketplace, rather than the AMA, had delivered up the financing structure – organized physicians proclaimed it vastly superior to any configuration entailing government funding or regulation. Still, behind the public pronouncements, the AMA perspective on health insurance was schizophrenic: some members continued to oppose prepaid services while physicians who did support insurance disagreed about the merits of nonprofit versus commercial plans. Mired in these disputes, AMA leaders neglected to seek ways to reform the insurance company model for lower costs or more efficient service delivery.

Even as the AMA publicized the feats and accomplishments of health insurance, doctors continued to resist medical prepayment. During the 1940s, while physician leaders were arguing that the growth of voluntary insurance proved federal reform unnecessary, AMA leader Morris Fishbein was simultaneously penning *JAMA* articles that disparaged prepaid medicine. Fishbein's enduring hostility toward insurance helped secure his dismissal in 1949. Still, even after his departure, some AMA officials continued to assert that insurance benefits should be restricted to prevent third parties from completely taking over health care financing.[130] During the 1950s, in response to the reform proposals offered under Eisenhower, abundant *JAMA* articles and almost every AMA meeting featured a medical leader warning that if physicians failed to support a sweeping expansion of health insurance, then the federal government would intervene in medicine.[131] Meanwhile, a vocal minority of physician members persisted in carping about third-party financiers. Some doctors complained that completing insurance forms and accounting for patient treatments undermined professional independence. As late as 1955, the House of Delegates was entertaining a resolution that accused insurance programs that compensated physicians according to set fee schedules – that is, Blue Shield plans – of drawing inspiration from the "Soviet model."[132]

Against this backdrop of lukewarm support and outright antagonism for insurance, doctors who did back voluntary prepayment often divided over whether to privilege nonprofit or commercial coverage. One physician faction argued that, because they were controlled by medical societies, only nonprofit Blue Shield plans could adequately safeguard professional standing. Indeed, the association's original 1938 resolution authorizing health care prepayment required that insurers obtain medical society approval for the policies that they sold. Then, during the 1940s, AMA officials launched a Seal of Acceptance program that only endorsed medical-society-supervised Blue Shield insurance. The physician leaders of Blue Shield in New York carried their support for nonprofits even further by labeling doctors who filled out commercial insurance forms as "traitors" who were "willing to sell out their colleagues."[133] The need to encourage and grow voluntary insurance during the Truman reform debates put a stop to this line of reasoning.

In 1949, the House of Delegates voted to formally recognize commercial or for-profit insurance, maintaining that the AMA had "no intention of giving preferential standing to any type of voluntary plan."[134] Prior to this resolution, commercial companies were able to issue health insurance because they used indemnity benefits, which created funding linkages between insurers and policyholders rather than between insurers and physicians. Official AMA approval legitimized commercial policies and cleared up lingering uncertainty among industry executives.[135]

Some physicians argued that doctors should favor commercial insurance over nonprofit policies. As we have seen, AMA leaders appreciated the initial endeavor of commercial firms to persuade consumers that insurance was a limited mechanism, meant only to cover catastrophic costs.[136] And commercial indemnity coverage provided stronger fortification for professional autonomy than did nonprofit service benefits, which entailed direct insurer-physician reimbursements. Moreover, the explicit for-profit status of insurance companies reassured doctors who worried about nonprofit administrators assuming the mantle of patient or community advocates.[137] Finally, AMA leaders found their most reliable political collaborators among commercial insurers. Because almost all moderate reform initiatives had potential to harm the for-profit industry's competitive standing in relation to nonprofits, commercial executives consistently joined the AMA to oppose them.

To fight political reforms, the AMA needed both nonprofit and commercial insurance to flourish. However, the larger issue of prepaid medical care, like so many other issues, became entangled in the association's organizational morass, and physicians failed to establish cohesive policies to proactively guide the market's evolution. In 1943, the House of Delegates created the Council on Medical Service to establish insurance requirements and work with Blue Shield. As an organizational arm of the House of Delegates, the council operated largely without board input.[138] In 1954, to constrain the power that delegates exercised through the council, the Board of Trustees founded the Commission on Medical Care Plans to investigate whether insurance was promoting "the proper interests of the medical profession."[139] In other words, the Council on Medical Service and the newly formed commission shared the same mandate.

Rather than sorting through the confusion, AMA leaders simply retreated from actively shaping health care financing by terminating the Seal of Acceptance program in 1954.[140] Several years later, the Heller Report chided AMA leaders for failing to set insurance policy standards and losing a critical opportunity to steer the health care market's direction.[141]

Once the AMA designated the insurance company model the only suitable form of medical prepayment, physicians ceded every opportunity to move the health care economy toward more efficient and inexpensive care. AMA leaders went through the motions of expressing interest in economic matters. They created councils and committees to study insurance and appointed representatives to confer with insurers. They also knew what they did not like: any third-party financing that might infringe upon physician autonomy or pay. This reactionary, backward-looking stance of AMA leaders left to insurance companies the primary responsibility for developing the health care market and also created political difficulties as policymakers looked for ways to make medical services more accessible.

CONCLUSION

During the postwar era, the AMA wielded significant political and cultural power. Nevertheless, peeling away the façade of vaunted AMA strength and evaluating the association's inner workings allows us to observe the political, organizational, and economic strategies that steadily eroded the influence of organized physicians. After the defeat of Truman's health care proposal, association officials not only mismanaged lobbying efforts but also took uncompromising stands on a broad assortment of legislation. Unrestrained political activity drew unfavorable publicity, and the AMA began losing important legislative battles, such as the campaign to prevent Social Security's expansion. Although these circumstances functioned as warning signs pointing to declining physician power, the association's elite and divided leadership, penchant for fabricating excessive objectives, and cumbersome bureaucracy obscured the AMA's collective vision. Amid frequent political skirmishes and a dysfunctional organizational structure, member discord escalated and apathy thrived. All the while, in the most important arena – the health care economy – physician leaders dithered to the point of relinquishing market development to third parties. These developments would later haunt the AMA when it emerged significantly weakened from Medicare battles and when insurance companies began acquiring political and economic authority at the expense of doctors.

4

Organized for Profit: The Hidden Influence of Insurance Companies and the HIAA

Although sometimes sponsored by property and casualty firms, commercial health insurance developed primarily out of the life insurance industry. During the first half of the twentieth century, life insurance associations provided the main political voice for commercial health insurers. Life insurance and health insurance executives often worked together within companies or, depending on the firm's structure, were one and the same person. Even after health insurers broke away to establish an independent trade association during the 1950s, they continued to coordinate political and economic activities with life insurers. Thus, a brief examination of the history of life insurance reveals the institutional genealogy of health care underwriters and sheds light on the choices they made to support and expand the insurance company model.

Because their industry explicitly pursued profits and contained gigantic, wealthy corporations, commercial insurers never obtained the cultural authority of organized physicians nor the political and societal goodwill accorded to nonprofit insurance leaders. Life insurers therefore assumed a pragmatic stance toward health care reform. Unwilling to squander the influence they did possess on a vicious political campaign and predominantly concerned with protecting their life and disability underwriting lines, industry representatives opposed Truman's reform proposal in a restrained, dispassionate manner. And although insurers united to resist nationalized health care, they divided when confronted with formulating a position toward moderate reform initiatives. Executives who primarily worked in health insurance viewed even the most tempered federal programs as perilous for their business interests and consequently followed a more hard-line conservative tack than life insurers. This political

disagreement, combined with the continual succession of reform proposals under Eisenhower, helped convince health insurers that they
required an independent trade association.

In 1956, they founded the Health Insurance Association of America
(HIAA) – a streamlined organization steered by a powerful leadership.[1]
Under the HIAA, the health insurance industry assumed an ultra-
conservative political disposition, opposing all federal reform initiatives,
no matter how limited. However, to account for negative cultural conceptions about big-business power, association officials adopted a low-visibility
political approach. In contrast to the publicity-grabbing American Medical
Association (AMA), HIAA representatives deliberately lobbied policymakers discreetly, away from the public eye.

HIAA member companies also focused significant energy and assets on
intensively developing the market in a manner calculated to strengthen
their claims about the superiority of private coverage over either
government-managed or federally regulated insurance. Fearing that even
modest federal reforms would subsidize their competitors and either
reduce or completely destroy their share of the insurance market, member
firms followed HIAA instructions to radically spread and liberalize coverage. As HIAA members hurriedly constructed the private sector, they
embedded a distinctive set of arrangements – the insurance company
model – into the health care system. They did so recognizing that their
actions flouted actuarial forecasts that linked coverage expansion through
such provisions to rapidly rising medical service costs.

This chapter maps the institutional development that supported and, at
times, jump-started that process, examining how the HIAA acquired the
capacity to convert federal political pressure into on-the-ground private
sector expansion. Indeed, insurance companies offer a stark contrast to
organized physicians. Because a mammoth, sprawling organization
hampered AMA leaders' ability to assess the broader political and economic context within which they operated, they made poor decisions that
weakened their influence. Meanwhile, HIAA leaders created a nimble and
effective association to guide members toward increasing political and
market power.

LIFE INSURERS AND POLITICAL EXPEDIENCY: THE ROOTS OF HEALTH INSURANCE

Life insurers sold a product constructed from political materials – from
legal rulings, state regulations, and the outcome of public investigations.

This reality shaped the industry's fortunes during its rough-and-tumble nineteenth-century history, as insurance firms struggled to acquire political favor and governmental objectives divided company leaders. When government authority expanded from the state to the national level during the twentieth century, insurance executives learned to be wary about assertively engaging in the federal political realm, lest they provoke a public backlash and retaliation from policymakers. Moreover, recognizing that some government policies had the potential to augment industry profits, many life insurers assumed moderate, pragmatic ideological positions. These characteristics, coupled with the fact that underwriters questioned the wisdom of even participating in the financially risky health care field, explain why commercial insurers entered the conflict over Truman's proposal cautiously, presenting a reserved, subdued resistance.

One can practically trace life insurance sales along a graph depicting U.S. industrial development. During the nineteenth century, consumers began to value life insurance for its ability to mitigate some of the risks attendant to mass industrialization. The growth of employment outside the home and reduction in family-centered sources of revenue, such as agricultural income, rendered the male breadwinner's death potentially more financially catastrophic than in previous periods. Additionally, rapid urbanization and increased mobility weakened the cradle of reciprocal caretaking relationships in which families and communities had long nestled.[2]

Despite its utility, commercial life insurance followed a rocky developmental course. Noncommercial groups experimented with elemental forms of life insurance during the eighteenth century. For example, fraternal orders, particularly Masonic Lodges, began paying member burial expenses out of dues collections. At the beginning of the nineteenth century, entrepreneurs replicated this logic to establish commercial life insurance companies. A few firms managed to survive the Panic of 1819 and, thereafter, life insurance sales grew steadily, reaching more than $1 million in total coverage by the early 1830s.[3] During the 1840s and 1850s, the industry reached a notable maturation point when insurers acquired sufficient data to construct reliable mortality tables and, concomitantly, the calculations necessary to improve risk pooling among population groups.[4] Further enhancing their product's appeal, insurers secured state laws that permitted widows and children to collect policy benefits ahead of other claimants to the deceased's estate.[5] However, the industry encountered serious difficulties when, around midcentury, states began enacting distinctive, burdensome insurance regulations. State guidelines governed a host of insurance activities, ranging from reserve requirements and permissible avenues of investment to agent licensing and premium taxes. By erecting barriers to growth across state lines, these regulations undermined two crucial stabilizers for insurance underwriting – high capital formation and diverse, geographically dispersed risk pools.[6] Taking advantage of state regulatory protections, numerous small firms entered the market and competition intensified. Conditions for substandard underwriting and fraud ripened. During the great economic downturn of the 1870s, many poorly funded operations folded.[7]

This environment helped nurture, at the end of the nineteenth century, the rise of massive companies with the necessary resources to meet the regulatory requirements of various states and, correspondingly, to aggregate far-flung risk groups. Moreover, all firms, whatever their size, attempted to survive difficult economic conditions by entering the field of burial insurance, a type of coverage that had previously been the domain of fraternal and mutual aid associations. This development made life insurance into a product for the masses: even if consumers could not afford "ordinary" policies, which maintained a family for years after the breadwinner's death, they could escape a pauper's funeral with small weekly payments toward burial or "industrial" insurance. Life insurance sales rose precipitously.[8]

Against this backdrop, the life insurance industry divided politically according to size.[9] The largest life insurance companies were located in the Northeast. Between the 1860s and the first decades of the twentieth century, these leading firms lobbied Congress and launched judicial challenges in an effort to exchange fragmented state governing frameworks for uniform federal regulation. Northeastern insurers were sorely disappointed when their 1869 Supreme Court case contesting licensing requirements in Virginia failed. Justices deciding the *Paul v. Virginia* case found that "though parties may be domiciled in different states," insurance contracts were "not interstate transactions" and therefore not subject to federal legislation.[10] In contrast, the leaders of small and medium-sized enterprises – predominantly located in the South and West – endorsed state regulatory jurisdiction. Rather than directly competing against the northeastern giants, they preferred channeling resources toward state policymakers who could erect regulatory shelters.[11]

The division between large and smaller firms manifested in separate trade groups. Founded in 1906, the Association of Life Insurance Presidents – later renamed the Life Insurance Association of America (LIAA) – was primarily composed of huge northeastern companies that collectively accounted for approximately two-thirds of all policies in force.[12] To no avail, the association continued petitioning policymakers and the courts for federal regulation.[13] Also in 1906, more than thirty small southern and western companies created the American Life Convention (ALC). The ALC fought legislation for federal supervision, which they argued would "be sprung by the large Eastern companies" in an attempt "to crush the life out of the Western companies."[14]

Meanwhile, immense, wealthy companies attracted public suspicion and negative attention toward the industry, at times with good reason. In 1905, New York officials launched a special review of all insurance companies operating within the state. What became known as the Armstrong investigation uncovered interlocking directorates, dishonest sales practices, heavy-handed lobbying, and undue influence over the state insurance department, among other disreputable activities.[15] The Armstrong hearings inspired public inquests around the country, and stricter state regulations followed.[16]

Foreshadowing the extraordinary efforts that health insurers would undertake to improve their product's reputation at midcentury, life insurers went to great lengths to repair their cultural standing and gain back subscribers lost during the Armstrong scandals. Both the LIAA and ALC sponsored advertisements, placed magazine articles, and published pamphlets emphasizing the industry's financial stability and spotlighting the peace of mind that families with insurance enjoyed.[17] Representatives from both associations worked closely with state regulators to develop laws designed to drive out fraudulent and marginal companies. Northeastern firms banded together to assume the policies of more than thirty companies that were unable, because of financial stress or fraud, to fulfill subscriber obligations.[18] The largest industry enterprise, Metropolitan Life Insurance of New York, initiated a decades-long program that, in an effort to protect policyholders and often at the behest of state regulators, regularly purchased failing companies.[19] Leading firms also launched public health campaigns that simultaneously boosted the industry's image while serving customer needs and reducing policyholder mortality rates due to infectious ailments. A multicompany bureau was established to provide subscriber medical exams and send representatives to discuss any identified health problems with the policyholder's doctor. Metropolitan dispatched nurses to tend to sick policyholders, primarily by instructing their families on hygiene and caretaking duties. The company carried out a massive health education drive that, through leaflets and advertisements, informed the general public about topics ranging from the "care of children" to "flies and filth." Combined with the millions of dollars that the firm spent on disease research, these operations made Metropolitan, according to scholar William Rothstein, "the nation's health department in the eyes of millions of Americans."[20]

In the midst of these endeavors, life insurers faced a political challenge that threatened to eliminate their core product. In 1915, a reform group, the American Association for Labor Legislation (AALL), published a model state bill to supply workers with a range of assistance, including health insurance, stipends to cover income lost during illness, and funeral benefits. Industry leaders particularly feared the proposed burial benefits, which, if enacted, would destroy their thriving industrial insurance business. To orchestrate resistance to the legislation, executives founded the IESA. IESA funneled resources into state organizing efforts, especially in California and New York where AALL legislation came closest to passage. In league with AMA medical societies, fraternal orders, and mutual aid associations, insurers penned newspaper editorials and distributed thousands of pamphlets to persuade voters that compulsory health and burial insurance were "socialistic" and "German-inspired."[21] After successfully defeating the AALL measures, IESA went on to coordinate numerous state political activities on behalf of insurance companies.

In addition to IESA, industry leaders established two associations to study and promote the rudimentary forms of health insurance that they sponsored: the Bureau of Accident and Health Underwriters (Bureau) and the Health and Accident Underwriters Conference (Conference). The Bureau primarily represented stock casualty companies in the Northeast while the Conference had a broader membership of almost every type of insurance company. Reflecting insurer reluctance to sell more expansive forms of health care coverage, the associations mainly focused on issues associated with disability and accident policies.[22]

During the 1930s, the outpouring of programs and legislation from the nation's capital compelled insurance executives to shift their attention from state to federal developments. Myriad legislative initiatives affected the industry. The Reconstruction Finance Corporation displaced potential insurance company investments by funding some of the lowest risk, in terms of profitability, municipal construction projects and businesses. Additionally, by restructuring the home mortgage market, the Federal Housing Administration altered one of the industry's primary investment channels.[23] But preoccupied with the financial crisis and fearful that political publicity would provoke government scrutiny, insurers declined to widely broadcast any negative opinions they harbored about economic reforms. When the Committee on Economic Security (CES) began developing the Social Security Act, most industry leaders remained silent, despite the impact that old-age payments might have on the sale of pension products and long-term annuities. Indeed, several industry executives and actuaries worked as consultants and assisted with CES investigations. In 1935, LIAA members voted to take no action either for or against the pending legislation. Where insurers did contest the measure, the opposition was, according to one executive, "isolated, personal, and lacking industry sanction or support."[24]

Although the ALC was traditionally inclined to espouse more anti-government positions than the LIAA, at least in regard to federal legislation, the politics of the two associations began to converge. Both associations evolved to include most life insurance firms among their membership, with almost all eastern companies joining the ALC by 1940. Moreover, the LIAA reversed its position on federal regulation. Because federal policymakers had begun to more vigorously intervene in the economy and because many of the problems created by fragmented state regulatory regimes had been ironed out with uniform model laws, northeastern insurers united with their western and southern brethren to defend state jurisdiction.[25]

Notwithstanding this newfound industry-wide consensus, federal policymakers launched a sustained assault against state regulatory prerogatives. Between 1938 and 1941, a joint congressional-executive committee created to investigate "monopoly powers" aimed heavy political fire at insurers.[26] Temporary National Economic Committee (TNEC) officials not only probed alleged antitrust activities among insurance companies but also did so in an attention-grabbing manner that, at times, portrayed the entire industry as unethical. Worried about additional political attacks and deteriorating public relations, insurers defended themselves using measured language. Confirming the legitimacy of government inquiries into fraud and corruption, ALC President C. A. Craig emphasized that insurers should complain about "the manner of the investigation, rather than the fact of the investigation."[27] TNEC representatives cited sizeable insurance company profits, potentially risky investments, and suspiciously similar policy prices as reasons that the industry required federal supervision. The Justice Department followed up with an antitrust suit against fire insurance companies.[28] In the 1944 *U.S. v. South-Eastern Underwriters Association* case, the Supreme Court overturned *Paul v. Virginia* and, with it, exclusive state authority to police insurance companies. The ruling threatened to topple, in one blow, the decades of energy and resources that both state policymakers and insurance representatives had sunk into crafting regulatory regimes. Congress responded by passing the 1945 McCarran-Ferguson Act, which blocked federal legislation from interfering with state insurance regulations. However, by deeming federal law applicable to insurance in matters that state law neglected to govern, the act failed to completely eliminate industry uncertainty. Indeed, throughout the postwar era insurers fought Federal Trade Commission attempts to acquire jurisdiction over industry advertising.[29]

This repertoire of political experiences persuaded insurers to adopt a pragmatic view of federal legislation. On one hand, insurers had a long history of encountering political hostility, and the recent TNEC investigations had impaired their public image. On the other hand, some New Deal legislation had improved the industry's welfare. Federal Housing Administration programs stabilized the mortgage market, which benefited insurance company investments. And Social Security payments for the elderly created a floor upon which insurance companies constructed a booming market of supplemental pension products. Acknowledging that industry wealth roused public misgivings and that government legislation could either injure or assist sector profitability, insurers shunned rigid ideological stands that could lead them into open political warfare. Instead, executives staked out practical positions on each issue and employed positive messaging to convince voters and policymakers to accept their views. Thus, even as insurers attempted to prevent social insurance expansion during the 1940s, they praised the Social Security program for being "orderly, dignified, and reliable."[30]

Insurers fought universal health care, but not because they had extensive fear of losing the medical insurance business. Chapter 1 detailed how, during the 1930s and 1940s, business requests for employee coverage and a desire to thwart federal reform initiatives pulled commercial companies into health insurance. The industry entered the field reluctantly, determined to offer only severely limited policies, such as hospitalization and catastrophic coverage. Given the financial risks associated with the insurance company model, losing health care coverage to a federal program would have been a relief to many underwriters. Nevertheless, industry leaders opposed federally managed health insurance as part of a broader campaign to contain Social Security and because they believed that a significantly enlarged welfare state would create a pattern of robust – and thus harmful for business – government intervention across the entire economy.

During deliberations over Truman's plan, industry representatives assumed a moderate tone and centered their political activities on favorably comparing private insurance to government-managed insurance. While organized doctors stridently screamed "socialized medicine," insurers restricted such terms to private conversations, carefully tempering any language deployed for public consumption.[31] Industry press releases and consumer literature were largely devoid of ideological arguments and instead focused on the "spectacular growth" of health insurance, boasting, for example, that hospitalization coverage had jumped from 52 million subscribers in 1947 to almost 61 million policyholders in 1948.[32] The 1949 statement of Ray Murphy, who testified before the Senate on behalf of the LIAA and ALC, exemplified the industry's approach. Murphy maintained that although the proposed legislation represented "a radical departure" from the voluntary system, he would nevertheless "confine" his comments "to the portions of that subject which are most closely related to our experience." The Equitable vice president then reviewed actuarial data to cast doubt on the government's ability to provide universal coverage "on a sound basis" and also presented statistics demonstrating the rapid advance of voluntary insurance.[33] Given the AMA's extraordinary campaigning efforts, commercial insurers did not have to exert much energy to be on the winning side of the political battle.

Although it was defeated, Truman's initiative left a durable imprint on commercial insurance companies. The criticism that reformers lodged against the paltry benefits of commercial coverage profoundly influenced industry attitudes toward health insurance. Executives recognized that to continue proclaiming private coverage more advantageous for consumers than government programming, they would have to broaden benefits beyond partial hospitalization coverage. Indeed, during the Truman debates, insurers expanded their offerings to include, among other products, major medical policies, which, although they required large deductibles, covered physician as well as hospital bills. Soon after, they began exploring how to liberalize major medical coverage by lowering deductibles and coinsurance requirements. By 1951, referencing the necessity of "fighting against Government interference," insurance executives were retreating from their insistence that policies remain restricted to catastrophic expenses.[34]

Reviewing the cultural standing and political background of the life insurance industry illuminates why, by the 1930s and 1940s, commercial insurers were exhibiting a mild and mannered political demeanor.

Insurers came to believe that widespread publicity would only harm their industry and, therefore, saw growing and augmenting health insurance as a more politically acceptable route toward defeating unwanted federal legislation. However, unlike the experience that life insurers had with some federal programs, medical insurers soon discovered that each and every proposed health care reform promised to damage their business interests. They consequently adopted a much more conservative political outlook.

INDUSTRY DIVISION AND BIRTH OF THE HIAA

The decision to oppose Truman's plan for nationalized medicine had been relatively simple for industry leaders. However, during Eisenhower's presidency they had to devise a political approach toward moderate reform overtures. Handling proposals for limited federal involvement in health care financing proved tricky. Although commercial insurers had long shunned a strictly conservative, anti-government posture, all of the proposed reforms appeared likely to introduce federal regulation of their industry and to significantly shrink their market share in what was now an established underwriting line.

The complexity of the problem manifested itself in industry disputes over Eisenhower's reform initiative. The president's reinsurance legislation sought to partially subsidize losses incurred by companies that expanded health care coverage, either by liberalizing policy benefits or by covering high-risk groups. After settling on the reinsurance proposal in 1953, the administration began courting industry support. Officials in the Department of Health, Education, and Welfare (HEW) convened a task force of insurance executives, and Eisenhower held a White House luncheon to convince key leaders that his program offered the best strategy for undermining the possibility of socialized medicine. Although insurers expressed reservations during task force deliberations, the president's personal appeal proved difficult to resist.[35] A prominent group of executives, including the LIAA's leadership, decided to back the measure. They argued that the industry could not afford to oppose a Republican president. Parroting an administration talking point, LIAA President Louis W. Dawson contended that the plan had "the merit of offering assistance to private companies, rather than pre-empting their field."[36] Life insurers also hoped that their support would convince Eisenhower to check Social Security expansion, thereby safeguarding the profitability of the industry's disability insurance and pension products.[37] LIAA lobbyist Eugene

Thore showcased the position as socially responsible, explaining to the press that a "sound attitude toward government is vital." He declared that a "business that continuously negates all welfare legislation without offering alternative suggestions may sterilize its constructive powers and alienate itself from the public and the government."[38] As members of the ideologically moderate northeastern wing of the industry, the presidents of Connecticut General Life Insurance and John Hancock Mutual Life Insurance sent letters to congressional members advocating Eisenhower's plan.[39]

These demonstrations of support for government reinsurance plunged the industry into division and "crisis."[40] By this point, commercial health insurance was far more entrenched than during the Truman presidency: certain companies and executives had poured substantial resources into developing the product and were committed to protecting it. Executives involved in medical underwriting and insurers who held more ideologically conservative beliefs protested that industry representatives had capitulated to a scheme that not only threatened to introduce federal regulation of insurance but also imperiled the entire health care underwriting business. According to the proposed legislation, administrators in a new federal agency, the Health Services Corporation, would decide which companies had losses that merited subsidization. Commercial health insurers feared, quite rationally, that government officials would award industry competitors – nonprofit plans and prepaid groups – more generous funding because they claimed to pursue socially responsible, community-oriented objectives. Opponents of federal reinsurance also worried that the Health Services Corporation would, as had the Social Security Administration, turn into a beachhead for reform-oriented policymakers seeking additional powers over medical financing and care. Since government reinsurance was unable to make "insurable what is not an insurable risk" and would cover only two-thirds of company losses, adversaries claimed that the program would inevitably fail to expand coverage significantly. Such a development, they asserted, would set the stage for future policymakers to enlarge the program, which would likely include mandating specific benefits and setting price controls.[41]

Edwin J. Faulkner led the resistance to federal reinsurance. Demonstrating the insurance industry's internal turmoil, Faulkner testified against the measure as a representative of the Chamber of Commerce. The insurance executive warned congressional members that the program would fall far short of stated objectives:

Government reinsurance of health insurance plans would introduce no magic into the field of financing health care costs. . . . Reinsurance does not reduce the cost of insurance. Reinsurance does not make insurance available to any class of risk . . . not now within the capability of voluntary insurance to reach.[42]

The outcry from health underwriting interests forced life insurance leaders to walk back the political assurances they had previously given Eisenhower. Testifying on behalf of both the LIAA and the ALC, Aetna Vice President Henry Beers praised the "many sound principles" in the legislation and commended the administration for attempting to find "constructive methods for stimulating private initiative." "However," continued Beers, "since the plan is new and so many important details are yet unknown and therefore many uncertainties remain unresolved, we are not in a position to go on record in favor of the bill at this time."[43]

Health insurers emerged victorious from the legislative row over reinsurance; however, the episode convinced them that they required an independent association to represent their political affairs.[44] Not only were they at odds politically with life insurers, but also they needed a unified organization that could sort through the differing concerns of numerous health insurance companies to define and defend the industry's "common interest."[45] By the early 1950s, approximately eight hundred commercial companies offered some form of medical insurance.[46] Many trade associations represented these enterprises, which, among others, included the LIAA, the ALC, the Insurance Economics Society of America (IESA), the Bureau of Accident and Health Underwriters (Bureau), and the Health and Accident Underwriters Conference (Conference).

Health insurers considered strengthening one of these existing organizations, but each group lacked either the support or institutional capacity necessary to serve as the industry's primary trade association. Though IESA leaders had proven themselves effective and forceful scrappers in state politics, executives worried that their brash style would incite hostility among federal policymakers and earn negative publicity for the industry nationwide.[47] The only two groups that dealt explicitly with medical policies – the Bureau and Conference – had been established decades earlier to study disability and accident coverage, which were far more circumscribed underwriting lines than the postwar health insurance product. The two associations had difficulty managing the evolution and growth of medical insurance, as evidenced by how leaders extemporaneously added committees as new issues arose. The Bureau, for example, swelled from nine committees in 1945 to forty-three committees by 1955.[48] Furthermore, the effectiveness of both

associations was hampered by size, organizational overlap, and competition for member company resources.[49]

While in the middle of combating government reinsurance, Faulkner
began orchestrating support for a new trade association. Faulkner had
long been a leading voice in the medical underwriting sector. During the
1930s, he served as president of the Conference and then as executive
board chairman. His firm, the Nebraska-based Woodmen Accident
and Life Company, underwrote a respectable amount of life insurance
but increasingly focused on health care policies. Premium income placed
the company among the top 5 percent of commercial health insurance
enterprises.[50] Drawing upon his industry-wide reputation, Faulkner
persuaded Bureau and Conference leaders to consider creating a new,
integrated organization. "Accident and sickness insurance has spoken
from many mouths, to the confusion of both the public and the industry,"
argued Faulkner. He warned that without the establishment of a single
organization to manage the politics of health care, life insurance
associations would "undertake more aggressive programs in the field."[51]
Faulkner's colleagues understood his underlying message: if they failed to
create an independent trade group, then life insurers would use the
health care industry as a bargaining chip to accomplish their own political
goals. Moreover, the only way that health insurers could mount the
stringently conservative political resistance that many believed was
necessary to protect their business was by creating a separate trade
association.

The increasing complexities of both the market and the political environment convinced medical underwriters to peaceably secede from life
interests to pursue their own objectives. In 1954, the Bureau, Conference,
LIAA, ALC, and several additional insurance groups dispatched representatives to meet under the umbrella of the Joint Committee on Health
Insurance, formed for the purposes of launching a new trade association.[52] At the same time, the Bureau and Conference began issuing joint
policy statements and hired a full-time lobbyist to live in Washington.
In 1956, the Bureau and Conference suspended operations and their
member companies established the HIAA.[53]

The HIAA's organizational features provided leaders with the capacity
and flexibility necessary to match industry ambitions. The association
commanded large financial resources owing to corporate dues, which
were based on the amount of health insurance each company underwrote.[54] HIAA officials used these resources efficiently by channeling
them into four well-defined areas of activity: lobbying, self-governance,

expertise, and public relations. Moreover, because they created their organization at midcentury, health insurance leaders were unimpeded by the burdens that shackled mature associations, such as sorting through the competing claims of different committees and bureaucratic enclaves or managing numerous ancillary commitments that drained focus away from fundamental pursuits. HIAA lawyers scrutinized government legislation and proposals in Chicago, researchers and actuaries carried out studies in New York, and lobbyists resided in the nation's capital. Nonetheless, staff members among these three offices probably numbered fewer than twenty-five.[55]

Centralized leadership enabled the HIAA to apply cohesive direction to a vast industry. The HIAA represented companies responsible for approximately 85 percent of all commercial health insurance. To elect the association's officers and Board of Directors, each firm cast votes that, like dues payments, were weighted according to the company's medical insurance volume. Candidates were drawn from among the executives of constituent companies. The Board of Directors formulated association policy and coordinated activities by working with ten standing committees as well as ad hoc committees, which were appointed as new issues arose.[56] The committees, primarily composed of executives from large companies, carried out in-depth research to support the political and economic strategies that they recommended to the board. Although company representatives met once a year to vote on policy matters, the association's positions were largely sorted out ahead of time by board and committee members. This structure allowed the most respected firms and executives to provide unified, authoritative guidance for the commercial health insurance sector.

From this governing base, Faulkner, the HIAA's first president and most prominent postwar leader, joined with like-minded colleagues to convince health insurers to adopt ultra-conservative political policies. A native Nebraskan, Faulkner grew up imbued with conservative midwestern values. His grandfather founded Woodmen Accident and Life Company in 1890. Faulkner's father, Ted, who also served as president of the company, was renowned for his work ethic and Sundays spent at the office. Edwin – or "Eddie," as his friends called him – maintained an "A" average at the University of Nebraska while participating in more than a dozen campus activities and working summers for his grandfather's firm. After receiving an MBA from Wharton, Faulkner returned to the insurance business in Lincoln. When he ascended to the presidency of Woodmen Life in 1938, he was only twenty-seven years old and probably the youngest insurance executive in the country. During the war, Faulkner took an extended leave from his company to coordinate aircraft production for the Air Force from Washington, D.C.; his accomplishments earned him the rank of lieutenant colonel. Small in stature but handsome and dashing, Faulkner was accustomed to being taken seriously. He was the type of man who believed most societal ills could be remedied by liberally applying a salve that mixed hard work and capitalism with a dash of Henry Ford's entrepreneurial spirit. The executive loathed the "supine compliance" that ideologically moderate businessmen had assumed – that posture, he argued, had permitted the "creeping paralysis of socialism" into American life. Advancing his beliefs in a soft-spoken, dignified manner, Faulkner urged fellow executives to stand resolutely against all government "meddling" in the health care sector.[57]

By distancing themselves from life insurers, HIAA leaders could join with organized physicians to combat all health care reforms, no matter how moderate. However, the HIAA's organizational configuration sharply diverged from that of physicians. While the AMA's fragmented leadership struggled to manage countless committees and a bloated bureaucracy that chased after hundreds of objectives, HIAA founders created an efficiently operated, powerful association that bolstered insurers as they surveyed the health care landscape and calculated how to carve out a central position for their industry.

THE HIAA AND FEDERAL POLITICS: THE HIDDEN STRATEGY

HIAA leaders not only employed different organizational methods than the AMA, they also embraced a distinct political style. Recognizing their inability to harness the cultural cachet of physicians or claim the broad social goals of nonprofit plans, HIAA leaders shaped their approach to account for the propensity of large corporations to attract political scrutiny. Because even modest health care reforms would have subjected commercial firms to federal regulation and severely undercut their competitive position, HIAA officials opposed all government intercessions into health care. But they did so using techniques devised to protect their public image. They conveyed the same restrained, moderate tone that insurance leaders had exhibited during the Truman reform debates. Additionally, HIAA leaders deliberately fought reform proposals in a concealed, behind-the-scenes manner. So adept was the HIAA strategy of avoiding political publicity that scholars have heaped lavish attention on organized physicians while largely neglecting the influence that commercial insurers had over the fate of health care reform.

As commercial financiers of medical care, insurers were vulnerable to the criticism that they valued profits over the health needs of patients. Union leaders, health care reformers, progressive policymakers, and some segments of the media disparaged insurers for selling high-priced coverage with meager benefits. For example, an exposé in *The Saturday Evening Post* discussed what some observers jestingly called "Fourth of July" policies. Such health insurance, explained the article, "sounds good, but is so limited that it will provide coverage for only the most rare events – like being trampled by a bull elephant on Main Street at high noon on the Fourth of July."[58] Unscrupulous operators, though a small portion of the industry, validated this critique. As health insurance became increasingly popular, mail-order and fly-by-night companies peddled marginal products with misleading advertisements. Insurance firms that made outrageous claims – marketing, for example, policies for ages "1 to 75" and promising large payments "for each sickness or accident" – usually canceled coverage as soon as the subscriber became ill.[59]

Still licking their wounds from the damaging TNEC hearings, industry leaders received another political flogging when, in 1955, the Federal Trade Commission (FTC) launched an investigation into the deceptive and false advertising practices of health insurance companies. Faulkner protested that "the sensational publicity accorded the FTC announcement" had "left serious misconceptions among the uninformed." Insurers complained that government officials sought to exploit the actions of a few companies to make a case for placing the entire industry under federal, rather than state, authority.[60] The FTC investigation initiated yet another round of legal skirmishes over regulatory jurisdiction.[61] With the industry locked in a fierce battle to maintain state governing prerogatives, politically conservative insurers argued that averting federal supervision required the industry to defeat even modest health care reforms.[62]

Faulkner and his political cohort also contended that because commercial insurers had precious little public goodwill upon which to trade, policymakers would invariably design health care reforms and programming initiatives to undermine their industry. Substantiating this assertion, insurers fought a litany of legislative measures throughout the 1950s that promised to reshuffle the health care economy in ways that would have harmed their companies while privileging their market rivals. A sampling of these proposals included Eisenhower's reinsurance legislation, the Wolverton-Kaiser bill to subsidize prepaid doctor groups, and the

Flanders-Ives plan to create universal coverage using nonprofit insurance. Since it seemed probable that any political compromise would significantly weaken the commercial industry's market standing, even ideologically moderate executives who were ordinarily inclined to cooperate with policymakers were deterred from doing so.

Although determined to defeat all health care legislation, insurance leaders had to tread carefully upon the political stage. Because commercial insurers had the least cultural status among private health interests, industry officials quickly ruled out direct political attacks as unpromising and perilous. Neither could they overtly lobby federal officials, as the appearance of close connections between policymakers and large, wealthy businesses would have been unseemly. Indeed, when a 1947 Gallup Poll asked voters if corporations should be allowed to directly participate in political contests by making campaign contributions, an overwhelming 72 percent of them answered "no."[63]

To accommodate this political setting, HIAA leaders deployed two main strategies to rout legislative reforms. First, before the public, they promoted the success of voluntary insurance. The HIAA expended roughly a quarter of a million dollars annually to publicize the advantages of commercial coverage. For example, advertisements in *The Atlantic Monthly* and *Harper's* pictured content families who could "rest comfortably" knowing that their savings were secure from the risk of illness. Through the Health Insurance Institute, a subsidiary of the HIAA, industry officials sent articles and editorials to news outlets. These essays countered reformer criticisms by documenting the rapid growth of insurance in terms of both policyholder numbers and more generous benefits.[64] "We felt our only defense ... was performance," explained the HIAA's principal lobbyist, "[c]ompanies don't have very much political leverage."[65]

Behind this public display, as the second plank of their political program, HIAA leaders implemented a low visibility lobbying approach designed to prevent charges of undue corporate influence in governmental affairs. Unlike the AMA, the HIAA rarely, if ever, issued political proclamations that went beyond praising the accomplishments of private insurance. When congressional hearings required HIAA representatives to publicly oppose a bill, they steered clear of inflammatory language and focused their testimony on highlighting the swift spread of commercial health coverage. Additionally, HIAA leaders tapped Robert Neal as their chief lobbyist. The choice of Neal, an industry insider who hailed from the Midwest, allowed insurers to operate under the media's radar. Insurers decided against selecting a prominent individual or politician, because a high-profile appointment would link insurance companies, in the citizenry's mind, with political activities and would "imply that the business" had "some scandalous situations" that necessitated "an outside and impartial giant to handle."[66] Meanwhile, industry representatives ingratiated themselves with the administration officials, legislators, and congressional staff members whom they lobbied by supplying them with valuable insurance data and underwriting expertise. Wilbur Cohen, a celebrated reformer and policymaker who served in the Social Security Administration before becoming HEW secretary under President Lyndon B. Johnson, observed that HIAA leaders survived many legislative battles without generating a "residue of anti-insurance company feeling" by cooperating with officials and eschewing belligerent political tactics.[67]

HIAA representatives met with administration and congressional officials to provide health insurance information and make their legislative views known; however, they avoided applying direct political pressure from their D.C. office. When industry leaders sought to affect a policy outcome, they identified key congressmen and encouraged the "vote back home" – that is, the executives, managers, and sales associates of insurance companies in their districts – to either write or meet with their representatives.[68] Neal explained why the HIAA shunned heavy-handed lobbying on Capitol Hill and large-scale organizing, which would have involved insurers across the country blanketing Congress with letters and telegrams:

I don't think that Senators and Representatives care to talk to us [representatives of the national HIAA organization]. They're interested in what their people back home think. The only successful way to get views across is from the grassroots. And we never go in for post card lobbying or anything of that kind. It's a waste of time. We just stick pretty well to basics ... the representatives here are representing their constituents [insurance company employees in their district], and it's their views that they're interested in.[69]

HIAA leaders understood that legislators had little to gain from appearing to bow to pressure from national industry groups or titan corporations. However, insurance firms in their districts had at their command voting employees and either active or potential campaign contributors.

Commercial insurers also took cover behind the AMA's political shield. For example, industry executives who opposed government reinsurance traveled to Chicago to ensure that AMA leaders would fully deploy their political machine to contest Eisenhower's measure.[70] Indeed they did. At times, AMA leaders extended commercial insurers political protection as a reward for staunchly resisting all government involvement in health care. Organized physicians even protested obscure legislation on behalf of their allies, such as a federal proposal to prohibit insurers from terminating subscriber policies after three years of coverage. Echoing a major industry concern, AMA leaders declared that "the regulation of insurance companies is a matter for the individual state governments."[71]

HIAA leaders skillfully exercised political influence without attracting public attention. Promotional campaigns that boasted of industry accomplishments in financing health care reassured consumers that insurance companies could meet their needs. Meanwhile, industry representatives quietly but effectively beat back political efforts to modify the insurance company model. Alternative delivery models, including prepaid physician groups and union welfare funds, continued to operate but, without the support of organized doctors or federal subsidies, soon faded in the public imagination as primary channels for arranging health care. Nonetheless, marketing and political operations could not, on their own, completely shape public notions about how funding for medical services should be packaged. HIAA officials also had to manage industry activities so that insurance company products appeared ubiquitous in the marketplace.

THE HIAA ORGANIZES THE MARKET

Conflicting company interests and interfirm competition often weaken trade associations.[72] This danger hung over the HIAA because the organization represented a wide range of underwriting businesses: life insurance, property and casualty, stock, mutual, small, midsized, and gigantic companies. Yet member firms united under strong HIAA governance, including directives for industry-wide economic cooperation, because loss of business from federal action loomed larger than individual market rivalries. Through conference speeches, industry meetings, and trade literature, HIAA leaders repeatedly – almost incessantly – warned members that if they failed to rapidly expand and liberalize coverage, government forces would intervene to trample the commercial health insurance sector.[73] HIAA member companies therefore consented to strict ethical requirements, shared sensitive data with each other, and complied with association guidance on the types of insurance products they formulated and sold. These activities greatly increased policyholder numbers and also redefined the function of insurance, converting it from a niche product that partially covered catastrophic expenses into a mass consumer good that paid for a majority of health care costs.

Industry governance raised potential antitrust issues. As insurers fought to maintain state regulation, antitrust allegations presented a potential opening for policymakers attempting to introduce federal industry oversight. HIAA founders conferred with legal experts and at least one lawyer counseled them not to institute strict ethical obligations, cautioning that antitrust action could be brought against the association if a company claimed that membership exclusion caused competitive disadvantage.[74] However, bad publicity caused by deceptive insurance practices and the need to develop the market in a manner that mitigated political critiques persuaded HIAA leaders to forge ahead with their plan for rigorous member regulation.[75] "It is easy to conclude that a monopoly is a stifling concept," argued one HIAA official. He continued: "It is also easy to see that speculative and cut-throat competition can tend toward chaos and economic disaster. A trade association which reduces friction and adds some stability through circulating information and setting standards may be the balance wheel between the two extremes."[76]

HIAA direction imposed a large degree of uniformity on industry practices. Association rules standardized policy design and content, marketing practices, and how companies collected and disbursed subscriber payments.[77] HIAA representatives also worked with the National Association of Insurance Commissioners to retool state laws governing medical insurance. HIAA leaders instructed members to lobby their domiciliary states to adopt these model laws and to obey them even where weaker regulations prevailed. The Uniform Individual Accident and Sickness Policy Provisions Law ensured that contracts were easy to understand and devoid of obscure language and coverage exclusions. Fair Trade Practices Acts prohibited false advertising.[78] The HIAA's ethical standards went further than the model laws. Association rules prohibited companies from discrediting other insurance firms in advertisements, heavily marketing experimental policies without knowing whether the company could finance the product over the long term, delaying subscriber payments, or making claims that implied "that benefits are larger or broader than is actually the case, also the use of essentially valueless benefits, and of policies or coverages with unreasonable restrictions, limitations, exceptions, reductions, and exclusions."[79] HIAA leaders implemented these parameters to reassure consumers about the security of commercial coverage – particularly subscribers who purchased insurance individually and, unlike corporate benefits specialists and union officials, lacked the expertise to evaluate complex policy details.

The HIAA monitored member compliance with both association and state regulations. A Membership and Ethical Standards Committee examined company applications to join the HIAA and investigated firms accused of violating the association's guidelines. To demonstrate an upstanding reputation, companies applying for membership had to provide the committee with state insurance department evaluations and actuarial data proving financial stability.[80] Member firms were obligated to maintain a catalog of consumer grievances and faced expulsion if state authorities reported "an abnormal record of complaints in relation to its volume of claims."[81]

In addition to accepting strict supervision, HIAA companies collaborated to improve underwriting expertise. During the immediate postwar period, knowledge about health care underwriting was shallow. Life insurance required actuaries to assess the probability of incurring one claim at a predetermined amount, while health insurance involved numerous claims, thousands of possible conditions, and various payment levels for each service and procedure. Insurers, moreover, lacked illness-specific morbidity statistics. Consequently, well into the 1950s, actuaries could only provide loose estimates of the reserve amounts necessary to support policy offerings.[82] Through the HIAA, companies aggregated their policy experience to begin constructing morbidity tables. Whether using rudimentary or, by the 1960s, more reliable data, underwriters observed the difficulty of financing medical care according to the insurance company model – gloomy actuarial forecasts always advised against further coverage expansion.

In an attempt to surmount these financial projections and continue advancing health insurance, HIAA members shared information about internal company operations. Company leaders went beyond the traditional industry practice of circulating actuarial statistics; they also divulged extensive business intelligence despite the hazards of disclosing such information to market competitors. In HIAA forums, executives revealed what steps their companies took to introduce new products, how they marketed health care policies, and the financing difficulties they encountered.[83] "Your progress in the past has been hampered due to little tendency to cooperate and pool experience and knowledge for improvement," stated one HIAA official. He continued: "Thanks in large part to this fine organization we have largely put aside such provincial attitudes."[84]

Regimenting company practices and developing underwriting and operational expertise only carried the industry so far toward the goal of broadening health insurance to head off federal reform. Ultimately, insurers had to reconceptualize axiomatic principles of underwriting risk. Up through the early 1950s, insurers could rapidly increase coverage rates by multiplying the number of highly restricted policies they sold to employee groups and healthy, young individuals. It then became apparent that insurers would have to reevaluate long-held risk avoidance strategies in order to make the political case that, first, consumers enjoyed benefits that were just as generous as any type of coverage conceived under government proposals and that, second, the industry could continue swelling the ranks of the insured. Accordingly, companies fundamentally altered their products so that they covered more medical procedures – particularly for employee groups, which usually contained healthier subscribers than the general population. Under these new policies, insured care often included diagnostic exams, laboratory tests, and routine office visits, which were the very types of services that patients would be more likely to demand and physicians would be more likely to provide if paid for by a third party. Additionally, underwriters experimented with expanding the individual insurance market to include subscribers with substandard health.

Underwriting ever more generous group policies was necessary, both to keep federal power at bay and to compete with nonprofit plans, which had a reputation for offering liberal benefits. One of the very first categories of health insurance that commercial companies had offered was hospital coverage. Once employee groups obtained hospitalization policies, they then sought surgical and regular medical coverage. Physician services were not covered by hospitalization policies, so surgical insurance afforded compensation for surgeons. Regular medical or medical policies covered physician services delivered inside and, increasingly, outside the hospital, thus moving insurers further away from more financially stable products that only reimbursed patient bills in case of an accident or serious, unforeseen illness. In 1949, commercial firms covered about five million subscribers with regular medical benefits. By the early 1960s, for-profit companies had raised that number tenfold.[85] With the introduction of comprehensive policies, the categories of hospital, surgical, and medical insurance gradually blurred. Ironically, the major medical or catastrophic policies that commercial leaders had initially formulated to limit insurance became vehicles for broadening coverage. In 1955, General Electric became the first prominent company to provide employees with comprehensive health benefits when New York Life agreed to underwrite a reconceived version of major medical. By significantly lowering the deductible and coinsurance requirements associated with major medical, New York Life began covering routine health services as well as a larger portion of catastrophic costs.[86] Within four years, more than seven million group subscribers had comprehensive commercial benefits and insurers were reporting "phenomenal" growth.[87] Major medical offered an additional avenue for generating comprehensive insurance. Employee groups began layering commercial major medical policies atop the basic or first-dollar policies of nonprofit plans to create all-inclusive coverage.[88] While these packages represented the gold standard in health insurance, they shaped the entire market by setting a benchmark toward which most policies would evolve. The innovation created a pattern that became so deeply ingrained in the market that modern consumers have difficulty imagining health insurance as anything other than a mechanism for paying most medical bills.

At the same time, HIAA leaders worked to make medical insurance a product not only for the employed, but also for the masses, including individuals with substandard health. Growing individual coverage presented particular difficulties. In the market for individual policies, adverse selection exacerbated cost problems associated with the insurance company model. Because consumers prone to illness bought insurance in greater numbers than did their healthy peers, individual coverage experienced exceptionally high rates of service utilization. To tackle this problem and organize industry efforts to enlarge the individual-purchase market, HIAA officials established a task force in 1957 to study high-risk subscribers.[89] The investigation only confirmed what insurers already knew: financial quandaries would accompany any augmentation of individual coverage. HIAA leaders nevertheless forged ahead. "Skillfully underwritten [insurance]," Faulkner contended, "is no longer an excuse for hesitancy or timidity."[90] Reflecting this view, delegates at the HIAA's 1958 annual meeting approved directives instructing companies to both minimize policy cancellations and offer coverage to the sick and elderly:

Insurers ... should continue to accelerate their progress in minimizing the refusal of renewal solely because of deterioration of health after issuance. ... Every insurer offering health care coverages should ... promptly make available to insurable adults policies which are guaranteed renewable for life. ... Every insurer ... should promptly take steps if it is not presently doing so to offer insurance coverage to persons now over age 65. ... It is essential that adequate voluntary health insurance be available to broad classes of physically impaired people.[91]

Although they lacked actuarial forecasts that could ease the profitmaking concerns of company executives, HIAA leaders continually prodded members, asserting that failure to broaden individual coverage would invite government reform. Faulkner maintained that "if private enterprise is to prevail," the "social nature of our business requires us to shoulder our share of providing protection for the less desirable type of risk and benefit."[92]

Scholars who assume that commercial companies cherry-picked healthy employee groups out of the broader insurance pool and left nonprofits to cover higher-risk individuals have somewhat mischaracterized the industry's behavior.[93] By 1960, commercial companies sold approximately 40 percent of their hospitalization policies to individuals.[94] Moreover, during the 1950s, about three-fifths of HIAA companies took steps to limit the quantity of subscriber renewals they would refuse due to declining health. More than seventy firms introduced policies that were guaranteed renewable for life – though, of course, premium prices could rise.[95] In sum, to undermine arguments in favor of government intervention in their field, commercial leaders had to demonstrate their industry's social responsibility and pursuit of the public interest; they attempted to accomplish this mission by insuring a significant portion of the individual-purchase market, including some high-risk subscribers.

At the end of the 1950s, when reformers ramped up their campaign to supply aged citizens with health insurance through Social Security, HIAA firms employed extraordinary measures to combat the legislation. Insurance companies began permitting workers with policies supplied through their employer to retain coverage upon retirement. Unions aided this project by convincing employers to fund either all or some of retirees' insurance costs.[96] Some HIAA firms authorized subscribers, for an additional fee, to include elderly parents as dependents when they purchased family coverage. Most strikingly, HIAA representatives lobbied state governments to grant antitrust exemptions to companies that joined together to collectively finance and administer operations for the express purpose of insuring customers over age 65. Enabling laws permitted commercial firms to establish and heavily publicize "State 65" programs, such as Connecticut 65 and Western 65.[97] Through these endeavors, the percentage of elderly citizens with some form of health insurance, whether commercial or nonprofit, rose from 26 percent in 1952 to approximately 60 percent by the end of 1962.[98] These policies usually only provided partial coverage for a limited number of hospitalization days; still, the coverage growth is noteworthy when one considers health care utilization rates among the elderly and the financial risks that companies assumed to insure them.

Only one decade prior, not a single insurer – not even Faulkner himself – would have fathomed a massive industry effort to supply the elderly with health care policies. Although they had entered the market with much trepidation during the 1930s and 1940s, by the 1950s, industry leaders envisioned the health care market built around the insurance company model, with their businesses at the center of that system. As they sought this objective, HIAA leaders employed both the organizational wherewithal and the threat of alternative political scenarios to persuade traditionally cautious insurance executives to brazenly challenge fundamental underwriting principles and gamble with company profits. The venture reaped significant returns – as HIAA members developed the medical financing market and consumers became increasingly familiar with commercial coverage, insurance company products acquired both cultural and political legitimacy.

THE COST DILEMMA

The success that HIAA firms enjoyed in rapidly organizing the health care market could not conceal the related problem of skyrocketing costs. Commercial underwriters expanded health insurance until they ran up against the insurmountable wall of moral hazard – a wall heightened and reinforced by a financing model that incentivized physicians to boost service supply. Surging medical costs made it increasingly difficult for individual subscribers, who lacked employer contributions, to afford insurance. Moreover, flagging profits led industry leaders to question their commitment to insuring the elderly.

Wagering that broader benefits and coverage would yield durable political rewards, industry leaders, throughout the 1950s and into the 1960s, urged companies to partially neglect short-term profits. Large firms had the most capacity to ignore negative actuarial prognostications because they could subsidize health care losses with profits from other underwriting lines. Indeed, some executives regarded medical policies as "door openers" or "loss leaders" that were primarily valuable for helping their firms win lucrative employee group pension and life insurance accounts. Other insurers grumbled; one executive complained that "insurance companies have acted like philanthropic organizations in recent years, paying out more money in claims and expenses than they've collected."[99] HIAA officials responded by arguing that once the health insurance market had matured, the pressure for federal reform would weaken and insurers would be permitted to more vigorously pursue profits. The key, asserted Faulkner, was rendering their business impervious to government intrusion: "the one salvation for free enterprise lies in peerless performance that will satisfy the needs of the American people."[100]

When this line of reasoning began to lose influence, HIAA leaders fell back on issuing stern orders. The field of aged coverage illustrates the association's tack. The conflict over federally funded elderly health benefits stretched on for almost eight years between 1957, when the Forand bill was introduced, and 1965, when Medicare passed. Whenever the issue of government aged insurance flared up, HIAA leaders issued communiqués urging members to protect the industry by joining the fight against government-run medicine. In one instance, the Board of Directors asked company executives to "review their programs, methods, and products in order to determine whether they are adequate in contributing their full share to the challenge with which private insurance is faced."[101] HIAA instructions were at times dire:

THE URGENCY WAS NEVER SO GREAT NOR THE TIME AVAILABLE FOR DEMONSTRATING OUR CAPACITY SO SHORT. TO AVOID A COMPULSORY GOVERNMENTAL PROGRAM THE HEALTH AND ACCIDENT INSURANCE INDUSTRY MUST ACT EFFECTIVELY DURING THE MONTHS IMMEDIATELY AHEAD. WE NO LONGER HAVE YEARS IN WHICH TO PROVE OUR CASE. IT MUST BE DONE IN MONTHS.[102]

Despite the leadership's forceful tone, the power of such edicts waned as insurance executives weighed them against diminishing corporate revenues.

By the early 1960s, insurers began regarding the State 65 initiatives as failures. The costs associated with the insurance company model had made covering regular policyholders difficult enough. Seniors not only had significantly higher rates of illness but usually lacked employer subsidies to offset coverage costs. Although the industry, in league with nonprofit plans, more than doubled elderly coverage rates between 1958 and 1961, exorbitantly high policy prices subsequently slowed that growth.[103] Experience allowed insurers to develop more sophisticated morbidity tables for aged subscribers, but the data only underscored why there "wasn't any great wave of enthusiasm to go into this."[104] As financial losses connected to elderly insurance mounted, even the executives who had initially offered State 65 programs wholehearted support began to consider withdrawing their companies from the plans.[105]

For-profit insurers made enormous strides in their drive to expand health insurance until they became mired in the intractable problem of covering the sick and aged. While commercial insurers lost this battle – or ultimately retreated from it – their efforts to spread voluntary coverage won the war. By positioning commercial financing at the heart of the market, HIAA firms increased the likelihood that government reforms, whether for federal employee benefits or elderly coverage, would accommodate the insurance company model despite its many flaws.

CONCLUSION

During the 1940s, commercial executives participated in the medical field with an abundance of wariness and reluctance; moreover, the insurance company model still represented but one of numerous possible ways of arranging the health care system. By 1965, the insurance company model had become the dominant means of financing and delivering medical services. The HIAA directed and disciplined commercial insurance companies through this dramatic evolution. HIAA leaders pursued industry objectives from a position of strength – atop a prosperous, efficient organization that exercised political power quietly, without attracting public attention or hostility. Meanwhile, member firms expended considerable resources attempting to fulfill HIAA instructions to convert health insurance into a mass consumer product with ever more generous benefits coverage. Animating industry activities through every tricky and financially risky step was the belief that if they failed to prove the voluntary market's vitality, then the federal government would regulate and possibly eradicate the commercial health insurance business. Together, the HIAA's organizational, political, and economic strategies helped commercial insurance firms create an institutional framework for health care that, by the 1960s, appeared to the public and policymakers as familiar, even natural – an outcome of market forces rather than the result of public sector objectives intermingled with collective associational governance and cooperative industry action.

5

The Conflicted Construction of Blue Shield: Caught between Blue Cross and the AMA

Blue Shield plans – or nonprofit medical plans – were conceived and birthed out of both Blue Cross and American Medical Association (AMA) actions. Indeed, before becoming known as "Blue Shield" programs, they were initially called "medical society plans." Both Blue Cross and AMA leaders sought to cultivate the plans in a manner that would help them achieve their organization's goals. However, because Blue Cross and AMA objectives frequently conflicted, the developmental story of Blue Shield resembles that of a child pulled between two parents in a custody battle.[1]

Since the formation of the first Blue Cross program in 1929, AMA leaders had viewed nonprofit hospital plans with aversion. Although organized doctors begrudgingly approved nonprofit hospital insurance in 1937, AMA leaders expressly forbade Blue Cross from underwriting the services of physicians. Two years later, doctors founded the first medical society plan. These programs sold insurance for physician care, including surgical and regular medical or medical policies. Blue Cross leaders wished to bundle and jointly market their hospital coverage with medical society policies, which would subsequently be promoted under the brand name of "Blue Shield" to correspond with the "Blue Cross" label. Blue Cross desperately needed Blue Shield, both to compete with the products of commercial insurance companies and to bolster the image of nonprofit plans as community service agencies that offered uniformly priced, generous coverage for a comprehensive range of health services beyond hospital care.

National AMA leaders tolerated constituent medical societies establishing prepaid programs, because they needed to display the strength of voluntary insurance to thwart government reform proposals. After organized doctors finally consented to health insurance, the only organizations that could comply with the AMA's stringent third-party financing guidelines were commercial insurance companies and Blue Shield plans. Nonetheless, fearing outside influence over health care, AMA officials continued to harbor misgivings about the insurance company model that they themselves had created. Compounding these tensions, the community-oriented bearing of Blue Cross posed a significant challenge to physician professional aims. The idea of Blue Shield administrators internalizing the Blue Cross ideology and then trying to subordinate physicians to the mandates of social responsibility – whether in the service of hospitals, consumers, labor unions, or government officials – heightened apprehensions among AMA members. So although AMA medical societies organized and supervised nonprofit plans, many physician leaders and rank-and-file doctors attempted to hinder Blue Shield's progress every step of the way.

The conflicting ambitions of Blue Cross and AMA leaders played out in the evolution of the National Association of Blue Shield Plans (NABSP). Founded under AMA auspices, the NABSP coordinated the efforts of nonprofit medical plans across the country. In order to manufacture a nationally uniform product that could compete with commercial insurance, NABSP leaders sought to enhance their governing power and impose order on a jumbled group of disparate plans. Working at cross-purposes, AMA leaders tried to undercut the NABSP to preserve medical society domination of local plans and to prevent Blue Shield from forging a sturdier partnership with Blue Cross. However, by hampering the ability of nonprofit medical plans to expand and stabilize financially, doctors practically pushed Blue Shield leaders into the Blue Cross camp where they could secure help to pursue their market objectives.

Federal politics and programming ultimately delivered the boost that Blue Shield plans needed to scale AMA-constructed barriers to growth and network integration. To obstruct health care reform proposals, AMA leaders had to authorize Blue Shield programs to liberalize benefits and broaden policyholder counts, even where such developments imperiled physician professional autonomy. Moreover, participation in the Federal Employees Health Benefits Program (FEHBP) required that NABSP leaders consolidate authority over local plans so they could negotiate with D.C. officials and provide uniform benefits to government workers employed throughout the country. In these ways, the political setting allowed Blue Shield to mature from an ersatz third party, largely controlled by physicians, into a more cohesive and sovereign federation of health care financiers.[2]

THE COMPLICATED CHILDHOOD OF BLUE SHIELD

Early Blue Shield leaders faced an institutional morass. Several organizations helped establish Blue Shield programs, and each had a different notion about the purpose of medical plans. Medical societies created prepayment programs to beat back federal and state proposals for health care reform and to maintain some control over the rapidly growing insurance market. Blue Cross leaders assisted medical society plans so they could package physician service coverage with their hospitalization policies. National AMA leaders endorsed medical society plans to aid their battle against government reform – not because they wanted to make health services more accessible or because they wished to compete with prepaid groups and insurance companies. Forged out of necessity rather than election, Blue Shield leaders encountered opposition from all quarters. At the local level, they engaged in turf altercations with medical societies and Blue Cross plans. At the national level, AMA officials helped them establish a trade association and then withdrew support when plan leaders began consorting too closely with Blue Cross.

Just as hospitals heavily influenced Blue Cross operations, physicians deployed substantial authority over Blue Shield, earning it the moniker of "the doctors' plan." State and county medical societies launched most plans. The California Medical Association inaugurated the movement by founding a statewide program at the end of the 1930s. By the early 1950s, physicians in almost every state had started a prepayment plan.[3] Medical societies usually supplied seed money or startup loans, and plan executive secretaries and other high-level administrators were frequently physicians and AMA members. Most critically, medical societies supervised plans through governing board appointments. In 1951, for example, physicians held approximately three-fifths of Blue Shield governing board positions nationwide. The remaining seats were reserved for the "public" but were primarily filled with medical and hospital employees who worked closely with doctors.[4] Thus, at least initially, plan governing boards behaved predominantly as watchdogs for the profession, monitoring administrative, policy benefit, and fee schedule changes to ensure that they complied with physician mores.

Blue Cross provided a crucial platform for the sale of medical society policies. During the 1940s, Blue Cross plans came under intense pressure as consumers, particularly the corporate managers and union officials who managed employee benefits, pressed hospital nonprofits to also offer surgical and medical policies, both of which covered physician services. Commercial insurance companies could provide these policies by sending indemnity payments directly to policyholders; however, the AMA had banned Blue Cross from funding physician services in any form. Some Blue Cross administrators grew so concerned about their competitive vulnerability that they negotiated with insurance companies to package commercial coverage for physician care with their nonprofit hospitalization policies.[5] Other Blue Cross plans defied the AMA and provoked the wrath of physicians by sponsoring medical coverage. Medical society plans resolved this quandary. Blue Cross leaders could market an all-inclusive product by bundling their hospital coverage with the policies offered by area physicians.

Thus, local Blue Cross administrators helped establish and direct what soon became known as "Blue Shield" programs. Pragmatic motives – that is, lack of experience with prepayment plans – impelled medical society leaders and Blue Shield governing boards to accept Blue Cross guidance. The administrators and staff of nonprofit hospital plans supplied Blue Shield with expertise and an existing organizational base; they performed operations for medical programs that ranged from advertising and billing to enrollment activities. In each locality, power-sharing agreements spelled out how Blue Cross and Blue Shield officials would divide responsibilities. Some programs even shared staff members.[6] Because of this partnership, Blue Cross left a deep imprint on the institutional configuration of medical plans. Like their counterparts, most Blue Shield programs secured state enabling legislation for nonprofit status, priced policies using uniform community rates, and emphasized first-dollar rather than last-dollar or catastrophic coverage.

Moreover, just as Blue Cross had unique monetary arrangements with hospitals, Blue Shield plans made demands of physicians that rendered them distinct from insurance companies and, at times, roused doctor concerns. Like Blue Cross, Blue Shield sold service benefits. Although Blue Shield paid physicians on a fee-for-service basis, service benefits required doctors to accept a fixed payment for each service or procedure they delivered, so that subscribers could receive paid-in-full care and avoid out-of-pocket costs. However, because of physician resistance, medical nonprofits offered service benefits far less frequently than Blue Cross. In the mid-1940s, only twenty-one out of forty-four medical society plans extended service benefits. The remaining programs relied on indemnity benefits, which allowed physicians to set their own service prices and bill patients for supplementary payments in addition to Blue Shield reimbursements. Among the plans that did provide service benefits, the coverage was usually reserved for subscribers under stipulated incomes.[7] In some areas, income ceilings permitted middle-class policyholders to access service benefits; in other areas, physicians considered them a charitable allowance, to be set aside only for lower-middle-class or poor patients.[8] Throughout the postwar period, Blue Shield leaders continually urged medical societies to either introduce or expand service benefits.

In addition to service benefits, Blue Shield also compelled doctors to accommodate direct third-party funding. Even where plans only employed indemnity benefits, they usually, unlike insurance companies, sent payments to physicians rather than to subscribers.[9] Direct financing obligated physicians to underwrite Blue Shield. If a plan lacked resources to fully remunerate doctors, then administrators apportioned funds according to physician service amounts. Once the plan was running in the black, doctors received their outstanding compensation.[10] Collective bankrolling by physicians was vital to the survival of Blue Shield and explains how many fiscally floundering plans continued to operate. Significantly, direct plan–doctor financing constructed a foundation from which Blue Shield leaders would gradually, over the course of subsequent decades, implement cost control measures and begin to reduce physician autonomy.

Fearing just such an eventuality and displeased with Blue Shield payment conditions, some doctors attacked nonprofit plans. After the Pennsylvania Medical Society launched a prepaid program, a constituent county society narrowly defeated a resolution to withdraw from the state association.[11] Many New York doctors only supported their medical society's plan because it countered "unfair competition against the individual physician," which Blue Cross had instigated by selling policies that covered the services of surgeons, anesthesiologists, and pathologists.[12] Alameda County physicians dissented from the California Medical Association, charging that Blue Shield was akin to socialism because "an agency" determined service fees.[13] When Michigan Blue Cross helped the Detroit Medical Society create prepayment policies for the employees of automakers, a group of physicians formed an anti–Blue Shield organization. They hung plaques in their waiting rooms stating that they would not accept Blue Shield checks. To keep the plan alive, nonprofit staffers filled a car trunk with money and drove around to physician offices, settling subscriber bills in cash.[14]

Blue Shield leaders also encountered difficulties working with Blue Cross. Sharing operational duties produced a great deal of interplan dissension. One early nonprofit leader reported that the "history of Blue Cross and Blue Shield in these areas often has been one of undercover conflict, occasionally erupting into public view."[15] Each director struggled to obtain more authority for his program, personnel sometimes answered to two sets of bosses, and local physicians and hospitals frequently sniped at each other through the organizational conduits provided by nonprofit plans. Another administrator recalled that there were "two boards, two sets of managements, rivalries, animosities, some days, and I'm ashamed to say this to you, pure unadulterated hatred of each other."[16]

Adding to local ill will, national AMA leaders nursed anxieties about medical society plans, even though they had officially endorsed them in 1942. Yet, through the 1940s and into the 1950s, Blue Shield coverage spread like flames to dry grass. This growth, coupled with the need to prevent government-funded medicine, compelled physician leaders to reluctantly accept Blue Shield. Indeed, because Blue Shield had to be sturdy enough to answer the criticism of policymakers intent on reforming health care, AMA officials agreed to aid the fledgling plans.

To establish a durable relationship with the AMA and to protect themselves from Blue Cross meddling, medical plan leaders began exploring the creation of a national trade association. Medical society plans also needed an integrative mechanism – a national organization capable of standardizing numerous policies and generating a cohesive product for large employee groups that spanned the geographical boundaries of individual programs. To accomplish similar purposes, hospital plans had joined with the American Hospital Association to form the Blue Cross Association in 1937. Dr. Arthur Offerman, a founder of Blue Shield of Nebraska, recalled that he and his colleagues "saw what the Blue Cross plans had done in developing their national coordinating agency" and "went to the AMA for assistance."[17] In 1944, the AMA's House of Delegates directed the Council on Medical Service to create a "nationwide organization of locally administered prepayment medical plans."[18] Two years later, AMA and Blue Shield leaders unveiled Associated Medical Care Plans (AMCP). The AMA furnished the association with $25,000 in startup costs and office space in its Chicago headquarters.

AMCP duties included promulgating membership standards, orchestrating combined plan activities, advising local administrators, managing national promotions, and collecting statistics. The Blue Shield

Commission acted as the association's Board of Directors and elected the president. To populate the commission, plans were divided into eleven geographical districts. Each district nominated two commissioners, one of whom had to be a physician. The AMA appointed an additional three commissioners and, collectively, the plans elected six commissioners, four of whom had to be medical doctors.[19] Plan representatives voted on association matters during annual meetings, and votes were weighted to reflect each program's share of subscribers. Plan membership dues were also calculated according to policyholder volume. Within the first several years of its operation, sixty-eight plans joined the AMCP.[20]

From the beginning, relations between the AMA and AMCP were strained. Leading the attacks against AMCP was Morris Fishbein, the powerful *Journal of the American Medical Association (JAMA)* editor who heavily influenced the policies of organized physicians until his ouster in 1949. Fishbein and his conservative allies grudgingly conceded that calls for federal reform required physicians to accept medical insurance. They questioned, however, why the AMA should become involved with medical underwriting rather than leaving the field to commercial insurance companies.[21]

The nonprofit designation of plans also agitated AMA officials. In 1946, the Council on Medical Service drew up standards that prepaid plans had to follow to receive the AMA's "Seal of Acceptance." These parameters required that plans obtain medical society approval and offer patients "free choice of doctor," which, in reality, meant that programs had to secure the participation of at least 51 percent of area physicians.[22] AMCP bylaws incorporated these guidelines and included an additional measure obligating all member plans to operate as nonprofits. AMA leaders became incensed when they realized that the stipulation precluded AMCP membership for medical society plans underwritten by insurance companies in Ohio, Indiana, Washington, and Wisconsin. Calling on AMCP officials to modify their policy, a Council on Medical Service report protested that the "profit motive is the wholesome driving force of private enterprise."[23] Although AMCP leaders wanted to maintain friendly relations with AMA officials, they also desired to govern a sovereign association. The doctors and nonphysician personnel who became Blue Shield leaders tended to be committed to medical prepayment as an independent concept. Particularly for the national leadership, Blue Shield was worth developing as a socially responsible economic project – not merely as a political concession that had to be tolerated. AMCP officials thus sought to defend a portion of their autonomy from the AMA by drawing a line in the sand and insisting that member plans acquire nonprofit standing. AMA leaders interpreted the commitment to nonprofit status as an indication that AMCP leaders wished to align themselves more closely with Blue Cross than with organized doctors.

Additional AMCP actions raised similar concerns. In 1947, AMCP adopted a national emblem – a serpent and staff on a blue shield that paired well with the blue cross logo of nonprofit hospital plans. The Council on Medical Service balked: "It is inconceivable to us that any group of state medical society plans should band together to exclude other state medical society programs by patenting a term, name, symbol, or product."[24] AMA leaders had created the AMCP to behave as a wholly dependent association, as a channel through which Council on Medical Service orders would filter down to plans. "AMCP was never intended as a policy making body," objected a Council report. "It was supposed to do a coordinating job with <u>all</u> plans approved by the AMA."[25]

AMA leaders reacted to the AMCP's show of independence by withdrawing support. Rather than assisting the AMCP, Council on Medical Service members continually grumbled about how quickly Blue Shield plans were growing. One nonprofit insurance leader complained that "[e]very concession and act of cooperation gained from the Council by AMCP has been through strenuous efforts and more or less knock down drag out fights."[26] Less than one year after the association's founding, the Council on Medical Service began refusing to admit AMCP directors into their meetings. And AMA-appointed representatives stopped attending Blue Shield Commission meetings. At the end of 1947, physician leaders asked AMCP officials to move out of AMA headquarters.[27] They added insult to injury by purchasing hospital insurance for Chicago employees from Blue Cross but obtaining medical coverage, not from the local Blue Shield plan, but from a commercial carrier. Furthermore, when physicians started heavily promoting voluntary insurance to defeat Truman's health care proposal, AMA pamphlets and press releases declined to mention "Blue Shield." They either highlighted physician efforts under the label of "AMCP" or referenced voluntary health insurance as a whole.[28]

AMCP officials exacerbated this strife when they entered into talks to explore the possibility of forming a national organization with the Blue Cross Association (BCA). In 1947, AMCP and BCA representatives began meeting to discuss dual mergers: a combined trade association and a national insurance company. The trade association would harmonize Blue Cross and Blue Shield interests. The insurance company, which would be collectively owned and operated by Blue Cross and Blue

Shield plans, would package hospital and medical policies together, negotiate large contracts on behalf of member programs, and conduct national enrollment and advertising campaigns.[29] Piggybacking on large Blue Cross accounts would facilitate even swifter Blue Shield expansion: while medical nonprofits had less than eight million subscribers in 1947, hospital nonprofits had almost 30 million members.[30] Moreover, a combined enrollment company would help nonprofits compete more vigorously against the insurance companies that had begun raiding corporate accounts long held by Blue Cross. Unlike nonprofits, which used community rating, commercial insurance firms used experience rating – calculating prices according to each group's likelihood of consuming care – to offer employee accounts less expensive coverage. Insurance companies also delivered nationally uniform policies that seamlessly merged hospital and physician coverage. Not only had pricier nonprofit benefits begun to deter businesses seeking employee insurance, but corporations with personnel spread across many regions were discouraged by complicated policies underwritten by a patchwork of local plans with varying benefits and different administrative procedures.[31]

Still, the national partnership was a tough sell to local plan administrators who valued self-rule. To placate physician concerns about Blue Cross domination of Blue Shield, Dr. Paul Hawley, a major general who had directed European medical operations during World War II, was selected to lead the combined association. AMCP and BCA officials also exploited the political atmosphere to persuade plan administrators, doctors, and hospital officials to accept the integrated insurance company. National leaders argued that blanketing the country with generous, uniform nonprofit policies would strengthen the case of voluntary insurance. When presenting the merger proposal to plan leaders, Hawley emphasized that its approval would "demonstrate that our program can meet the needs of the public so well that they will not heed the misleading siren song of those who would put Government into the health insurance business."[32]

The 1948 meeting of Blue Cross and Blue Shield plan representatives laid bare the difficulty of forging a national alliance. Plan leaders had no desire to place their domains under joint, national rule. According to a participant at the failed conference, the "Blue Cross group was saying, 'I'm not going to let any doctors tell us how to run a hospital.' The Blue Shield group was saying, 'I'm not going to let any guy who doesn't know anything about medicine tell me how to practice.'"[33]

The AMA sealed the coffin burying Blue Cross and Blue Shield merger efforts. The Council on Medical Service warned the House of Delegates that a combined venture would curtail physician authority over prepayment plans and strengthen Blue Cross interests:

The question has arisen as to whether the proponents of this proposal are interested in a national enrollment agency to obtain national accounts or if they desire, in this proposed insurance company, a medium whereby they can deal directly, and not through the individual state society and the A.M.A., with "big" labor and with the government funds such as those available in government programs for poor relief.[34]

Delegates voted against the proposed union.[35]

Then, in 1949, the House of Delegates voted to sever official connections between the AMA and AMCP.[36] After the separation, the AMCP became the NABSP.[37] Although national AMA leaders cut formal ties with Blue Shield, they stressed that medical societies would continue to supervise local programs. An AMA report reminded nonprofit officials that all "matters of policy concerning medical service plans should rest in the hands of physicians."[38]

Flanked by Blue Cross and the AMA, early Blue Shield leaders found themselves dodging arrows from both directions. On one side, joint operational arrangements often created friction between local Blue Cross and Blue Shield plans, making the leaders of medical programs hesitant to partner nationally with hospital nonprofits. On the other side, AMA leaders hindered Blue Shield's growth and development. AMA officials believed that as long as the NABSP remained weak and local medical societies kept plans on a short leash, they could keep Blue Shield tethered to physician professional goals and restrain the threatening influence of Blue Cross.

DOCTORS AND THE PROBLEM OF BLUE CROSS

Suspicion of Blue Cross motivated much of AMA leaders' concern about medical society plans. AMA leaders worried that because Blue Cross was larger and more economically powerful than Blue Shield, hospital plan objectives would overshadow and eventually begin to govern medical plans.[39] Physicians mistrusted Blue Cross because plan administrators exhibited little concern for how third-party financing might diminish doctor professional sovereignty. Specifically, Blue Cross plans presented an institutional pathway for gaining authority over physicians to four groups – hospitals, nonprofit administrators, unions, and government officials.

The close connection between Blue Cross and hospitals troubled AMA leaders. As hierarchical bureaucracies managed by lay administrators, hospitals had long posed a potential hazard to doctor power and autonomy. During the first half of the twentieth century, organized physicians exerted significant influence over hospitals because the AMA certified physician internship programs and was actively involved with the Joint Commission on Accreditation of Hospitals. Hospitals relied on physician interns as a cheap source of labor and on practicing doctors to both provide charity care and admit paying patients. Consequently, hospital administrators and governing boards generally bowed to AMA directives and medical society requests.

After World War II, hospitals slowly acquired independence, in part, because of the growing need of doctors to practice in large, multifaceted medical facilities. Generous federal funding, directed through the 1946 Hill-Burton Act and government grants for medical research, spawned a proliferation of hospitals, including huge, urban medical school–hospital centers. Doctors exercised authority over medical school–hospitals through accreditation activities and powerful medical chiefs and physician-professors whose research brought in grant money. Where excess hospital capacity existed, usually in suburban areas, physicians retained their dominance because they admitted and served the middle-class and insured patients vital for increasing revenues. However, in localities with a limited supply of beds, new physicians, particularly general practitioners, found it increasingly difficult to obtain hospital admitting privileges. Moreover, community physicians complained that medical care had become too "hospital-oriented." Doctors required medical facilities to provide surgical care, and many specialized health services entailed a broad array of new technologies, equipment, and laboratory tests available only in hospitals. As hospital capacities expanded to include diagnostic and outpatient services, the AMA and American Hospital Association engaged in numerous verbal skirmishes, with physician leaders reiterating long-time prohibitions against medical facilities "practicing medicine" or profiting from doctor labor.[40]

In the middle of this shifting power line, as physicians began losing their hold over medical facilities, AMA leaders worried that hospital administrators would exploit Blue Cross to gain control over Blue Shield and doctors. The sentiment among doctors, quipped an early Blue Cross leader, was that "'if it comes to a question of working for the hospitals or working for the government, I think I would take the government any-time.'"[41] When tensions flared up between organized physicians and hospitals, NABSP leaders claimed neutrality. However, when Blue Shield officials asserted that a plan "should not permit itself to be used by either one or the other party to such a controversy," they only reinforced the belief among AMA leaders that medical nonprofits could not be counted on to wholeheartedly support the doctor's position.[42]

Doctors fostered additional apprehensions about the influence of Blue Cross over Blue Shield. Physicians linked Blue Cross leaders' celebratory embrace of nonprofit principles with "socialistic" endeavors to undermine profit-driven health care.[43] Since the 1930s, Blue Cross leaders had flaunted their plans as models of "voluntarism" or the "third way" – they described hospital nonprofits as part of a grand "social movement" designed to meet community health care needs in a manner superior to either government-managed arrangements or market-based ventures.[44] Exhibiting their eschewal of commercialism, Blue Cross leaders instructed employees to avoid using insurance company terminology. Rather than "policyholders," Blue Cross had "members." Instead of "salesmen," they had "enrollment representatives."[45] Emblematic of this ideology, Oklahoma Blue Cross leader Ralph Bethel questioned the connection between health care and "the profit making system," reasoning that "[c]hurches could never operate on a profit system." "The incentive to make a profit," argued Bethel, "over-rules the giving of full quality of care."[46] Harold Maybee, a founder of the Delaware Blue Cross plan, recalled the ethos that existed among early plan leaders who believed they were on a mission to make health care broadly accessible: "[w]e were positively messianic in our ardor."[47] Remarking on how plan administrators, when describing the Blue Cross movement, often used terminology reserved for the realm of the sacrosanct, one leader joked that "the only mistake our forefathers made" was "not converting it to a religion."[48] Although medical societies organized their insurance plans with nonprofit designation, the decision generally reflected practical concerns about avoiding taxes and reserve requirements rather than a philosophical perspective. Thus, when national Blue Shield leaders, through NABSP rules, required plans to obtain nonprofit status, AMA officials interpreted the decision as an institutional shift toward Blue Cross values.

AMA leaders worried that administrators who viewed prepaid plans as instruments of public service would have few qualms about running over physician prerogatives to fulfill community goals. As we have seen in previous chapters, AMA leaders initially hoped to limit insurance but modified their attitudes, at least publicly, to position the voluntary sector as more attractive to consumers than any type of government health care program pitched by reformers. So even as they championed the growth and liberalization of insurance to block federal reform, AMA leaders questioned Blue Cross motives. Blue Cross leaders enthusiastically pursued increasingly generous insurance coverage and service benefits as a civic obligation, not simply because, as was the case with doctors and commercial insurers, the political environment compelled them to do so. The conflicting pressures under which AMA officials operated manifested as they simultaneously promoted the expansion of voluntary insurance while also warning members that comprehensive insurance, which required no out-of-pocket patient expenses, jeopardized professional independence and incomes:

Any plan which promises "complete medical service" for fixed payments must sooner or later maintain financial solvency by reducing the quality or the quantity of the medical service and by skimping payments to physicians.[49]

Hence, when nonprofit administrators declared that the labor of health care providers "rightly belong[s] in ... service to the public on a nonprofit basis," they exacerbated AMA trepidations about Blue Cross and, by extension, Blue Shield.[50]

AMA leaders also resented the alliance between Blue Cross and unions. Top labor officials – including United Automobile Workers (UAW) and Congress of Industrial Organizations (CIO) leaders Harry Becker and Walter Reuther – favored nonprofit organization in health care. Union representatives held Blue Cross governing board positions and, when negotiating worker benefits, frequently demanded nonprofit coverage in lieu of commercial policies.[51] In areas with high union affiliation rates, labor leaders exercised their clout at the company bargaining table to attempt to shape Blue Shield policies, demanding, for example, that medical plans liberalize coverage or lose their account to a commercial firm. At times, unions openly battled doctors over such issues. In one instance, a CIO affiliate in Akron, Ohio, launched a public campaign, complete with newspaper advertisements, urging physicians to allow the local Blue Shield plan to furnish service benefits. Protesting that doctors were "gouging the public," the union published statistics showing that under indemnity benefits, area medical fees had risen 300 percent between 1939 and 1952. Physicians refused to bargain with CIO officials, but the decision pit them against approximately half a million U.S. Rubber, Firestone Tire, Goodrich, and Goodyear workers and their families.[52]

Although labor leaders began scolding Blue Cross for lavishly funding hospitals, they primarily blamed physicians for escalating health care costs. During the 1950s, the bond between Blue Cross and unions frayed because of rapidly rising premium prices and, concomitantly, nonprofit plans' inability to continue offering community rating. Still, labor officials maintained close connections to Blue Cross and often used their influence to argue that health care costs should be constrained by reducing physician autonomy; doctors, they asserted, not only set service fees but also determined when medical and hospital care were necessary.[53] When a UAW representative objected that Blue Cross leaders were "losing control of their program because they are not masters in their own home," he tellingly declined to admonish hospitals or hospital administrators but instead charged that it was "the doctor who has control."[54] Such statements alternately angered and disquieted physician leaders.

Finally, AMA officials nurtured animosity toward Blue Cross because many of the nonprofit's national and local plan leaders supported federal financing for health care.[55] The hospitals with which Blue Cross partnered had a long history of accepting charitable and government contributions, primarily at the local municipal level. In 1943, the American Hospital Association staked out a political stand to the left of physicians by endorsing federal grants to states for hospital construction and for indigent medical care.[56] They soon realized those aims. During the late 1940s, as the objective of swathing the population in generous coverage produced financial difficulties for nonprofit plans, a significant faction of Blue Cross leaders began advocating federal grants-in-aid for state insurance programs to benefit the poor. They subsequently pursued a similar solution to cover the elderly. By lobbying for these proposals throughout the Eisenhower administration and by supporting other moderate reform initiatives such as federal reinsurance, Blue Cross officials exasperated AMA leaders.

The ever-present danger of government involvement in health care restrained AMA officials from publicly rebuking Blue Cross, either for their relations with hospitals and unions or for their ideological positions. Indeed, the nonprofit had spearheaded the very voluntary insurance movement that now represented organized medicine's primary defense against federal reform. So AMA leaders proclaimed the dynamism and vitality of voluntary coverage while concealing their deep animosity toward Blue Cross. This resentment animated AMA refusals to strengthen or support Blue Shield in ways that might afford Blue Cross an opportunity to obtain additional power over health care.

SELLING BLUE SHIELD TO DOCTORS

Physicians held Blue Shield's fate in their hands; plans required the permission of medical societies to adjust policy benefits and provider reimbursement rates or to significantly modify administrative procedures. Securing physician approval, particularly to expand service benefits, was often difficult. To persuade doctors to allow more generous policy coverage, Blue Shield administrators depicted their plans as instruments of physician professional goals and reliable guardians of provider sovereignty. Additionally, Blue Shield leaders continually reminded AMA officials and rank-and-file members that their case against federal reform rested on the strength of voluntary insurance, which required that nonprofit plans liberalize coverage and attract additional policyholders. By tying their actions to the fight against government intervention in health care, Blue Shield leaders overcame a good deal of physician grousing and dramatically enlarged coverage.

Physician–Blue Shield relations varied from area to area. As we have seen in previous chapters, doctors divided over whether supporting nonprofit or commercial insurance was preferable. Blue Shield participation rates reflected regional predilections. In 1951, for example, only the barest majority of doctors in North Dakota and Virginia agreed to accept Blue Shield coverage; meanwhile, almost 100 percent of physicians joined nonprofit plans in Florida and Colorado.[57]

In most locales, regardless of provider participation rates, doctors either carped about or outright fought Blue Shield requests to broaden service benefits or expand policy coverage to include additional types of medical care. Referring to service benefits, an AMA ally argued that the "physician must be assured that fixed fees shall not extend above the low-income group." He continued: "If they do, his incentive will be destroyed."[58] Physicians in the South and Southwest mounted the most resistance to service benefits. In these areas, doctors viewed the coverage as a charitable obligation – that is, if they permitted service benefits at all. Hostility toward service benefits was not, however, confined to the South. During the early 1950s, Blue Shield of Minnesota almost triggered a physician boycott when administrators raised subscriber income ceilings from $3,600 to $5,000, thereby offering service benefits to middle-class families. Although the state medical society ratified the change, about four hundred physicians threatened to resign from the plan.[59]

Nevertheless, to compete more effectively against insurance companies, Blue Shield leaders persistently sought policy liberalizations. Furnishing service benefits for a wide range of care would allow Blue Shield leaders to differentiate their policies from commercial products and match the Blue Cross reputation for generous coverage. Indeed, because Blue Cross and Blue Shield polices were frequently sold together, medical coverage limitations were quite glaring to prospective consumers. Blue Shield leaders sought, at minimum, to make service benefits available to middle-class consumers. "In too many places, Blue Shield is either an indemnity plan or has woefully inadequate service benefits," complained a nonprofit administrator. He continued: "Because of this, there's a good deal of public dissatisfaction with the plans. And such dissatisfaction is grist for the commercial companies' mill."[60] NABSP leaders highlighted the fact that in the Northeast, where plans had the most liberal benefits, medical non-profits had a larger market share than commercial companies. This finding was noteworthy considering that at the same time – during the latter half of the 1950s – for-profit insurers dominated the market nationally, account-ing for approximately 62 percent of surgical and medical policies.[61]

To convince medical societies to allow policy liberalizations, Blue Shield leaders strove to improve their standing among physicians. They argued that doctors should seek the competitive advantage of nonprofits to safeguard their prerogatives from commercial insurers who had little understanding of health care. In contrast to for-profit firms, claimed Blue Shield spokesmen, nonprofit plans offered a medium through which physicians could structure the medical system to fit professional conceptions:

Blue Shield hopes to strengthen the doctor's traditional way of practicing medi-cine, not to change it or destroy it. ... Blue Shield deserves the doctor's whole-hearted support because it is fashioned in the doctor's own image; it is his own creation; and it is designed to strengthen the freedoms that he and his patients want to keep strong and safe.[62]

Accordingly, nonprofit leaders portrayed commercial insurers as corpor-ate rogues who cared only for revenue. "The doctor," stated one Blue Shield director, "would naturally prefer to deal with ... an enterprise designed for the benefit of the patient and the physician, rather than with one organized to make a profit for someone else."[63]

Blue Shield administrators also played upon physician political fears to elicit support.[64] They contended that only robust nonprofit plans could defeat federal reform. When James Bryan, a New Jersey plan adminis-trator, penned an article opposing Eisenhower's reinsurance measure, he used the opportunity to tie physician political fortunes to liberal nonprofit benefits and Blue Shield growth:

[I]t is clearly up to the profession to provide a truly satisfactory medical security program. It would be fatal to fall too far short of this goal. For if we succeed only in giving everyone a partial and inadequate coverage, or if we fail to make our program available to every important segment of the population, we will aggravate the demand for a comprehensive Government system.[65]

Nonprofit leaders maintained that because insurance companies lacked social responsibility and direct professional backing, simply multiplying commercial policies could never effectively quell the demand for more generous and equitable coverage, which was driving calls for federal involvement in health care. However, they asserted, government legislative initiatives would crumble if confronted by a strong "non-profit community enterprise, sponsored by the medical profession in cooperation with labor, industry and the general public."[66]

Indeed, political pressure obliged doctors to accept liberalized nonprofit coverage – just as they had to permit, however unhappily, ever more generous commercial insurance. Whereas in 1947, less than half of medical plans supplied service benefits, by 1958, almost 80 percent of Blue Shield programs did so. In 1947, less than 10 percent of Blue Shield plans furnished service benefits to all subscribers regardless of income. By 1958, over one-quarter of plans provided this coverage universally. Furthermore, among plans that offered service benefits according to income, administrators progressively raised salary limits to incorporate a higher proportion of subscribers. By 1965, it was not unusual for plans to sell service benefits to middle-class, including upper-middle-class, consumers.[67] Although many doctors resented these coverage expansions, they accepted them to advance their political argument about the attractiveness of voluntary insurance.

Additionally, Blue Shield policies were typically broadened from only covering surgical bills and in-hospital physician services to also covering office visits, diagnostic procedures, and additional outpatient care. To generate comprehensive insurance coverage, during the latter half of the 1950s, nonprofits began bundling their traditional first-dollar or "basic" policies with major medical policies. Nonprofit leaders, particularly Blue Cross administrators, were reluctant to offer major medical because they had long championed first-dollar benefits and disparaged the last-dollar or catastrophic coverage of commercial insurers. Moreover, because major medical policies covered a percentage of total catastrophic costs, they represented a "philosophical departure from the idea that a sick person should receive the services he needed rather than a dollar 'allowance' to purchase services."[68] Nonetheless, both political and competitive pressure drove Blue Cross and Blue Shield to adopt major medical benefits. Blues leaders needed a response to political criticism that nonprofit benefits ran out too quickly, leaving acutely ill individuals with large medical bills. Moreover, union leaders and corporate managers began viewing catastrophic coverage as an important supplement to basic plans; commercial insurers were using it as a "door-opener" to group accounts that nonprofits had managed for years. Nonprofit plans in Texas, Massachusetts, Wisconsin, Hawaii, and Washington, D.C., were among the first to sell major medical policies.[69] These programs let consumers use service benefits for first-dollar costs, pay a bridge deductible of $200 or $300 once those benefits ran out, and then resume coverage with indemnity reimbursements through major medical. By 1961, twenty-five Blue Shield plans provided some type of catastrophic coverage.[70] By the mid-1960s, the average Blue Shield policy underwrote 77 percent of the customer's total physician bills. The most generous plans covered 90 percent of subscriber medical costs, while the most conservative programs paid about 60 percent.[71]

Furthermore, like commercial insurers, Blue Cross and Blue Shield plans made exceptional efforts to expand individual coverage. Nonprofit plans customarily held community-wide open enrollment periods. They also launched special operations to register hard-to-reach rural residents and migrant workers.[72] As federal debates over insurance for the aged intensified, NABSP leaders, with AMA encouragement, urged all plans to establish and rapidly grow programs for the elderly. To help Blue Shield create low-priced policies for the elderly poor, AMA leaders instructed physicians to accept reduced nonprofit service fees. Blues plans also liberalized conversion privileges for retiring members of employee groups.[73] In 1958, only four Blue Shield plans permitted individuals over 65 to enroll; by the following year, plans representing approximately 90 percent of subscribers had either begun developing or marketing coverage for senior citizens.[74]

Blue Shield overcame physician objections to broader coverage and policy expansions by presenting them as antidotes to federal interference in health care. Indeed, political pressure fostered the standardization of health insurance. As commercial companies began insuring routine, first-dollar costs and Blues plans began offering coverage for catastrophic costs, their policies increasingly resembled one another. However, because of the unwieldy and inefficient insurance company model, enlarging coverage presented both groups with a bevy of financial and administrative difficulties. Blue Shield administrators bore the additional burden of continually attempting to mollify AMA officials and rank-and-file practitioners, reassuring them that they would never exploit their direct funding relationship or use of service benefits to undercut doctors' professional values. This, of course, was a promise that they ultimately could not keep.

BLUE SHIELD ATTEMPTS TO CONSOLIDATE

During the 1950s, the Blue Cross Association increasingly centralized power over local plans while the NABSP's development lagged far behind. BCA leaders confronted resistance from hospitals and local plan administrators as they integrated and systematized their network. However, NABSP officials encountered more ferocious opposition to similar efforts because doctors believed, quite rightly, that thwarting Blue Shield consolidation was crucial to keeping plans under medical society and, thus, physician governance. Although Blue Shield desperately needed a nationally uniform product to compete with commercial companies for large corporate accounts, national leaders struggled to convince medical societies and local administrators to cede autonomy to the NABSP.

After rejecting the BCA-NABSP attempt to establish a joint corporation during the late 1940s, the AMA approved a national enrollment firm dedicated solely to Blue Shield. In 1950, forty-three of the existing sixty-eight Blue Shield plans contributed startup capital to found Medical Indemnity of America (MIA).[75] MIA was a stock insurance company owned by Blue Shield plans.[76] Its primary function was to bundle various plan benefits together to generate master policies that could be marketed to large accounts, usually businesses, with geographically dispersed subscribers. Physicians and administrators agreed to MIA's formation because it made few demands on local autonomy. Plans chose whether to participate in each account and, if they elected to do so, set their own premium rates and determined whether they would support the entire master contract or only a portion of it. MIA was tasked with underwriting any sections of the contract that local plans refused.[77] Meanwhile, Blue Cross created Health Services Incorporated (HSI) to perform a similar role.

As they attempted to tackle the national competitive needs of nonprofits, MIA and HSI leaders tried to mimic the unified corporation that local plans and the AMA had only recently vetoed. The two firms rented adjoining office space in Chicago and shared staff members. When MIA and HSI packaged medical and hospital benefits together in a contract, each company underwrote half of the risk and administrative overhead. The two firms also established the Joint Operating Committee, which sponsored conferences to educate local plan leaders about the role of MIA and HSI in procuring and servicing large accounts.[78]

Despite MIA-HSI cooperation, local plans undermined their objective of creating nationally uniform policies. Because they had little of their own financial capital, the two companies required enthusiastic plan participation and sponsorship to succeed. Such support was not forthcoming. At the Joint Operating Committee's first meeting in 1954, national leaders previewed ensuing difficulties when they examined a survey of local Blue Cross and Blue Shield administrators. The survey revealed just how little backing the national organizations had – plan administrators refused to look beyond parochial concerns or narrow interests. "[A]n expression of opinions as divergent as these," lamented one national leader, "makes the rendering of firm recommendations impossible."[79] Blue Shield plans proved to be particularly uncooperative; they frequently declined to adopt benefits according to the MIA-HSI schedule. MIA officials sometimes convinced local administrators to participate in an account only to see medical society leaders veto plan involvement because they disliked the contract's administrative terms or use of service benefits. Physicians who jealously guarded their control over plan operations branded the MIA "a grab for power" by national leaders.[80] A frustrated NABSP representative commented that it "was as if General Mills tried to do a national business while each of its local plants made cake-mixes by its own formula."[81]

To help the NABSP rise above this imbroglio and centralize authority, the Blue Shield Commission elected John Castellucci president in 1955. Identified as a leader who could "[b]ring people together," Castellucci's conciliatory style befitted a fledgling organization attempting to placate the formidable AMA. Born in Maine, Castellucci moved with his parents to Detroit while he was in high school. After dropping out of medical school, Castellucci attended Detroit College of Law, as he explained in an interview, "to please my family." He recounted: "we all had to be professional people." Determined not to practice law, he obtained his degree and then sampled various jobs to find a suitable career. In 1943, upon learning about Michigan's nonprofit medical program, the thirty-five-year-old talked the plan's president into hiring him as a claims processor. From that position, he rose quickly through the ranks, soon becoming a professional relations consultant for the NABSP. A bit thick in appearance with once-dark receding hair, bushy eyebrows, and sagging jowls, Castellucci's soft, kind eyes revealed his agreeable personality.[82]

As president, Castellucci worked hard to consolidate the association's power over local plans, but he did so cautiously, taking great care to "stay out of their [physicians'] straightaways." He advised member plans not to employ nurses who might be likely, given their medical training, to question the treatments for which physicians sought reimbursement. To exhibit deference to physician expertise, Castellucci went as far as purposefully mispronouncing medical terms when in the company of doctors. The association president also cultivated the image of Blue Shield as the doctors' helpmeet, ready and willing to develop the health care economy in a manner that would support professional interests. He urged plans to intensively develop provider relations programs that would regularly dispatch representatives to physician offices and medical society meetings to discuss the advantages of Blue Shield and answer questions.[83]

Castellucci's careful approach could be seen in the NABSP's incremental efforts to bring local plans under national direction. In 1956, NABSP officials began lobbying local leaders to adopt a narrow sliver of standard benefits; from that contractual foundation, they hoped to gradually develop more detailed, nationally uniform policies. The "Minimum Benefits for National Accounts" agreement allowed local plans to continue setting their own physician compensation rates and prices but compelled them to underwrite certain policy features, including age limits, qualifying diseases, and waiting periods.[84] At a meeting convened to discuss the matter, Blue Shield executives unanimously agreed to recommend that their plan governing boards approve the program. Physician concern about the agreement prompted a nonprofit leader to pen an article in *Medical Economics* reassuring doctors that "[i]f you've heard rumors that Blue Shield will be 'going national,' discount them." He explained that the "doctors who run your local plan will still have the say about income ceilings and schedules of payment."[85] Such arguments failed to soothe the uneasiness of physicians and, by extension, plan governing boards. By 1958, NABSP leaders had persuaded only thirty-nine out of sixty-six plan boards to endorse the Minimum Benefits program.[86] Moreover, by refusing to set realistic underwriting rates, plans participating in the agreement continued to impede national accounts acquisition.[87]

Physicians and local administrators even attempted to hinder an NABSP advertising campaign. At their 1956 annual conference, plan representatives agreed to increase membership dues to support a national publicity program. New Jersey Blue Shield's Board of Governors subsequently voted against the dues increase, citing financial problems. Dr. Royal A. Schaaf, the plan's president, claimed that the advertising operation put the cart before the horse: "Blue Shield does not have anything to offer on a national level that applies uniformly to Blue Shield

Plans except the name."[88] In a rare show of authority, Castellucci responded that the association could not decrease dues for one plan.[89]

In the face of stiff-necked resistance to plan coordination, nonprofit leaders developed ad hoc methods to supply contracts for large accounts. Under the "syndicate" system, local plans that won an account extending beyond their service area contracted with other plans to offer uniform benefits at an average rate. If a plan in one of the included geographic areas refused to participate, then MIA stepped in to support that portion of the contract. Although similar to the MIA-HSI system, the syndicate model placated local leaders and physicians by preventing authority from aggregating at the national level.[90] Nevertheless, Blue Shield continued to encounter difficulties marketing syndicate contracts because, according to an NABSP spokesman, they involved a "hodgepodge of adjustments, sub-underwritings, special clauses, and what-have-yours."[91]

While Blue Shield leaders fought to impose order on a network of incongruent programs, federal legislation smoothed the way for Blue Cross consolidation. After a Department of Defense survey found that military members and their families were having difficulty accessing care at federal health facilities, Congress passed legislation to remedy the problem. The 1956 law created the Civilian Health and Medical Program of the Uniformed Services (CHAMPUS). CHAMPUS permitted service members and their dependents to obtain government-funded health care from private hospitals and physicians.[92] The BCA managed the CHAMPUS account for nonprofit hospital plans, thus forcing local administrators to accept national association guidelines in order to service the lucrative contract.[93] Because the Department of Defense financed all underwriting risks and administrative expenses, BCA leaders were able to avoid the complicated, conflict-filled ratemaking and benefit structure negotiations that had frustrated previous attempts to standardize national contracts. CHAMPUS accelerated the evolution of Blue Cross into a network of integrated, nationally regulated plans. The program "really demonstrated it was possible for this kind of a thing to work," explained a Blue Cross official.[94]

National Blue Shield leaders hoped to administer the nonprofit medical portion of the CHAMPUS account through the NABSP or MIA, but AMA officials insisted that Department of Defense officials contract individually with local plans and medical societies. Although participating Blue Shield plans had to adopt standard policy benefits to participate in CHAMPUS, they avoided empowering the NABSP.[95] Still, doctors were not satisfied. Fearing that a more united BCA would gain additional leverage over the strategies and general outlook of Blue Shield, physician leaders protested that CHAMPUS had strengthened the Blue Cross network.[96] Castellucci, who had once vowed to make the NABSP more than "a catering service" for annual plan meetings, was deeply disappointed that doctors rejected his association's bid to administer the federal account. He realized, moreover, that the centralization of Blue Cross had only heightened physician wariness of Blue Shield.[97]

Each time NABSP leaders attempted to make a step toward consolidating their network, physicians dug in their heels and pulled Blue Shield plans back. AMA leaders even complained about increased cooperation among Blue Cross plans. Although many local nonprofit administrators shared the AMA's fear of bolstering the NABSP, the refusal of physicians to allow even the smallest amount of national contract uniformity and their apparent willingness to cripple Blue Shield financially began to create frustration among plan leaders.

BLUE SHIELD'S COMPETITIVE AND FINANCIAL POSITION

Although Blue Shield witnessed phenomenal growth – about 10 percent annually during the 1950s – the plans never dominated the market for surgical and regular medical policies like Blue Cross had for hospital policies during the 1930s and 1940s.[98] This limitation was partly due to the later establishment of medical plans, during a period when insurance companies were also entering or had already entered the health care field. However, Blue Shield competitive woes were largely driven by the network's inability to provide uniform products across numerous plan areas and medical nonprofits' failure to offer coverage benefits substantial enough to favorably counter the cheaper and increasingly generous policies of commercial insurers. Disregard for sound underwriting techniques further sapped Blue Shield's vitality, and many plans faced chronic financial problems.

Blue Shield plans initially experienced rapid development by building atop Blue Cross success. Nonprofit representatives often convinced employee account managers to add surgical or medical policies or both to their hospital benefits for a supplementary fee. However, where group account managers considered Blue Shield benefits independently, they frequently found that nonprofit medical plans offered a mediocre, high-priced product. As insurance companies liberalized their policies, the Blue Shield brand, particularly where plans clung to indemnity benefits, had less to distinguish itself from commercial products. Moreover, corporate managers and union officials complained about the administrative difficulties that accompanied Blue Shield policies spanning the territory of more than one plan.[99] Union leaders frequently overlooked such inconveniences to push for more generous Blue Cross coverage and advance their ideological predilections for nonprofit enterprise. However, in the eyes of many union officials, Blue Shield's more restricted benefits proved that the plans functioned as little more than devices for physician financial gain. Because they marketed expensive benefits with operational complexities that vexed business managers and a philosophical taint that irked labor leaders, Blue Shield plans lost competitive ground in the group market. During the 1950s, particularly toward the end of the decade, many important group accounts, ranging from Sears Roebuck to the railroad unions, began abandoning Blue Shield for less expensive, nationally standardized commercial policies.[100] David Dolnick, a chief negotiator with the AFL, explained that his members were "just as well off with commercial companies and ... indemnity contracts, because I think we can get it cheaper and I think we can get more uniform service."[101]

Blue Shield garnered praise – from labor officials, progressive policymakers, and customers alike – for using community rating. However, community rating only further destabilized plans' financial standing. Selling uniformly priced policies to all consumers within a given region and age category required a massive subscriber base so that healthy policyholders could offset the costs of insuring sicker members. Blue Cross enjoyed such conditions during the 1930s and 1940s when commercial firms hesitated to enter or fully commit to the market. Once commercial companies began promoting medical insurance, they used experience rating to offer relatively healthy customers lower-priced policies.[102] The competition left many nonprofits with a dangerously high proportion of sick, expensive-to-insure subscribers.[103] Already straining to overcome the fiscal difficulties inherent to the insurance company model, most nonprofit programs discarded community rating by the end of the 1950s. The move left nonprofit administrators, particularly Blue Cross leaders, lamenting that they had betrayed cherished social goals and feeling as if they "were going against motherhood."[104]

Neglect of basic tenets of insurance also contributed to Blue Shield's anemic pecuniary condition. Nonprofit leaders chided for-profit companies for hesitating to underwrite health insurance and then entering the field with an abundance of caution. Yet the commercial industry's behavior reflected a rational fear of the costs associated with the insurance company model and a more sophisticated understanding of actuarial principles. Describing how early nonprofit plans determined the financial reserves necessary to support policy offerings, one administrator proudly explained that "there were no statistics or actuarial bases, it was merely an idea."[105] At the time, commercial insurers also lacked dependable actuarial data; however, nonprofit leaders evinced a more reckless, seat-of-the-pants attitude. Even at the end of the 1950s, once commercial insurers had begun constructing reliable morbidity tables, nonprofit administrators continued to lean too heavily on "whims and fancies" rather than statistical formulations.[106]

The history of Blue Cross and Blue Shield is littered with stories of plans that either went bankrupt or, more commonly, barely survived. For example, during the 1940s, even as the plan was growing "like wildfire," Michigan Blue Shield almost went under. Although autoworkers and their families eagerly purchased Blue Shield coverage, nonprofit leaders had neglected to establish adequate financial reserves or to implement utilization restraints. By the end of 1942, the plan was almost half a million dollars in the red. During the same decade, plans in New York, New Mexico, Kansas, and Illinois barely escaped bankruptcy.[107] Between 1948 and 1958, as commercial insurers gained market share, growing to account for more than three-fifths of all medical coverage, the collective balance sheet of Blue Shield plans deteriorated. Net revenues fell from 8.6 percent of total income to 1.3 percent. Moreover, as Blue Shield liberalized benefits, subscriber claims rose from 77 percent to almost 87 percent of premium income, leaving less room for administrative overhead. Many Blue Shield plans spent years on the margins of financial viability.[108]

Yet Blue Shield stayed afloat and continued to expand. Blue Cross hospitalization policies continued to aid the sale of nonprofit medical benefits. Additionally, physician underwriting allowed cash-strapped plans to temporarily reduce doctor payments until they could raise sufficient revenues. Tax-exempt status and low administration costs provided additional financial buoys.[109] Furthermore, Blue Shield plans that employed indemnity payments enjoyed a monetary advantage over Blue Cross. To underwrite full service benefits, Blue Cross had to completely reimburse hospitals for costs that increased significantly every year. Indemnity payments, in contrast, obliged consumers to share the burden of rising physician fees.

A host of characteristics combined to deplete the financial potency of Blue Shield: lack of national account uniformity, intense commercial competition, haphazard actuarial techniques, and – paramount among all of these features – the inherent costliness of the insurance company model. However, many Blue Shield leaders saw one main problem at the center of profitability issues – doctor resistance. If the AMA had permitted Blue Shield to consolidate, medical nonprofits might have acquired sturdier footing in the marketplace. Physicians could have energetically promoted Blue Shield policies or cooperated to allow service benefits liberalization at more reasonable costs. Instead, by persistently impeding Blue Shield attempts to compete for business, physicians drove medical nonprofits out of their orbit of influence.

GROWING AWAY FROM THE AMA

Since its founding, the NABSP had not only acquiesced to most physician economic concerns, but also, as we have seen in previous chapters, dutifully backed AMA political positions. By the end of the 1950s, Blue Shield exhibited mounting independence in both arenas. Individual plans were growing too large and complex for medical societies to capably govern their operations. And in regard to politics, nonprofit leaders chanted the party line with less enthusiasm. Blue Shield leaders did not dare rebel openly against organized physicians. However, the AMA's unduly rigid control had created the very reality that physicians had so desperately wished to avoid – increasingly autonomous, expanding plans that more closely identified with Blue Cross than with medical societies.

Medical societies lacked the expertise and resources necessary to manage swiftly evolving plans. In 1955, a nonprofit administrator explained how the burgeoning workload associated with Blue Shield supervision had generated friction between plans and physicians:

They [medical society leaders] long for the old days when they could pass on the salaries of the help and review most of the interesting cases in the course of a monthly board meeting. Instead, they are now asked to digest ponderous actuarial analyses. They're required to place their trust in specialists and consultants in fields far beyond their ken. Some of these erstwhile leaders suggest that Blue Shield "stabilize" enrollment, that it eschew the drive for expansion.[110]

Several years later, AMA President Louis Bauer bemoaned Blue Shield's increasing sovereignty: "[s]ome of our plans are no longer doctors' plans except in name." He continued: "Not all of this is Blue Shield's fault, but often it is the fault of the medical society in letting control of the plan slip out of its hands."[111]

Additionally, political pressure allowed nonprofits to begin removing some of the shackles of provider domination. Critics of voluntary insurance blamed swiftly increasing nonprofit coverage prices on the influence of service providers. Physicians were accused of exploiting Blue Shield to reward themselves generous fees and the liberty to supply unnecessary services. The critique compelled both Blue Cross and Blue Shield to decrease the number of governing board seats reserved for provider representatives. Between 1960 and 1965, public representation on Blue Shield governing boards rose from about 26 percent to 31 percent. Although this variation may appear minor and although public representatives were initially swayed or outvoted quite easily by physicians, adjustments in the composition of governing boards nevertheless marked a significant change. Thereafter, both the number of board seats reserved for doctors and the influence of area physicians over nonprofit operations declined steadily.[112]

Additionally, physicians with sympathy or even active support for the nonprofit movement increasingly occupied governing board seats. President Bauer reminded members that medical societies, not plan administrators, were to appoint physicians to Blue Shield governing boards; he urged these representatives to fiercely defend professional autonomy from third-party encroachment.[113] Accommodating these directives was not always easy. Governing board seats were not highly sought-after positions. Medical societies suffering from member apathy and chronic meeting under-attendance often filled board positions with any doctor willing to accept the role.

Blue Shield also produced a cadre of physician-administrators whose objectives failed to match those of the AMA. This process occurred as administrators began defining their professional identity more through Blue Shield success than through their standing among doctors. Frank L. Feierabend provides one such example. Before assuming the presidency of the Kansas City, Missouri, plan, Feierabend was an orthopedic physician and active member of his local medical society. During the 1940s, he traveled the country advising medical societies on how to establish nonprofit plans, not simply as an AMA functionary hoping to ameliorate physician political troubles, but primarily because he believed that the programs were "morally good."[114] In an article that appeared in the *JAMA*, Feierabend argued that doctors should wholeheartedly support Blue Shield because every "physician has the obligation to make his special talent available to all the people."[115] As an NABSP founder, Feierabend endured overt AMA antagonism. The experience only deepened his resolve to use Blue Shield as an instrument to bring physicians in line with broader societal trends. "There are still some ... [who] feel that I'm not going to have some fellow come along and tell me what I can charge for taking out an appendix," Feierabend observed. "But you have to be realistic," he maintained, "[i]f the majority of the people like it, that is what we are going to get."[116] Another example of a doctor who linked his career to Blue Shield fortunes was James Bryan. Bryan served as the executive secretary of the Medical Society of New Jersey. After becoming chief administrator of New Jersey Blue Shield, Bryan unapologetically promoted nonprofit plans. He regularly wrote articles and gave speeches encouraging physicians to permit benefits liberalization and support Blue Shield growth.[117]

Adding to the economic and organizational issues dividing the AMA and Blue Shield, political relations began to breed conflict. Outwardly, physicians and Blue Shield appeared to be fast political comrades. Behind this public image, AMA officials observed that medical nonprofits were falling under the sway of "liberal" Blue Cross leaders. During the federal reform debates of the 1940s and early 1950s, Blue Shield repudiated Blue Cross policy stances to instead fortify the position of organized physicians. Because they worked closely with physicians and were often doctors themselves, Blue Shield leaders tended to hold more conservative beliefs than their Blue Cross counterparts. However, some Blue Shield leaders – particularly nonphysician managers, administrators who worked closely with Blue Cross, and those holding national positions – were attracted to moderate reform proposals that promised steady income streams and also to alleviate the financial burdens associated with covering the elderly, poor, and chronically ill. As these leaders gained more influence, they slowly unraveled Blue Shield's political alliance with the AMA. When AMA officials requested Blue Shield support for one of their most significant political operations – defeating the Social Security disability program – they were sorely disappointed. Blue Shield commissioners refused to defend the AMA's platform during their annual meeting with Blue Cross:

> There was unanimous recognition that the proposal [to oppose Social Security Disability Insurance] would be to the detriment of Blue Cross and Blue Shield, but also since in a way the proposal did not relate directly to us, we should not bring it out for discussion in a joint session and with the possible resulting publicity and thus place the Plans in the position of being accused of political action or meddling in legislation which did not directly affect us.[118]

Blue Shield leaders agreed to lobby legislators privately, but the arrangement failed to placate AMA officials. As the decade came to a close and organized physicians geared up for a full-scale offensive against Medicare, they realized that Blue Shield leaders lacked passion for the cause.[119]

After years of seeking succor from physicians but instead receiving scorn, Blue Shield leaders became, at best, halfhearted collaborators in AMA economic and political operations. As plans functioned with progressively more self-determination and less concern for physician professional demands, Blue Shield also began to lean away from AMA political preferences. For many NABSP leaders, shoring up their alliance with Blue Cross began to hold more appeal.

CENTRALIZING BLUE SHIELD THROUGH FEDERAL PROGRAMS

The 1959 FEHBP, which provided medical insurance for government workers, gave national Blue Shield leaders the developmental breakthrough that they had long sought. Federal officials insisted on conducting account relations with only one set of Blue Shield representatives, thus compelling local plan administrators, after years of noncooperation and defiance, to submit to a uniform national contract. Managing the federal account inaugurated a new era for Blue Shield: the NABSP grew powerful enough to forge a more homogenous, integrated network and begin cultivating closer relations with Blue Cross.

To obtain a portion of the massive FEHBP account, NABSP leaders had to convince legislators that their plans could sponsor a standardized contract covering federal employees located across the country. In congressional hearings, Blue Shield representatives optimistically testified that plans were "able through such mechanisms as our national accounts agreement to offer uniformity of benefits very widely."[120] This sanguine declaration hid a cacophonous behind-the-scenes dispute, in which plan leaders threatened not to participate if the program neglected their demands. The director of NABSP marketing, Ed Werner, recalled the disagreements:

[W]e were hearing, "Well we can't accept that, our board won't accept that.". . . I said "Gentlemen, it's bigger than any of us. We don't dare tell the government that we can't respond, and [I] doubt that you want to take the risk to tell the government that you won't let us."[121]

NABSP leaders shrewdly exploited the political fears of plan administrators and physicians. They emphasized that failure to support the FEHBP would validate the criticism of progressive policymakers about grave weaknesses in the voluntary insurance sector.

After years of congressional hearings and political debates, representatives of the Blue Cross Association and the NABSP sat down with federal officials to write FEHBP legislation. The process did not lend itself to democratic trade association procedures. Although lacking formal authority to do so, NABSP leaders negotiated policy terms, rate struc- tures, and administrative methods on behalf of the entire network. "[P]lans would have to work together like they had never worked together before, they would have to agree to a commonality that they had never agreed to before," recollected Werner. He continued: "it was scary ... we were going to have to shove it down their throats."[122] Castellucci recalled that after negotiating the deal, BCA and NABSP leaders "sat back and waited for the noise, but none came."[123]

Physicians and local administrators capitulated to the arrangement because the FEHBP bolstered plan efforts to fulfill essential political and financial goals. AMA leaders backed the federal program because it replicated and thus legitimized the private sector model of employer- provided health insurance. The AMA had to assent to NABSP centraliza- tion because the legislation – heavily influenced, of course, by national Blue Shield leaders – required that one representative manage the account for all plans. Meanwhile, local plans endorsed the FEHBP contract, because they could not afford to lose such a large, profitable account. Indeed, federal contributions toward health care coverage encouraged employees to choose service benefits over commercial indemnity policies, thus granting Blue Cross and Blue Shield the lion's share of program subscribers.[124]

The FEHBP marked a crucial turning point for Blue Shield, enabling national leaders to begin building a sense of collective destiny among member plans. To smooth the transfer of authority from the local to the national level, NABSP leaders held regional meetings where they ironed out program details and produced a master contract.[125] MIA assumed responsibility for underwriting any portions of the contract refused by local plans. However, national leaders induced cooperation by obliging plans to donate funds to MIA, regardless of whether they chose to service the FEHBP account.[126] The experience emboldened NABSP leaders to begin mandating that plans participate in additional standardized con- tracts. The process of plan integration, nevertheless, evolved gradually and was still replete with conflict. Moreover, the NABSP's organizational maturation continued to lag behind that of the BCA.[127] In 1960, the Blue Cross Association instituted a rule that required hospital plans to support national accounts at uniform rates.[128] Lawyers who studied the proposal for the Blue Cross plan in Texas pointed out that "while the local organization may be theoretically autonomous, as a practical matter it will not be."[129] Although Blue Shield remained a much looser confederation of plans than Blue Cross, BCA centralization paved the way for the NABSP's future developmental progress.

As the Blue Shield network slowly consolidated, both local administrators and national officials increasingly looked to Blue Cross for leadership. Because Blue Cross officials desired Blue Shield's advancement to support their own market objectives, they frequently offered their sibling plans moral sustenance where medical societies failed to do so. Furthermore, Blue Cross leaders provided Blue Shield employees with practical guidance in administrative matters, such as claim payment procedures or enrollment activities – that is, if they weren't already managing those processes on behalf of the medical plan. In some localities, as hospital plans and medical plans increasingly freed themselves from service provider influence, nonprofit leaders contemplated unification. During the first half of the 1970s, Blue Cross and Blue Shield programs in Kansas City, Oklahoma, South Carolina, New Mexico, and New York combined their operations. In 1977, national nonprofit leaders revisited the idea, originally formulated in the 1940s, of merging their associations. This time it was successful: the BCA and NABSP united to create the Blue Cross and Blue Shield Association.[130]

In this way, federal policy, though functioning in an indirect manner, profoundly shaped nonprofit development and helped make AMA leaders' worst fears a reality. Two decades of AMA attempts to constrain Blue Shield had failed to keep the organization from maturing into a fully autonomous third party. As we will see in the following chapter, this organizational progression ended up reversing the financier-provider relationship: to control costs, Blue Shield plans gradually constructed a supervisory platform from which they could oversee and scrutinize physician work.

CONCLUSION

As organized physicians prepared to battle Medicare, Blue Shield appeared, as it always had, firmly under the AMA's command. However, through incremental advances and sub-rosa rumblings, Blue Shield had changed. Because the AMA obstructed Blue Shield's development and delivered stern tongue lashings whenever plans stepped out of line, medical nonprofits were growing up to rebel against the parent who had raised them. AMA officials learned, once again, that no amount of wishful thinking could freeze an institution in time. Just as they could not preserve the nineteenth-century model of medical practice, physician leaders discovered that a fluctuating, ever-varying market – especially one that was heavily influenced by the political sphere – required that Blue Shield evolve. Ultimately, the AMA's need to advocate voluntary insurance prevented physicians from continuing to suppress the growth of nonprofit insurance and the NABSP's control over constituent plans. Nonetheless, just like physicians had predicted, as Blue Shield plans gained collective strength, they realized the determination to assert their independence from doctors and seek a more robust alliance with Blue Cross.

During the postwar period the AMA, Health Insurance Association of America (HIAA), and NABSP adopted divergent political, organizational, and economic strategies to accomplish the same overriding goal. Association leaders attempted to enhance their members' social standing and cultural power by expanding – or, in the case of physicians, endorsing and publicly supporting – the insurance company model. Over the course of two short decades, the insurance company model grew to structure federal policy debates, configure financing relationships, organize the delivery of care, and dictate how private interests would subsequently acquire political and economic influence. To fully understand this transformation, we must examine the health care system more deeply, plumbing beneath federal politics and national trade associations to inspect organizations at the grassroots.

6

Corporate Health Care: From Cost Controls to Medical Decision Making

This chapter exposes how decisions made at the national level – among federal policymakers and professional and trade association leaders – filtered down to transform ground-level organizations. Tracing the effects of the insurance company model into the heart of America's health care system illuminates its inefficient and costly nature. By examining individual insurance companies, nonprofit plans, medical societies, hospitals, and physician offices, we can see how they both generated and responded to skyrocketing costs. As these groups erected an institutional network to support the insurance company model, they cemented in place a patchwork of faulty incentives and misplaced resources that could continually be modified at the edges or shifted slightly but never fundamentally rooted out and reformed.

The insurance company model drove costs by separating the delivery of care from the financing of care. Service providers became detached from concerns about the economical use of the health care system's assets. Because a third party paid the medical bills, insured patients could request unnecessary services while doctors and hospitals had pecuniary incentive to supply as much high-priced care as possible.[1] The dictates of organized medicine compelled insurers to reward doctors and hospitals for providing services and procedures, even when they did so in an excessive or arbitrary manner. At a deeper level, as delivering more insured services and securing larger insurance payments became the simplest route for earning money, physicians and hospitals lost the motivation to increase revenues by improving productivity – by restructuring the delivery of care, enhancing labor division, or more effectively and efficiently applying technological innovations.

Health care costs have been the subject of much scholarly inquiry. Many economists attribute rising costs to technological advances. However, such analysis renders technology an independent, socially defining force that acts upon health care without reference to the actions and needs of service providers, patients, and insurers.[2] With proper payment incentives, hospitals and physicians would have found ways of using medical technology so that, as in other economic sectors, as demand rose, the price of services based on such innovations would have fallen and become more readily available.[3] Some scholars have observed that the 1965 Medicare and Medicaid programs prompted cost surges by dramatically escalating demand – much of it quite appropriate – for health services.[4] Furthermore, since World War II, physicians have increasingly practiced "defensive medicine," which has entailed providing excessive services and procedures to protect themselves from potential malpractice suits.[5] While these factors have certainly exacerbated cost problems, they are not the principal sources of system troubles. Indeed, how these features contribute to higher costs often relates to the manner in which they interact with the insurance company model. Medicare has created a massive cost strain, not only because the elderly consume so much health care but also because policymakers nested the program within insurance company payment structures and institutions. Moreover, while the United States hosts a particularly litigious citizenry, malpractice suits can also be linked to consumer dissatisfaction with health care arrangements that have at times been oriented more heavily toward insurance reimbursement processes than patient care.[6]

At the beginning of the postwar period, insurers simply passed along cost increases to purchasers, particularly to businesses that bought employee group coverage. However, by the end of the 1950s, business leaders, labor officials, and state insurance regulators were demanding that insurers and service providers enact reforms to depress rising prices. Framing these developments was the constant possibility of federal intervention in health care. Indeed, negative publicity about inflated service prices and unnecessary utilization compelled physicians to begin accepting insurance company cost containment procedures – though they did so grudgingly and with many objections.

Ultimately, insurers and physicians began to narrow the wide organizational chasm that separated them – in an attempt to control costs, the two groups built overlapping institutions to negotiate their financing relationship. This development placed health care within a pseudo-corporate structure.[7] The medical system acquired corporate qualities as insurers extended their authority over the delivery of care: they became experts in the practice of medicine, introduced cost containment measures, and assumed a supervisory position over physician and hospital service provision. The full implications of this arrangement would take decades to develop; nevertheless, the process whereby insurers gained power over service providers was initiated during the 1950s. Nor did this institutional progression occur in an orderly or straightforward manner. The course of implementing cost controls unfolded along a circuitous, obstacle-laden route replete with continual confrontations between the financiers and the providers of health care. Yet by the 1970s, physicians and hospitals had organized their practices to support insurance company policies and requirements, including cost containment procedures. In this way, insurance companies expanded their role from simply underwriting the risks associated with health services consumption to also managing the actual delivery of medical care.[8]

EXPLAINING COST PROBLEMS

As the insurance company model evolved along the median between free enterprise and government control, it evaded the correctional forces intrinsic to each system. Markets discipline through price. In properly functioning markets, prices convey information about supply and demand to consumers and producers. If demand increases for a particular service, prices rise, thus signaling to consumers to buy prudently. Price increases also encourage providers to enter the market, which, by raising service supply, drives down prices. In government-directed systems, officials hold down prices by setting agency or regional budgets. Under the insurance company model, the liability of paying for care was transferred from patients to insurance organizations, thereby altering the perception of prices in the minds of consumers, sending an artificial signal that they had been lowered. Meanwhile, insurance companies lacked effective means of regulating physicians and hospitals. Consequently, neither markets nor the government controlled provider fee setting or service supply.

As the principle of moral hazard dictated, assigning a significant portion of the medical cost burden to insurance companies encouraged some policyholders to demand excessive health care because they were more likely to seek out medical care and, when they did so, demand more services and procedures than they otherwise would have in the absence of insurance. Policyholders with what one journalist facetiously labeled "premium payer's syndrome" requested unnecessary care to wring as much value as possible out of their insurance.[9] Furthermore, and entirely separate from the problem of unwarranted utilization, commercial indemnity benefits were particularly susceptible to fraud because insurers sent payments to compensate for accessed health care directly to policyholders. An insurer explained that physicians "found it difficult to handle the patients who came to their offices and stated, 'Well, look Doctor, why don't you put down that you saw me for two additional visits? You know, Dr. So-and-so, down the street will do it.'"[10]

Despite the inclination of some insured patients to overutilize health services – and, among many fewer, even perpetrate fraud – they were not responsible for rising costs. Doctors stood guard – or were supposed to stand guard – at the gateway of medical care. Only physicians had the requisite expertise to decide whether a procedure or hospital admission was necessary. However, fee-for-service compensation rewarded physicians for increasing the quantity of services they supplied. And doctors could easily rationalize additional office visits, supplementary procedures, or "the works" in diagnostic services as essential for proper care. Between 1945 and 1960, the number of services that physicians ordered to support each hospital admission surged sixfold.[11] New technologies and procedures accounted for a good portion of this growth; however, the insurance company model fueled the increase as well.[12]

Indeed, unwarranted surgery became a national dilemma during this period. Viewed positively, insurance improved professional practices and techniques – surgeries previously considered difficult or impossible to perform because of costs became routine as patients acquired insurance to fund them. Unfortunately, easy access to per-service compensation for high-priced procedures motivated unethical physicians to convince insured patients that they required surgery even when they did not. In the early 1950s, a pathologist discovered that 76 out of 200 hysterectomies performed in his midwestern hospital were unnecessary. In Seattle, an examination of 187 hysterectomies revealed that at least 46 of the women could have avoided the procedure without any deleterious health results.[13] In a 1953 *U.S. News & World Report* article, the president of the American College of Surgeons, Dr. Paul Hawley, charged that as performing operations simply to collect insurance fees became more attractive, some physicians were removing healthy organs in 60 to 70 percent of the appendectomies that they performed.[14]

Similarly, the insurance company model drove climbing hospital admission rates. While modern technologies and procedures attracted patients to hospitals, insurance also helped change perceptions about

"the appropriate setting for the treatment of illness."[15] Particularly
through the 1950s, many insurance policies declined to cover certain
services unless they were performed in the hospital. Moreover, shielded
from the full weight of medical costs, some patients more actively sought
hospital care. Insurance reports and media accounts brimmed with stories
of doctors admitting patients to the hospital for frivolous reasons – to give
stressed professionals a break from the office or families time off from
caring for a nonacutely ill grandparent.[16] *Reader's Digest* carried the
following anecdote in 1954:

A young Tennessee couple told their family physician last fall that they wanted to
take a second honeymoon but had no place to leave little Bobby and Nancy.
"We'll fix that," said the doctor, "Bring them to the hospital." The children
enjoyed toys, books, a convalescent playground, dietetically prepared meals and
24-hour-a-day professional supervision. The doctor, charging at regular patient's
rates, collected this highly skilled baby-sitting fee from the family's hospital-
insurance company.[17]

An investigation conducted by Michigan Blue Cross during the early 1950s
determined that one-fifth of subscriber hospital days were unnecessary and
28 percent of admissions involved some element of "faulty use."[18] Later in
the decade, a nationwide study found that on an annual basis, per one
hundred individuals, uninsured persons spent an average of seventy days in
the hospital while insured patients racked up one hundred days.[19]

Because doctors furnished the insured patients vital for profitability,
hospital administrators were reluctant to restrict admissions or institute
cost controls. In an influential 1959 study, Milton Roemer and Max
Shain found a correlation between an area's hospital bed supply and the
number of hospital days that insured patients accessed. According to
"Roemer's Law," hospitals in communities with excess beds freely distributed physician admitting privileges to draw additional patients.[20]
Furthermore, loose, unstandardized accounting methods permitted hospitals to inflate service prices. Hospitals typically charged Blue Cross the
"cost" of care, which, depending on the region, could include expenses
ranging from personnel training to charity services. By allowing administrators to recoup a good deal of their expense outlays from Blue Cross,
cost reimbursements encouraged hospitals to invest heavily in facility
construction and medical equipment, irrespective of usage frequency or
existing area supply.[21] Notwithstanding generous nonprofit cost payments, hospitals often compensated for money "lost" on Blue Cross
patients by billing commercial policyholders higher per-diem prices and
for many extraneous charges.[22]

Third-party funding in combination with doctors' traditional reliance on sliding fee scales produced a ready vehicle for physician bill padding. Because doctors had always taken the patient's ability to pay into account when calculating fees, many practitioners inflated service prices for insurance subscribers. Bill padding diminished the value of indemnity policies. For example, a 1950s Indiana investigation revealed that approximately half of the indemnity policyholders under study were charged higher fees than uninsured patients. In 1953, the Blue Shield plan in California discovered that about two hundred physicians accounted for more than $1 million in excessive fees. In particularly egregious cases, doctors charged patients their customary fee plus any indemnity payment they received.[23] While the insurance narrative is rife with stories of overt bill padding, third-party financiers expressed more apprehension about incremental price increases, which were difficult, if not impossible, to stop and which induced even the most honest physicians to raise their fees to match prevailing rates. "I am not greatly concerned about flagrant abuses (and we've seen some)," stated Jay Ketchum, President of Michigan Blue Shield. He continued, explaining that "small, gradual increases per unit of service will, when multiplied by millions of individual cases, accumulate a total which will inflate costs beyond the point of toleration by the people."[24]

Overutilization and bill padding spawned swiftly escalating health care costs. Between the late 1940s, when the insurance company model began to take root in the market, and the early 1960s, medical care costs climbed 61 percent, outpacing price increases in all other goods categories.[25] Well-known health care analysts Anne R. Somers and Herman M. Somers estimated that medical expenditures in real dollars increased more than 80 percent per person between 1948 and 1958:

The dramatic rise in the costs of medical care is well known. However measured – on the basis of national, per capita, or unit costs, in current or constant dollars, considering only medical services or all medical items, over the long run or the short run, as a proportion of gross national product or of personal disposable income – the rise has been far greater than for the cost of living as a whole.[26]

Reflecting this trend, insurers frequently raised policy prices, sometimes by double-digit percentages. In 1952 alone, John Hancock, Aetna, and Prudential each increased group hospital and surgical premiums between 15 and 17 percent.[27] In 1958, Blue Cross plans sought price increases of 26 percent in Kentucky, 33 percent in Delaware, and 34 percent in New York.[28] In 1962, Equitable hoisted major medical premiums an astounding 45 percent.[29]

Under these circumstances, denouncing insurance subscribers – or, in the minds of many, ailing patients – for rising costs could only make health interests appear heartless and aggravate negative publicity. Even the usually tone deaf American Medical Association (AMA) backed away from this strategy after a brief trial. Nonetheless, fearing that cost controls would erode physician independence and incomes, AMA leaders mounted a campaign to convince the public that health care prices were not a serious problem.

THE AMA AND COST CONTAINMENT

The issue of health care costs underscores one reason that organized physicians were dragged kicking and screaming toward accommodating insurance during the late 1930s. AMA leaders understood that once third parties controlled the capital flowing through the health care system then doctors would occupy a defensive position, both professionally and economically. Cost containment measures would inevitably entail diminished doctor sovereignty. To avert this scenario, as insurance began to spread during the postwar era, physician leaders denied the cost crisis and any doctor involvement in creating it. Once the political costs of this tack became too great, organized doctors gradually and with great aversion began ceding authority to insurers.

AMA leaders initially responded to medical service cost problems by expending considerable resources to refute their existence. In *Journal of the American Medical Association (JAMA)* articles, consumer pamphlets, and newspaper editorials, physicians contended that health care prices had not risen significantly. AMA President John Cline accused policymakers of using "obsolete material and inaccurate figures" to gin up a fictional "health emergency."[30] A favorite AMA-sponsored argument was that consumers spent more on recreation and tobacco than on health care.[31] When AMA publications did admit to rising costs, they transferred responsibility from physicians to other factors. "The major reason for the more rapid increase of medical care expenditures was an extra million and a quarter 'bundles of joy,'" maintained Frank Dickinson.[32] As director of the AMA's Bureau of Medical Economic Research, Dickinson managed approximately sixty staff members who produced reports that "exploded statistical myths" about costs.[33] Alternately, these studies linked high health care prices to modern technology, hospital costs, and excessive demand spurred by insurance.[34] "Health insurance was never meant to relieve the insured person from any individual responsibility for financing his health care costs," protested AMA President David Allman.[35]

Blame shifting failed to fix the public relations fiasco entangling physicians. Each time the press ran an exposé on health care costs or policyholders complained about rising premiums, the likelihood of government reform grew. In addition to the coverage that unwarranted surgery and hospitalization received, popular publications, such as *Reader's Digest* and *The Saturday Evening Post*, repeatedly spotlighted how physicians inflated medical bills and oversupplied services.[36] *Life* magazine featured a lengthy article that inquired, "Are the doctors and hospitals robbing us?"[37] Physicians received a more favorable portrayal in the 1930s and 1940s Dr. *Kildare* movies, which, during the 1960s were turned into a T.V. series that provided a launching pad for additional medical shows presenting doctors as everyday heroes, such as *Marcus Welby M.D.* Nevertheless, in the fluctuating landscape of public opinion, these positive representations could not completely undo the damage of critical media depictions. Painting a troubling picture for doctors was a 1950s AMA survey of three hundred Illinois families. Summarizing the attitudes of many participants, one respondent characterized physicians as "a bunch of grafters." Another asserted that "[u]ntil a doctor has a Cadillac, he's not satisfied."[38] In 1955, the AMA hired Ben Gaffin and Associates to conduct a national poll. The firm found that although most citizens trusted their physician to charge fair prices and provide appropriate care, eight out of ten respondents described him as "different" from other doctors.[39] Even as they complained that physicians had "been subjected to years of the most vicious, systematized campaign of vilification ever waged," AMA leaders realized that the status quo could not hold.[40]

Meanwhile, insurers presented AMA leaders with incontrovertible evidence of physician overutilization and fee padding. These interactions did not always unfold smoothly. In a 1957 closed-door meeting with AMA leaders, insurance executives respectfully, indeed timidly, requested help resolving cost problems. The AMA's general manager, Dr. Francis Blasingame, countered with an impassioned monologue condemning commercial insurers – organized physicians' closest economic and political allies – for failing to adequately educate policyholders about the function of insurance and for refusing to contest federal reforms in a sufficiently forceful and public manner. Attempting to return to the subject of cost containment, Health Insurance Association of America (HIAA) leader Edwin J. Faulkner waited for the applause of Blasingame's fellow physicians to subside before responding with a deferential "Thank you doctor."[41] Despite such tantrums, AMA leaders reluctantly conceded that insurance companies had "displayed reasonable evidence that there are several instances wherein charges for professional services have not been rendered on the basis of the insured's circumstance independent of insurance." AMA officials cautioned members that "[i]f these indisputable and self-evident facts are not embraced by the entire membership of the profession, then it will have dealt irreparable harm to the whole [voluntary insurance] movement."[42]

To mend the image of doctors in relation to costs, AMA leaders showcased several efforts to constrain health expenditures. They, for example, established the Commission on the Costs of Medical Care. In 1960, to examine research conducted by the commission and to discuss cost concerns with all relevant actors, the AMA sponsored the National Congress on Prepaid Health Insurance. Physician leaders invited representatives from insurance companies, nonprofit plans, businesses, and labor groups to participate in the Chicago conference.[43] Around the same time, *JAMA* and *AMA News* began publishing "Let's Use, Not Abuse" articles to educate doctors about how fee padding and excessive service provision damaged voluntary insurance.[44] Despite these endeavors, the primary cost containment role of national physician leaders amounted to setting a moral tone – that is, after numerous media and political hits, finally acknowledging that health care prices were a legitimate issue and that doctors had to take action.

More meaningful cost control activities had to be spearheaded at the grassroots. At the end of the 1940s, in a bid to improve public relations, national leaders had instructed medical societies to establish grievance committees. They tasked these committees with reviewing insurer and patient complaints about physicians who behaved unethically, whether by providing substandard care or overcharging for services.[45] The system proved weak. Insurers labeled grievance committees "unworkable"; although they could sometimes handle instances of the most blatant physician abuse, they rarely evaluated allegations and tended to provide cover for doctors when they did.[46] For example, the Medical Society of Virginia created a statewide grievance committee in 1949. Throughout the following decade, the committee sporadically examined cases appealed from county societies where similarly little attention was accorded the process and where few patients even knew that grievance committees existed.[47] Particularly in small societies with well-acquainted members, doctors were unwilling to question their colleagues or discipline fellow physicians.[48] "Too often, their tendency is to whitewash the doctor," observed a Blue Cross official.[49] During the early 1960s, as the AMA was enmeshed in Medicare debates and continually responding to charges that insurance for the elderly was far too expensive, national physician leaders added teeth – albeit baby teeth – to grievance committees. They ordered constituent societies to strengthen their review procedures and enhance disciplinary actions for physicians caught misusing insurance.[50]

The national leadership also turned to medical societies to bring a measure of regularity to physician fees. Medical society representatives negotiated with Blue Shield to establish the fixed payments that service benefits entailed and with commercial companies to develop indemnity fee schedules. However, individual physicians determined most of their charges, particularly where Blue Shield was an indemnity program. Doctors could "balance bill" patients with indemnity benefits for whatever costs the insurance policy failed to reimburse. As we have seen, the inconsistency of physician pricing, combined with insurance policies that rapidly lost value because of rising service costs, generated patient grumbling and negative press. This public frustration convinced some medical society leaders to consider methods for standardizing doctor fees.[51] In 1956, after studying the charges of thousands of doctors, the California Medical Association created the Relative Value Scale (RVS). The RVS systematized fees while avoiding fixed prices. The scale set point values for each service and procedure, according to the degree of difficulty and time it took to perform.[52] Physician fees continued to vary, depending on the dollar value each doctor assigned to an RVS point. Ostensibly, these values reflected the doctor's experience and training. The national AMA spent years developing an RVS, but in 1958 the House of Delegates voted against implementation. Rather than enacting a universal scale, delegates recommended that constituent societies assemble schedules that reflected regional practices.[53] By 1961, medical societies in thirteen states and Washington, D.C., had adopted an RVS.[54]

In an attempt to keep claims review and fee setting processes securely under physician purview and out of the hands of third parties, AMA leaders permitted a few diluted cost control measures. At the national level, they made some elaborate displays to exhibit concern about rising prices; however, their main contribution to the project of cost containment consisted in giving medical societies the green light to take action. Insurance companies and nonprofit plans seized upon this development to cultivate more robust practices.

COMMERCIAL INSURANCE COMPANIES AND COST CONTAINMENT

Commercial insurers, more so than their nonprofit cousins, were disinclined to implement cost control procedures. Nonprofits sold service benefits, which required plans to directly reimburse doctors and hospitals in order to cover the full cost of each service or procedure. Organized physicians forbade for-profit companies from selling service benefits, and commercial leaders gladly accepted this proscription. They preferred indemnity benefits – such coverage kept insurers far removed from the delivery of health care because they furnished policyholders, not service providers, with payments. However, runaway costs gradually altered insurer attitudes about involvement in medical care. At the same time that insurance company balance sheets weakened, key industry clients, including business and labor leaders, demanded that underwriters take steps to control costs. Moreover, by the end of the 1950s, escalating service prices began to hinder industry efforts to resist government reform by expanding and liberalizing policy benefits. These factors incrementally drew insurance companies into the health care system where, in an attempt to constrain costs, they began to monitor service delivery.

Rising insurance rates attracted unfavorable political attention and public scrutiny and also raised the hackles of group customers. Although employer contributions to worker coverage allowed insurers to increase prices without unduly vexing policyholders within the group, union and business leaders took notice. During account meetings, labor officials and corporate managers complained to insurers about rising premiums and health care costs. For example, union leaders often argued that indemnity fees produced "more money in circulation to pay higher doctor bills, with the patient no better off."[55] Labor and business representatives also aired their views at insurance industry conferences. During a 1958 insurance forum, Jerome Pollack of the United Automobile Workers (UAW) bluntly told commercial insurers "to admit" that "they do influence medical practice." He urged insurers to overcome their qualms about involvement in health care and begin instituting cost controls: "certain provisions should be adopted because they encourage good practice, and others rejected because they stimulate bad practice."[56] At another industry meeting, Malcolm L. Denise, a Human Resources Manager with Ford Motor Company, warned that businesses would not turn a blind eye to cost increases: "As customers interested in value received, employers have a responsibility to see that the consumers' needs and interests are accorded real weight."[57] The leaders of small and mid-size companies also joined the conversation. By banding together, they enlarged their influence and applied it to prod insurers for cost containment. At the end of the 1950s, a Tulsa businessman formed the Employers' Health Care Council to represent twenty-one firms comprising more than 200,000 workers and their dependents. As the 1960s opened, similar councils were established in Chicago, Cleveland, Houston, New York City, and Pittsburgh.[58] Businesses also attempted to effect cost controls through local chambers of commerce.[59]

Despite this pressure, insurers had no desire to become engaged with the delivery of medical care. Political considerations had already compelled them to liberalize coverage far beyond their initial intentions. Insurers hoped that, at minimum, they could keep their companies removed from the inner workings of physician offices and hospitals. Executives commonly expressed the belief that the "physician's fee is a matter for agreement between himself and his patient and is no more to be dictated than any other phase of the practice of medicine."[60] So axiomatic was this adage that insurers continued repeating it – even after they began supervising physician activities.

Insurers initially evaded involvement in medical care by aiming cost containment measures at policyholders. To educate consumers about "the problem of control," the HIAA and allied industry groups distributed thousands of pamphlets to women's clubs, chambers of commerce, and civic organizations. One tract explained that when patients requested "unnecessary or overlong hospital stays, unneeded medical service, or health luxuries," they pushed up insurance prices for everyone.[61] Instructing policyholders yielded few results, and insurers were left relying on two primary means of checking patient demand – deductibles and coinsurance. Insurers hoped that if consumers shouldered a significant portion of the medical bill, then they would scrutinize physician and hospital fees and refrain from requesting excessive care.[62] Climbing utilization rates demonstrated that this approach was ineffectual. Moreover, the political project of expanding coverage benefits prevented insurers from depending too heavily on deductibles and coinsurance. Insurers gradually recognized that to constrain costs, they would have to enter the realm of health care delivery.

Meanwhile, generous coverage impelled insurers deeper into the medical system, requiring them to process vast quantities of claims, begin directly financing service providers, and, along with these activities, observe the cost problems caused by physician – not policyholder – behavior. Major medical policies illustrate these trends. Rather than paying subscribers an indemnity fee per covered service, major medical covered a percentage of aggregate health care bills. When insurers first introduced major medical, the policies offered the barest of coverage, only paying a portion of hospital and perhaps surgeon charges. As insurers liberalized major medical to cover additional services, including care delivered outside the hospital, they began processing many more claims from a broader network of providers.[63] At the same time, doctors began seeking direct compensation from insurers to avoid the encumbrances of collecting fees from patients. Insurance companies and many physicians, against the advice of AMA leaders, established direct funding connections. However, the AMA prohibited commercial companies (unlike nonprofit plans) from using fixed fee schedules. Insurers therefore resolved to pay a portion of whatever charge the physician submitted, as long as it was "usual, customary, and reasonable" (UCR). Predictably, physician bills tendered under major medical spiraled out of control, outstripping the usual norms of rapidly mounting costs. One survey found that 70 percent of California doctors significantly increased fees to exploit UCR arrangements. The outspoken editor of the *Los Angeles County Medical Society Bulletin*, Dr. Gerald Shaw, declared that UCR payments had "led doctors in the direction of wholesale petty and grand larceny."[64]

The health insurance enterprise had quickly become far more than industry leaders had bargained for; the amount of operational capacity necessary to support medical coverage expanded dramatically between 1945 and 1955, surpassing the requirements of life insurance and pension products. Some insurance companies, such as Lincoln National and Metropolitan, horizontally integrated health insurance functions into existing divisions. New York Life, for example, assigned health insurance marketing, claims processing, billing, and underwriting activities to its life insurance units. However, because health insurance generated so many claims and entailed distinct underwriting logic, some companies established separate departments to manage medical coverage. Signaling the route along which the industry would move, Prudential created an Accident and Sickness branch so staff and executives could focus entirely on supporting health care products.[65]

Regional decentralization helped insurance companies begin to implement cost containment measures. Large companies opened offices throughout the country, which facilitated claims investigations and service provider contact. Prudential decentralized in 1948, initially to improve policyholder services but subsequently to support activities involving hospitals and physicians.[66] During the 1950s, Equitable set up ninety-four offices around the nation to handle sales and policyholder concerns. These offices also allowed employees to participate in industry programs, further discussed below, which were designed to strengthen provider oversight.[67] In local Aetna offices, staff members began examining health insurance claims for vague medical explanations, hospital admissions without diagnoses, and unusually long hospital stays. Because they were positioned close to service providers, Aetna representatives could readily consult doctors and hospitals when questions arose. Commenting on how these interactions alerted physicians to the presence of insurer surveillance, an Aetna executive explained that "[t]his system is in itself a form of cost control."[68]

To manage cost containment efforts, insurance companies transformed the role of medical directors. Medical directors, who were typically physicians, had traditionally helped companies assess the risks of underwriting applicants and policyholders for both life and health insurance. Executives naturally turned to these staff doctors to handle delicate cost control discussions with physicians. Indeed, arguing that only a doctor had the necessary expertise to judge claims and review UCR fees, medical society leaders often demanded that insurance companies hire physician consultants.[69] Accordingly, medical directors were often appointed to supervise departments that evaluated claims and conducted provider relations.[70]

Insurers also constructed avenues of provider communication at the industry level. In 1946, trade association leaders and executives of the largest companies formed the Health Insurance Council (HIC) to manage affairs with organized physicians and hospitals. After the HIAA was created, it assumed primary responsibility for the HIC. For many years, HIC leaders directed their energies toward designing standardized claim forms for industry-wide usage, in order to reduce physician paperwork and streamline hospital admissions.[71] During this period, the HIC's primary contribution toward cost regulation consisted of educational pamphlets targeted toward physicians, which gingerly requested that practitioners not arbitrarily raise prices or provide unwarranted care.[72] In 1957, HIC leaders bolstered containment efforts by unveiling a network of local organizations. Throughout the country, hundreds of insurance company employees, from firms both large and small, staffed and directed local HICs. Insurers attempted to mollify physicians by stressing that constituent councils only served to enhance provider relations by identifying "problems or points of irritation." In reality, they also pursued cost controls.[73] Local HIC staffers wrote articles for medical society journals and spoke at physician meetings, continually, though cautiously, reminding physicians that "[i]nsurance does not increase the ability of the patient to pay."[74]

By the 1960s, local HICs were working with medical societies to introduce more stringent claims review measures. Stating that "neither grievance nor [existing] review committees have been as effective as they might have been," national HIC Chairman Arthur Browning contended that "some way must be found to determine when these charges are excessive and, if possible, some enforcement procedure should be developed."[75] This process evolved differently in each region. In Texas, the statewide HIC decentralized further. City and county HICs sponsored workshops for insurance representatives, physician leaders, and hospital administrators to discuss common problems, including health care costs.[76] The state from which AMA leader Francis Blasingame hailed, hosted a particularly intractable group of physicians. They were so hostile to insurance company influence that they protested *Texas State Journal of Medicine* articles politely suggesting that physicians charge reasonable fees.[77] Moreover, although Texas Medical Association bylaws mandated that all constituent societies sponsor grievance committees, physicians rarely reviewed patient, much less insurance company, complaints.[78] However, under the weight of bad publicity and impending Medicare legislation, doctors began to buckle. In 1963, physician leaders reluctantly authorized local HICs to form committees to regularly examine insurance claims.[79] The Texas Medical Association instructed county societies to assist these activities by strengthening grievance committee procedures and arbitrating physician–insurer disputes.[80] Though a tentative beginning, insurance companies began assembling the institutions necessary to monitor physicians in one of the most unfriendly regions of the country.

When HIC representatives approached the New York County Medical Society about creating regular claims review practices, physician leaders stonewalled their request, directing them to use the existing, ineffective grievance committee. HIC officials responded by encouraging local companies to route all questionable claims through the grievance committee. As committee members struggled to manage the flood of submitted claims, the process was exposed as "totally unsatisfactory." In 1962, after consulting with HIC representatives, medical society leaders established the Review Committee on Medical Insurance. Two panels, each composed of five doctors, met in alternate months to examine claims for "reasonable" charges and appropriate services. To "educate" physicians about what types of behavior merited reprimand, the medical society began publishing case examples in *New York Medicine*.[81] By 1965, local

HICs had facilitated the founding of 35 medical society committees capable of reviewing UCR claims.[82] An HIC director observed with satisfaction that the "[medical] societies are gradually accepting the fact that the insurance companies are in this picture as a third party."[83]

HIC activities helped insurers acquire the expertise necessary to intensify claims evaluation independent of physician assistance. HIC officials encouraged medical societies to develop RVSs as a basis for claims assessments. Where they refused, companies forged ahead of physicians; for example, Continental Casualty and Home Life of New York created their own RVS schedules.[84] Along with uniform claim forms and review committee findings, the RVS allowed insurers to standardize medical nomenclature and diagnosis definitions.[85] Universal medical terminology permitted companies to code claim forms for computer analysis and begin generating reliable morbidity tables.[86] With these data, insurers developed additional benchmarks to detect overutilization. New York Life established a "loss control engineering operation" to study the relationship between specific diagnoses and delivered health services.[87] Similarly, in 1960, the HIAA initiated a nationwide survey to determine how disease categories related to provider charges and utilization.[88] Insurers input information gleaned from such investigations into computers, which identified claims that fell outside stipulated parameters. Computers also tracked individual physician fee profiles for UCR payments.[89] By the mid-1960s, few insurance companies simply paid tendered claims. Most firms checked for reasonable charges; consistency between diagnosis and treatment; as well as the appropriateness of hospital admissions, lengths of stay, and delivered procedures.

In addition to reviewing claims ex post facto, insurers introduced preemptive containment measures. Insurance companies launched authorization programs that required doctors to obtain permission before admitting patients to the hospital. Admission certificates indicated the number of days the patient's insurance coverage would be active based on diagnosis.[90] Some companies obliged physicians to "certify" at varying intervals – for example, every ten days – the need for patients to remain in the hospital.[91] In 1960, a Liberty Mutual executive called on his colleagues to mimic the practices of property insurers, who both produced and insisted upon the adoption of specific building codes in order to prevent fires:

We all know what research into the causes of fires and into ways of minimizing the causes of fires has accomplished in reducing the cost of fire losses. ... However, in group sickness and accident insurance ... there has been ... all too little [research] on the much greater possible savings through a better use of good medicine, both preventative and curative. Is this lay interference in the practice of medicine? Actually, it is not interference. It is cooperation.[92]

Only five years earlier, no commercial insurer would have thought – or dared, given the AMA's likely reaction – to publicly state that insurance companies should have an active role in shaping health care.

Group client demands and political necessity pushed commercial insurers, against their inclinations, to assume responsibility for monitoring health services. To manage this task, insurers built connections between their companies and doctors and hospitals – they created communication channels, provider relations activities, fee review processes, and medical care evaluations. Through these institutional linkages, insurers slowly shifted the scales of economic power to endow themselves with a measure of supervisory authority. Nevertheless, because commercial insurers were hesitant to become involved in health care, they remained several steps behind nonprofits in the arena of cost controls.

BLUE CROSS AND BLUE SHIELD AND COST CONTAINMENT

Two features of nonprofit plans allowed them to enact more rigorous cost containment procedures than for-profit firms. First, nonprofit plans were established as local operations while commercial companies were headquartered in the Northeast or other places distant from service providers. The geographical positioning of Blue Cross and Blue Shield plans cast a shadow over each area's medical community. Although local HICs and firm decentralization partially bridged the distance between commercial financiers and providers, for-profit insurers were never able to replicate the homegrown dominance of nonprofit plans.

Second, Blue Cross and Blue Shield – as the "hospitals' plans" and "doctors' plans" respectively – forged sturdy institutional bonds with service providers much earlier than did commercial companies. Hospitals and medical societies helped establish and supervise Blues plans. Moreover, service benefits, which fully covered each unit of health care for subscribers, required plans to send payments directly to hospitals and physicians. Even where Blue Shield used indemnity benefits instead of service benefits, plans usually reimbursed physicians directly. Nonprofit representatives also interacted with service providers much more frequently than did commercial insurers. Blue Shield employed doctors, reserved a majority of governing board seats for them, negotiated fee schedules with medical societies, dispatched representatives to physician meetings, and frequently issued provider communications. This intermingling gave nonprofit leaders substantial expertise. While commercial insurers enjoyed advanced actuarial and business acumen, nonprofit leaders had more knowledge about health care – a fuller understanding of both service delivery and the culture of medicine.

Despite – and sometimes because of – the close relationship between nonprofits and physicians, instituting cost restraints generated conflict. Doctors rebelled. But forces external to health insurance and service delivery finally compelled them to yield. As businesses and labor groups protested rising insurance prices and both state and federal policymakers cited cost issues as a reason to intervene in health care, physicians begrudgingly relinquished grants of authority to nonprofit plans.

In comparison with commercial insurance companies and particularly during the first decades of the movement, nonprofit financing and administrative operations were unsophisticated. In most areas, Blue Cross managed all or the majority of Blue Shield's administrative functions. During the 1940s, Blue Cross of Minnesota employed only a director, bookkeeper, and secretary. Marketing consisted of the director promoting the plan on the radio and then racing back to the office to answer phones and sign up customers. The bookkeeper's organizational system relied on shoeboxes: one held subscriber contracts and another contained plan revenues – that is, bundles of cash.[93] Nonprofits also lagged behind insurance company technology. Commercial firms began purchasing computers between the war's end and the mid-1950s. Meanwhile, as the 1950s began, Philadelphia Blue Cross, one of the nation's largest nonprofit plans, still managed all administrative tasks manually. To process a claim, employees examined a master record to ascertain the subscriber's benefits eligibility. The medical director then evaluated the claim and, using a fee schedule, calculated how much to reimburse the physician.[94]

To handle the rapid growth of insurance, nonprofit plans had to intensively develop their organizational capabilities. Toward the end of the decade, nonprofit plans caught up with commercial firms in the field of computing. In 1957, Blue Cross of Western Pennsylvania purchased IBM equipment to automate subscriber files, utilization records, and claims reports.[95] Computers encouraged nonprofit administrators, who had long trailed commercial insurers in underwriting proficiency, to direct more attention toward actuarial tables and risk formulations. Like commercial companies, nonprofit administrators used their "automatic machines" to assign code numbers to disease categories and develop utilization patterns for each diagnosis.[96] Now instead of manually checking each claim, staff members only inspected cases that computers flagged for having charges or services inconsistent with stated diagnoses.[97] Medical directors began focusing their attention toward higher-level activities than processing individual claims; they usually managed departments that handled both provider reimbursements and relations. Nurses, because of their medical knowledge, were often hired to staff the claims units in these departments. With increasing frequency, whenever a payment request seemed aberrant, claims representatives contacted hospitals and physicians to obtain additional information and medical records.[98] During the 1960s, Blue Cross plans installed Teletype communications, which allowed hospitals to directly notify plans, within minutes, of an admitted patient's diagnosis and payment information. With these data, claims representatives issued admission authorizations and preapproved the patient's number of covered hospital days.[99]

Although nonprofit plans trailed commercial firms in many facets of the insurance business, they led the way in provider relations. While commercial companies were sending indemnity payments to policyholders and attempting to sidestep involvement in health care well into the late 1950s, nonprofit plans directly financed and frequently communicated with service providers from their earliest days of operation, usually starting in the 1940s. Through monthly newsletters, leaflets mailed with reimbursement checks, and dedicated space in state medical society and hospital journals, plans issued provider guidelines while attempting to build goodwill. In Philadelphia, Blue Shield used monthly newsletters to instruct physicians on how to complete insurance forms, where to obtain the latest fee schedule, and whom to contact with claims questions. They also entreated physicians to resist providing unnecessary services.[100] To reinforce the argument that Blue Shield was "not just another insurance company," but an organization designed to meet physician needs, promotional literature often featured doctors serving as governing board members or medical society leaders negotiating with plan representatives.[101] The plan's newsletter highlighted physicians who worked for Blue Shield, such as surgeon James Z. Appel, who served without compensation as the plan's vice president.[102] Moreover, approximately ten to twenty years before commercial firms inaugurated similar though weaker programs, Blue Shield plans created Provider Relations Departments, supervised by physician medical directors.[103] In 1950, representatives of the Blue Shield office in Philadelphia began traveling the plan's territory, visiting physician offices "to establish friendly relations." These visits allowed provider representatives to train the doctor and his staff on how to manage paperwork procedures or to inquire about specific claims. Provider representatives also attended medical society and hospital staff meetings to answer questions and explain policy directives.[104]

The close interconnections between Blue Shield and physicians produced two widely varying situations, depending on the locality. In some areas, Blue Shield was captured by the medical society and subservient to physician demands – at least initially. Texas illustrates this pattern. In 1954, after years of ignoring cost issues, the Texas Medical Association and Texas Hospital Association responded to negative publicity by appointing a committee to study rising nonprofit premiums. Rather than investigating provider bill padding and overutilization, the committee hung the entire cost containment project upon the frail reed of hospital services coordination. Certainly, delays in scheduling labs or diagnostic tests and difficulties reserving surgery facilities increased patient hospital stays. However, they represented a secondary issue driving health care cost increases. Undergirding poor services coordination was the fundamental problem of how Blue Cross paid hospitals – not for enacting productivity improvements, but for simply spending additional resources to justify higher "cost" of care formulations. Yet to even secure the committee's formation, Walter R. McBee, Executive Director of the state's Blue Cross and Blue Shield plans, had to reassure the Texas Medical Association's president that "the committee will have very little interest in claims."[105] The state medical society president was none other than future AMA General Manager Dr. Blasingame. The only cost control tool granted to nonprofit plan leaders was communicating with physicians through newsletters and medical society journal articles. As we have seen, Texas physicians even bristled at recommendations that they exercise discretion when setting fees or supplying services. When Blue Cross and Blue Shield introduced major medical coverage in 1956, average physician fees jumped approximately 25 percent in less than one year.[106] Additionally, the plan's anemic cost containment methods fostered fraud. Nonprofit administrators discovered that groups of doctors in several hospitals were systematically padding bills and filing fictitious claims. The overcharges amounted to almost half a million dollars in losses at each hospital. Blue Cross and Blue Shield attempted to recover the money but declined to take any punitive measures against the hospitals or the physicians. McBee's comment reveals the magnitude of physician control: "I assume it is up to the doctors as to whether any action is to be taken."[107] Unsurprisingly, nonprofit premiums skyrocketed in Texas; in some years, they increased more than 20 percent. After a massive rate hike in 1957, the plan lost some of its largest employee accounts, including Shell Chemicals and Ethyl Corporation.[108] Similar to the circumstances surrounding the commercial industry's local HICs, it wasn't until the 1960s, when physicians were under extreme duress due to the prospect of Medicare's passage, that Texas physicians finally acquiesced to claims utilization and billing reviews.

In other areas of the country, strong institutional ties between non-profits and service providers allowed plans to implement aggressive cost containment measures. In the following pages, we will examine how these developments unfolded so that by the 1960s, many nonprofits – particularly plans located outside the South – applied far more stringent cost controls than did commercial insurance companies.

When they were founded in the 1940s, a number of Blue Shield plans created claims review committees. Nonprofit leaders organized these committees primarily to reassure doctors; they explained that any claims disputes would be evaluated, not by insurers or actuaries, but by fellow physicians. Some plans handled claims assessments in house, using physician-staffers or doctor consultants. Blue Shield of Iowa hosted an internal "Special Physicians' Committee." In Omaha, Blue Cross and Blue Shield installed a joint review committee composed of board members, most of whom were doctors. In other cases, medical societies established review committees. Blue Shield of Baltimore conferred with four panels; each consisted of eight doctors appointed by the medical society.[109]

Initially touted as devices for protecting physician interests, these committees evolved into instruments of cost containment. For example, during the 1940s, Blue Shield of New York introduced the Physicians' Review Committee. In 1951, to improve deteriorating provider relations, plan leaders weakened the committee's original cost control objectives by replacing physician-employees with privately practicing doctors. Rather than eradicating unscrupulous practices, the committee ruled in favor of either maintaining or even raising physician reimbursements in approximately 55 percent of the claims that nonprofit administrators contested. Soon, however, policyholders began approaching the committee with complaints about excessive doctor fees and unnecessary procedures. Negative publicity forced New York's medical society to assent to stricter third-party regulations. By 1960, the Physicians' Review Committee had reoriented its focus. Rather than emphasizing doctor concerns, members principally examined claims to identify and eliminate fee padding and overutilization; they now sided far more often with nonprofit adminis-trators. To aid this process, Blue Shield dispatched auditors to investigate hospital and physician medical records.[110] Similarly, the Pennsylvania Medical Society originally formed its Blue Shield Committee as a venue for doctor complaints. By the 1960s, the strengthened and renamed Pennsylvania Physicians' Review Board regularly appraised nonprofit claims for provider errors. For example, in 1964, the board denied fee disbursements for more than twelve hundred out of thirty thousand hospital admissions.[111]

With so many physicians and nurses filling their ranks, nonprofit staffers, compared to commercial insurers, possessed a broader baseline knowledge of health care, which helped them spot fee padding and over-utilization. Service providers had to scale additional obstacles to contest the decisions of third-party financiers represented by one of their own. For example, Dr. William Harer was president of the Pennsylvania Medical Society before becoming medical director of Philadelphia Blue Cross. Local newspapers labeled Harer "the Blue Cross watchdog" because he devised thorough claims assessment procedures and methods for rooting out unnecessary hospital admissions.[112] Physicians wishing to dispute these measures had to challenge a doctor whose peers had previously elected him to the state society's highest position.

Because hospital services represented the most expensive medical care, Blue Cross became the heaviest mallet driving cost containment processes into the system. Although nonprofit hospital plans were prohibited from funding doctors' care, the cost constraints that Blue Cross applied to hospitals translated into physician controls by means of limited admitting privileges, restricted access to facility services, and utilization reviews. As a financier of hospital services, Blue Cross exercised near monopsony power; in most areas of the country, the nonprofit represented approximately half of each facility's revenue.[113] Fragmentation among commercial insurers as purchasers of hospital care undermined their influence; however, Blue Cross activities worked to the advantage of all third-party financiers. Blue Cross wielded its economic clout to standardize hospital budgets, dampen facility construction, and either initiate or strengthen utilization review procedures.

To more carefully evaluate claims payments, Blue Cross administrators had to impose order on traditionally haphazard hospital accounting techniques. Nonprofit plans based reimbursements on nebulous, hospital-generated "cost" of care calculations, which were particularly susceptible to abuse. During the 1950s and 1960s, nonprofit leaders began requiring that hospitals use accepted accounting practices. Uniform accounting enabled Blue Cross officials to dissect hospital budgets and object to unnecessary outlays, such as expensive medical equipment that was already abundantly available within the hospital's locality.[114]

Blue Cross leaders also attempted to decrease hospital costs by employing insights from Roemer's Law. They understood that unchecked facility expansion fueled excessive hospital admissions and utilization. At the end of the 1950s, area-wide planning councils began to determine whether new hospitals should be constructed, based on the region's population and health service needs. Planning councils created by state or municipal authorities could deny government funding or licenses and permits to unsanctioned hospital construction. Local HIC and Blue Cross representatives joined these councils.[115] Where planning activities lacked governmental sanction, nonprofit leaders established their own organizations, pledging to refuse Blue Cross compensation to any hospitals that opened without authorization. In 1955, there were only two hospital planning agencies in the country. By 1965, there were almost sixty.[116]

Blue Cross also encouraged hospitals to institute utilization review (UR) committees. In 1949, after reading newspaper accounts about excessive surgery and unethical behavior in his facility, a New Jersey hospital administrator formed a "tissue committee." The committee's name derived from the practice of testing tissue after surgery to determine whether the removed organ contained a pathology. The idea spread.[117] In one hospital, for example, the implementation of review procedures decreased the percentage of healthy appendix removals from 28 percent to an acceptable rate of between 8 and 9 percent.[118] Tissue committees developed into UR committees as they broadened their mandates to assess the medical necessity of additional forms of surgery as well as hospital admissions, lengths of stay, and laboratory and diagnostic testing. Because of AMA insistence, UR committees were almost always composed of physicians. Nonetheless, Blue Cross drove their establishment and growth. During hospital contract negotiations, Blue Cross officials secured agreements for the formation of UR committees and, where they already existed, pushed for them to undertake additional evaluation tasks. By the mid-1960s, forty-six out of seventy-six Blue Cross plans had either helped inaugurate or were actively assisting hospital review processes.[119] Where permitted, commercial insurers submitted questionable claims and communicated matters of concern to UR committees. However, even where service providers barred commercial insurance representatives from interacting with UR committees, industry leaders welcomed their development. "The mere fact that every surgeon knows that his record will be reviewed in the coming month stimulates him to stop and take stock before he attempts to proceed with his operation," observed a commercial executive.[120]

Although helpful, the close institutional affiliation between nonprofit plans and service providers could not, on its own, significantly augment third-party authority over health care. Because of service provider and particularly physician opposition to regulation, the march toward cost control regimes spawned frequent conflicts and, to stay on course, required the prodding of businesses, labor unions, and government officials. Nonprofit plans in Michigan and Pennsylvania illustrate this process.

The Blue Cross and Blue Shield plans in Michigan garnered national publicity for rising premiums and unscrupulous service provider behavior. In 1954, the University of Michigan School of Public Health issued a report that severely damaged the image of physicians in the state. Several years earlier, the professor supervising the investigation had resigned, protesting the state medical society's "lack of co-operation." Replacing the original director was Walter J. McNerney, a young professor who would later become president of the Blue Cross Association. Despite physician opposition, McNerney persevered and completed the study. Among many unfavorable findings, McNerney's report uncovered improper hospital admissions in 31 percent of twelve thousand examined cases.[121] Two years later, Blue Cross triggered an uproar when, as some nonprofit plans were directed to do under their enabling legislation, administrators applied to the state insurance commission to raise premium prices – they requested a 23 percent hike. State regulators granted Blue Cross a 15 percent increase and formed a special commission to examine health care costs. Meanwhile, UAW leader Walter Reuther accused "fee-hungry doctors" of cheating nonprofit subscribers.[122] Citing skyrocketing premiums and service benefits only available to workers under certain incomes, UAW officials declared their intention to establish a prepaid physician group in Detroit. Reuther contended that by regulating physician compensation and utilization, the plan would bring down costs and virtually eliminate out-of-pocket expenses for subscribers. The UAW's actions demonstrate how cost problems frayed the longstanding alliance between labor and Blue Cross. Labor's prepaid group presented a grave challenge to Blue Cross and Blue Shield, which had almost 3.5 million Michigan subscribers, more than half of whom belonged to the UAW.[123]

Blue Shield responded to the negative publicity by announcing additional coverage for outpatient services: administrators hoped to weaken physicians' motivation to hospitalize patients simply to activate insurance. With the approval of the state medical society, Blue Shield also increased the service benefits income ceiling to $7,500, thus allowing families at the upper end of the middle class to purchase the coverage. While failing to resolve cost problems or bring down insurance rates, service benefits somewhat shielded policyholders from rising prices by covering the full cost of each unit of care. The change required doctors to accept a greater proportion of fixed fees. Physicians dissented. "This contract is in accordance with the dictates of an omnipotent union," charged one doctor. Members of the state's internal medicine society and at least one AMA county society threatened to collectively withdraw from Blue Shield.[124]

Yet labor was not the only group pressing for cost controls during the 1950s and 1960s. Within a fifteen-year period, the Michigan Department of Insurance launched several cost inquiries. And in 1964, Republican Governor George Romney created the Action Committee on Health Care to investigate escalating medical service prices.[125] Business leaders who purchased employee group coverage also complained. Out of fifteen Blue Shield Governing Board seats reserved for "the public," businessmen held six. From these positions, they persistently lobbied for the adoption of cost containment measures. Writing in the medical society's journal, *Michigan Medicine*, the president of the national Chamber of Commerce, Robert P. Gerholz, called on doctors to strengthen utilization review activities. Citing "unwise and excess use of our health facilities," Gerholz blamed rising costs on physicians.[126]

Furthermore, business, labor, and civic group leaders began collaborating with Blue Cross to depress the growth of hospital costs. In 1956, they joined together to establish the Greater Detroit Area Hospital Council to evaluate whether proposed medical facility construction matched local needs. Council members warned would-be hospital founders that without their organization's approval, they would be denied local charity and community chest funds as well as contracting privileges with Blue Cross. By the 1960s, community leaders were working with Michigan Blue Cross officials on seven planning councils throughout the state.[127] When a hospital was built in Mount Clemens in defiance of one council's decision, Blue Cross denied the facility network participation. The hospital sued, but Michigan courts sided with Blue Cross.[128] Within a two-year period during the early 1960s, Michigan planning councils rejected fifty out of seventy-eight hospital construction requests.[129] Tightening area bed supplies reduced the availability of physician admitting privileges and the need for hospital administrators to kowtow to doctor demands as they grubbed for too few patients.

With so many groups assailing physicians – including their traditional allies among Republicans and business leaders – and with federal political debates over aged insurance at a fever pitch, the Michigan State Medical Society could no longer afford to remain obdurate. Physician leaders reasoned that they could either regulate themselves to constrain costs or allow negative publicity to escalate until the government – whether state or federal – intervened.[130] After discussions with Blue Shield officials, medical society leaders conceded the ineffectiveness of existing grievance committees and instructed constituent societies to establish new committees dedicated to regular claims evaluation. Physician leaders encouraged both nonprofit and commercial insurers to submit for appraisal invoices with inordinate fees, overutilization – where "medical care rendered deviates from the accepted practice" – and even borderline questionable claims.[131] Because of the considerable time needed to assess so many claims, insurers agreed to remunerate committee physicians. Throughout the state, medical societies created a system of judicial boards to discipline members found abusing insurance, either with membership revocation or a report to the licensing board.[132] A number of physicians condemned the new policies; one doctor accused medical society leaders of being "a conscience-stricken group riddled by guilt obsession and groveling in its attempt at placating discreditors." Medical society President Oliver B. McGillicuddy rebutted detractors by arguing that refusal to cooperate with insurers would only guarantee government-managed medicine: "continuance of the American system of private practice is dependent, in a large measure, on the success or failure of voluntary health insurance."[133]

The case of Blue Cross and Blue Shield plans in Pennsylvania also reveals the decisive role that groups outside health care played in compelling physicians to accept cost control procedures. Pennsylvania nonprofits created one of the strictest containment programs in the country, goaded along, as in Michigan, by business and union leaders. Overutilization and fee padding by Pennsylvania physicians damaged their collective reputation and angered nonprofit insurance clients. Noting how rapidly the value of indemnity policies – whether nonprofit or commercial – deteriorated in the state, one journalist reported that "labor and industry representatives believe that many doctors have two fee schedules: one for patients without insurance, and a second and higher scale for patients with insurance."[134] Like the UAW in Michigan, the United Mine Workers (UMW) announced plans to create a prepaid physician group to provide subscribers with more benefits at lower costs.[135]

However, the heaviest truncheon hanging over Pennsylvania doctors was the state insurance commissioner. The enabling laws under which nonprofits operated accorded state officials varying degrees of power to modify subscriber contracts. Thirty-five states required plans to notify officials of premium increases while twenty-four states had authority to regulate policy prices.[136] At the end of the 1950s, state officials in New York, Maryland, Massachusetts, and Indiana demanded meaningful cost controls in exchange for granting higher premiums.[137] New Jersey's insurance commissioner declared that he had reached the "inescapable conclusion that the medical influences, as they are exerted by doctors individually, in staff, and through their professional bodies, are five times as great a factor in the increase in hospital costs as all the other influences the hospitals have to encounter."[138] In Pennsylvania, Blues plans had frequently raised policy prices, sometimes by double-digit percentages from one year to the next. In 1958, Blue Cross requested state approval for a 21 percent rate increase. After eighteen days of testimony – which included a bevy of business leaders, labor officials, and subscribers complaining about physician fee padding and overutilization – Pennsylvania Insurance Commissioner Francis R. Smith authorized a 15 percent hike. Smith informed nonprofits that further premium increases would not be forthcoming until they implemented significant cost regulations; he also ordered Blue Shield to appoint more laymen to its governing board and to help Blue Cross establish review committees.[139]

Subsequently, Pennsylvania Medical Society leaders took extraordinary steps to restrain costs and utilization. They emphasized that because news of a doctor's unethical behavior traveled "like wildfire" among the "enemies" of organized medicine, physicians had to scrupulously check such conduct.[140] Some doctors grew irate, contending that labor unions and state authorities were encouraging "piecemeal socialization by third-party plans."[141] However, negative publicity, which nurtured an adverse political environment, helped physician leaders tamp down such protests: "we cannot remain merely defensive," they argued.[142] Financial self-interest also motivated physician action. As promised, the insurance commissioner refused to grant Blue Shield additional rate increases, and plan administrators froze fee schedules. Pennsylvania nonprofits were already notorious for awarding providers particularly low reimbursements. Indeed, the plan's national reputation for low fees had emboldened doctors to overuse services and charge indemnity policyholders extra to "make up" for what they perceived as money lost on patients with service benefits. Medical society leaders hoped that self-policing would ameliorate the situation: if doctors controlled fee padding and utilization, then Blue Shield could afford to pay more.[143]

Representatives of the state medical society worked with Pennsylvania Blue Shield and Blue Cross of Western Pennsylvania, headquartered in Pittsburgh, to develop RVSs.[144] Physician leaders also began sponsoring conferences with business and union representatives to discuss policy benefits and cost controls.[145] Most significantly, in 1963, the Pennsylvania Medical Society helped launch the "Marshall Plan," named after its sponsor, Dr. Matthew Marshall. Under the plan, the Allegheny County Medical Society, which included the Pittsburgh region, established four committees. One committee advised Blue Shield on which physicians qualified for compensation for delivering outpatient diagnostic services. To guard against excessive utilization of these services, particularly by doctors who owned diagnostic or lab facilities, the medical society began monitoring practitioners to determine who should be eligible to provide them as insured benefits. A second committee examined the UCR fees charged under major medical policies. The third committee evaluated all additional claims submitted by third-party payers. Between 1959 and 1961, members reviewed approximately two thousand nonprofit and 160 commercial claims for inflated fees and unnecessary utilization. The final committee under the Marshall Plan helped establish hospital review processes.[146]

To accomplish the work of the fourth committee, medical society officials partnered with Blue Cross of Western Pennsylvania to introduce the Hospital Utilization Project. Project financing came from Blue Cross, the Pennsylvania and Allegheny County Medical Societies, and the United Steelworkers of America. Area businesses chipped in $250,000.[147] After surveying existing review procedures, project leaders instructed each area hospital on how to either create or strengthen evaluation committees. By the end of 1963, all area hospitals had significantly intensified cost containment procedures, and sixteen hospitals were experimenting with the most rigorous approach, which project officials planned to apply statewide. In these hospitals, a specially trained lay assistant reviewed patient charts and pulled those with incomplete information, unusual delays between diagnosis and surgery or other procedures, and potentially unnecessary admissions or overlong stays. These records went to a UR committee. In one hospital, twenty-one physicians and one administrator met each week to evaluate selected charts. If the committee found improper utilization, the doctor was notified in writing. If the offending physician was defiant or continued to misuse services, the committee notified his (or now sometimes, but still rarely, her) department chair. "This might not sound like very effective disciplinary action, but it is," explained a physician and UR committee chair. He continued: "When 22 of your fellow staff members decide you're guilty of improper utilization or have otherwise mismanaged a case, you're going to reconsider your handling of it."[148]

In a dramatic departure from most previous review activities, committee members freely admitted to treading upon sacred physician terrain – they challenged individual expertise by appraising the quality of medical care.[149] The Hospital Utilization Project consulted with panels of distinguished physicians from each major specialty to develop treatment guidelines for the fifty most common diagnoses. Nonprofit leaders developed tables that listed each diagnosis with its average length of stay, associated tests and procedures, and appropriate specialist consultations. UR committees used these data to guide their assessments and spot problematic cases.[150] Physicians complained that these practices undermined the individuality of personal care. One doctor contended that if such measures proliferated, physicians would be compelled "to adapt to pre-established blueprints for hospital stays, standardized for each disease regardless of clinical course."[151] Nevertheless, as officials with the Hospital Utilization Project prepared educational materials to distribute nationally, they titled one pamphlet "A Program of Improved Medical Service," signaling their conviction that review processes and third party controls enhanced physician-provided care.[152]

Responding to physician "resentment of the committee as a policing body," Pennsylvania Medical Society leaders repeatedly explained that the new measures maintained professional control while reassuring the public and policymakers that patients received high quality care at the lowest possible costs.[153] Nonetheless, some doctors persisted in calling those who supported the plan "socialists and radicals."[154] Recalcitrant physicians believed themselves vindicated when medical society leaders reported a distressing trend in nonprofit relations: there "was a growing estrangement between the two organizations, with a tendency of Blue Shield to assert increasing independence." The "diminishing responsiveness of Blue Shield administrators to the expressed concerns and desires of" medical society leaders testified to a new day in physician-insurer interactions.[155] Doctors began to realize that financiers – the ones who paid the piper – would also call the tune.

The western Pennsylvania project was more than an experiment; it was a milestone along the road toward insurer regulation of the health care system. Project details were widely reported in medical and insurance industry publications, raising concerns among doctors and hospital administrators nationwide. Representatives of commercial insurance companies participated in the western Pennsylvania program and took away valuable lessons to share at HIC and HIAA meetings. Blue Cross plans in Ohio and New York replicated the Pennsylvania experiment, requiring hospitals to establish similarly stringent UR processes or face contract cancellation.[156] During this period, the national organizations to which local plans belonged – the Blue Cross Association (BCA) and the National Association of Blue Shield Plans (NABSP) – grew steadily more powerful. As BCA and NABSP leaders increased their authority over member plans, they disseminated cost control information and considered standardizing containment measures nationally.[157] By 1965, sixty-three out of seventy-six Blue Cross plans regularly evaluated claims for hospital admission appropriateness; fifty-one assessed whether delivered services matched diagnoses.[158] Walter J. McNerney, who had left the University of Michigan to assume the post of BCA president, candidly discussed the intention of nonprofit leaders to manage health care delivery:

Most of us in Blue Cross are becoming convinced that one of our greatest challenges is to create and support active programs which will discipline the amount, appropriateness and effectiveness of care being rendered to the American people.[159]

The fears of AMA leaders who had opposed Blue Cross during the 1930s had been realized: by financing hospital services, plan administrators had gradually acquired influence over physician practices. Exacerbating AMA worries, the 1960s witnessed a steep decline in the degree of guidance exerted by physicians over Blue Shield, both nationally and at the local level. In sum, the supervisory relationship was incrementally inverted so that nonprofits began overseeing a good deal of service provider labor.

Compared to commercial insurance companies, nonprofit plans were physically, financially, and professionally closer to doctors. The offspring of medical societies, Blue Shield plans grew up to exploit these close ties by gradually appropriating authority from their patrons and joining with Blue Cross to do so. Blue Shield leaders referred to their organizations as "the doctors' plans" with waning frequency. And physicians utterly lacked the ability to reverse these developments, having come to rely far too heavily on nonprofit payments as a source of income and on the voluntary insurance emblem that Blue Cross and Blue Shield brandished to ward off government reform. Furthermore, nonprofit leaders pursued cost containment in the name of "the public interest." That is, regulations that diminished physician autonomy positioned third-party financiers on the side of consumers, businesses, unions, and government officials.

DOCTORS: PROFESSIONAL EVOLUTION THROUGH THE INSURANCE COMPANY MODEL

During the postwar period, doctors had a fairly heroic professional reputation, thanks to their association with cutting-edge scientific advances and to their skills directed toward the crucial tasks of healing and saving lives. Physicians also enjoyed a financial golden age, enriched by a growing number of insured patients and the clamor for modern medicine. And they exercised broad autonomy when compared to the third-party restrictions they face today. Yet, as we have seen, negative publicity about fee padding and the delivery of unnecessary care had somewhat tarnished their shining professional image. Indeed, because of their high salaries, doctors were often typecast as Cadillac-driving, country-club-attending, leave-the-office-at-four golfers. Furthermore, medical practice was changing rapidly. Physicians were no longer the solitary rulers of their domain. Insurance progressively ordered the realm within which doctors labored, altering the way they delivered care and earned money.

As the insurance company model became entrenched, the doctor's pecuniary standing increasingly derived from two factors. First, a physician's income level stemmed from the relationship between his particular medical specialty and insurance company fee schedules. Second, revenue streams heavily relied upon the doctor's capacity to organize commercial relationships – in other words, on his ability to serve a mass-demand market while interacting with insurance company incentives, rules, and regulations. The insurance company model did not independently produce medical specialization or the physician's professional evolution into a businessman. However, it crucially engaged and accentuated both of these trends.

The insurance company model accelerated the pace of physician specialization. Specialization commenced during the nineteenth century with surgery, obstetrics, and psychiatry and gained ground during the twentieth century because concentrating on one field allowed physicians to keep abreast of voluminous, rapidly advancing medical knowledge and techniques.[160] Before the widespread introduction of insurance, patients had to weigh whether accessing specialist care warranted paying more than the general practitioner's fee. Specialists consequently competed vigorously to attract wealthy and upper-middle-class patients.[161] Health insurance rendered specialty care more broadly available. Although this development was positive in many ways, the insurance company model distorted the market by providing higher reimbursements for specialist services while, at the same time, reducing physician competition – the one mechanism that had regulated and constrained service supply. Because a third party paid all or a portion of the medical bill, policyholders had incentive to consult higher-priced specialists even when the expertise of a general practitioner would have sufficed.[162] Under the insurance company model's pattern of fragmented care, patients were largely left to make this determination on their own. Among doctors, ample patient demand and lenient third-party regulation created a relatively low-risk path to elevated salaries. Between 1949 – when insurance began taking hold as a popular product – and 1960, the number of specialists grew 64 percent. By 1960, the overall composition of the physician pool reflected this increase: the majority of doctors – 56 percent – were now specialists.[163] This adjustment reflected both the demands of burgeoning medical knowledge and technological innovations as well as the influence of insurance company arrangements.

So critical was third-party compensation to this development that securing particularized insurance fee schedules became part of the legitimization process for medical specialties. Because of their supplementary internship training and board credentialing, specialists earned higher insurance payments, even when they supplied the same service or procedure as a general practitioner. Thus, to fully establish their field, specialty boards had to obtain insurance company recognition and their own fee schedule. The case of internal medicine highlights this situation. Although they performed many of the same services as general practitioners, internists spent additional time on patient procedures and examinations. Patients often consulted them to solve complex diagnostic cases. Contending that their skills and expertise merited larger reimbursements than did the routine care of general practitioners, internists lobbied insurers throughout the 1950s to grant them a dedicated fee schedule. "If internal medicine is to survive," argued Dr. Herbert Berge, President of the New York State Society of Internal Medicine, "these carriers must recognize us. They must offer our patients coverage for our specialized care." By the 1960s, insurance companies began complying with internist demands.[164]

Because they received lower fees, general practitioners often complained that insurers undervalued their skills. A general practitioner who devoted one hour to diagnosing a patient might collect one-tenth

the payment that a surgeon received for spending fifteen minutes removing an appendix.[165] One general practitioner recounted how, after
working all night in the hospital caring for a patient, "doing chemistries,
labs, this and that," the insurance company sent him a paltry emolument.
He recalled his outrage: "So I called them up and I said, 'You know, the
trouble with you is if you don't use a knife ... you don't get paid. ... If
you don't do the procedures like that and you just use your head, you
don't get paid.'"[166] Insurance fee arrangements also abetted the
narrowing of the general practitioner's field. Many general practitioners
found that delivering babies and performing basic surgeries, such as
appendectomies and tonsillectomies, were not worth the time away from
the office, particularly when they received less remuneration than specialists for the same service.[167] While this development partially reflected the
demands of ever more effective and efficient specialty medicine, insurance
company practices hastened the transition.

By influencing how doctors earned income, insurance not only stimulated medical specialization but also expanded the physician's role as a
businessman.[168] During the nineteenth century, the doctoring enterprise
largely depended on attracting patients through individual reputation
and interpersonal relationships. By the mid-twentieth century, physicians
could draw upon the profession's collective cultural standing. Given the
intimate nature of health care, which entails physical contact and individuals presenting their bodies for medical scrutiny, doctors continued to
cultivate personal relations as a means of appealing to patients. However,
the dual forces of industrialization and insurance compelled physicians to
also accommodate bureaucratic and commercial organization. Physicians
who worked chiefly within hospitals – a common route for certain specialties, such as anesthesiology and radiology – had to navigate progressively
more ordered, hierarchical relationships. Privately practicing doctors interacted more frequently with hospitals while, in the community, the way
they earned money and how much they earned increasingly derived from
business skills: the ability to manage larger patient loads; divide labor
effectively; and master third-party payment processes, which ranged from
claims form accounting to utilization review procedures. Establishing a
professional office facilitated the accomplishment of these tasks.

Setting up an office was one of the most arduous tasks doctors undertook. After graduating from medical school and spending several years
earning modest intern salaries, many physicians without family resources
had to acquire sizeable loans to start their practices. This capital was
essential for obtaining office space, purchasing medical and office

equipment, and hiring a nurse or administrative assistant.[169] One doctor reported that he borrowed $30,000 to start his Richmond, Virginia, practice in 1958, a substantial sum considering that, at the time, median U.S. household income hovered around $5,000 a year.[170] As physicians encountered mounting business exigencies, medical practice consulting firms carved out a profitable niche. Consultants advised physicians to set aside approximately 40 percent of gross income to sustain operating expenses.[171] Because of the large investment required to run an office and because inexperienced physicians lacked a stable patient base, during the first few years of practice, doctors frequently lived "sort of hand-to-mouth."[172] These difficulties persuaded some doctors to begin their careers working for an established practice, usually with one or two physicians in the same medical specialty. Nonetheless, because of their earnings prospects, doctors who chose to launch their own practices generally found financing more readily available than other small business owners.

Doctors placed small signs in front of their offices to announce their presence. Otherwise, because AMA medical ethics prohibited physician advertising, they employed indirect means to attract patients. A doctor's office might appeal to patients if it provided ample parking or was located near a bus line. Less experienced physicians often supplemented their incomes and brought in new patients by administering medical exams to life insurance applicants. Recently graduated physicians or practitioners new to an area could circulate their names among patient pools by filling in for established doctors on call nights or when they took a vacation. Additionally, many physicians joined civic clubs and community organizations to subtly promote their practices.[173]

During the immediate postwar years, competition for patients could be intense, particularly in urban areas; thus many doctors, especially those just beginning to practice, migrated to the suburbs. The newly constructed highways and abundance of mortgage credit that enticed middle-class families to suburbia also drew physicians who wanted to "build more fruitful practices and lead less harried lives."[174] A general practitioner explained why he left Washington, D.C., after almost five years of practice to open an office in the northern Virginia suburb of Vienna:

D.C. had thousands of doctors. It was loaded with doctors. And there were medical buildings all over the place. So you were just another needle in the haystack. But there was a need for doctors in northern Virginia at that time. I'm very satisfied with what I did, because in a year or two I was making more than I made in D.C. As a matter of fact, my first year there, I did twice as much as I ever did in Washington.[175]

Because of competitive conditions, general practitioners were usually the first group of physicians to move to the suburbs; specialists soon followed.

Offices permitted doctors to take advantage of economies of scale by seeing as many patients as possible – particularly insured patients. Before insurance became popular, a doctor's earnings generally reflected the wealth of his patients. Because sliding fee scales encouraged doctors to charge the affluent handsome fees, a practitioner could focus on appealing to the correct clientele rather than attracting a large patient base. As consumers acquired insurance, they began to expect – though, as we have seen, did not always receive – more standardized medical fees, formulated irrespective of socioeconomic class or insured status. Physician charges did gradually become more uniform with the spread of insurance, and the simplest way for practitioners to augment income was by delivering more services to more patients. In an office, doctors could efficiently order their time to accomplish this objective. As physicians made fewer house calls and became increasingly office-based, they initially held open practice hours, inviting patients to show up unannounced and wait to be seen. Introducing appointment schedules allowed doctors to balance their service delivery pace and see more patients, often between twenty and thirty a day. The time physicians had for casual conversation and friendly chitchat decreased; doctors attempted to confine appointments, especially for routine illnesses, to between fifteen and twenty minutes.[176] To reduce time expended per patient, consultants advised practitioners to distribute leaflets with medical advice for common diagnoses, such as arthritis or the flu. In larger practices, physicians began relying on nurses or medical aides to review patient care instructions, handle additional questions, and follow up with individuals by phone.[177] Many physicians still dedicated certain hours each week to house calls, particularly for elderly patients; but growing patient pools gradually eroded this practice. Insurance coverage contributed to the decline of house calls: third parties labeled such services a "luxury" and refused to cover them. Moreover, doctors could provide patients with more services – which they hoped were billable to an insurance company – in their offices, where they often had x-ray machines, liver-functioning labs, and basal metabolism devices.[178]

Insurance also helped transform the maintenance of physician accounts and medical records. Along with tax laws and larger patient loads, insurance compelled doctors to modernize accounting techniques. During the 1940s and 1950s, most physicians abandoned the custom of informally noting patient accounts in debit books and instead adopted modern bookkeeping procedures based on double entry standards, which helped them keep track of operational expenses; patient payments; and third-party financing, including multiple insuring organizations and methods of reimbursement.[179] Physicians also revamped patient medical records. One explained the customary approach: "Little 3×5 cards and the date. 'Feb 15th, nosebleed.' Nothing fancy about it. I just put down a simple thing."[180] The need to justify care to insurers ended such casual methods. Physicians began logging diagnosis details, delivered services and procedures, and the time it took to perform each treatment – so as to have on hand thorough records to fill out claims forms and in case insurance representatives called or visited with follow up questions. Increasingly, physicians and their staff used dictating-transcribing machines and electric typewriters to complete medical records and claims.[181]

The growing complexity of medical practice, including proliferating insurance company requirements, prompted physicians to hire aides or secretaries – who, in the male-dominated world of the 1950s and 1960s, were frequently referred to as the doctor's "girl" or "girl Friday."[182] In a small practice, a physician might hire a nurse to handle both adminis-trative responsibilities and some medical duties. Increasingly, however, physicians hired dedicated administrators and reserved nurses, who gener-ally commanded higher salaries, for medical care. By 1956, only 19 percent of doctors worked alone while 40 percent had one administrative assistant or nurse, 23 percent had two, and 18 percent had three or more.[183] Being "an executive in his office – not a man-of-all-work," allowed physicians to focus their costly-to-acquire expertise on delivering medical services.[184] Lower-skilled workers could handle at least a portion of the paperwork, phone communications, collection duties, and bookkeeping. Medical sec-retaries familiarized themselves with the most popular insurance policies in their area and the services they covered. They learned to ask patients questions unrelated to medical care: Did they have an insurance card? Did their income qualify them for Blue Shield service benefits? At times, they directly managed insurer relations, calling companies with questions about an outstanding claim or meeting with plan representatives to learn about new form submission or review processes.[185]

As insurance became the lifeblood of physician incomes, claim forms emerged as the doctor's favorite complaint. Initially, each insurance com-pany used its own form with distinct formatting and medical questions. According to one survey, commercial insurers had twenty-six different ways of asking for the patient's diagnosis and forty-two methods of inquiring about the prognosis. To reduce physician confusion, most commercial firms adopted the HIC's standardized claim form by the end of the 1950s.[186] But this development failed to stem the tide of forms, and doctors devoted a growing number of work hours to filling out insurance claims. Some doctors scheduled time cushions between each appointment to complete the forms.[187] One physician reported that, about four times a week, he returned to the office after dinner to spend two to three hours processing paperwork.[188] Another doctor explained the havoc that descended upon his practice when he failed to implement a systematic process for handling claims:

> The rain of paper work was almost continuous. Scarcely a day passed that some 'little' mistake we'd made didn't explode into a big one. We seemed constantly to be billing patients who were covered by their health insurance – and failing to bill others who weren't. We were forever neglecting to report services for which I should have been paid, thereby snarling the bookkeeping and losing money due. How much time we wasted answering requests from the plans for further information I couldn't even estimate.[189]

As the principal communications link between insurers and physicians and the means by which doctors accounted for their work to secure reimbursements, insurance forms became extremely important to the health care system's functioning.

Physicians learned that how they responded to insurance queries determined their earnings, particularly as claim forms became the cornerstone of cost containment measures. By the 1960s, physicians not only provided written descriptions of care but also supplied code numbers associated with diagnosis and procedure categories. These codes allowed computers to track individual billing and treatment practices and deny payments in cases of suspected fee padding or overutilization.[190] During medical society meetings, in the hospital break room, and on the golf course, doctors discussed key phrases and code numbers to help them extract "fair" reimbursements from insurers. These practices were sometimes innocent enough: "Wording those things was very important," explained one doctor, "because if they weren't worded precisely, specifically, why then the insurance company wouldn't pay for them."[191] Another physician gave a different account for why he sometimes altered his service descriptions:

> A lot of people want to come in for physicals. But the insurance company doesn't pay for physicals. You have to have a disease. You have to have an abnormality. So you almost had to make up something so you would get paid. Because you'd do the whole physical and you're not getting a dime if it's just a normal physical exam.[192]

Such anecdotes reveal that doctors often viewed overutilization and fee padding – when and if they recognized they were performing these activities – as ways to offset what they considered unreasonable third-party payment procedures.

Moreover, because physician charges were partially detached from competitive market forces, fee determinations became an increasingly arbitrary and sometimes confusing process for physicians. Under indemnity and major medical policies, which allowed physicians to disregard fee schedules, doctors could elevate their prices to compensate for any number of perceived financial burdens, ranging from charity care to an insufficient number of patients. The bad publicity associated with extravagant physician charges convinced many state and local medical societies to adopt RVSs, which, though they avoided setting specific fees, structured physician pricing by designating points to reflect the varying complexity of each service and the time and skill level required to perform it. Doctors were increasingly advised to discuss costs with patients before beginning a procedure and to itemize bills so that patients understood what they or their insurance policies were paying for.[193] The most frequently proffered guidance on price setting, from medical society leaders and management consultants, appeared reasonable: "Don't undercut the average and don't go above it. You don't want your fees to set you apart from the other doctors in town."[194] Unfortunately, this advice encouraged even the most ethical physicians to inflate charges simply to keep track with their peers. And as insurance companies introduced "usual, customary, and reasonable" payments, they unwittingly tempted doctors to significantly hike fees lest they be prohibited from doing so at a later date.[195]

With growing frequency, doctors accepted direct payments, not only from nonprofit plans, but also from commercial insurance companies "on assignment." Depending on the stability and affluence of their customer base, physicians wrote off between 10 and 40 percent of patient bills as uncollectible.[196] Because of the difficulty and expense of collecting patient fees and because some insurance subscribers chose to pocket indemnity checks rather than pay their medical bills, a number of physicians, flouting the preferences of AMA leaders, lobbied insurance companies for direct compensation.[197] By the mid-1960s, physicians received between 30 and 70 percent of their income directly from insurance companies.[198] These direct financing linkages severed doctor-patient monetary relationships and became crucial conduits through which insurance companies intensified cost containment measures.

As cost controls spread, doctors recognized that every service delivered to an insured patient was open to scrutiny by third-party payers. Insurer-provider communication intensified, and physicians not only managed forms but also received phone calls and visits from insurance representatives requesting additional information. Provider representatives also put questionable claims before medical society and hospital review committees. One doctor recounted his unpleasant experience before a hospital utilization review committee in Richmond, Virginia during the 1960s:

> I remember at Memorial being called up one time because I didn't order a BUN [a blood urea nitrogen level test] on a patient. And many thought the patient needed a BUN. ... If it was inappropriate, then they would call you. 'Why did you order this test doctor?' So that was no fun. So ... you made damn sure they [the treatments] were appropriate and you hoped you met all the criteria. ... Why didn't I order a BUN? It was my judgment that the patient didn't need it. I told them, I said he didn't need the BUN. ... It's a standard test you order on anybody over 40, but not a young person.[199]

As this case demonstrates, the claims review processes initiated and sustained by third-party financiers quickly moved beyond simple cost calculation and utilization assessments to also standardizing and regulating the quality of medical care.

Into the 1960s and thereafter, physicians continued receiving substantial salaries. Moreover, the profession's close association with scientific advances maintained and augmented the social standing of doctors. Physicians also preserved their collective cultural authority, their influence to define, as a group, illness categories and standards of care. Yet the individual latitude of doctors within the workplace – wherever they delivered care – contracted so that they increasingly complied with uniform prices and payments and even regimented treatment blueprints. As medicine became progressively bureaucratized, the art of doctoring dwindled.

CONCLUSION

The insurance company model fundamentally skewed the actions and motivations of health care actors. It required insuring agencies to finance services for which they could not regulate the demand or the supply. And the model obliged physicians to shift their focus, at least partially, from competing for patients by providing high-quality, reasonably priced services to concentrating more intently on insurance company directives and payment procedures. Though intended to resolve these problems, the cost containment methods formulated during the 1950s and 1960s worked like tattered pieces of fabric tethering massive support beams – they provided feeble reinforcement for the system, mostly by helping private interests enhance the facade of voluntary insurance. However, cost control procedures failed to substantially constrain prices or more logically order health care. Each time third-party payers employed a new measure, service providers shifted costs and overutilization elsewhere.

Nevertheless, cost containment practices repositioned the locus of economic power in health care. Cost regulations aided the medical system's conversion into a corporate structure that granted insurers increasing authority over service providers. While physicians assiduously resisted attempts to diminish their autonomy, commercial and nonprofit insurers cited business, labor, and governmental concerns to justify their oversight. With this transition, third-party insurers assumed a role far beyond simply financing services – they began to supervise medical care delivery and, more broadly, to manage the health care system, which entailed coordinating features ranging from hospital construction to physician payments.

Though fraught with dissension and generating flawed outcomes, as private interests developed the institutional underpinnings of the insurance company model, they produced an additional, crucial result. Their activities gradually transformed a model that was once recognized as inherently defective and costly into a culturally legitimate and familiar form – what many would begin to identify as a "natural" outgrowth of market processes. At the grassroots, where individuals encountered the health care system, a dense network of organizations, people, and ideas evolved to maintain and nurture insurance company arrangements. Insurers and service providers tailored their daily routines to fit the framework. Patients and insurance customers grew accustomed to the system's peculiarities. Moreover, each set of actors began to filter their beliefs about the health care system – whether reform-oriented or bent on protecting the status quo – through the insurance company model. Private health interests, politicians, voters, patients, and policyholders forgot the historical alternatives and had difficulty imagining health care as anything other than an insurance-company–dominated system.

7

The Politics of Medicare, 1957–1965

After decades of attempting to achieve meaningful health care reform, policymakers passed Medicare in 1965. Reformers attained this goal by conclusively demonstrating to voters and politicians that voluntary health interests had failed to uphold their side of soft corporatist arrangements. Since the 1940s, policymakers had articulated clear objectives for the health care sector, demanding that private interests satisfy a consumer ideal – that is, mass-produced insurance that granted policyholders liberal access to modern medicine. Under the terms of the soft corporatist understanding, policymakers would intercede in the health care system if the voluntary sector failed to achieve this goal. Through professional and trade associations, health care leaders were able to impel physicians, insurance companies, and nonprofit plans a long way toward fulfilling the politically enunciated consumer ideal. Yet overcoming the cost problems inherent in the insurance company model proved exceedingly difficult. Carrying the additional burden of elderly policyholders, who required high levels of medical care, strained the insurance company framework to its breaking point. The situation convinced a majority of policymakers and voters to support a program of federally funded aged insurance.

Although the Forand bill for elderly hospital benefits was introduced in 1957 and Medicare did not pass until 1965, the delay reflected divergent views about how to define the program rather than widespread opposition to government-financed health insurance for seniors. Both Democrats and Republicans offered proposals for federally funded aged insurance.[1] However, because the plan that won passage would influence whether and how far future politicians could move toward developing the program into a centrally managed, universal health care system, policy-makers engaged in fierce disputes over the issues of means testing, Social Security financing, and the degree of insurance company participation.

Nevertheless, all Medicare proposals, whether offered by liberal or conservative politicians, anticipated using the institutions that physicians and insurers had already created to structure the voluntary market. Even policymakers who viewed the program as a means toward eventually nationalizing health care recognized that they had to adopt the insurance company model because the federal government lacked the capacity and expertise to reorder the system's now thoroughly embedded organizational pattern. Furthermore, replicating private sector arrangements allowed advocates to promote Medicare as ideologically moderate – they could argue that the program would not only aid the vulnerable and deserving aged population but would also employ culturally familiar institutions.

After two decades of policymakers attempting to either undermine or displace the insurance company model, politicians designed the most significant health care program of the century in a manner that bestowed official legitimacy upon that very model. Policymakers appointed insurance companies and nonprofit plans to administer Medicare and act as fiscal intermediaries, which included handling service provider communications, conducting utilization reviews, and determining fee-for-service physician reimbursements as well as hospital cost payments. Although the government would finance and direct Medicare, federal funding and ordinances would reach physician offices and hospitals through the institutional conduits of the insurance company.[2]

During Medicare debates, private interest groups negotiated with government officials over the positions their members would assume within the program. These negotiations occurred either formally, when representatives from each side sat down to discuss program terms, or, as was more common under soft corporatist arrangements, informally through political debates and before the public eye as each side articulated a message and the other responded. American Medical Association (AMA) leaders discovered the significant harm that lay in resisting the realities of the soft corporatist pact. Because private interests had failed to satisfy consumer desires in the aged market, organized physicians' traditional tactic of ferociously battling government reform made them appear out of step with dominant political and societal perceptions and consequently undercut the AMA's reputation. Meanwhile, Health Insurance Association of America (HIAA) and National Association of Blue Shield Plans (NABSP) leaders declined to vigorously fight Medicare before the viewing public. Blue Cross Association (BCA) heads chose to support the Kennedy and Johnson administrations' proposals and worked with policymakers to shape the legislative details. These strategies of muted resistance and active support helped enhance insurers' political and economic standing over the long term.

Medicare represented the culmination of the soft corporatist provisions that had governed the health care system's development through preceding decades. After health care interests failed to uphold policymaker objectives in the field of elderly insurance coverage, federal officials intervened in the market. However, they designated these same private interests to operate as adjuncts of state power. Medicare benefits, while regulated and paid for by the government, were manufactured through the insurance company model. Thus, within a relatively short period, between the 1930s and 1960s, insurance companies evolved from system outsiders into the principal managers of both public and private health care.

THE INCREMENTAL STRATEGY

At the end of the 1950s, liberal policymakers and Social Security Administration (SSA) officials recognized that the private market was far too institutionally ingrained to convince voters and policymakers to adopt government-provided universal insurance.[3] So they sought to penetrate the voluntary market where organizational buildup was frailest and insert a federal program. By gradually expanding that program, they hoped to eventually acquire control over the health care system. Accordingly, reformers began spotlighting expensive, limited elderly medical coverage, arguing that such woeful private market conditions confirmed that only the federal government could deliver a health insurance product worthy of aging consumers.

Following the defeat of Truman's plan for universal health insurance, SSA policymakers embraced an incremental approach to achieving their objective. They began promoting medical coverage for a more limited, "deserving" group of individuals – namely, senior citizens. In 1952, their Democratic allies in Congress introduced legislation to provide Social Security recipients with hospital benefits. Truman's Commission on the Health Needs of the Nation endorsed the program. However, after Eisenhower was elected, the issue lay dormant while Republicans offered their own versions of health care reform.[4]

During Eisenhower's second term, after having steadily enlarged Social Security through expanded pension benefits and the addition of Disability Insurance in 1956, reformers were sufficiently emboldened to refocus on aged medical assistance. The social insurance director of the American Federation of Labor and Congress of Industrial Organizations (AFL-CIO), Nelson Cruikshank, joined SSA officials to write legislation providing health care coverage for senior citizens.[5] In 1957, the group convinced the fourth-ranking Democrat on the House Ways and Means Committee, Aime Forand (RI), to introduce a bill that proposed raising Social Security taxes in order to supply aged beneficiaries with surgical, hospital, and nursing home care.[6] The Forand bill had little chance of passage given Republican and conservative Democrat opposition, particularly from such quarters as the White House, the powerful House Ways and Means Chairman Wilbur Mills (D, AR), and influential Senate Finance Committee member Robert S. Kerr (D, OK).

Nonetheless, the Forand bill pushed the issue of elderly health care to the forefront of domestic policy debates. The supporters of every major reform proposal since World War II, whether Democrat or Republican, had argued that the private market was failing to fulfill a consumer ideal for health insurance products that amply displayed the nation's prosperous, consumption-oriented economy. After a decade of political debates and publicity about high-priced medical insurance with meager benefits, a similar message, which was now tailored to emphasize the cost burden on one distinct and "deserving" group, resonated deeply with voters and the policymaking community, not to mention the elderly who shared a common stake in Social Security. Advocates of Forand's legislation stressed that high premium prices combined with the elderly's limited earning power placed voluntary insurance outside the reach of many senior citizens.[7] They maintained that even aged citizens who could afford health insurance paid exorbitant prices for minimal benefits, usually bare-bones hospitalization coverage. "The question is not how many older people have private insurance, but how good is it?" asserted one SSA official.[8] Pro-reform politicians pledged that their program would cost less and provide more coverage benefits than the voluntary market.[9]

Reformers shrewdly took advantage of congressional hearings on the Forand bill to foster their contention that only the government could ensure satisfactory health coverage for the elderly. House Speaker Sam Rayburn (D, TX) threw his support behind the legislation with a story about how his brother had undergone an expensive cancer surgery followed by months of intensive medical care. "I had the money and was glad to do it," stated Rayburn. "But a lot of folks don't have the money and can't do it."[10] Representative Forand announced that he was "piling up bagfuls of mail" in favor of the measure.[11] From the House floor, the congressman derided the State 65 policies that insurers, in conjunction with the AMA, sold to seniors. Forand criticized their high prices and limited benefits, citing one policy that paid $10 a day for hospital costs. "Have any of my colleagues," he inquired, "any members of their families – or indeed any of our constituents – found a hospital room recently for $10 per day?"[12] Another avenue for garnering publicity came with the Senate's 1959 formation of the Subcommittee on Problems of the Aged and Aging. Subcommittee Chairman Patrick McNamara (D, MI) traveled the country, from Boston to San Francisco, conducting town-hall–style meetings to highlight the difficulty that elderly citizens on fixed incomes had purchasing health care.[13] *Time* magazine explained the complaint of many seniors:

In the past decade, medical costs for the aged have about doubled. Today the average couple over 65 spends $140 a year for medical care, or $700 if hospitalization is needed. But 57% of the aged have means of less than $1,000 a year, counting social security benefits.[14]

Eisenhower's Health, Education, and Welfare (HEW) secretary, Arthur S. Flemming, testified against the Forand measure during House Ways and Means hearings. Yet, even he conceded that insurance companies had failed to adequately cover an acceptable portion of the aged.[15]

Despite mounting agreement that the nation required some form of government programming for elderly health care, Forand's bill was easily bottled up in committee. Many Ways and Means members wished to side with their district's medical society, and Republican members had little reason to support a Democratic initiative. Moreover, Southern Democrats were wary of legislation that vested spending authority with the federal government rather than the states. Given the significant civil rights legislation being passed and discussed at the time, southerners were feeling especially sensitive about state prerogatives. They had just experienced the spectacle of Eisenhower sending the 101st Airborne Division into Little Rock to aid school desegregation. Recognizing that medical facility integration would accompany federally funded hospital care, Southern Democrats, including key Ways and Means Committee members, opposed Forand's measure.[16] Additionally, some committee members worried that costly medical benefits would upend Social Security's actuarial tables, thus undermining long-standing efforts to keep the program financially sound and politically reputable. For this reason, Ways and Means Chairman and conservative Arkansas Democrat Wilbur Mills would erect numerous obstacles to block aged insurance.[17]

In 1960, the Ways and Means Committee voted the Forand bill down by a margin of 17–8.[18] Yet it was becoming increasingly difficult for politicians to ignore the problem of elderly medical care. Policymakers and voters found that private interests had failed to uphold their end of the implicit political-consumer compact, which had always maintained that the government would intervene in health care wherever voluntary groups failed to mass produce generous insurance.

LATE 1950S: THE HESITANT OPPOSITION

As the premise that the voluntary market was failing to serve the elderly gained acceptance, some private health leaders advised their peers that reform was inevitable and urged them to reevaluate long-held political strategies. Leading members of the AMA, HIAA, Blue Cross, and Blue Shield warned that contesting medical aid for aged citizens would only generate bad publicity. Nevertheless, the AMA's dominant conservative faction convinced the leadership to stridently fight the Forand bill and similar measures. AMA representatives approached insurers about forging a coalition to forcefully combat the legislation; however, the Forand proposal sowed division among insurance company and nonprofit leaders, and many eyed an alliance with physicians warily.

The AMA's leadership paused momentarily before plunging into a full-scale war against the Forand bill. When the legislation first surfaced, Eisenhower's HEW secretary at the time, Marion Folsom, approached the AMA about finding a legislative compromise. Folsom counseled AMA leaders that at some point they would probably lose the issue of government-funded aged health care; so refusing to cooperate with policymakers would only forfeit an opportunity to shape the legislation to their liking.[19] As we have seen, the association was by no means a conservative monolith, and a healthy minority of physician leaders would have been amenable to Forand-type legislation. Conservative leader Francis Blasingame described the AMA's Board of Trustees as "divided ideologically into the right, left, and those in between," though perhaps what he characterized as "left" is what most observers at the time would have labeled "moderate."[20] The board entertained arguments from a faction of members who insisted that because federal medical benefits for the elderly were unavoidable, the AMA should collaborate with policymakers to enhance the position of doctors within the program.[21] Blasingame and his allies triumphed once again, persuading leaders that anything resembling the Forand measure would usher in government-managed medicine. Blasingame declared that the "surest way to total defeat is to say, we are now going to sit across the negotiating table and see what you will give us."[22] Recalling their victory against Truman, one physician boasted that "no one should underestimate the tremendous strength of medicine, that's the way we won last time."[23] The statement embodied the AMA's political strategy – arrogant, dated, and ultimately doomed.

Physician leaders then turned to their longtime political partners, enjoining commercial insurers to emphatically oppose the Forand proposal. At the HIAA's 1959 meeting, AMA President Leonard Larson exhorted the audience not to be manipulated by reformers who were attempting to woo them away from physicians: "backers of the bill hope to prevent the American Medical Association from establishing a united front with the insurance industry."[24] AMA representatives correctly sensed the wavering nerve of their companions: insurance leaders split over the appropriate course for the industry.[25] This division was deepened by the HIAA's decision to join forces with life insurance groups, which were led by executives who often viewed modest deployments of governmental authority with approval. Throughout the Medicare debates, HIAA leaders met with Life Insurance Association of America (LIAA) and American Life Convention (ALC) officials to consider and reconsider the industry's position toward government-funded elderly benefits.

Edwin J. Faulkner, chief of the HIAA's conservative wing, enthusiastically supported the AMA, reminding his peers that "compromise leads to further compromise and hence, eventually, to complete surrender."[26] Faulkner recommended that the HIAA, AMA, and Chamber of Commerce collectively launch a nationwide, Whitaker-and-Baxter-style campaign.[27] Just as they had done during the Truman debates, Faulkner and like-minded colleagues wished to massively promote the assertion that the voluntary market could deliver more to consumers than could the government. They contended that by 1970, approximately 90 percent of senior citizens would have private health insurance.[28] But at the same time, conservative HIAA leaders indicated the deficiency of their argument by continually, fervently – almost desperately – pressuring member firms to expand elderly coverage.[29] Faulkner characterized executives who refused to insure additional aged subscribers because of profitability concerns as "complacent and somnolent ... [and] living in an ivory tower."[30]

Ideologically moderate executives regarded conservative faith in voluntary efforts as naïve. The industry's endeavor to supply senior citizens with insurance was barely surviving. Although companies participating in State 65 plans had pooled financial and administrative resources to collectively underwrite aged coverage, they could not surmount the combined problems of innately expensive insurance company arrangements and the elderly's greater need for medical care. Around 1960, once commercial and nonprofit insurers had sold policies to almost three-fifths of senior citizens, growth in coverage rates slowed dramatically because of the high premium prices that accompanied even the most stripped-down contracts. Moreover, State 65 programs had become financially onerous for companies. For example, the Connecticut 65 plan lost more than half a million dollars during its first eighteen months of operation.[31] Nonprofit programs were also losing money, even though their aged policies were of much "lesser benefit quality" than "coverage of younger age groups."[32] A commercial executive voiced the thoughts of many when he remarked that a "basic question remains as to whether after age 65 is a proper field for insurance."[33]

A number of insurance leaders cautioned that disputing a program of elderly benefits would only generate bad publicity for the industry. "Few politicians will want to take on the doctors, but this same restraint will not apply in the case of large insurance corporations," averred LIAA lobbyist Eugene Thore. In a swipe directed at Faulkner, Thore continued: "If we fight ... to the last ditch and the last man as is being recommended in some quarters, we can foresee some serious long range damage to the insurance industry."[34] Insurers also feared the political costs of fostering unrealistic expectations. An industry insider argued that "overly optimistic testimony as to the accomplishments and prospects of voluntary health insurance in providing suitable coverage for the aged simply operates to alienate Congressmen." Underscoring the industry's central dilemma, he conceded that "voluntary insurance cannot do the full job."[35]

Despite such ongoing discussions, HIAA officials testified against the Forand measure during congressional hearings. Since the bill had little chance of passage, insurers saw no reason to break long-established political ties with the AMA and other conservative groups.[36] Moreover, correctly reading reformers' incremental strategy, insurers believed the program might serve as a foundation for government-managed, universal health care. Even leaders who favored political compromise stressed the necessity of shaping the program to hamper expansion efforts. Furthermore, after having spent decades defending state regulatory jurisdiction of insurance, executives feared that an elderly benefits program would effect federal supervision of their industry.[37] Finally, the Forand bill was risky to support because, like many of the reform measures that preceded it, the legislation privileged nonprofits, this time by designating Blue Cross and Blue Shield plans to monopolize benefits administration.[38] Insurers were nonetheless uneasy; they understood that the Forand proposal was merely the first battle of what promised to be a grueling political war.

As they worked to strengthen the wall of voluntary resistance to Forand-type legislation, AMA officials pinpointed the weakest links as the BCA and allied providers, represented by the American Hospital Association (AHA). BCA and AHA representatives had been lobbying for federal grants-in-aid to state insurance programs for years before Congressman Forand submitted his bill. Dr. Blasingame warned Blue Cross and AHA leaders that policymakers proposed the measure as a ploy to consolidate federal control over the entire health care system. "[Y]ou can't be a little bit in favor of the Forand approach without compromising your entire position," Blasingame argued.[39] Indeed, worried that politicians might exploit a limited program of government-funded health care to gradually nationalize insurance, BCA leaders had long objected both to centralized program management at the federal level and to financing medical benefits through Social Security. However, the 1958 Ways and Means Committee hearings revealed growing uncertainty among Blue Cross leaders over those key points. They declined to either support or oppose the Forand bill, even though the legislation recommended using the Social Security system. Rather than appear for questioning, BCA officials submitted a written statement affirming the need for some type of government funding: "Voluntary prepayment cannot, singlehandedly, provide hospital services to any substantial number of those already retired and not now covered by Blue Cross."[40] An AHA representative testified before the committee, promoting the association's preferred approach of federal grants to states. However, he indicated the increasing flexibility of organized hospitals toward Forand-type proposals by refraining to take a position on Social Security financing.[41]

Close affiliation with organized physicians predetermined the official stance of Blue Shield leaders against the Forand proposal. Nevertheless it is hardly surprising, especially given Blue Shield's shaky financial state, that many national association officers and some local plan leaders privately approved of the bill. Commenting on nonprofit efforts to insure the elderly, NABSP counsel Marv Reiter remarked, "Well hell, that went nowhere. All that did was show us what we couldn't do."[42] The surgical portion of Forand's program would have solved some fiscal problems for plans. Forand advocates also reasoned that if aged citizens had federal hospital and surgical insurance, then they would have more money available to purchase regular medical coverage. After the measure was introduced, the NABSP issued a report declaring that "Blue Shield should be in opposition" to Forand legislation.[43] The statement incensed AMA leaders and their supporters among conservative insurers: "These expressions from the Government Relations Committee of the Blue Shield Commission are so typical of the 'pussyfooting' and trying 'to ride both sides of the fence' with which one seems to be confronted in nearly every direction he turns."[44]

NABSP officials trod carefully, attempting to signal their political differences with the AMA while avoiding outright rebellion. In 1958 hearings before the Ways and Means Committee, the chairman of the Blue Shield Commission's Government Relations Committee, Dr. Donald Stubbs, placed Blue Shield ambivalence on full display. After delivering a dissertation on the history of medical care stretching back to the physicians employed in ancient Greek and Roman households, then listing nonprofit aged insurance programs and coverage rates, Stubbs ended his testimony by briefly and blandly informing congressmen that at their recent annual conference, Blue Shield plan representatives "went on record as being opposed to the enactment of H.R. 9467 [Forand legislation]."[45]

Private health interests vacillated over the most suitable game plan for the Forand bill. The AMA quickly settled into its usual adversarial mode and dragged along reluctant Blue Shield leaders. Meanwhile, commercial insurers and Blue Cross administrators contemplated both the financial losses associated with aged coverage and the negative publicity of combating reform. As private interests readied themselves for Medicare battles, even the most belligerent conservative leaders had to gather their courage – having already seen headlines proclaiming "Free Health Care for Aged Opposed," many realized that the political discourse could only degenerate and potentially maim those caught in the downward spiral.[46]

THE EVOLVING POLITICAL CONSENSUS

Republicans joined with conservative Democrats to contest the Forand bill on the grounds that it handed too much power to federal officials. However, legislative debates and media coverage compelled an increasing number of policymakers to acknowledge that the elderly required some form of federal aid to access health care. Leading Republicans thus offered alternatives to Forand's plan. Intense partisan conflict nevertheless remained, because policymakers understood that how the program was structured would shape the health care system's subsequent evolution, including prospects for universal insurance.

Although President Eisenhower criticized the Forand approach for failing to safeguard the voluntary sector, his administration soon expressed interest in providing health benefits for seniors. As the presidential election loomed, the apparent Republican nominee, Vice President Richard Nixon, urged Eisenhower to sponsor legislation that would demonstrate the party's concern about elderly medical care.[47]

Once Republicans decided to seek alternatives to Forand's proposal, political debates turned toward how aged benefits should be designed. It was an open secret that liberal policymakers intended to use the program as an entering wedge for a national health care system. Congressman Forand, publicly revealing more than SSA officials and allied legislators usually did, explained the strategy to a sympathetic audience of seniors and union members: "If we can only break through and get our foot inside the door, we can expand the program after that."[48] Politicians on both sides of this objective viewed three programmatic characteristics as significant to either limiting or enlarging government-managed health care: means testing, Social Security funding, and the level of insurance company involvement.

The first major issue of contention was whether beneficiaries should comply with means testing. Politicians on the left sought coverage for the entire aged population or, at minimum, all Social Security recipients. Broad program membership would generate extensive political support and encourage participants to think of their benefits as a right rather than a charitable donation. Pro-Forand policymakers characterized means testing as "degrading," arguing that only an inclusive program would permit seniors to "retain their dignity and self sufficiency."[49] Conservative politicians, in contrast, viewed means testing as a curb on program expansion.

Benefits financing was the second major issue that divided politicians. Those who championed robust reform insisted that citizens fund benefits through Social Security contributions in the form of increased payroll taxes. Social Security financing would lodge the program within an agency hosting officials who had long sought universal health care. Additionally, policymakers favored social insurance believing that they could more readily protect and augment benefits that recipients believed they had "earned" through dedicated payroll deductions.[50]

Many conservative politicians vehemently objected to the notion that Social Security was insurance.[51] "Under the payroll tax," argued Ways and Means member John W. Byrnes (R, WI), "an erroneous concept has been sold the people that they have paid for their benefits, that they have bought something as a matter of right." He continued: "under such a concept there is no flexibility to make changes because the people will tell you, 'We have bought this and you cannot make any change except to liberalize it.'"[52] Conversely, some moderate and conservative policymakers viewed Social Security financing as fiscally responsible and anti-inflationary. Ways and Means Chairman Wilbur Mills reasoned that payroll taxes would restrict future benefit hikes more so than general revenue financing, because policymakers would be able to clearly see where program costs outran earmarked funds.[53]

Finally, policymakers debated the extent to which insurance companies should participate in an elderly benefits program. Reformers seeking nationalized insurance wished to exclude private sector involvement and solely empower the federal government. However, by the end of the 1950s, they recognized that they had lost the race that pit government capacity against voluntary sector development. In the preceding decade, insurance companies had rapidly constructed the institutions necessary to finance insurance and to interact with service providers. Policymakers were consequently forced to consider how to employ insurers' expertise and organizational capabilities to deliver federal benefits. Moreover, by proposing to use insurance companies as program administrators, advocates could portray government-funded medical benefits as a modest addition to existing arrangements. Influential Social Security expert Wilbur Cohen advised fellow reformers that partnering with insurance companies would create a politically palatable program: "If we are going to make any headway in the hospitalization or medical field, I think we have to reluctantly admit that the only way we can get it is by accepting 'contracting out.'" He emphasized that the swift growth of private insurance had painted reformers into a corner: "Each month that goes by the voluntary plans expand and proliferate."[54] Ideology, nevertheless, shaped how legislators envisioned using the private sector. Republicans preferred either providing beneficiaries with subsidies to purchase their own coverage or granting federal resources to state-run programs for the purposes of buying insurance. Democrats favored using insurance companies to help officials administer a more centralized and regulated program.

Additionally, many liberal policymakers and labor leaders wished to exclude commercial firms and engage only nonprofit plans. Because they purportedly operated "in the public interest," Blue Cross and Blue Shield (though less so given its AMA affiliation) appealed to reformers. Indeed, the Forand bill proposed exclusive reliance on nonprofit plans to administer benefits.

Against this backdrop, Eisenhower proffered an elderly benefits program that managed to alienate both liberal and conservative policymakers. The president settled on a plan of federal subsidies, financed through general revenues, to match state funds for the purchase of private insurance for seniors with low to moderate incomes.[55] Although the program would have applied means testing, officials forecast that approximately 75 percent of elderly citizens would qualify for coverage. Beneficiaries would pay a small annual fee and a $250 deductible, after which insurance would cover 80 percent of all hospital, medical, and nursing home fees.[56] Liberal policymakers criticized the general revenue financing and means testing portions of the bill; however, a congressional Democrat observed that the generous benefits package made the Forand proposal "look like a piker."[57] Conservative Republicans and organized physicians opposed the legislation because of its expensive, liberal benefits and its objective of covering most senior citizens.[58] Meanwhile, commercial insurers worried that Eisenhower's plan "would in all likelihood lead eventually to a thoroughly undesirable system of complete, compulsory Federal health insurance."[59]

Senator Jacob Javits (R, NY) announced an additional alternative to the Forand bill. Despite being asked to shelve his plan to give the president's measure the full media spotlight, Javits forged ahead, leading a group of liberal Republicans, including Senators John Sherman Cooper (R, KY) and Hugh Scott (R, PA), to recommend state-administered exchanges financed through federal general revenues. Under the plan, senior citizens would choose either first-dollar coverage or catastrophic coverage from among numerous voluntary insurance policies. Premium prices would be scaled to the beneficiary's income.[60] Javits hoped to secure support from the large insurance companies domiciled in his home state of New York. However, insurers believed the proposed system would pave a broad avenue for reformers seeking to expand government-funded coverage to citizens under age 65.[61] They labeled the program "an administrative monstrosity" that would likely place their companies under federal control while resulting "principally in supplementing the Blues."[62] AMA leaders also assailed the legislation.

Republican gadfly and New York Governor Nelson Rockefeller joined with Representative John Lindsay (R, NY) to submit yet another proposition. Having recently dropped out of the presidential primaries, Rockefeller criticized the party's soon-to-be nominee, Richard Nixon, for promoting Eisenhower's "fiscally unsound" program.[63] Rockefeller-Lindsay legislation would have granted Social Security recipients a choice between either a government-administered plan or higher cash benefits to purchase private insurance.[64] AMA and insurance leaders worried that the suggested government plans would usher federal officials deep into the voluntary sector where they would begin regulating policy benefits and prices.[65] On the other side of the ideological divide, policymakers criticized the Rockefeller blueprint for failing to give the SSA sufficient control.[66] The proposal nonetheless made an impact; as he sought publicity for his idea, Rockefeller convinced thirty of his forty-three peers at the 1960 National Conference of Governors to vote in favor of aged medical benefits financed through Social Security. Once again, the press reported that a group of influential policymakers had endorsed government-funded elderly health care.[67]

The Republicans' inability to unite around a single program (and failure to win the 1960 presidential and congressional elections) weakened their bargaining position. Nevertheless, the parade of leading Republicans putting forth aged insurance proposals helped accustom voters to the idea of such a program and undercut physicians and insurers who claimed that the voluntary sector could adequately supply elderly coverage. Additionally, the Republican preference for maximizing the role of insurance companies reinforced the idea among Democrats that their plan had to accommodate the market's prevailing framework.

1960 SHOWDOWN

The dramatic 1960 congressional session featured numerous aged insurance proposals, presidential campaign debates, and two legislative chambers filled with politicians ready to declare their stand on the most important domestic issue of the day. Neither the Forand bill nor the Eisenhower plan gained passage through the fiscally conservative House Ways and Means Committee. After exploring alternative measures and finding that they had little backing, Chairman Mills joined with Senator Robert S. Kerr (D, OK) to put forth a scaled-down proposal. Kerr-Mills legislation pledged federal general revenues to create Medical Assistance for the Aged, a system of state programs that would supply the elderly poor with health services. Depending on the state's per capita income, the federal government would provide between 50 and 80 percent of program funding. The bill won Ways and Means approval and easily passed the House, 381–23.[68]

The legislation traveled to the Senate where both presidential candidates took up the issue as vital to advancing their electoral fortunes. Vice President Nixon endorsed the Javits bill while Senator John F. Kennedy promoted the Kennedy-Anderson Amendment (subsequently renamed King-Anderson). Contending that the Kerr-Mills program "simply does not go far enough," Kennedy tasked his vice presidential running mate, Majority Leader Lyndon B. Johnson, with rounding up votes in support of hospitalization insurance for all Social Security beneficiaries over age 68.[69] Both proposals were voted down, largely along party lines, with some conservative Democrats joining Republicans to defeat the Kennedy-Anderson initiative.[70]

Senators then passed Kerr-Mills by a vote of 91–2. The legislation sailed through because it proposed public benefits for the most vulnerable citizens – the elderly poor – and had both Democratic sponsorship and President Eisenhower's blessing. AMA and HIAA leaders had traditionally opposed federally subsidized health care, preferring that medical charity be funded and managed locally. However, the associations endorsed Kerr-Mills, both for public relations reasons and in the hopes of thwarting more substantial reform.[71]

Almost immediately after the passage of Kerr-Mills, politicians began attacking the program's deficiencies. On the campaign trail, both presidential contenders disparaged its limited reach while plugging their favored measure.[72] Kennedy and Nixon disagreed over the issues of Social Security financing and compulsory participation, yet their concurrence about the need for additional reform led the *New York Times* to report that "on most issues concerning health the two Presidential candidates agree."[73]

KING-ANDERSON: A "MIDDLE-OF-THE-ROAD" APPROACH

After Kennedy won the election, the King-Anderson bill, which the media labeled "Medicare," became his administration's preferred legislative vehicle for aged insurance reform. Liberal lawmakers, health care activists, and union officials supported the initiative because it proposed compulsory, non–means-tested benefits and Social Security financing. Reform advocates believed these characteristics would allow them to make the program into a stepping stone toward nationalized, universal health insurance. Nevertheless, policymakers carefully tailored King-Anderson so they could market it as politically moderate. To tamp down resistance from doctors, King-Anderson omitted the surgical benefits contained in the Forand bill, thus excluding all physician services and limiting coverage to hospital and nursing home care.[74] Most important, the legislation proposed using the existing, culturally recognizable organizations and processes that composed the insurance company model.

Administration officials and their allies promoted Medicare as a "middle-of-the road" solution to the problem of elderly health insurance.[75] Swinging fiercely at conservative criticism that they desired "socialized medicine," reformers retorted that such a system would entail government ownership of hospitals and government employment of physicians. They emphasized that their program, though managed by the SSA, would rest upon existing institutions. An oft-repeated point of Medicare advocates was that program participants would be able to choose their own doctor and hospital and continue interacting with the medical system in the manner to which they had grown accustomed.[76] Wilbur Cohen, now President Kennedy's assistant secretary of HEW and the primary overseer of Medicare's legislative content, masterfully sold the plan as ideologically temperate:

I am absolutely opposed to socialized medicine. ... There are, however, many people who sincerely believe that any form of governmental program for the financing of medical care is a form of socialized medicine. If you accept this definition then the Kerr-Mills program (including means-tested medical care for the elderly) is a form of socialized medicine and since the American Medical Association supports the Kerr-Mills program the conclusion must be that the AMA is in favor of socialized medicine.[77]

Administration officials also stressed that their measure used the "very conservative approach" of Social Security financing, which afforded beneficiaries coverage only after years of payroll contributions.[78]

This messaging appealed to middle-class voters. Many adults who cared for elderly parents welcomed the prospect of government aid to offset medical costs. King-Anderson proponents contended that, rather than paying medical bills for grandparents, families should be able to set aside money for their children's education.[79] Moreover, because administration officials went to such lengths to highlight the moderate nature of their program, consumers who favored Medicare did so without worrying that their own insurance or health care arrangements would be modified. "Private health insurance has made notable advances in recent years," President Kennedy stated, assuring voters that he embraced the prevailing system. He continued, maintaining that he merely wished to bring an additional group into the fold: "But older people, who need it most but can afford it least, are still unable to pay the high premiums."[80]

Leaders of Golden Ring Clubs and Senior Citizens' Councils, which evolved out of "Seniors for Kennedy" groups, often with financial assistance and guidance from unions or the Democratic Party, argued that they sought a politically mainstream program of earned benefits for deserving citizens. As representatives, or at least the declared representatives, of 17 million elderly voters – approximately 20 percent of the electorate – senior citizen groups captured the attention of politicians. Locally based clubs and councils held rallies, organized voter registration drives, distributed leaflets, conducted letter-writing campaigns, and sent members door to door during election seasons to convince citizens to vote for pro-Medicare politicians.[81] Aged activists underscored the politically moderate nature of King-Anderson when they charged hypocrisy among physicians who fought the legislation while accepting government funding for scientific research and medical school construction: "they apparently contend federal assistance is OK for doctors but a program that would help the aged pay their own doctor bills is bad for their patients."[82] Elderly crusaders also played to voter sympathies by depicting the pitiable position of senior citizens who, after decades of laboring in the workforce, had to submit to humiliating means tests in order to obtain medical care under Kerr-Mills provisions.[83] At rallies and meetings, they hung banners declaring, "Care with Dignity, Not Charity" and "We Want Dignity, Not Paupers' Oaths."[84]

By selling King-Anderson as a modest reform devised to protect needy, worthy citizens, the administration attracted broad public support. While polling data varied depending on the wording and specificity of the questioning, a majority of voters consistently favored Medicare-type legislation.[85] Even portions of the traditionally conservative business community sanctioned the plan. In 1960, *Business Week* endorsed Medicare while some local chambers of commerce split from the national organization to back the proposal.[86] Important Republican leaders also applauded King-Anderson. Arthur S. Flemming praised the program. Arthur Larson, who held various posts under Eisenhower and was widely viewed as the chief theoretician behind moderate Republicanism, advocated Medicare. Former HEW Secretary Marion Folsom dubbed the bill a "logical plan."[87] Other moderate Republicans withheld approval only because they preferred alternative legislation, particularly the Javits proposal.[88] Perhaps most stunning was the position of former AMA leader and staunch conservative Morris Fishbein. Explaining his support for Medicare, he stated that "[w]hen conditions become so severe [that] they can no longer be handled by private initiative, the Government must step in."[89]

Reformers sold Medicare as far removed from anything resembling government-managed medicine by configuring proposed arrangements around the insurance company model – beneficiaries would receive care from service providers who, on the back end, would follow customary procedures when they engaged with insurance companies operating as program administrators. Pro-Medicare policymakers also maximized the legislation's appeal by targeting a group frequently portrayed as both frail and deserving. This savvy promotional strategy put the AMA on the defensive, convinced HIAA leaders to remain relatively quiet, and persuaded Blue Cross to join the campaign for reform.

THE AMA'S WAR ON MEDICARE

Because most voters and policymakers viewed King-Anderson as an ideologically temperate way to assist senior citizens, the AMA's all-out war against the measure made doctors appear politically oblivious and detached from critical societal concerns. Liberal policymakers perceived the tactical error and moved in with a blistering defamation campaign that ensured the association's political defeat. As they continued advancing their anti-reform message, AMA leaders alienated the members on whom they depended for political strength and diminished the cultural standing that organized physicians had once derived from their image as knowledgeable, compassionate caregivers.

Recognizing that their opposition to Medicare would generate negative publicity, AMA leaders made overt demonstrations of concern for the elderly, for example, by spotlighting an eight-point program to improve conditions for aged citizens. This effort backfired. Although AMA recommendations acknowledged that seniors not classified as "poor" but lacking resources for medical care should receive public benefits, elements of the program calling for better-coordinated welfare assistance, nutritional education, and an end to compulsory retirement at age sixty-five failed to convince observers that doctors were prepared to address the grave problems facing aged citizens.[90] Nor did promoting Kerr-Mills programming help physicians appear sympathetic toward the elderly. By 1963, only thirty-two states had Kerr-Mills plans.[91]

And Medicare supporters warned seniors that Kerr-Mills benefits would only begin once they were destitute and prepared to submit to a means test. Addressing a union-organized political rally, Senator McNamara declared, "If we follow the advice of the AMA, then each senior citizen will become a bum! ... Every one of you will have to apply to welfare organizations and line up for charity doles." Critics also disparaged Kerr-Mills benefits, citing, as an illustration, one state that allotted the elderly indigent only ten days of hospital coverage a year.[92]

Rising medical costs also undermined AMA arguments. Physician leaders frequently asserted that 90 percent of elderly citizens would have health insurance by 1970.[93] However, widely publicized data on sky-rocketing insurance premiums and average senior citizen incomes contradicted their claim. The usual AMA gambits – establishing commissions, conducting research, releasing studies, and holding conferences about health care costs – did little to render insurance less expensive for high-risk elderly subscribers who purchased coverage individually and typically without employer contributions. Indeed, AMA officials came across as aloof and unconcerned about high insurance costs when they appeared in a CBS documentary titled "The Business of Health, Medicine, Money and Politics." Their case against government intervention in medicine failed to explain how seniors could access affordable health care.[94]

The AMA's combative style also cast organized physicians in a negative light. In 1961, AMA delegates threw down the gauntlet when they passed a resolution stating that organized physicians "will not be a willing party to implementing any system which we believe to be detrimental to the public welfare."[95] Some of this resistance stemmed from doctors who sought to defend what they believed were free market arrangements (though, as we have seen, they were not). However, some of the vitriol came from southern delegates determined to preserve hospital segregation and deny admitting privileges to black physicians.[96] Whatever the motivation, to many observers, the threat to violate the law over a program of elderly hospital benefits seemed extreme.

AMA leaders lost further credibility when they trotted out the familiar indictment of "socialized medicine." "Socialism can be garbed in the raiment of angels, but it is materialistic and evil in concept," proclaimed Blasingame.[97] However, with policymakers promoting King-Anderson as ideologically moderate, AMA rhetoric sounded inflated and melodramatic to many voters. *Good Housekeeping* gave the charge its seal of disapproval, publishing an article titled "Care for the Aged ... and This Nonsense about Socialized Medicine."[98] Several New York radio stations canceled advertising contracts with medical societies after spots characterizing Medicare as "socialized medicine" elicited listener complaints.[99] Cohen explained that the AMA's "socialism" charge played into the hands of reform advocates: "Crying 'Wolf! Wolf!' when there is no wolf is always a mistake."[100]

Nevertheless, organized doctors forged ahead with their Truman-era playbook, deploying vast resources to defeat Medicare. The AMA printed millions of pamphlets warning citizens about the dangers of King-Anderson, ran copious radio and TV announcements, and created a seventy-man speakers bureau to deliver talks to business groups and civic associations. The Woman's Auxiliary, composed primarily of doctors' wives, directed "Operation Coffee Cup" – members hosted small gatherings where they played recorded speeches, including *Ronald Reagan Speaks Out against Socialized Medicine*, and urged those in attendance to write their congressmen.[101] In 1961, partially in reaction to the AFL-CIO's formation of the Committee on Political Education (COPE), AMA leaders added a new page to their script by creating a political action committee, which allowed them to give campaign contributions to politicians. The American Medical Political Action Committee (AMPAC) solicited financial donations from individual doctors and businesses, but the bulk of its funding came from the AMA.[102]

Vast financial assets and a large organization scored an occasional AMA victory. In 1962, President Kennedy stumped for Medicare in New York's Madison Square Garden. On all three major networks, the president delivered extemporaneous, rambling remarks in what has been described as the worst performance of his career. Denied television time to rebut the president, the AMA rented the Garden the following night so that Dr. Edward Annis could appear in a paid spot on one network. A surgeon from Florida, Annis began his rise to prominence as a member of the AMA's speakers bureau. Through high-profile debates with labor leaders and Senator Hubert Humphrey (D, MN), he had acquired a reputation as an excellent orator with ultra-conservative principles. Dramatizing the fact that physicians lacked the president's star power – thus casting the AMA as David and pro-Medicare forces as Goliath – Annis's televised speech showed him addressing an empty stadium. The event won an enormous viewership and favorable publicity. The ascension of Annis to the AMA's presidency the following year signaled the association's enduring hard-line resistance to Medicare.[103]

Despite intermittent physician triumphs, champions of Medicare effectively portrayed the AMA as a backward-looking organization.

Abetting the efforts of Medicare proponents was the AMA's penchant for vociferous politicking, which had recently included the obstruction of both federal disability benefits and medical aid to servicemen. COPE distributed a pamphlet detailing past AMA positions, including the association's opposition to the Social Security Act and to free tuberculosis and cancer diagnostic centers, as well as its 1930s characterization of voluntary insurance as 'socialism, communism-inciting to revolution.' AMA leaders published a refutation, but sensing that they had hit a nerve, labor leaders dug in.[104] During a televised debate between Dr. Annis and Walter Reuther, the labor leader compared the AMA's prior stance against insurance to the contemporary Medicare battle: "you will think this one through, and a few years later you will be down the road on our side of this issue just as you were on the Blue Cross."[105]

The "campaign of vilification" extended beyond Medicare as critics sought to depict organized physicians as more concerned with pecuniary matters than with health care.[106] Opponents publicized the AMA's receipt of $10 million in research funds from the tobacco industry.[107] Although the association was preparing a leaflet to warn patients about the dangers of smoking, AMA leaders' refusal to support federal tobacco regulation all but placed a target on their backs and asked adversaries to fire. Similarly, detractors charged that in order to maintain high physician salaries, the AMA was restricting the supply of practitioners through its medical school credentialing activities.[108]

Reformers reaped considerable success in their attempt to represent organized physicians as villains who, for financial reasons, opposed compassionate, sensible reforms to assist the elderly. Observing how the Medicare crusade had damaged the profession's public image, an Illinois medical society official remarked that the "idea has developed that doctors are not really interested in the welfare of the people."[109] Indeed, a survey conducted by the Opinion Research Corporation found that a majority of respondents held unfavorable views about the AMA.[110]

The polemical atmosphere drained the AMA's political and organizing strength. Medicare battles required national goal setting backed by enthusiastic grassroots implementation. Under "Operation Hometown," association leaders directed constituent medical societies to appoint publicity chairmen, set up speakers bureaus, conduct congressional letter-writing campaigns, and create committees to coordinate political events with AMPAC and national AMA officials. Medical societies were also instructed to join with local industry groups, chambers of commerce, and civic associations to organize anti-Medicare operations.[111]

However, medical society leaders often had difficulty uniting and motivating members to carry out these activities.

Younger doctors, academics, salaried physicians working in hospitals, and ideologically moderate or left-leaning practitioners generally did not identify Medicare as a threat to their autonomy or livelihood.[112] Few doctors relished the prospect of telling their elderly patients that they opposed Medicare or of facing a backlash from locally organized Senior Citizens' Councils, some of which had begun picketing medical society meetings. Moreover, doctors recognized that a federal program could aid them monetarily. Most physicians gave seniors charity care and many accepted reduced payments from Blue Shield in order to prop up their aged insurance programs. As SSA Commissioner Robert Ball explained in a *New England Journal of Medicine* article, if the government financed elderly hospital care, then seniors would have more funds available to pay the physician's bill.[113]

As during the Truman debates, outside physician groups challenged the AMA's political position; this time they were more numerous and attracted more doctors. The Physicians' Committee for Health Care for the Aged through Social Security recruited nationally renowned doctors, such as pediatrician Benjamin Spock and heart surgeon Michael DeBakey.[114] A Physicians' Committee representative appeared before the AMA's House of Delegates to argue that King-Anderson was a "constructive, conservative approach" to meeting senior health care needs. When delegates responded with an eruption of verbal outbursts, organized doctors once again appeared unreasonable.[115] At the local level, physicians, including some AMA members, organized pro-Medicare groups. Even medical society officials betrayed the national leadership – from Atlanta to Los Angeles, they griped to the press. One complained that the AMA "is always against something."[116]

Rank-and-file discontent obliged the leadership to continually urge member fealty to the AMA's political platform. For example, at a 1961 legislative conference, AMA President E. Vincent Askey entreated members to "get on this nationwide team that we call the American Medical Association."[117] AMA leaders had four additional years of political battles remaining; yet already they had to enter the trenches and plead with soldiers not to desert. "Apathy," Blasingame later observed, "is the Society's [AMA's] major problem."[118]

The AMA's organizational structure exacerbated its troubles. Division of authority between the Board of Trustees and House of Delegates hindered the association's capacity to formulate the clear month-to-month strategies needed to rally the troops. One insider complained that although the board largely controlled political policy, trustees were "not ... in close contact with the House of Delegates nor the men at the 'grass roots.'"[119] Moreover, AMA field service staff sometimes clashed with AMPAC officials over appropriate political tactics, thus confusing medical society leaders. Compounding these organizational problems, federal lobbying fell under the province of Blasingame and his increasingly powerful assistant, Bert Howard, but AMPAC officials controlled campaign contributions. When the two factions failed to agree about whether a particular politician was a friend, potential friend, or foe, they bewildered policymakers and AMA members alike.[120] In 1964, an internal AMA report disclosed that communications between headquarters and constituent medical societies were strained.[121] As Medicare debates wore on, national leaders progressively lost the ability to rouse members into political action.

After having done so little to help generate inexpensive, widely available health care, the AMA's attacks against Medicare seemed hollow. As one commentator put it, they were "willing to take large credit for the population's increased longevity," but were less willing to take "responsibility for developing those programs needed to deal with the consequences of medical progress."[122] Left wondering what they were fighting for, many rank-and-file doctors laid down their weapons and refused to fight the bloody battle against public opinion. As the discord surrounding physicians intensified, commercial insurers increasingly questioned their political allegiance to the AMA.

THE HIAA WALKS THE LINE

After Kennedy was elected, commercial insurers continued duking it out behind the scenes to determine the HIAA's political strategy. On one side were conservative, hawkish, launch-a-massive-campaign, join-the-AMA leaders. On the other side were ideologically moderate executives, mostly from large northeastern companies, who wished to protect the industry's political reputation as well as corporate profits by supporting a limited government program of aged coverage. Insurers' customary political caution dictated a compromise. As with the Forand measure, HIAA officials adopted an approach of quiet resistance. Ultimately, they spent most of their time dodging the exchange of fire between pro-Medicare groups and the AMA.

Administration officials astutely played upon industry division and uncertainty. In 1960, Cohen took to the pages of the *Journal of*

Insurance to warn executives that fighting Medicare could invite political retaliation in the form of federal regulation of their industry.[123] However, as policymakers attempted to neutralize commercial insurers politically, they did so primarily by dangling monetary prizes before them. HEW and SSA representatives emphasized that King-Anderson offered insurance companies an escape from the financially hazardous market of elderly hospital coverage.[124] There was simply "no way for profit-making organizations to cover the high risk aged group without charging premiums that the vast majority of the aged cannot afford," stated HEW Undersecretary Ivan Nestingen.[125] Repeating a common theme of administration officials, Nestingen maintained that just as life insurers had profited by selling pension plans to augment Social Security benefits, Medicare would allow insurers to sell lucrative supplementary products: "Once the program is underway I predict that the private health insurance industry will blossom with new life in responding to its responsibilities and new opportunities, for we have learned that social and private insurance are complementary, rather than competitive."[126] Such contentions incited debates among insurers and provided ammunition for executives who preferred to work with policymakers in order to secure legislation that benefited industry interests.

Nonetheless, despite its potential advantages, King-Anderson simply presented too many risks to elicit an official endorsement from commercial insurers. Pro-Medicare forces might have tipped industry leaders toward support if they could have convinced them that the program would not be expanded. Insurers, moreover, worried about arrangements that would entangle their companies in complex webs of public and private authority, including federal rather than state regulation. And, as with every reform proposal they had battled, commercial insurers assumed the measure would benefit their nonprofit competitors.[127] Besides these business concerns, insurers ultimately determined that "there was nothing to be gained politically by a reversal of position."[128] AMA leaders would be livid if the HIAA abandoned them in the heat of battle.[129] "The conservative views of the life insurance business are well known," reasoned one executive, "and the espousal of any other philosophy would not be understood by our friends."[130] As representatives of large corporations and traditional allies of the AMA, Chamber of Commerce, and National Association of Manufacturers, HIAA officials believed that liberal policymakers would distrust them even if they did decide to back King-Anderson. Indeed, advocating Medicare, would put them in "danger of being shot at by both sides."[131]

After working through these issues with representatives of the life insurance industry, HIAA leaders settled into a position of formal, though timid, disapproval of Medicare. Insurers met with HEW and SSA officials to express their concerns and testified against King-Anderson during congressional hearings. However, to avoid political rigidity, association leaders directed Washington lobbyists not to operate "as though the only question was one of favoring or opposing Forand-type proposals."[132] They also restricted the scope of their criticism, primarily challenging Medicare on the grounds that administration officials were promulgating erroneous actuarial forecasts and that the program that would ultimately bankrupt the Social Security fund.[133] Presenting a narrow case limited to their field of expertise allowed HIAA leaders to play upon the apprehensions of fiscally conservative congressional members while sidestepping ideological arguments.

Insurers also refused to align their industry closely with one party.[134] The sole attempt of HIAA leaders to advance a legislative compromise demonstrates why. Insurers lobbied policymakers to grant the children of elderly citizens a tax deduction for assisting their parents with medical bills, including insurance premiums.[135] However, after the Republican National Committee picked up the suggestion, labeled it the Bow bill after Representative Frank Bow (R, OH), and began advertising it as preferable to President Kennedy's plan, HIAA leaders withdrew their support. Under the Republican proposal, citizens would receive either a tax credit or a voucher to purchase insurance.[136] Industry executives believed that vouchers would encourage politicians to eventually begin regulating insurance benefits and premium prices. Moreover, if Republicans claimed that insurers sanctioned their legislative alternative, the industry would likely draw negative publicity and potentially attract political retribution from liberal policymakers.[137]

Insurers assiduously steered clear of political controversy. The HIAA's principal lobbyist, Robert Neal, maintained contact with AMA General Manager Francis Blasingame to chart their associations' legislative positioning. But before public eyes, insurance leaders eschewed close affiliation with the overexposed AMA.[138] Insurers recognized that if physicians were sustaining heavy reputational losses for their assault against Medicare, then profitmaking, "big-business" groups would only fare worse. Most HIAA political materials avoided mentioning Medicare and instead attempted to create "a favorable attitude towards the health insurance business." Advertisements in *Look* and *Newsweek* emphasized the wide variety of insurance plans available for families and individuals, including the elderly.[139] The furthest the HIAA went in publicly opposing Medicare was a pamphlet titled "The King-Anderson Bill and What You Should Know about It." In comparison with Republican leaflets charging that reformers wanted to control doctors and hospitals, and AMA literature, which screamed "socialism," the HIAA missive struck a temperate tone. It listed the legislation's proposed benefits, costs, and tax increases. After briefly asserting that tax hikes would fail to cover program costs, the pamphlet quickly returned to positive messaging, touting Kerr-Mills assistance and State 65 plans.[140]

Because most politicians had little to gain from publicly identifying with "powerful corporate interests," HIAA officials decided against applying political pressure from within D.C. Instead, they continued operating on the principle that lobbying "can most effectively be undertaken by individual companies," the representatives of which could approach congressmen as job suppliers in their districts and as voters and campaign contributors.[141] HIAA leaders asked company officers to detail sums donated to their congressman, when they last spoke with him, and what political activities had been coordinated with local chambers of commerce and business groups. At key points during the Medicare debates, HIAA state legislative chairmen requested that company employees write their congressmen.[142] Discouraging inflammatory tactics, HIAA officials reminded company directors that "the rabble-rousing type of letter is nowhere near as effective as the plain folksy type of letter."[143]

Notwithstanding this cautious, carefully calculated resistance to Medicare, some insurers continued pressing for industry cooperation with federal officials. Exemplifying insurance executives receptive to King-Anderson was Orville F. Grahame, a politically moderate northeastern Republican. While representing the HIAA at a legislative meeting with LIAA and ALC officials, Grahame, Vice President of the Massachusetts-based Paul Revere Life Insurance Company, reminded his colleagues that they "were not a meeting of the John Birch Society" and "could not solve" their "problems by shouting in the rain spout."[144] Reinhard Hohaus, the executive vice president of Metropolitan Life Insurance Company, was another prominent, ideologically moderate insurer who served on several Social Security advisory boards. Hohaus advocated a Medicare compromise and championed Social Security funding as fiscally conservative.[145]

Revealing the fragility of the industry's Medicare opposition, some executives openly broke with the HIAA. Representatives of Nationwide Insurance testified before Congress in favor of King-Anderson. Murray

Lincoln of Nationwide told congressmen that private insurance could never adequately cover the elderly population.[146] Before an annual HIAA meeting, General American Life Insurance President Frederic M. Pierce argued that Medicare would enhance company profitmaking.[147] Similarly, the medical director of Continental Casualty pitched the program on the basis of industry prospects for selling supplementary coverage to beneficiaries:

> Back in 1935 many insurance firms predicted that if the social security program were enacted nobody would bother to buy life insurance as a financial hedge for their old age. But they were dead wrong and life insurance sales have soared to new highs. … Similarly, I think that if the President's health care of the aged bill is enacted, private companies will sell more health insurance than ever before.[148]

Well before Medicare's creation, large insurance companies began planning to market policies that seniors could purchase to shield them from program coverage gaps.[149]

After years of joining with the AMA to battle all federal health care reforms, no matter how minor the initiative, the public relations and monetary costs of that tack finally proved too high for commercial leaders. Although the HIAA formally contested Medicare, tepid campaigning and internal industry divisions that spilled out onto the political stage did little to deter the program's legislative course. Significantly, by avoiding intense political combat, insurers gave policymakers sufficient breathing room to consider appointing not only nonprofit plans but also commercial companies as Medicare administrators.

BLUE CROSS AND BLUE SHIELD PART WAYS

Approximately one year into the Kennedy administration, both the BCA and AHA were ready to support aged medical benefits financed through Social Security. This advocacy was vital as Blue Cross leaders provided the expertise policymakers needed to hammer out the details of what would be the most formalized feature of the health care system's soft corporatist arrangements. Meanwhile, the NABSP maintained its political affiliation with the AMA and officially, although halfheartedly, opposed Medicare.

As soon as Forand tendered his legislative proposal, influential Blue Cross leaders began urging the BCA to join the growing political consensus in favor of federally financed elderly benefits. The president of Colorado Blue Cross, Thomas Tierney, made this case before a 1959 meeting of his colleagues:

Mr. Eisenhower is now for it. Mr. Nixon is now for it. Mr. Kennedy is now for it. I don't know anybody in government who is against it, and I don't see how the nation's largest single health prepayment agency can quietly sit here and pretend no problem exists. ... We can't evade this issue.[150]

Revenue considerations figured prominently. BCA officials feared that challenging Medicare would threaten relations with labor unions and place some large nonprofit group accounts in jeopardy. Moreover, by the early 1960s, Blue Cross plans were reaping a financial windfall from participation in the Federal Employees Health Benefits Program.[151] This boon, when weighed with Medicare's promised reprieve from underwriting costly aged subscribers, caused many plan leaders to look toward Medicare expectantly.

At their 1961 annual meeting, the BCA's Executive Committee triggered heated debates when they placed a pro-King-Anderson resolution before plan representatives. Conservative plan leaders, who predominantly hailed from the South and Midwest, had long expressed discomfort with BCA lobbying efforts on behalf of federal funding for state insurance programs.[152] King-Anderson went even further by enshrining authority in Washington and in the SSA, where officials steadfastly sought national health insurance.[153] Reacting to arguments that Medicare was inevitable and that Blue Cross should maneuver to benefit as much as possible from the program, Harold Maybee, director of the Delaware plan, stated he was "disturbed": it "seems to me we are more intent on taking the position that will assure all of us of jobs when the United States takes over."[154]

Tipping the scales in favor of support for Medicare was newly hired BCA President Walter J. McNerney, who, though only thirty-five, was already a star in the hospital field. McNerney had run a University of Pittsburgh hospital before moving to the University of Michigan, where he founded the Program in Hospital Administration. In 1957, the professor won admiring national press for his comprehensive, nearly fifteen hundred–page study of Michigan Blue Cross and Blue Shield. An outspoken, affable glad-hander, McNerney convinced plan leaders to follow his straightforward Medicare strategy: since a program of aged medical benefits was unavoidable, nonprofits would negotiate with federal officials to obtain a lucrative administrative role.[155] "I see the government as being the best vehicle for establishing public goals," explained McNerney. "On the other side of it I think that the private sector ... can with the proper stimulus, do a better job of implementation."[156]

By 1962, a majority of plan representatives were ready to advance McNerney's vision. The BCA and AHA adopted joint resolutions endorsing King-Anderson. The resolutions called for Medicare to provide an administrative function for nonprofits, service benefits instead of cash payments (thereby cutting out commercial insurers), and freedom for Blue Cross plans to operate without government interference. The associations declined to comment on Social Security financing.[157]

BCA leaders immediately and aggressively began bartering for their legislative preferences. Because they had stepped out ahead of other private interests to back King-Anderson, Blue Cross and AHA leaders argued that government officials should "employ our facilities, our hospital agreements, our existing procedures, and our experience in the administration of any program which evolves."[158] By 1964, Congressman Mills and SSA officials were determined to establish Blue Cross as Medicare's sole program administrator.[159] They wanted to reward Blue Cross for publicly promoting Medicare, and, as we have seen, policymakers, from liberal to moderate, had long played favorites with nonprofits. According to Social Security Commissioner Robert Ball, "the public service orientation ... of many Blue Cross plans is generally lacking among commercial insurance carriers."[160] Furthermore, labor leaders pressured policymakers to bar commercial companies from administrative positions that would allow them to augment their "exorbitant profits" with government funding.[161] Though nonprofits would ultimately capture an overwhelming majority of the program's benefits administration, they were unable to hold onto the promised monopoly. Nevertheless, in exchange for this sought-after prize, Blue Cross representatives spent days, probably weeks, helping officials write legislation – their expertise was essential for crafting a Medicare program that was consistent with the insurance company model. BCA representatives helped policymakers shape legislative sections governing qualified service providers, participation contracts, reimbursement formulas, and utilization review procedures.[162]

Meanwhile, to toe the AMA's mark, Blue Shield leaders distanced themselves from Blue Cross political activities.[163] Yet the significance of this division was more apparent than real. Blue Shield only covered physician services, and throughout most of the debates, policymakers planned to restrict Medicare to hospital insurance. Moreover, many NABSP officials, including President John Castellucci, as well as some local plan leaders privately supported federally funded elderly benefits.[164] NABSP leaders therefore confined their official Medicare dissent to congressional testimony and occasional position pamphlets and protest letters, doing just enough to avoid enraging AMA leaders.

In the end, BCA leaders leveraged their support for Medicare to capture major administrative roles for nonprofit insurers, which would include Blue Shield plans once policymakers decided to expand the program to include physician services. On paper, Blue Shield leaders maintained their political pact with the AMA. However, behind doctors' backs, prominent Blue Shield officials winked and nodded at their nonprofit brethren, signaling their sympathy with the Blue Cross vision for federal directives and resources flowing through insurance plans into the health care system.

CONGRESSIONAL BATTLES AND THE MAKING OF MEDICARE

Medicare legislation endured many skirmishes before becoming law in 1965, yet the long delay did not occur because of overwhelming political opposition. Although some conservative policymakers continued to promote Kerr-Mills, many Republicans recognized its growing unpopularity and sought a more substantial aged insurance program. The almost eight-year distance between the Forand bill and Medicare's passage reflected both partisan efforts to score credit with voters and an ideological rift over the ability of future policymakers to expand benefits to additional segments of the population. Ultimately, the Democratic Party's 1964 electoral sweep allowed health care reformers to create their desired program, at least within the boundaries of the insurance company model. Private interest groups – the AMA, HIAA, BCA, and NABSP – were left scrambling to carve out positions that allowed their members to pursue revenues under the fewest federal requirements possible.

In 1962, President Kennedy helped reignite the drive for Medicare. When the Ways and Means Committee once again failed to vote King-Anderson through, Senators Javits and Clinton Anderson (D, NM) attempted to snatch the initiative out from under Chairman Mills by attaching a bipartisan amendment to a House-passed bill on welfare. The measure proposed financing benefits through Social Security but would have allowed seniors to opt out of government-administered benefits to purchase private insurance with federal vouchers. By a narrow vote of 52 to 48, the Senate tabled the amendment. Minutes later, President Kennedy appeared before news cameras to denounce the vote and pledge his determination to create a comprehensive program of aged medical benefits.[165]

Kennedy's support for Medicare became a powerful legacy when an assassin's bullet felled the young president in 1963. Indeed, Ways and Means Committee members received the news of Kennedy's death during hearings on King-Anderson. After a period of national mourning, many Americans turned their attention to honoring Kennedy by fulfilling his major policy goals. Partly for this reason and partly because voters, like policy-makers, were reaching a consensus about the inability of the private market to satisfactorily insure seniors, a 1964 opinion poll showed that almost two-thirds of the electorate not only favored elderly medical benefits but also supported an increase in Social Security taxes to finance the program.[166]

In 1964, Javits and a bipartisan group of senators advanced yet another compromise measure. Under the proposed amendment, aged citizens could elect either federal hospitalization benefits or increased Social Security payments for the purposes of buying insurance. To help them attract additional Republican support for the legislation, Javits and SSA officials courted commercial insurers. However, industry leaders remained resistant to any plan that would enmesh their companies in a network of governmental authority. Most executives amenable to reform preferred King-Anderson because the bill provided only hospital benefits and the administrative function could be left to Blue Cross.[167] Neverthe-less, the Javits proposal passed the Senate 49–44. Blasting the fiscal irresponsibility of the program and irritated that the legislation did not originate within his committee, Mills assembled the votes to torpedo the measure during the House-Senate conference.[168] Mills now understood that if he hoped to retain control of Medicare legislation, he would have to move quickly.

The Democrats' decisive 1964 electoral triumph, which won them large majorities in both legislative houses and earned Johnson the presi-dency, gave Mills ample room to maneuver and laid bare the AMA's deteriorating position. While AMPAC had spent approximately $400,000 to support candidates, the labor-backed COPE had allotted almost $1 million to political allies.[169] Furthermore, in a stinging reproach, Republican leaders complained that their party's association with the AMA had contributed to their electoral losses.[170]

King Belshazzar read the writing on the wall; AMA leaders chose to avert their eyes. At the AMA's 1964 winter meeting, the House of Delegates considered several resolutions to soften resistance to King-Anderson. However, physician officials insisted that only the poor should receive government benefits.[171] That December, they unveiled an initia-tive to liberalize Kerr-Mills.

Under the AMA's Eldercare proposal, states would help lower-income seniors purchase insurance by supplying stipends scaled to their earnings. The indigent would receive insurance gratis. Rather than undergoing means testing or state welfare agency investigations, as they did under Kerr-Mills programming, beneficiaries would simply provide a sworn statement of their income, excluding assets. Financing was to come from federal general revenues. A. Sidney Herlong (D, FL) and Thomas B. Curtis (R, MO), AMA allies on the House Ways and Means Committee, introduced the legislation and organized physicians allocated approximately $1 million to advertise the plan. Ominously, CBS and NBC declined to run Eldercare ads, deeming them "too controversial."[172]

The AMA touted Eldercare as offering "more benefits" than King-Anderson because, in addition to hospitalization coverage, state plans would provide insurance for physician services.[173] An AMA pamphlet boasted that "Yes, The Doctors' Eldercare Program offers better care than 'Medicare.'"[174] However, when AMA leaders asked HIAA officials to join their promotional campaign, insurers responded that it "would be unwise politically and as a matter of public relations." Recognizing the imprudence of taunting the now powerful Democrats for not proposing sufficient benefits, insurers tried to dissuade physicians from pursuing their advertising program, but to no avail.[175]

Republicans joined the AMA in characterizing King-Anderson as inadequate. Though the party's platform rejected Social Security financing and insisted on means testing, all major Republican alternatives – from the officially backed Bow measure to the buck-the-party Javits bids – included coverage for doctor bills. Even small-government-conservative Barry Goldwater (R, AZ), while campaigning for president, had derided King-Anderson for promising to provide elderly medical care but covering only hospital bills.[176] After the election, Republicans began promoting the Byrnes initiative, which proposed using general revenues to allow the elderly to purchase both hospital and medical insurance, with premium prices scaled to income.[177] In the winter of 1965, during Ways and Means hearings on Medicare, Republicans and AMA officials highlighted the paucity of King-Anderson benefits, while Representative Byrnes goaded Democrats by repeatedly calling his measure and Eldercare "Better Care."[178]

Mills's resolve to protect the Social Security fund had hindered the passage of elderly medical insurance for years, but the Ways and Means Committee chairman was now ready do far more than back King-Anderson. Seizing upon Republican and AMA critiques, Mills radically expanded the administration's measure. In a famous legislative feat that came to be known as the "three-layer cake," Mills asked Cohen to design a bill with a trio of programs. Part A mimicked King-Anderson by using Social Security financing to create a compulsory program that included sixty days of hospitalization coverage a year and limited nursing home benefits. Part B drew from Republican proposals and the Eldercare plan by covering physician bills, employing general revenues, and allowing seniors to choose whether to participate. The third layer, Title XIX or Medicaid, expanded Kerr-Mills grants-in-aid so that states could supply health insurance to indigent citizens regardless of age. The legislation passed the House 313–115.[179]

Passage of the House bill further enfeebled the AMA-HIAA-Blue Shield political coalition. Rather than joining together to devise a unified strategy before hearings began in the Senate Finance Committee, the associations adopted an every-man-for-himself approach. HIAA leaders were incensed by their allies' tactical blunders; they placed "responsibility on the American Medical Association and the Republican leadership for this all encompassing bill."[180] Some Blue Shield administrators shared commercial insurers' distaste for the legislation, while other NABSP leaders, similar to BCA and AHA officials, favored the measure.

In Senate hearings, AMA representatives protested the comprehensive nature of the legislation but, because of their prior backing of Eldercare, could really only dispute the lack of means testing and program management power concentrated at the federal level in the SSA. Realizing they were pinned down, physician leaders concentrated their remaining firepower on securing financing agreements that replicated prevailing arrangements. Now even more wary of hospital and AHA power, AMA leaders fought to keep radiologists, anesthesiologists, pathologists, and psychiatrists classified as autonomous physicians who could bill separately from hospitals. They ferociously attacked Senator Anderson's attempt to constrain program costs by modifying the House's provision for "customary and usual" and fee-for-service payments to physicians.[181] Similarly, AHA leaders insisted that hospitals receive "reasonable" cost reimbursements, which would require the government to partially finance such overhead expenses as the addition of new wings, equipment purchases, and charity cases. Ultimately, policymakers believed that they had to yield to service provider remuneration preferences in order to ensure their participation in Medicare.[182] By granting these demands, the final bill guaranteed that for service providers, Medicare would be a government-funded version of the existing insurance company model.

AMA leaders continued fuming and even required meetings with President Johnson to alleviate their apprehensions. But despite their prior threats, organized physicians acquiesced to working with government officials after Medicare's passage.[183] Facilitating the accord was a program that would increase demand for physician services while allowing doctors to charge generous fees. There was no mechanism for restraining costs, but that was the government's problem now.

For insurers, Senate hearings primarily revolved around their role in program administration. Blue Cross representatives appeared before senators to argue that their plans should administer Part A hospital benefits to the exclusion of commercial insurers. BCA leaders stressed their close relationships with hospitals while asserting that commercial companies lacked the capacity to handle the bill's administrative requirements (which they had conveniently written). Senator Anderson retorted, "It sounds to me that you are saying this bill is so complicated, let Blue Cross have it."[184] Anderson's comment reflected growing unease among policymakers about creating an administrative monopoly for nonprofit plans. Medicare's success would depend heavily on the ability of nongovernmental liaisons to run the program. As fiscal intermediaries responsible for payment determinations and utilization reviews, insurers would have substantial influence over Medicare spending.[185] Questioning their prior preferences, many liberal policymakers now worried that relying solely on nonprofit plans, which had governing boards dominated by service providers, was akin to putting the fox in charge of the hen house. SSA officials and Senator Anderson finally decided that competition among fiscal intermediaries would be crucial for managing costs because federal officials would at least retain authority to award administrative contracts according to individual firm performance.[186] However, convincing additional insurers to act as program administrators was not an easy task.

While BCA leaders were happy to assume complete control of Part A's hospital coverage, policymakers had some trouble corralling commercial companies and Blue Shield into Part B, to act as administrative liaisons between the government and physicians. The two groups displayed such "stand-offish" attitudes that, at one point, SSA officials considered designating state health departments to operate as program intermediaries.[187]

As the legislation moved from the House to the Senate, HIAA leaders split over whether they should lobby for administrative assignments. Some insurers worried that if their companies failed to secure intermediary functions, then Blue Cross and Blue Shield would forever monopolize the financially rewarding positions.[188] The heads of large companies displayed particular interest in acquiring administrative roles in Medicare. Equitable executives, for example, had already begun planning for the possibility of administering federal benefits.[189] On the other side of the argument, HIAA lobbyist Robert Neal declared that he "could not see why any company or companies would want the responsibility."[190] Conservative insurers contended that "under no circumstances should we endorse, or participate in, a program which does not give consideration to 'the difference between individuals who need assistance and those who, without hardship, meet their own needs.'"[191]

Manton Eddy, Senior Vice President of Connecticut General and President of the HIAA, appeared before the Senate Finance Committee on behalf of commercial insurers. The HIAA's strategy was simple. Eddy would first throw the industry at the mercy of legislators. If that move failed, he would seek intermediary roles for interested firms. Accordingly, Eddy pleaded with policymakers to strip Part B from Medicare. Labeling Part B "devastating," he requested that policymakers, in its place, allow insurance companies to sell physician coverage as supplemental policies without any governmental oversight or formal programming.[192] Once it became clear that his arguments were falling on deaf ears, Eddy relaxed the industry's long-established position against program involvement. When Senator Anderson questioned him about Medicare's administration, Eddy concurred that "it was a big piece of premium income to hand Blue Cross" and then proceeded to plug the performance of commercial firms in administering policies for the Federal Employees Health Benefits Program (FEHBP). Eddy contended that because the "profit system has a greater challenge to perform than the non-profit system," administration costs per FEHBP claim were only $1.26 for commercial insurers in comparison with $2.31 for Blue Cross plans.[193]

Meanwhile, with organized physicians reeling over the comprehensive measure that had passed the House, NABSP officials believed that openly negotiating for administrative positions in Medicare would be akin to pouring salt on the wounds of an injured animal. Blue Shield leaders recognized that as long as Part B remained in the legislation, nonprofit plans would obtain intermediary roles. So they attempted to mend the strained political relations between NABSP and AMA leaders and between the many local plans and medical societies quarreling over cost containment measures and Blue Shield's too-cozy relationship with Blue Cross. Showcasing their loyalty to the AMA, NABSP leaders informed the Senate Finance Committee that they could not participate in Medicare without "the active support of the practicing physicians."[194]

Before the public, the bill advanced steadily: the Finance Committee reported out the legislation in June, and the Senate passed Medicare the following month by a margin of 68–21. President Johnson signed the bill on July 30, 1965, with former President Truman at his side. Thanking his honored guest for "inspired leadership," which "made it historically possible for this day to come about," the president presented the aging Truman with the country's first Medicare card.[195]

Behind the fanfare, both HIAA and Blue Shield leaders, now with the AMA's consent, lined up to lobby for a portion of Medicare's remunerative administrative contracts. Policymakers would exercise more control over Medicare administrators than over FEHBP participants. However, unlike the FEHBP, and more financially advantageous for private interests, insurers would outsource the risk of underwriting beneficiaries – the actual costs of providing aged medical care would be the government's responsibility.

SSA officials examined potential program intermediaries based on their ability to supply the agency with statistical data, determine service provider charges, audit medical records, conduct utilization reviews, and, in general, provide "effective and efficient administration."[196] For each state, SSA officials identified the companies and nonprofit plans with the greatest administrative capacity, which were generally also the largest enterprises. From there, they balanced the requests of service providers with political horse-trading as congressmen forwarded their pet organizations for consideration. Because of their tight communications and financing connections with hospitals and, in particular, their experience reviewing "cost-based" hospital charges, Blue Cross plans dominated Medicare Part A, winning approximately 90 percent of intermediary contracts. SSA officials awarded Blue Shield almost 60 percent of administrative contracts under Part B, leaving the remaining portions of each program segment to commercial insurance companies.[197] Moreover, both nonprofit plans and commercial firms established profitable underwriting lines by creating supplemental or "Medigap" policies that helped seniors pay for Medicare deductibles and coinsurance as well as uncovered care.[198]

In the end, the marketplace's established structure severely restricted the choices available to the federal officials who created Medicare. Because of the private sector's superior organizational capacity and because program advocates sought the support of the public, moderate policymakers, and private health interests, they were compelled to configure Medicare to fit the insurance company framework. Within the institutional piping of that framework, insurers and physicians had failed to institute mechanisms for controlling costs. Now, however, massive amounts of federal resources would also be sloshing through those pipes.

CONCLUSION

Medicare's organization – based upon the insurance company model – granted official validity to an economic design that, during the 1940s and 1950s, was widely recognized as defective and costly. Now firmly ensconced at the center of the health care system, insurance companies financed private medical services while coordinating arrangements and supervising the delivery of care for both the public and private sectors.

Furthermore, by designating private interests semiformal appendages of the state, Medicare underscored the health care system's soft corporatist nature. In the decades leading up to Medicare, the environment of soft corporatism dictated that each interest group's economic power and political power would intimately inform and shape one another – passage of the federal program brought this system attribute into sharp relief. During the 1930s and 1940s, the AMA wielded enormous professional authority to impose a high-cost (among other problematic features) insurance company model on the health care market. Through repeated legislative reform attempts and almost unceasing political debates, policymakers pushed private interests to cover most Americans with generous insurance. However, the AMA's selection of an inherently expensive financing model guaranteed that physicians would gradually lose sovereignty to third parties seeking to control costs and, moreover, that private interests would never be able to meet political demands for an insurance product that covered the elderly. Unable to fully accept the consequences of the consumer-oriented compact between policymakers and the private sector, AMA leaders gradually undermined their political standing through frequent, sanguinary legislative battles.

The combat over Medicare left the association politically damaged. The AMA delegates called into special session after Medicare's passage rejected resolutions recommending that members refuse program participation. But a parade of newspaper headlines such as "A.M.A. Head Predicts Medicare Boycott" did little to bolster the diminished reputation of organized doctors.[199] After Medicare was created, polls showed that a majority of citizens believed that the AMA operated primarily to protect the financial interests of doctors rather than to advance medical science or safeguard patient welfare.[200] Throughout the rest of the 1960s and the

1970s, the AMA and constituent medical societies steadily declined in membership and, at the same time, experienced many protests and picketing from an array of groups, ranging from activists for nationalized medicine to advocates of African American and women doctors.[201] With the AMA weakened and physicians increasingly assembling through specialty societies – a development that further fractured the once monolithic and unified bulwark of organized doctors – politicians had more – not complete, but certainly growing – ability to seek health care reform.

Initially, physicians garnered large financial rewards from Medicare. It would be decades before the program would squeeze their market position. Nonetheless, both insurers and federal officials intensified their search for ways to regulate physicians – from Professional Standards Review Organizations (PSROs) in the 1970s to managed care regimes in the 1980s. Societal reverence for science and technology would maintain physician professional stature and incomes; however, at the same time, doctors increasingly lost autonomy to practice as they saw fit and witnessed a growing share of system revenues diverted to administration costs and third-party organizations.

In contrast, insurance companies emerged from the Medicare fight with augmented political and economic power. HIAA leaders' deliberate attempt to avoid political publicity allowed commercial firms to escape Medicare battles relatively unscathed. Although the NABSP had backed the AMA politically, it too skated through the debates without attracting undue public or policymaker attention. The decision of BCA leaders to support Medicare earned hospital nonprofits political favor. Insurance companies would soon come under heavy political fire for escalating health care and Medicare costs. However, they ably exploited this criticism to justify additional supervisory leverage over hospitals and physicians, both in the administration of Medicare and in the private sector. Although proposals for national insurance were seriously considered during the 1970s, skyrocketing medical costs combined with voter concerns about losing the employer-provided insurance and health care arrangements to which they had grown accustomed ended up dashing liberal hopes of creating universal coverage. Moreover, policymakers, now habituated to working within the constraints of the insurance company model, increasingly viewed health care costs not as a structural problem but as an issue that entailed finding new cost containment measures to bandage up the entrenched system. And cost containment processes almost always strengthened insurance company authority at the expense of service providers.

Medicare and Medicaid dramatically increased patient demand for health care and exacerbated the cost problems intrinsic to the insurance company model. Although exorbitant health care costs resulted as much from underlying inefficiencies as from rising service demand, many policymakers and health care scholars began linking the medical cost "crisis" to the establishment of these programs. These analyses obscured the shortcomings of the insurance company model and helped insurance companies appear to be "natural" features of "private" health care. Indeed, after Medicare's passage, it would become almost impossible to remove insurance companies from their position at the heart of the public-private health care system.

8

Epilogue: The Limits of "Comprehensive" Reform, 1965–2010

This story opened with organized physicians opposing all forms of prepaid health care except policies that fit the insurance company model. American Medical Association (AMA) leaders crafted the insurance company model during the 1930s and then insisted that each group of economic actors adjust their behavior to match its idiosyncratic conditions. Organized doctors required insurers to underwrite health care by supplying fees for each provided service and procedure. Moreover, under AMA stipulations, insurance policies could only cover care delivered by autonomous physicians who practiced individually, rather than in groups, particularly multispecialty groups. In a wager calculated to evade the confines of corporate bureaucratic organization, physicians placed all their chips – the authority they derived from economic standing, professional prestige, political influence, state licensing laws, and credentialing activities – on insurance company arrangements. It proved to be a poor gamble for society and, over time, for doctors themselves.

The insurance company model drove up medical costs and fragmented care. Moreover, the problems associated with insurance company financing provoked endless political attempts to repair deficiencies in the "voluntary" market. Though politicians repeatedly failed to achieve comprehensive reform, they created a soft corporatist environment by erecting federal standards – for mass coverage and generous benefits – that private interests, using the insurance company pattern, strove to fulfill and spotlight for public display. After approximately two decades of organizational buildup around the insurance company model, this distinct form of health care financing and delivery gained additional weight when policymakers structured the Federal Employees Health Benefits Program (FEHBP) and Medicare around its institutional provisions.

Over time, the health care narrative evolved to be less about physician power and more about the dominance of insurance companies and third-party financiers. Spiraling costs drove insurers and, after Medicare's passage, government officials to attempt to close the institutional gap that separated them, the financiers, from doctors and hospitals. Third parties implemented cost containment measures, which entailed insurers wading into the medical delivery process to supervise physician work and regulate provider remuneration. This process unfolded gradually and generated substantial conflict as organized physicians still retained a good deal of influence, which they wielded in political fights and in battles against third-party payers. Nonetheless, the very outcome that AMA leaders initially sought to prevent had come to fruition – physicians were now bound within a corporate structure of their own, inadvertent making.

HEALTH CARE REFORM, 1965–2010

After Medicare was introduced, health care reform proposals revolved around attempts to either nationalize coverage or constrain costs. However, the incorporation of the insurance company model into the Medicare program established an unshakable precedent. Through each subsequent round of political deliberations and legislative initiatives, the insurance company model emerged victorious. An additional, crucial development occurred with Medicare's enactment: the flagging alliance between physicians and insurers completely fractured. As financiers and providers increasingly saw each other as adversaries, federal policy assumed a more overtly corporatist flavor and reform debates became proxies through which doctors and insurers bickered over their principal-agent relationship. Organized doctors moderated ideologically to accept some types of government programming; now resisting insurance company regulations increasingly consumed their politicking. Meanwhile, as the financiers of health care, insurance companies and federal policymakers jointly assumed the task of instituting cost control measures that would reduce physician independence and pay.

Private Health Interests amid Crisis

After 1965, voters and policymakers discussed health care using terms customarily reserved for national catastrophes. Medicare and Medicaid generated an enormous increase in the demand for health services – much of which was justified and served to expose the extent of previously unmet needs. Nonetheless, the influx of new patients into the health care system magnified the forces of moral hazard and amplified provider incentives to pad bills and oversupply services. By 1970, physician fees were growing at twice the rate of average consumer price increases while hospital charges were rising five times more rapidly.[1] The "massive crisis" and "soaring" costs of a system "teetering on the brink of disaster" dismayed voters and policymakers and triggered a litany of questions about the shortcomings of U.S. health care.[2] Medicaid patients and insured individuals residing in rural or inner-city areas had difficulty finding general practitioners to provide them care.[3] The working poor, who often failed to qualify for Medicaid, also lacked regular access to medical services. Media accounts probing the quality and distribution of care highlighted the nation's elevated infant mortality rate, especially among minority groups.[4] These conditions led three-fourths of respondents to a 1970 survey to agree with the following statement: "There is a crisis in health care in the United States."[5]

Rapidly rising costs strained insurance companies. Between 1969 and 1976, the twenty largest health insurance companies, which accounted for approximately 70 percent of group coverage, reported average annual losses in four out of seven years.[6] Surging health care prices also put insurance leaders on the political hot seat as federal policymakers questioned their ability to manage service providers, particularly in their position as Medicare administrators. At the end of the 1960s, insurers were called before Congress to account for service provider abuses under Medicare and to explain their plans for constraining overall costs. Senator Edward M. Kennedy (D, MA) charged that there was "strong evidence that the insurance industry had neither the ability nor the will to control costs or promote efficiency in the health system."[7] Industry executives objected that they too were victims of hospital and physician fees. One executive protested that "[i]nsurers have suffered grievously from the skyrocketing hospital and medical costs of the past decade. It is surely enlightened self-interest to seek out and to foster all practical antidotes to this malaise."[8] Mounting political scrutiny encouraged insurers to sever their long-time partnership with doctors and publicly shift the blame for system failings onto service providers.

Despite difficult economic conditions and criticism from policymakers, insurers strengthened their overall market standing and political power during the 1970s, especially in relation to physicians and hospitals.

The intermediary role of insurance companies in Medicare supplied financial rewards without the risks of underwriting elderly subscribers. The program also created a floor of benefits upon which the industry constructed a profitable market of supplementary coverage for seniors. These pecuniary advantages helped stabilize the industry as companies lost money on other health care underwriting lines. Moreover, as the custodians of private insurance and as Medicare administrators, company executives and nonprofit leaders shared a purpose with federal officials – to depress costs by undercutting service provider autonomy.

In the nonprofit sector, Blues leaders could bolster their authority over providers only by first diminishing the influence that local doctors and hospitals had over each plan's procedures, policy offerings, and reimbursements. To demonstrate their commitment to cost containment and to improve public and political relations, nonprofits began dramatically reducing the number of provider representatives on their governing boards. Medical societies saw their control over Blue Shield plans dwindle. And a wave of mergers swept through local Blue Cross and Blue Shield plans as administrators sought ways to decrease operating costs. At the national level, nonprofit leaders resurrected the idea of consolidating the Blue Cross Association (BCA) and the National Association of Blue Shield Plans (NABSP). The objectives of the two associations were more closely aligned than ever: hospital and medical plans not only had similar operational issues and competitive difficulties but also faced political scrutiny brought on by rising costs and questions about their performance as Medicare administrators. A key issue driving negotiations was the goal of unifying processes across both plan networks to help nonprofits apply robust cost containment measures and rein in service providers. In 1977, the BCA and NABSP merged. Walter J. McNerney, who had long championed the implementation of more aggressive service provider controls, assumed the presidency of the Blue Cross and Blue Shield Association (BCBSA).[9]

Meanwhile, organized physicians suffered a decline in market and political clout. The nation's fascination with science and medical technology offered doctors a fortress of professional protection; but cost control procedures, whether instituted by insurance companies or federal programs, reduced physician independence and earning power. Moreover, the passage of Medicare inaugurated a new phase in health care politics. AMA leaders' determination to spend every ounce of political capital opposing Medicare generated so much negative publicity that, subsequently, politicians had less apprehension about confronting the association, particularly those policymakers who questioned its legitimacy as the mouthpiece of the entire doctoring profession.

Political setbacks spawned intense conflict within the AMA. In a move that harkened back to Morris Fishbein's dismissal, the Board of Trustees overthrew the association's chief political strategist and director of the conservative wing, Francis Blasingame.[10] Members then attempted to repair the AMA's public persona by installing ideologically moderate leaders. The House of Delegates, for example, declined to create a spokesman position for nationally known conservative ideologue Edward Annis. And in 1969, the newly elected president, Dwight Wilbur, upended decades of AMA political rhetoric when he announced that access to health care was a "right."[11]

Despite the association's new tone, turbulent times buffeted the AMA leadership. During the 1960s and 1970s, groups such as the National Welfare Rights Organization and the Medical Committee for Human Rights protested and even stormed into and interrupted AMA meetings. One activist alleged that the AMA's opposition to universal insurance had earned it the moniker of "American Murder Association."[12] At another meeting, a young doctor burned his membership card while calling on physicians to offer "free equal care for all."[13] As rights-based politics gained ground during the 1970s, groups ranging from folk medicine practitioners to feminists challenged the expertise of doctors who had traditionally dismissed alternative health practices and women's medical issues (scandals over unnecessary hysterectomies, discussed in Chapter 6, helped fuel this criticism). Representatives of the Student American Medical Association (SAMA) and young member physicians, many of whom endorsed their generation's revolt against "the establishment," spurred the formation of a liberal faction within the AMA.[14]

With the AMA's cultural reputation deteriorating and specialty medical societies standing by, ready to accept doctors either disaffected from or apathetic toward the association, membership numbers declined. The AMA still represented approximately 65 percent of doctors during the 1960s. By 1971, however, membership had fallen to less than half of all physicians. Thereafter, AMA affiliation rates steadily shrank.[15]

National Health Insurance

Runaway costs coupled with the AMA's fragile political position created an opportunity for liberal policymakers and activists to achieve far-reaching reforms. In 1968, United Automobile Workers (UAW)

President Walter Reuther declared that the medical cost "crisis" could only be remedied by nationalizing health care and restructuring the market for efficiency. Reuther rallied leading public figures to create the Committee of One Hundred for National Health Insurance. Senator Kennedy took up the cause in 1969. By the early 1970s, Congress had a variety of National Health Insurance (NHI) proposals before it, including legislation offered by Senator Kennedy and Representative Martha W. Griffiths (D, MI) to create a universal, government-managed program. Unlike most of the reform initiatives proffered throughout the decade, Kennedy-Griffiths legislation sought to eradicate the insurance company model by placing the entire population into one program, funding the establishment of prepaid groups, and obliging service providers to operate within federally mandated regional budgets.[16]

To counter the Kennedy-Griffiths plan, President Richard Nixon proposed the Comprehensive Health Insurance Program (CHIP) in 1971. Grounded in the insurance company model, CHIP would have mandated employer-supplied insurance, expanded Medicaid, and enhanced Medicare coverage. In 1973 and 1974, the Nixon administration reintroduced the same basic plan.[17] Similarly, insurers and physicians fought single-payer, government-administered medicine by assenting to a greater federal presence in health care – but only within the boundaries of the existing insurance company model.

The burdens of financing health care combined with the benefits that commercial insurance companies derived from federal programs such as the FEHBP and Medicare altered the views of industry leaders about government-supported coverage. In 1969, commercial insurers formulated a proposal for national health care, recommending that employers receive supplementary tax reductions in exchange for providing workers with insurance that conformed to generous and expensive benefit standards. Under the Health Insurance Association of America (HIAA) plan, businesses that failed to offer such coverage would lose 50 percent of the tax deduction that they already received for supplying fringe benefits. The initiative also called for policymakers to augment Medicaid. As a cost containment measure, insurers requested additional federal funding for medical education to increase the supply of physicians, reasoning that a larger practitioner pool would drive down service prices and make doctors – under pressure to compete for patients – more willing to submit to insurance company regulations in return for accessing their subscriber networks.[18] Finally, insurers advocated government-subsidized ambulatory facilities to decrease hospital admissions. HIAA suggestions were packaged in the Burleson-McIntyre bill.[19] Some executives, particularly those representing large companies, stood ready to accommodate whatever plan passed. Aetna and Equitable, among other firms, lined up to secure administrative roles in any potential NHI program. Even the Kennedy-Griffiths legislation, if slightly modified, would have allowed insurers to earn lucrative administrative fees while transferring the risks of underwriting health services to the government.[20]

Blue Cross leaders opted not to endorse a specific legislative proposal, but asserted that they were equipped to administer whichever program policymakers created. NABSP officials initially remained quiet on the subject, but by 1973, John Castellucci's successor, Ned Parish, was working with BCA leaders to prepare for national health insurance. As comprehensive reform appeared imminent in 1974, national leaders distributed pamphlets instructing local administrators on how to ready their plans for NHI.[21] Playing the same role they assumed during Medicare discussions, Blue Cross leaders, throughout the decade, provided government officials with expertise about health care financing and delivery and also helped draft legislation.[22]

As soon as NHI debates began, AMA officials designed and publicized their own reform package. Alluding to the Medicare debacle, a representative explained that association leaders had come to believe that "the AMA was at a disadvantage if all it could do was sit on the sidelines and throw slings and arrows at the proposals other people made." AMA leaders now "[a]greed that there was a role for the federal government and for the federal dollar in the financing of health care."[23] In 1968, the House of Delegates approved "Medicredit," which called for combining income tax credits and federal subsidies to ensure that all citizens could purchase health care coverage.[24]

The country came closest to obtaining universal insurance in 1974 when Senator Kennedy partnered with House Ways and Means Committee Chairman Wilbur Mills (D, AR) to create a compromise measure that resembled a liberalized version of the president's CHIP plan. The plan faltered because labor leaders were unhappy with the concessions given to craft the bill and Republicans saw no reason, in the midst of increasing Watergate allegations, to go out on a limb politically and support Nixon's proposal.[25]

In 1978, Kennedy mounted another drive for comprehensive reform. The Massachusetts senator proposed a unified national system that would operate under government-imposed budgets. Attempting to pick up additional political backing, Kennedy now sought a system situated firmly within the insurance company model; it called for employer mandates to purchase worker coverage and a recommendation that insurance companies administer the program. However, the legislation was soon buried beneath Kennedy's political disagreements with Jimmy Carter, not to mention the senator's attempt to overthrow the president in primary elections.[26] Ultimately, cost concerns, voter hesitancy to commit to a national system, and the proliferation of NHI plans defeated the ability of any one program to gain sufficient support for passage.

Legislating Cost Controls

While the issue of universal health insurance occupied the political foreground, policymakers established measures to restrain cost growth within existing arrangements.[27] These containment mechanisms focused almost exclusively on restricting service provider sovereignty. In 1971, as inflation became an overriding domestic concern, President Nixon instituted price controls across the economy, including upper limits on doctor fees and hospital rates. Health care price controls lasted longer than the restrictions placed on other economic sectors. When the ceilings were finally lifted in 1975, medical care costs surged ahead 12.5 percent in one year.[28]

In 1972, Congress passed legislation to slow the rise of spending in government health care programs, particularly Medicare. They created Professional Standards Review Organizations (PSROs) to regularize and strengthen service provider utilization and payment evaluation processes. AMA leaders condemned the government's intrusion into medical review procedures and secured physician control of PSROs.[29] Nonetheless, federal policy had validated the legitimacy of third parties regulating hospitals and doctors.[30]

In 1973, at the Nixon administration's urging, Congress passed legislation to provide federal loans and grants for the creation of Health Maintenance Organizations (HMOs). HMOs were an attempt to quash rising costs by integrating health care financing and delivery. Under HMOs, third parties formed especially robust funding and management relations with service providers. This occurred either because the financier (such as Kaiser Permanente) hired physicians and paid them a salary to serve patients or because the financier contracted with select physicians, promising them a pool of patients if they observed stricter care guidelines and accepted either lower fee-for-service payments or capitation reimbursements. Harking back to the many prepaid experiments that populated the market before World War II, federal officials envisioned numerous organizations – including businesses, physician groups, consumer associations, unions, and insurance companies – establishing and running HMOs. However, because the legislation heavily regulated government-subsidized HMOs, they were hard to get off the ground. Consequently, the reform failed to restructure the health care economy in any meaningful way.[31] Instead, the legislation buttressed insurers psychologically, encouraging them not only to experiment with HMOs, but also, and more important, to embrace tighter service provider relationships.

The debates surrounding HMO legislation exhibit how federal policy ordered physician-insurer skirmishes. The AMA opposed the act because HMOs amplified third-party power to the detriment of provider autonomy. Commercial insurance leaders initially resisted HMO legislation, but they reversed their position once they recognized that the program would, if nothing else, create a precedent for enhanced insurer authority over physicians.[32] Blue Cross had begun investigating and establishing HMO arrangements during the 1960s, and BCA leaders supported any bill that would subsidize their efforts.[33]

Congress applied other band-aids to the chronically ill insurance company model. The National Health Planning and Resources Development Act of 1974 created new layers of government regulation, including Health Systems Agencies (HSAs), which were local boards composed of doctors, hospital administrators, and – occupying a majority of seats – consumer representatives. To restrict the medical facility capacity in each area and thereby restrain costs, HSAs evaluated local health care conditions before issuing official authorizations or "certificates of need" to organizations seeking to build or expand hospitals. HSAs established nationally the hospital planning processes that civic groups, insurance companies, and Blue Cross plans had initiated during the 1950s and that some state governments had begun enacting into law during the 1960s.[34]

Amid legislative encounters that pit financiers seeking to contain costs against service providers attempting to retain sovereignty, insurance leaders tried to convince the public that responsibility for rising health care prices rested with doctors and hospitals. For instance, an Aetna advertisement featured a cartoon with a patient on an operating table surrounded by a surgeon and nurses. As the surgeon readied his scalpel, the patient popped up to argue about the service fee. Blue Cross and Blue Shield sponsored ads picturing a baby girl and the query, "By the time she can have a baby of her own, will she be able to afford to?"[35] Through such advertisements as well as subscriber leaflets and pamphlets, insurance companies publicized their activities to control costs by using provider fee-tracking systems, utilization review committees, and second opinion programs for surgery patients.[36] Dr. James H. Sammons, the AMA's executive vice president, denounced "the oversimplification of the cost problem in the advertisements I have seen." He continued: "Emotionalizing and scapegoating isn't going to improve things."[37] Despite AMA protests, cost problems had emboldened insurers to the point of publicly criticizing, even shaming physicians.

Managed Care on the Road toward Comprehensive Reform

The term "managed care" came into use to describe how insurers bundled together various techniques to reduce health service expenditures; the phrase gained prominence at the end of the 1970s as the cost containment efforts of third-party financiers became more visible to the public. Precedents for managed care stretched back to the immediate postwar era when insurers began acquiring the medical expertise necessary to monitor the appropriateness of delivered services. Managed care encompassed many of the processes that insurers began employing during the 1950s and 1960s, including utilization reviews and treatment blueprints, but also incorporated new procedures such as reimbursement methods designed to decrease provider incentives to oversupply care.[38]

The development of managed care demonstrates the increasingly symbiotic relationship between federal programming and private industry evolution. For example, in 1972, Congress authorized "prospective payment" trials in state health care programs. At the same time, under intense political pressure to dampen costs, Blue Cross began experimenting with similar measures by affixing preset hospital reimbursements to each patient diagnosis category. In the 1983 Social Security Amendments, policymakers adopted this approach to alter the way Medicare compensated hospitals. Instead of paying "costs" of care, Medicare began using Diagnosis-Related Groups (DRGs) to remunerate hospitals with a fixed fee according to the patient's diagnosis.[39]

Encouraged by the adoption of DRGs, the development of HMOs, and strengthened utilization review activities, insurers spread managed care techniques throughout the health care system during the 1980s. Under managed care regimes in the voluntary market, financiers usually assembled physician networks, which they matched with large policyholder groups. In return for the market share, doctors agreed to accept more rigorous utilization reviews; reduced payments or capitation fees;

and additional cost containment regulations, ranging from treatment guidelines to the appointment of general practitioners as "gatekeepers" who regulated patient access to physician specialists. Managed care practices attracted criticism for interfering with medical care and for denying patients necessary services.[40] Nonetheless, in the national quest to curb health care costs, the power of third-party payers, whether governmental or private, continued to grow.

President Bill Clinton's 1993 attempt to create universal health care once again showcased how service providers and insurance companies attempted to harness legislative initiatives to advance their market standing vis-à-vis one another. To enter into negotiations with federal officials and advance their program preferences, both the AMA and HIAA endorsed universal coverage by means of employer mandates. In exchange for backing the administration's proposal, AMA leaders requested safeguards to protect physician autonomy and pay from federal regulation and from insurance company authority. Although AMA leaders participated in discussions with the president's health care task force, they ultimately objected to national spending limits and cost containment measures that would "limit choices by patients and physicians . . . and lead to Federal control of medical education and the physician work force."[41]

The Clinton plan threw the HIAA into turmoil. Unsurprisingly, executives of large companies assumed their organizations would benefit from a program that required businesses to purchase employee insurance and that brought new customers into state-run exchanges. While the federal government would heavily regulate their industry and product offerings, these insurers believed they would reap net gains from federal guidelines granting them additional control over service providers. However, small and medium-sized companies feared that requirements to cover all risk groups and offer expensive benefits would shut them out of the market. The intra-associational dispute led the "big five" – Cigna, Aetna, Metropolitan, Travelers, and Prudential – to abandon their smaller brethren and resign from the HIAA. Meanwhile, HIAA leaders launched a fierce campaign against the Clinton proposal, including television advertisements now famous as the "Harry and Louise" commercials. The ads featured a middle-class couple at their kitchen table discussing the Clinton blueprint and lamenting the power that government bureaucrats would have in shaping insurance policies and limiting consumer choice. Some analysts have cited the commercials as influential in turning public opinion against the legislation and helping secure its demise.[42]

COMPREHENSIVE REFORM AND THE HEALTH CARE SYSTEM

March 23, 2010, marked the culmination of more than a century of efforts to give government a major role in running the health care system. When President Barack Obama signed the Patient Protection and Affordable Care Act (ACA) in the East Room of the White House, hundreds of Democratic lawmakers cheered the most momentous social legislation enacted since President Johnson's Great Society.[43] To achieve near universal coverage, the ACA would expand Medicaid, institute a tax penalty on most consumers who failed to purchase insurance, and create state exchanges in which insurance companies would sell products with federally stipulated benefits and regulated administrative expenses.

The Democratic Party's health care reform spurred sizable grassroots counter-organization and passed without garnering Republican votes.[44] The ACA's passage provoked Tea Party protests, election slogans calling for repeal, and state-led judicial challenges. Yet, neither organized physicians nor insurance companies led resistance to what came to be called "Obamacare."

During legislative debates, the AMA, BCBSA, and the HIAA's new incarnation – America's Health Insurance Plans (AHIP) – endorsed both universal coverage and a prohibition against denying insurance to applicants with preexisting health conditions.[45] With Democrats controlling both congressional houses and a freshly elected, young, popular media darling and first African American president in the White House, private interests sensed the inevitability of reform. Having flirted with comprehensive reform for decades, AMA, BCBSA, and AHIP leaders now sought to build societal goodwill and political capital by announcing their support for the administration's endeavor. Private health care leaders hoped this strategy would allow them to influence legislative details to favor their interests.

Once again, reform legislation became a vehicle for private interests to improve their position within the health care system's corporate arrangements. The HIAA's 2003 consolidation with a trade group that represented the interests of managed care organizations indicated that commercial insurers, now under the flag of AHIP, would seek even more authority to regulate service providers. During ACA debates, AHIP leaders requested that policymakers enact federal regulations for electronic recordkeeping and "value-based reimbursements," tools that would augment their ability to manage medical care by tying doctor compensation to compliance with ever more detailed insurance company directives.[46] Additionally, to improve their industry's financial strength, insurers sought malpractice legal reforms and an individual mandate that would oblige young, healthy citizens to purchase policies and thereby offset the costs of insuring sicker and older subscribers. Blue Cross and Blue Shield leaders also sought legislative provisions to enhance their market power and their influence over medical care delivery. However, both AHIP and BCBSA officials lobbied against the administration's attempt to create a new government-sponsored plan. Liberal politicians tendered this plan, known as the public option, with the intent of weakening insurance companies over time. Meanwhile, AMA leaders offered to support the administration in exchange for measures to protect their Medicare payment levels, prevent insurance company interference in health care services, and effect a reduction in physician paperwork.[47] These negotiations foreshadowed what will likely occur now that the ACA has passed – the system's corporatist features will become more pronounced as insurers and physicians increasingly haggle over the terms of their relationship at the government's bargaining table.

Despite the political uproar surrounding the ACA, many citizens, including the legislation's opponents, acknowledged the need for some type of reform. Indeed, ACA antagonists were most effective raising the specter of how federal programming would worsen health care rather than boasting about prevailing arrangements. Poor service distribution, fragmented care, and uneven service quality had long characterized U.S. medicine. But policymakers and voters were primarily concerned about the uninsured and the exorbitant costs that ranked American health care as the world's most expensive. These flaws helped push the ACA over the finish line. And the program has thus far proven resilient, withstanding presidential and congressional contests as well as significant court challenges.

The ACA built new rooms atop a defective, jerry-built edifice. The public option would have put the nation firmly on the path toward a nationalized, universal system by creating a government-managed plan and using regulations and mandates to enfeeble and eventually drive out private coverage. Readers can decide for themselves the wisdom of creating a centralized system. Nonetheless, because the ACA failed to secure fundamental, structural reform, it will be unable to rein in costs while also maintaining or improving the quality of care. Indeed, this narrative has illustrated how a fusion of public and private power constructed an institutionally tangled health care system that, even under the banner of comprehensive reform, policymakers were ultimately unable to rescue from the insurance company model.

Endnote Abbreviations

BCBS D.C. Archives	Blue Cross and Blue Shield Archives, Washington, D.C.
BCBS Philadelphia Archives	Independence Blue Cross Archives, Philadelphia, PA
Blasingame Papers	F. J. L. Blasingame Papers, Truman G. Blocker Jr. History of Medicine Collections, University of Texas Medical Branch, Galveston, TX
CCMC	Committee on the Costs of Medical Care
CCOHC	Social Security Project, Columbia Center of Oral History Collection, Columbia University, New York, NY
Cunningham Papers	Robert M. Cunningham Jr. Papers, private collection, Gaithersburg, MD
Faulkner Papers	E. J. Faulkner Papers, Archives and Special Collections, University of Nebraska-Lincoln Libraries
Equitable Archives	AXA Equitable Life Insurance Company Archives, New York, NY
Grahame Papers	Orville Francis Grahame Papers, University of Iowa Special Collections, Iowa City, IA
HEW	Records of the Department of Health, Education, and Welfare (National Archives, College Park, MD)
JAMA	*Journal of the American Medical Association*
JHPPL	*Journal of Health Policy, Politics, and Law*

Michael M. Davis Collection	Microfilm Reels of the Committee for the Nation's Health Records, Michael M. Davis Collection, in the New York Academy of Medicine, U.S. National Library of Medicine, Bethesda, MD
NARA	National Archives, College Park, MD
SSA	Records of the Social Security Administration (National Archives, College Park, MD)
SSA Archives	Social Security Archives, Baltimore, MD

Notes

Introduction

1 Organization for Economic Cooperation and Development, "OECD Health Data 2013," June 27, 2013, http://stats.oecd.org/Index.aspx?DataSetCode=-SHA.html (accessed November 4, 2013). As of 2013, the percentage of GDP various countries spent on health care was as follows: United States, 17.7%; the Netherlands, 11.9%; France 11.6%; Germany, 11.3%; Canada, 11.2%; Switzerland, 11%.

2 For works that examine historical alternatives to the insurance company model, see, for example, Jennifer Klein, *For All These Rights: Business, Labor, and the Shaping of America's Public-Private Welfare State* (Princeton, 2003); Paul Starr, *The Social Transformation of American Medicine: The Rise of a Sovereign Profession and the Making of a Vast Industry* (New York, 1982), 198–215, 290–334.

3 N.B. that using "voluntary" and "private" as synonyms does paper over significant variations between nonprofit insurance plans and commercial or for-profit insurance companies. Nonprofit insurers, particularly early Blue Cross leaders, attempted to distinguish their plans as "voluntary," as constituting a "third sector" that was distinct from both the private sector and the governmental or "compulsory" sector. These nonprofit leaders claimed to supply health care coverage as a civic duty, in pursuit of the public interest and eschewing profitmaking motives. Because of their declared objectives, most nonprofit plans operated under state enabling laws that exempted them from paying taxes or complying with commercial insurance regulations. The differences between nonprofit plans and commercial insurance firms are discussed throughout this narrative and particularly in Chapter 5. See Lawrence D. Brown, "Capture and Culture: Organizational Identity in New York Blue Cross," *Journal of Health Policy, Politics, and Law* (hereafter *JHPPL*) 16 (winter 1991): 651–70; Daniel Fox, David Rosner, and Rosemary A. Stevens, "Introduction: Between Public and

Private: Half a Century of Blue Cross and Blue Shield in New York," *JHPPL* 16 (winter 1991): 643–50; Robert Cunningham III and Robert M. Cunningham, Jr., *The Blues: A History of the Blue Cross and Blue Shield System* (DeKalb, IL, 1997), 28–32.

4 American health care has long been viewed through a dichotomous framework that categorizes systems as either government-run or based on private markets. Most health care studies attempt to uncover why the United States embarked on a different path from western and northern European countries, which have universal, centrally managed systems. These scholarly treatments reveal how comprehensive reform has been impeded by distinctive American political features, such as the nation's decentralized system of governance, divided among federal, state, and local authorities. Some authors point to deep-seated political ideology and the tenacity of classical liberal concerns to explain the failure of nationalized health care. Other scholars demonstrate how, during the first half of the twentieth century, federal agencies had less governing capacity than the well-funded and sophisticated bureaucracies housed in corporations, trade associations, and professional organizations. Indeed, the strength of private health interests, particularly the American Medical Association, is a central premise in these studies. This scholarship has been crucial to understanding the most visible political conflicts over health care. Such analyses, however, tend to neglect significant developmental features; in seeking to explain what the system lacks, this mode of examination often overlooks how the U.S. health care system assumed its unique public–private form. Representative works include Daniel Hirshfield, *The Lost Reform: The Campaign for Compulsory Health Insurance in the United States from 1932 to 1943* (Cambridge, MA, 1970); Monte M. Poen, *Harry S. Truman versus the Medical Lobby: The Genesis of Medicare* (Columbia, MO, 1979); Ronald L. Numbers, *Almost Persuaded: American Physicians and Compulsory Health Insurance, 1912–1920* (Baltimore, 1978); Beatrix Hoffman, *The Wages of Sickness: The Politics of Health Insurance in Progressive America* (Chapel Hill, NC, 2001). For studies grounded in the state's institutional structure, see Theda Skocpol, *Protecting Soldiers and Mothers: The Political Origins of American Social Policy* (Cambridge, MA, 1992); Sven Steinmo and Jon Watts, "It's the Institutions, Stupid! Why Comprehensive National Health Insurance Always Fails in America," *JHPPL* 20 (summer 1995): 329–72. For analysis that focuses on public attitudes and ideology, see Lawrence R. Jacobs, *The Health of Nations: Public Opinion and the Making of American and British Health Policy* (Ithaca, NY, 1993). For historical treatments that examine the power of private interests in shaping the health care system, see Colin Gordon, *Dead on Arrival: The Politics of Health Care in Twentieth-Century America* (Princeton, 2003); Robert Alford, *Health Care Politics: Ideological and Interest Group Barriers to Reform* (Chicago, 1976); Vicente Navarro, *Medicine under Capitalism* (New York, 1976); Richard Harris, *A Sacred Trust: The Story of America's Most Powerful Lobby – Organized Medicine* (Baltimore, 1969); Jill Quadagno, *One Nation Uninsured: Why the U.S. Has*

No National Health Insurance (New York, 2005). Admittedly, my attempt to categorize these works is somewhat crude. Many of these excellent monographs go far beyond single variable explanations of why the United States lacks a nationalized health care system. For example, while Colin Gordon emphasizes the importance of private interests in blocking health care reform, he also explores race, gender, and the rapid development of voluntary insurance.

A second category of scholarship blurs the line between public and private health care. Jacob Hacker demonstrates how conservative politicians fought comprehensive reform by directing federal subsidies toward employer-provided medical insurance. Federal tax policy granted valuable write-offs to businesses that purchased fringe benefits, including health insurance, for workers. Jacob S. Hacker, *The Divided Welfare State: The Battle over Public and Private Social Benefits in the United States* (New York, 2002). For additional studies of government-subsidized benefits delivered through private institutions, see Klein, *For All These Rights*; Beth Stevens, "Blurring the Boundaries: How the Federal Government Has Encouraged Welfare Benefits in the Private Sector," in *The Politics of Social Policy in the United States*, ed. Margaret Weir, Ann Shola Orloff, and Theda Skocpol (Princeton, 1997); Marie Gottschalk, *The Shadow Welfare State: Labor, Business, and the Politics of Health Care in the United States* (Ithaca, NY, 2000); Andrew Morris, *The Limits of Voluntarism: Charity and Welfare from the New Deal through the Great Society* (New York, 2009).

5 For traditional accounts that identify cost problems as a post-Medicare phenomenon, see Rashi Fein, *Medical Care, Medical Costs: The Search for a Health Insurance Policy*, 2nd ed. (Cambridge, MA, 1989); Karen Davis, Gerard F. Anderson, Diane Rowland, and Earl P. Steinberg, *Health Care Cost Containment* (Baltimore, 1990); Quadagno, *One Nation Uninsured*, chapter 4. Scholars have recently begun revising this argument to demonstrate that health care costs were a significant economic problem and political issue before Medicare's passage. See Klein, *For All These Rights*, 217–18, 242–43; David J. Rothman, "The Public Presentation of Blue Cross, 1935–1965," *JHPPL* 16 (winter 1991): 684–87.

Some scholars blame technological advances for rising health care costs. See, for example, David Mechanic, *The Growth of Bureaucratic Medicine* (New York, 1976); Joseph P. Newhouse, "Medical Care Costs: How Much Welfare Loss?" *Journal of Economic Perspectives* 6 (summer 1992): 3–21; Sherry Glied, *Chronic Condition: Why Health Reform Fails* (Cambridge, MA, 1998); David M. Cutler and Mark McClellan, "Is Technological Change in Medicine Worth It?" *Health Affairs* 20 (September/October 2001): 11–29; Sherry Glied, "Health Care Costs: On the Rise Again," *Journal of Economic Perspectives* 17 (spring 2003): 125–48. However, such analyses make technology a determining force, detached from the decisions and financial incentives of service providers, patients, insurers, and businesses. For a discussion of how health care markets function in relation to the efficient use of technology, see Victor Fuchs, *The Health Economy* (Cambridge, MA, 1986), 29–31, 107.

6 Odin W. Anderson, Patricia Collette, Jacob J. Feldman, *Changes in Family Medical Care Expenditures and Voluntary Insurance: A Five-Year Resurvey* (Cambridge, MA, 1963), 100–101; Anne R. Somers and Herman M. Somers, "Coverage, Costs, and Controls in Voluntary Health Insurance," *Public Health Reports* 76 (January 1961): 4–5.

7 For a discussion of how this model differs from insurance arrangements in other countries, see Chapter 1, note 63.

8 On the transition from individual physician practice to ever increasing insurance company power through managed care regimes, see David Dranove, *The Economic Evolution of American Health Care* (Princeton, 2000); Starr, *Social Transformation of American Medicine*, 420–49.

9 In 2003, the HIAA merged with the American Association of Health Plans to form AHIP.

10 On trade associations, see David B. Truman, *The Governmental Process*, 2nd ed. (Berkeley, 1993); Robert H. Wiebe, *The Search for Order, 1877–1920* (New York, 1967); Louis Galambos, *Competition and Cooperation: The Emergence of a National Trade Association* (Baltimore, 1966); Robert M. Collins, *The Business Response to Keynes, 1929–1964* (New York, 1981); James Q. Wilson, *Political Organizations*, 2nd ed. (Princeton, 1995).

11 To quote Jennifer Klein, "The terms *public* and *private* are not mutually exclusive." Klein, *For All These Rights*, 5. See Marc Allen Eisner, *The American Political Economy: Institutional Evolution of Market and State*, 2nd ed. (New York, 2014); Brian Balogh, *Between the Cycles: Essays on the Evolution of Twentieth-Century American Governance* (University of Pennsylvania Press, forthcoming).

12 This work augments the historical institutional approach by highlighting structural connections between the state and society or between policymakers and interest groups, which have behaved as interdependent actors shaping the political economy. For example, Peter B. Evans, Dietrich Rueschemeyer, and Theda Skocpol, eds., *Bringing the State Back In* (New York, 1985); Stephen Skowronek, *Building a New American State: The Expansion of National Administrative Capacities, 1877–1920* (New York, 1982); Daniel Carpenter, *The Forging of Bureaucratic Autonomy: Reputations, Networks, and Policy Innovation in Executive Agencies, 1862–1928* (Princeton, 2001); Sven Steinmo, Kathleen Thelen, and Frank Longstreth, eds., *Structuring Politics: Historical Institutionalism in Comparative Analysis* (New York, 1992); Elizabeth Sanders, *Roots of Reform: Farmers, Workers, and the American State, 1877–1917* (Chicago, 1999); Richard Franklin Bensel, *The Political Economy of American Industrialization, 1877–1900* (New York, 2000); Elizabeth S. Clemens, *The People's Lobby: Organizational Innovation and the Rise of Interest Group Politics in the United States, 1890–1925* (Chicago, 1997); Ellen M. Immergut, *Health Politics: Interests and Institutions in Western Europe* (New York, 1992); Brian Balogh, *A Government Out of Sight: The Mystery of National Authority in Nineteenth-Century America* (New York, 2009).

   Also important for this analysis is the "organizational synthesis" in American history, which places great importance on the late-nineteenth-century transition from community, inter-personal, and informal relationships to a society dominated by national bureaucratic organizations – corporations, trade associations, and labor unions. The timing of this shift was particularly important because, in most economic sectors, the private sector had more organizational capacity and expertise than did the federal government. See Wiebe, *Search for Order*; Louis Galambos, "The Emerging Organizational Synthesis in Modern American History," *Business History Review* 44 (autumn 1970): 279–90; Louis Galambos, "Technology, Political Economy, and Professionalization: Central Themes of the Organizational Synthesis," *Business History Review* 57 (winter 1983): 471–93; Brian Balogh, "Reorganizing the Organizational Synthesis: Federal-Professional Relations in Modern America," *Studies in American Political Development* 5 (spring 1991): 119–72; Alfred D. Chandler, Jr., *The Visible Hand: The Managerial Revolution in American Business* (Cambridge, MA, 1977); Jerry Israel, ed., *Building the Organizational Society: Essays on Associational Activities in Modern America* (New York, 1972).

13 Karl Polanyi is credited with introducing the concept of socially embedded markets, which he argued assumed their institutional form as much from a country's government and religion as they did from a negotiated pattern of exchange. Karl Polanyi, *The Great Transformation: The Political and Economic Origins of Our Time* (New York, 1944); Polanyi, "The Economy as Instituted Process," in *Trade and Markets in Early Empires*, ed. Polanyi, Conrad M. Arensberg, and H. W. Pearson (New York, 1957), 243–70.

14 Ellis W. Hawley, "The Discovery of a 'Corporate Liberalism,'" *Business History Review* 52 (autumn 1978): 309–20; Howard J. Wiarda, *Corporatism and Comparative Politics: The Other Great "Ism"* (Armonk, NY, 1997); Wolfgang Streeck and Philippe C. Schmitter, eds., *Private Interest Government: Beyond Market and State* (Los Angeles, 1985). For examinations of various models of capitalism, see Peter Hall and David Soskice, eds., *Varieties of Capitalism: The Institutional Foundations of Comparative Advantage* (New York, 2001); Wolfgang Streeck and Kozo Yamamura, eds., *The Origins of Nonliberal Capitalism: Germany and Japan in Comparison* (Ithaca, NY, 2001); David Coates, *Models of Capitalism: Growth and Stagnation in the Modern Era* (Cambridge, MA 2000); Cathie Jo Martin and Duane Swank, *The Political Construction of Business Interests* (New York, 2012).

15 Douglass C. North, *Institutions, Institutional Change and Economic Performance* (New York, 1990), 3.

16 North, *Institutions, Institutional Change*; Paul Pierson, "Review: When Effect Becomes Cause: Policy Feedback and Political Change," *World Politics* 45 (July 1993): 595–628; Paul Pierson, "Increasing Returns, Path Dependence, and the Study of Politics," *American Political Science Review* 94 (June 2000): 251–67; Hacker, *Divided Welfare State*, 24–27, 52–62, 291–92; Elizabeth S. Clemens and James M. Cook, "Politics and Institutionalism: Explaining Durability and Change," *Annual Review of Sociology* 25 (August 1999): 441–66; James Mahoney, "Path Dependence in Historical Sociology," *Theory and Society* 29 (August 2000): 507–48.

17 The question of whether or not physicians have lost professional standing has spawned a debate in the literature on professions. Although some scholars do,

I would not characterize physicians as "proletarianized." As an occupation, physicians continue to enjoy professional prestige, largely because of their connection to science and technology and their ability to use innovations in those fields to improve individual health. Nonetheless, physicians have incrementally lost professional autonomy and pay. While most doctors, particularly specialists, continue to enjoy relatively high salaries, insurance companies have redirected a significant portion of the medical dollar away from service delivery and into administration. Moreover, the AMA has lost considerable political authority.

On physicians' loss of political, economic, and cultural authority, see, for example, Frederic Wolinsky, "The Professional Dominance, Deprofessionalization, Proletarianization, and Corporatization Perspectives: An Overview and Synthesis," in *The Changing Medical Profession: An International Perspective*, ed. Frederic Hafferty and John B. McKinlay (New York, 1993), 1612–16; Mark Schlesinger, "A Loss of Faith: The Sources of Reduced Political Legitimacy for the American Medical Profession," *Milbank Quarterly* 80 (June 2002): 185–235; Eliot Freidson, *Professionalism, The Third Logic: On the Practice of Knowledge* (Chicago, 2001); Mark Schlesinger, Bradford Gray, and Kristin Perreira, "Medical Professionalism under Managed Care: The Pros and Cons of Utilization Review," *Health Affairs* 16 (January 1997): 106–24; Ralph R. Reed and Daryl Evans, "The Deprofessionalization of Medicine: Causes, Effects and Responses," *Journal of the American Medical Association* (hereafter *JAMA*) 258 (December 1987): 3279–82; Starr, *Social Transformation of American Medicine*, 379–80, 444–49.

For scholarship that posits that physicians have retained considerable political and professional strength, see Robert J. Blendon, Tracey S. Hyams, and John M. Benson, "Bridging the Gap between Expert and Public Views on Health Care Reform," *JAMA* 269 (May 1993): 2573–78; Thomas Haskell, "Introduction," in *The Authority of Experts*, ed. Thomas Haskell (Bloomington, IN, 1984), ix–xxxix; David Mechanic, "Sources of Countervailing Power in Medicine," *JHPPL* 16 (fall 1991): 485–521; Eliot Freidson, *Profession of Medicine: A Study of the Sociology of Applied Knowledge* (New York, 1970). Note that Freidson's views about physician professional dominance changed over the course of several decades, as expressed in *Professionalism, The Third Logic* (above).

1 Background: Physicians Choose the Insurance Company Model, Late Nineteenth Century to the 1940s

1 Paul Starr, *The Social Transformation of American Medicine: The Rise of a Sovereign Profession and the Making of a Vast Industry* (New York, 1982), 13–15.
2 Magali Sarfatti Larson, *The Rise of Professionalism: A Sociological Analysis* (Berkeley, 1977), 20.
3 Scholars ranging from neo-Marxists to classical liberals have critically explored how the AMA's power, particularly over licensing and medical schools, endowed association leaders with the ability to restrict the supply of doctors, increase physician incomes, and shape professional conceptions.

Larson, *The Rise of Professionalism*; Jeffrey L. Berlant, *Professions and Monopoly: A Study of Medicine in the United States and Great Britain* (Berkeley, 1975); Robert R. Alford, *Health Care Politics: Ideological and Interest Group Barriers to Reform* (Chicago, 1975); Milton Friedman, *Capitalism and Freedom*, 3rd ed. (Chicago, 2002), 137–60. One school of sociological literature presents a more optimistic view of professional governance, as a "third way" between government control and the unpredictability of free markets: for example, Talcott Parsons, "Professions," in *International Encyclopedia of the Social Sciences*, ed. David L. Sills (New York, 1968), 536–47; Eliot Freidson, *Professionalism, The Third Logic: On the Practice of Knowledge* (Chicago, 2001). See also economist Kenneth Arrow's classic essay, "Uncertainty and the Welfare Economics of Medical Care," *American Economic Review* 53 (December 1963): 941–69.

4 These physicians were often referred to as "regular," "orthodox," or "allopathic" doctors as opposed to, for example, "eclectic" or "homeopathic" doctors.

5 This discussion of physician practices during the nineteenth and early twentieth centuries is drawn from the following works: Starr, *Social Transformation of American Medicine*, 65–81; William G. Rothstein, *American Physicians in the Nineteenth Century* (Baltimore, 1972); John Duffy, *From Humors to Medical Science: A History of American Medicine* (Chicago, 1993); George Rosen, *The Structure of American Medical Practice, 1875–1941* (Philadelphia, 1983), chapter 1; Steven M. Stowe, *Doctoring the South: Southern Physicians and Everyday Medicine in the Mid-Nineteenth Century* (Chapel Hill, NC, 2004); Steven M. Stowe, *A Southern Practice: The Diary and Autobiography of Charles A. Hentz, M.D.* (Charlottesville, VA, 2000); Joseph F. Kett, *The Formation of the American Medical Profession: The Role of Institutions, 1780–1860* (New Haven, CT, 1968); Judith Walzer Leavitt, "'A Worrying Profession': The Domestic Environment of Medical Practice in Mid-Nineteenth-Century America," *Bulletin of the History of Medicine* 69 (spring 1995): 1–29; D. W. Cathell, *Book on the Physician Himself*, 12th ed. (Philadelphia, 1913); Mary B. Spahr, "Medicine's Neglected Control Lever," *Medical Economics* 28 (March 1951): 193–209; Charles C. Dennie, "Old Doc," *Virginia Medical Monthly* 83 (July 1956): 278–84.

6 Cathell, *Book on the Physician Himself*, 40–41.

7 Quoted in Stowe, *Doctoring the South*, 110.

8 Cathell, *Book on the Physician Himself*, 232.

9 Ibid., 233, see also 146–54, 231–34; Starr, *Social Transformation of American Medicine*, 85–88.

10 Cathell, *Book on the Physician Himself*, 24–27.

11 Starr, *Social Transformation of American Medicine*, 81–85; "Does It Pay to Be a Doctor?" *JAMA* 42 (January 23, 1904): 247.

12 James C. Mohr, *Licensed to Practice: The Supreme Court Defines the American Medical Profession* (Baltimore, 2013); Starr, *Social Transformation of American Medicine*, 102–12. Some of these state laws established alternative licensing boards to permit "irregular" doctors to continue practicing medicine.

13 Duffy, *From Humors to Medical Science*, chapter 13; Starr, *Social Transformation of American Medicine*, 112–23.

14 William G. Rothstein, *American Medical Schools and the Practice of Medicine: A History* (New York, 1987), 144–49; American Medical Association, *A History of the Council on Medical Education and Hospitals, 1904–1959* (Chicago, 1960); "Medical Education – A Review of Fifteen Years' Progress," *JAMA* 65 (August 21, 1915): 717.

15 Duffy, *From Humors to Medical Science*, 183–84; Starr, *Social Transformation of American Medicine*, 147–69; Charles E. Rosenberg, *The Care of Strangers: The Rise of America's Hospital System* (New York, 1987), 9; Rosemary Stevens, *In Sickness and in Wealth: American Hospitals in the Twentieth Century*, 2nd ed. (Baltimore, 1999), 19, 21–23, 39.

16 The Committee on the Costs of Medical Care (hereafter CCMC), *Medical Care for the American People*, no. 28 (Washington, D.C., 1932), 13–21; Starr, *Social Transformation of American Medicine*, 142–43, 257–60.

17 Starr, *Social Transformation of American Medicine*, 206–209; George Rosen, "Contract or Lodge Practice and Its Influence on Medical Attitudes to Health Insurance," *American Journal of Public Health* 67 (April 1977): 374–78; David T. Beito, *From Mutual Aid to the Welfare State: Fraternal Societies and Social Services, 1890–1967* (Chapel Hill, NC, 1999); Rosen, *Structure of American Medical Practice*, 98–103.

18 Mark Aldrich, "Train Wrecks to Typhoid Fever: The Development of Railroad Medicine Organizations, 1850 to World War I," *Bulletin of the History of Medicine* 75 (summer 2001): 254–89.

19 Starr, *Social Transformation of American Medicine*, 200–206; Stuart D. Brandes, *American Welfare Capitalism, 1880–1920* (Chicago, 1976), 92–102; Christopher Sellers, "The Public Health Service's Office of Industrial Hygiene and the Transformation of Industrial Medicine," *Bulletin of the History of Medicine* 65 (spring 1991): 45–53.

20 CCMC, *Medical Care for the American People*, 80–81.

21 Paul de Kruif, *Kaiser Wakes the Doctors* (New York, 1943); Rickey Hendricks, *A Model for National Health Care: The History of Kaiser Permanente* (New Brunswick, NJ, 1993); Jennifer Klein, *For All These Rights: Business, Labor, and the Shaping of America's Public-Private Welfare State* (Princeton, 2003), 191–97; Starr, *Social Transformation of American Medicine*, 321–27.

22 Klein, *For All These Rights*, 132–33, 135; Starr, *Social Transformation of American Medicine*, 302–4; Michael R. Grey, *New Deal Medicine: The Rural Health Programs of the Farm Security Administration* (Baltimore, 2002), 14–15, 42–47, 53–57; James Peter Warbasse, *The Doctor and the Public* (New York, 1935), 514–23.

23 C. Rufus Rorem, interview by Lewis Weeks, transcript, 1983, Robert M. Cunningham Jr. Papers, private collection, Gaithersburg, MD (hereafter Cunningham Papers).

24 Robert Cunningham III and Robert M. Cunningham, Jr., *The Blues: A History of the Blue Cross and Blue Shield System* (DeKalb, IL, 1997), 36–37; Starr, *Social Transformation of American Medicine*, 162–69.

25 Cunningham, *The Blues*, 32.

26 John E. Murray, *Origins of American Health Insurance: A History of Industrial Sickness Funds* (New Haven, CT, 2007).

27 Klein, *For All these Rights*, 149–61; Raymond Munts, *Bargaining for Health: Labor Unions, Health Insurance and Medical Care* (Madison, WI, 1967), 3–6; Ivana Krajcinovic, *From Company Doctors to Managed Care: The United Mine Workers' Experiment* (Ithaca, NY, 1997).

28 Starr, *Social Transformation of American Medicine*, 210–13; Helen Clapesattle, *The Doctors Mayo*, 2nd ed. (Minneapolis, MN, 1955).

29 American Medical Association Bureau of Medical Economics, *Group Practice* (Chicago, 1933), 13–17.

30 Rosen, *Structure of American Medical Practice*, 94, 104–5; Starr, *Social Transformation of American Medicine*, 207–8.

31 Mary Ross, "The Case of the Ross-Loos Clinic," *Survey Graphic*, June 1935, 300, 304; Starr, *Social Transformation of American Medicine*, 200–213, 301–5, 321–27; Klein, *For All These Rights*, 122–25, 130–31.

32 The Committee on the Costs of Medical Care (CCMC), which was composed of leading health care experts, studied various medical delivery arrangements for approximately four years between 1928 and 1932. The committee's final report recommended that the health care system be organized around prepaid doctor groups because they offered high-quality care by implementing peer evaluation of physician work and by coordinating the services of general practitioners and specialists. CCMC, *Medical Care for the American People*, 109–20. After the CCMC report, health care reformers continued to promote prepaid groups on the basis of quality care. For example, according to journalist Mary Ross, "group work ... has been of great importance in raising standards of medical service, since it gives doctors an opportunity to pool their skill and knowledge so that all benefit from a range of experience which no man could gain alone." Ross, "The Case of the Ross-Loos Clinic," 301.

33 CCMC, *Medical Care for the American People*, 76–79. Additionally, because physicians joined together to invest in and share equipment, laboratories, and offices, group practice lowered the overhead costs associated with medical care delivery.

34 Robert H. Wiebe, *The Search for Order, 1877–1920* (New York, 1967), especially 111–16; Richard Hofstadter, *The Age of Reform* (New York, 1955), 148–64.

35 "Principles of Medical Ethics of the American Medical Association. Adopted by the House of Delegates at Atlantic City, N.J., June 4, 1912," *Annals of the American Academy of Political and Social Science* 101 (May 1922): 260–65; Leonard L. Landis, *The Physician and the People* (New York, 1924), 5–9, 97–170; R. G. Leland, "Contract Practice," *California and Western Medicine* 36 (April 1932): 234–41.

36 A. Bascom Croom, "Commercialism Pervading the Medical Profession – A Study of the Man and a Remedy for the Evil," *Transactions of the Tri-State Medical Association of the Carolinas and Virginia* (Raleigh, NC, 1911), 147–51; James G. Burrow, *AMA: Voice of American Medicine* (Baltimore, 1963), 108–26, 255–68, 364, 396.

37 "A Physician and Surgeons Hospital Association," *JAMA* 99 (November 26, 1932): 1867–68; Nathan B. Van Etten, "Better Health for America," *JAMA* 114 (June 15, 1940): 2347–50; "The Insurance Principle in the Practice of Medicine," *JAMA* 102 (May 12, 1934): 1612–18; "The 'Elastic Element' in Sickness Insurance," *JAMA* 115 (October 19, 1940): 1369; Irvin Abell, "The Aims of the Medical Profession as They Relate to the Public," *JAMA* 110 (June 18, 1938): 2041–44; Starr, *Social Transformation of American Medicine*, 215–18.

38 Quoted in Morris Fishbein, *A History of the American Medical Association, 1847 to 1947* (Philadelphia, 1947), 346–47.

39 Ibid., 385.

40 For example, "A Physician and Surgeons Hospital Association," 1867–68; "Insurance Contract Practice," *JAMA* 103 (July 28, 1934): 263–64; Leland, "Contract Practice," 234–41. See also Donald L. Madison, "Preserving Individualism in the Organizational Society: 'Cooperation' and American Medical Practice, 1900–1920," *Bulletin of the History of Medicine* 70 (fall 1996): 442–83.

41 Quoted in Burrow, *AMA*, 172.

42 Quoted in Ibid., 242, see also 239–40. See also Melchior Payli, *Compulsory Medical Care and the Welfare State* (Chicago, 1949), 28–33; Nathan Sinai, Odin W. Anderson, and Melvin L. Dollar, *Health Insurance in the United States* (New York, 1946), 22–24; Edgar Sydenstricker, "Group Medicine or Health Insurance – Which Comes First?" in *Free Medical Care: Socialized Medicine*, ed. E. C. Buehler (New York, 1936), 305–9; A. G. Christie, *Economic Problems of Medicine* (New York, 1935), 130–33.

43 CCMC, *Medical Care for the American People*, 103–44. On the CCMC, see also Daniel Fox, *Health Policies, Health Politics: The British and American Experience, 1911–1965* (Princeton, 1986), 45–51; Klein, *For All These Rights*, 120–26; Starr, *Social Transformation of American Medicine*, 261–66.

44 "The Committee on the Costs of Medical Care," *JAMA* 99 (December 3, 1932): 1950; Lewellyn F. Barker, "Investigations and Conclusions of the CCMC," *JAMA* 100 (March 25, 1933): 863–67.

45 "Americanism versus Sovietism for the American People," *JAMA* 99 (December 10, 1932): 2034–35.

46 The AMA physicians who controlled state boards also demonstrated prejudice against black doctors. They frequently either rejected African American candidates outright or erected additional test-taking barriers to discourage their licensure. This discrimination occurred particularly in the South but also in other parts of the country where organized doctors resented the competition and lower service fees of black physicians. David E. Bernstein, *Only One Place of Redress: African Americans, Labor Regulations, and the Courts* (Durham, NC, 2001), 41–44. Similarly, women were often precluded from obtaining medical licenses, either because of state laws or because of the preferences of board authorities. To study medicine, black physicians usually attended either Howard University or Meharry Medical College while women had to obtain admission to male-dominated medical schools.

47 Medical malpractice suits became a problem for doctors starting around the mid-nineteenth century. Malpractice insurance to protect physicians was introduced at the end of the century. And at the beginning of the twentieth century, some medical societies created their own malpractice defense funds. James C. Mohr, "American Medical Malpractice Litigation in Historical Perspective," *JAMA* 283 (April 5, 2000): 1731–37; Starr, *Social Transformation of American Medicine*, 111–12. See also James C. Mohr, *Doctors and the Law: Medical Jurisprudence in Nineteenth-Century America* (New York, 1993).

48 "Insurance Contract Practice," 263–64.

49 For examples of medical society oppression of doctors involved in alternative delivery models, see Landis, *The Physician and the People*, 5–9, 97–170; James Rorty, *American Medicine Mobilizes* (New York, 1939), 131–55; Edward D. Berkowitz and Wendy Wolff, *Group Health Association: A Portrait of a Health Maintenance Organization* (Philadelphia, 1988), 25–28, 30–36.

It appears that many physicians would have gladly participated in prepayment and group experiments. According to a 1938 Gallup poll, 75 percent of surveyed doctors favored prepaid health plans or insurance. Fifty-three percent of physicians agreed that group practice improved medical care. However, it is difficult to precisely gauge doctor support for prepaid groups because polling results varied depending on how practitioners were queried. For example, in one survey, 67 percent of physicians reported that they were opposed to the reorganization of medical practice. Just what they believed that reorganization would entail is unclear. Oliver Garceau, *The Political Life of the American Medical Association* (Cambridge, MA, 1941), 133–37. The Michigan State Medical Society and American College of Surgeons endorsed prepayment plans in 1934. Burrow, *AMA*, 235. See also Klein, *For All These Rights*, 155–56.

50 Ross, "The Case of the Ross-Loos Clinic," 300, 304; Klein, *For All these Rights*, 130–31.

51 "Medicine: Cooperative Doctor," *Time*, May 1, 1939, www.time.com/time/magazine/article/0,9171,761173-2,00.html (accessed June 22, 2013); Rorty, *American Medicine Mobilizes*, chapter 11; Starr, *Social Transformation of American Medicine*, 303–4; Michael Shadid, *A Doctor for the People; An Autobiography of the Founder of America's First Co-operative Hospital* (New York, 1939).

52 David Blumenthal and James A. Morone, *The Heart of Power: Health and Politics in the Oval Office* (Berkeley, 2009), 28–56; Jacob S. Hacker, *The Divided Welfare State: The Battle over Public and Private Social Benefits in the United States* (New York, 2002), 206–12; Starr, *Social Transformation of American Medicine*, 266–79; Odin W. Anderson, "Compulsory Medical Care Insurance, 1910–1950," *Annals of the American Academy of Political and Social Science* 273 (January 1951): 110–11.

53 Interdepartmental Committee to Coordinate Health and Welfare Activities, "A National Health Program" (*Proceedings of the National Health Conference*, Washington, D.C., 1938), 36, 62; Anderson, "Compulsory Medical Care Insurance," 110–11; Blumenthal and Morone, *The Heart of Power*, 40–49.

54 Arthur J. Altmeyer, *The Formative Years of Social Security* (Madison, WI, 1966), 96.
55 Berkowitz and Wolff, *Group Health Association*, 25–28, 30–36, 47–54; Starr, *Social Transformation of American Medicine*, 305–6; Burrow, AMA, 247–49.
56 "A.M.A. is Indicted as Trust Blocking Group Medicine," *New York Times*, December 21, 1938, 1, 21 for quotes.
57 "Doctors Draft Plan to Rival GHA, Refute Trust Charge," *Washington Post*, August 2, 1938, 1, 4 for quote. See also Morris Fishbein, *Morris Fishbein, M.D.: An Autobiography* (New York, 1969), 212–24.
58 The AMA's 1934 statement on voluntary insurance is often inaccurately characterized as the association's official acceptance of insurance or prepaid plans. The 1934 position was formulated *only* to allow constituent medical societies to work with state and local governments that employed Federal Emergency Relief Administration funding to create health care programs for the poor. The guidelines also provided direction for medical society representatives who negotiated with Resettlement Administration and Farm Security Administration officials on behalf of local doctors to provide health services for rural residents. In addition to being bound by federal law, the AMA leadership approved these programs because of the financial stress that physicians were experiencing during the Great Depression. By 1933, the average income of physicians had fallen to 53 percent of the 1929 figure. Simon Kuznets and Milton Friedman, "Income from Independent Practice, 1929–1936," *National Bureau of Economic Research Bulletin* (February 5, 1939): 8.
  Among the AMA's ten 1934 guidelines, rule six was as follows: "However the cost of medical service may be distributed, the immediate cost should be borne by the patient if able to pay at the time the service is rendered." AMA leaders reminded members that the association's cooperation with federal legislation did "not constitute in any sense of the word an endorsement of health insurance, either voluntary or compulsory." Quoted in "Extension of Medical Service to the Indigent," *JAMA* 108 (January 16, 1937): 209–10. See also "The 'Elastic Element' in Sickness Insurance," 1369; "County Medical Societies and Medical Service," *JAMA* 110 (February 12, 1938): 512; Klein, *For All These Rights*, 132–33, 155–56; Grey, *New Deal Medicine*. On the hostility of the national association and some constituent medical societies toward New Deal programming, see Michael M. Davis, *America Organizes Medicine* (New York, 1941), 92; "The Ascent of the Medical Profession," *JAMA* 106 (January 25, 1936): 297–99; Rorty, *American Medicine Mobilizes*, 147–55.One reason that some scholars trace organized physicians' acceptance of voluntary insurance back to 1934 is that, for public relations reasons, in an attempt to counter "the misrepresentation of the Association's attitude toward voluntary health insurance," the AMA subsequently published pamphlets and articles that obscured their historical positions. For example, Frank G. Dickinson, *A Brief History of the Attitude of the American Medical Association toward Voluntary Health Insurance* (Chicago, 1949), 3, 20–24; *Voluntary Prepayment Medical Benefit Plans* (Chicago, 1953), 10.

59 Burrow, *AMA*, 219–21, 246–47; Starr, *Social Transformation of American Medicine*, 276, 306. Note the resolution's ambivalent wording as recorded in a *JAMA* editorial: delegates approved "the *principle* of cash indemnity insurance." Quoted in Fishbein, *Morris Fishbein*, 211.

60 The agency's founding 1935 legislation created the Social Security Board, which was renamed the Social Security Administration in 1946.

61 Starr, *Social Transformation of American Medicine*, 277–81; Klein, *For All These Rights*, 172–77.

62 Berkowitz and Wolff, *Group Health Association*, 52–54.

63 The "insurance company model" is unique to the United States. Other countries, such as Germany, Switzerland, and France also have health care systems that employ insurance companies or sickness funds, which perform similar third-party financing functions. However, several characteristics, at least two of which have been effected through government regulation, have produced divergent health care economies in these countries.

First, in countries that engage insurance companies to coordinate health care, there has traditionally been, compared to the United States, less institutional (and, for that matter, geographical) distance between insurers and service providers. For example, in Germany, social insurance was born at the end of the nineteenth century out of a system of mutual aid societies and sickness funds, many of which directly hired physicians, paid them salaries, and closely supervised their provision of care. During the 1920s and 1930s, the government permitted physicians to begin bargaining collectively, through their regional associations, with these insuring organizations. However, compensation was still limited to capitation (per-patient) fees and constrained by fixed budgets that sickness funds paid to the regional associations representing doctors. Sickness funds, moreover, continued to monitor and regulate physician care and service utilization. While the particulars of this model have changed throughout the last century, insurers and governmental authorities have always retained far more control over physician work and pay than did third-party financiers in the United States. As this narrative will show, insurers in the United States spent decades attempting to acquire service provider oversight.

Second, in nations where insurance companies play a large role in the health care system, administration costs are generally much lower than in the United States. Even where the country includes a multiplicity of insurance groups and agencies, government regulations have standardized payment procedures, reporting measures, and monitoring processes across the system, thus permitting both financiers and service providers to spend less time on administrative tasks and associated complications. In Switzerland, for example, the government regulates policy benefits and physician compensation, thus homogenizing operational practices across numerous insurance companies. Additionally, mandated open enrollment periods and community rating have decreased the administrative costs associated with selling individualized, experience-rated policies.

Third, in other countries that incorporate third-party insurers, policymakers have had far more latitude to enact system-wide cost containment measures. It appears significant that nations that rely on third-party insuring agencies also rank among the most expensive, after the United States, health care systems in the world. Yet because government policymakers already have management authority over these systems, they have generally had more capacity than U.S. officials to enact cost control reforms. For example, similar to U.S. arrangements, the French health care system has historically featured fee-for-service payments for doctors and a high degree of physician autonomy. Third-party insurers – in this case, nonprofit sickness insurance funds – have been financed through payroll contributions and closely regulated by the government. As health care spending escalated over the twentieth century, policymakers negotiated lower fee schedules, constrained hospital budgets, and limited the scope of insurance coverage. Since the 1990s, physicians have followed more detailed medical care guidelines and now face penalties for exceeding spending targets. Nevertheless, costs continue to present grave problems for the French health care system. Moreover, a two-tier system of providers has developed, with one set of physicians agreeing to accept negotiated fee schedules as full payment and a second set levying charges in addition to fee schedules, which wealthier patients cover with supplementary insurance policies.

See Deborah A. Stone, *The Limits of Professional Power: National Health Care in the Federal Republic of Germany* (Chicago, 1980); Regina E. Herzlinger and Ramin Parsa-Parsi, "Consumer-Driven Health Care: Lessons from Switzerland," *JAMA* 292 (September 8, 2004): 1213–20; Uwe Reinhardt, "The Swiss Health System: Regulated Competition without Managed Care," *JAMA* 292 (September 8, 2004): 1227–31; Paul V. Dutton, *Differential Diagnosis: A Comparative History of Health Care Problems and Solutions in the United States and France* (Ithaca, NY, 2007); Lawrence D. Brown, "The Role of Regulation in Health Care Policy," in *Lessons from Europe? What Americans Can Learn from European Public Policies*, ed. R. Daniel Keleman (Thousand Oaks, CA, 2015), 43–57.

64 Starr, *Social Transformation of American Medicine*, 204, 305–6; "Right of Corporation to Practice Medicine," *Yale Law Journal* 48 (December 1938): 346–51.

65 "Proceedings of the House of Delegates," *JAMA* 111 (July 2, 1938): 59.

66 Starr, *Social Transformation of American Medicine*, 25–26.

67 It can also be argued that, by undermining market competition among physicians, indemnity payments and fee-for-service compensation have exacerbated the problem of uneven doctor distribution. If physicians had been forced to compete for employment (from a prepaid group, consumer cooperative, or hospital) or for patients based on well-advertised fees, then many younger, less-experienced, or poorer-quality doctors would have been driven away from metropolitan and suburban regions to practice in underserved districts, usually rural and, later in the century, inner-city areas. However, instead of switching geographical markets to attract a stable patient base, doctors practicing under indemnity and fee-for-service regimes could serve fewer patients and rely on inflated pricing and overutilization to cushion their bottom line.

68 "Cutting the Doctor's Bill to Fit," *JAMA* 116 (January 18, 1941): 417. See also "The 'Elastic Element' in Sickness Insurance," 1369; Burrow, *AMA*, 251.

69 Cunningham, *The Blues*, 58.

70 Klein, *For All These Rights*; Munts, *Bargaining for Health*; Marie Gottschalk, *The Shadow Welfare State: Labor, Business, and the Politics of Health Care in the United States* (Ithaca, NY, 2000); Colin Gordon, *Dead on Arrival: The Politics of Health Care in Twentieth-Century America* (Princeton, 2003), 60–67; Hacker, *Divided Welfare State*, chapters 4 and 5. Hacker and Klein challenge the standard narrative, which asserts that the World War II wage freeze was a primary factor leading to the rapid spread of employer-provided health insurance. Hacker argues that tax breaks to businesses were far more important than the wage freeze. Klein points out that the War Labor Board did not approve fringe benefits until 1943, and, thereafter, the Board rarely approved union requests for additional benefits or more liberal policies. Indeed, medical coverage data do not indicate unusual growth between 1943 and 1945. Hacker, *Divided Welfare State*, 218–19; Klein, *For All These Rights*, 179–83; *Source Book of Health Insurance Data* (New York, 1959), 11.

71 Gordon, *Dead on Arrival*, 62–63; Hacker, *Divided Welfare State*, 228–31.

72 Harry M. Johnson, "Major Medical Expense Insurance," *Journal of Risk and Insurance* 32 (June 1965): 211–14; Munts, *Bargaining for Health*, 7; Starr, *Social Transformation of American Medicine*, 201. A few companies began selling hospitalization insurance during the early twentieth century, but the coverage was very limited and not widespread.

73 For a discussion of moral hazard and how health insurance is different from other forms of insurance because it subsidizes frequently accessed services rather than unexpected occurrences, see Mark V. Pauly, *Medical Care at Public Expense: A Study in Applied Welfare Economics* (New York, 1971). For an alternative view positing that businessmen used such underwriting arguments as moral hazard and risk classification to oppose redistributive policies, fragment the market for profit, and exclude people who needed coverage, see Deborah Stone, "Beyond Moral Hazard: Insurance as Moral Opportunity," in *Embracing Risk: The Changing Culture of Insurance and Responsibility*, ed. Tom Baker and Jonathan Simon (Chicago, 2002), 52–79. See also Stone, "The Struggle for the Soul of Health Insurance," *JHPPL* 18 (summer 1993): 287–317.

74 Quoted in C. Rufus Rorem.

75 Johnson, "Major Medical Expense Insurance," 214. Adding to insurer hesitancy to enter the health care field, many insurance companies lost money on disability policies during the early 1930s. Premium prices had not been set high enough; benefits were too generous; and as the unemployment rate rose, policyholder claims increased precipitously. E. J. Faulkner, "The Insurance Company Approach to Health Insurance in the United States" (*International Insurance Conference of the Wharton School of Finance and Commerce*, Philadelphia, May 22, 1957), Series 9, Box 72, E. J. Faulkner Papers, Archives and Special Collections, University of Nebraska–Lincoln Libraries (hereafter Faulkner Papers).

76 Memo for M. Davis, "Hospitalization Benefits," October 8, 1930, Box 34, RG4, AXA Equitable Life Insurance Company Archives, New York, NY (hereafter Equitable Archives).

77 Johnson, "Major Medical Expense Insurance," 214; "Vice President Graham Memorandum," August 6, 1934, Box 34B, RG4, Equitable Archives;

Faulkner, "The Insurance Company Approach to Health Insurance"; Klein, *For All These Rights*, 208–9; Gordon, *Dead on Arrival*, 56–57.

78 Klein, *For All These Rights*, 211–12; To the President, "Medical Reimbursement Insurance," February 14, 1945, Box 34C, RG 4, Equitable Archives for quote; "Keeping Up with the Social Planners," *National Underwriter* 47 (January 1, 1943): 10; Travis T. Wallace, "Address of the President" (*Health Insurance Association of America Annual Meeting*, Philadelphia, May 4, 1959).

79 Johnson, "Major Medical Expense Insurance," 214–15.

80 Ibid., 215; "Liberty Mutual Catastrophe Medical Plan," *National Underwriter*, 1949, Box 42A, RG4, Equitable Archives.

81 "The In-Hospital Major Expense Policy," July 1, 1951, Box 41 C, RG4, Equitable Archives; "Prudential Plans Illness Coverage," *New York Times*, June 20, 1951, Box 41C, RG4, Equitable Archives; "Private Health Insurance through the Centuries," *Perspective* (summer 1984): 29, Cunningham Papers; Faulkner, "The Insurance Company Approach to Health Insurance." In 1943 or 1944 (sources differ on the dates), a few of the largest insurance companies began underwriting "medical policies," which covered physician services delivered outside the hospital. However, these policies were not widely available until the end of the decade when the Truman health care debates gained energy. See the following chapter. "Private Health Insurance through the Centuries," 29; Morton D. Miller, "Group Medical Expense Insurance," February 7, 1951, Box 32A, RG 4, Equitable Archives.

82 Arthur J. Offerman, interview by Odin W. Anderson, transcript, March 26, 1971, Cunningham Papers; Faulkner, "The Insurance Company Approach to Health Insurance.

83 "A.L.C. President Comments on New Role of A. & H.," *National Underwriter* 57 (May 8, 1953): 26.

84 Christie, *Economic Problems of Medicine*, 120–27; Starr, *Social Transformation of American Medicine*, 204–6; Jerome Schwartz, "Early History of Prepaid Medical Plans," *Bulletin of the History of Medicine* 39 (September–October 1965): 450–75; "History of the Bureaus and Washington Physicians Service" (photocopy, n.d.), Cunningham Papers.

85 In 1935, the California Medical Association passed a resolution endorsing state-run compulsory insurance. One year later, a more conservative faction of physicians won the association's leadership posts and the medical society reversed its position. Howard Hassard, "Fifty Years in Law and Medicine: An Oral History" (1985): 21–31, Cunningham Papers; A. J. Viseltear, "Public Health: Then and Now: Compulsory Health Insurance in California, 1934–1935," *American Journal of Public Health* 61 (October 1971): 2115–26.

86 Hassard, "Fifty Years in Law and Medicine," 30–31; California Physicians Service, *Voluntary Health Care by California Physicians Service: A Blue Shield Plan* (San Francisco, CA, 1950), 6–8; Cunningham, *The Blues*, 45–47.

87 Among Blue Shield plans, CPS would be among the most liberal in terms of making service benefits available. The program's salary cap permitted approximately 90 percent of California families to qualify for service benefits.

See Chapter 5. Louis S. Reed, *Blue Cross and Medical Service Plans* (Washington, D.C., 1947), 163.
88 Hassard, "Fifty Years in Law and Medicine," 34; Cunningham, *The Blues*, 45–46.
89 Cunningham, *The Blues*, 47–55; *Source Book of Health Insurance Data*, 14.
90 Burrow, *AMA*, 408–9.

2 Federal Reform Politics: Implanting the Insurance Company Model, 1945–1960

1 Ellis W. Hawley, "The Discovery of a 'Corporate Liberalism,'" *Business History Review* 52 (autumn 1978): 309–20. Hawley describes a "corporative system" as one in which "the state properly functions as coordinator, assistant, and midwife rather than director or regulator." In "such as system," writes Hawley, "there are deep interpenetrations between state and society, and enjoying a special status is an enlightened social elite, capable of perceiving social needs and imperatives and assisting social groups to meet them through enlightened concerts of interests." Howard J. Wiarda, *Corporatism and Comparative Politics: The Other Great "Ism"* (Armonk, NY, 1997), viii–xi, 6–7, chapter 6. Wiarda argues that "the U.S. system is one of limited corporatism, of partial corporatism, of mixed liberal and corporatist influences" (p. 148). Wiarda defines corporatism to include a strong state, a limited number of structured interests groups, and interest groups that function as state entities (pp. 6–7). The concept of "soft corporatism" allows for a less robust state, durable but sometimes informal ties between the state and interest groups, and more conflict between the state and voluntary groups than is seen under corporatism. Crucially, and as we will see in subsequent chapters, the trade associations under study were able to coordinate the actions of their members to reflect decisions made at the national level. Additionally, as in formal corporatist regimes, the government awarded these associations significant authority within their economic sectors. However, because of the fragmented nature of U.S. government power, this authority often came from state governments. State licensing laws endowed the AMA with regulatory power over the health care market. Insurance trade associations often collaborated with state officials to write industry governing codes, laws, and guidelines. And nonprofit Blue Cross and Blue Shield plans secured state enabling legislation to operate. These state-level concessions granted interest groups substantial control over the national marketplace as well as a dominant voice in federal health care politics. In Chapter 7, we will examine how U.S. corporatism became more explicit when policymakers shaped Medicare to incorporate the insurance company model and also designated insurance companies and nonprofit plans to act as program administrators. See also Ellis W. Hawley, "Herbert Hoover, the Commerce Secretariat, and the Vision of an 'Associative State,'" *Journal of American History* 61 (June 1974): 116–40; Robert Griffith, "Dwight D. Eisenhower and the Corporate Commonwealth," *American Historical Review* 87 (February 1982): 87–122; Robert M. Collins, *The Business Response to Keynes, 1929–1964* (New York,

1981); Wolfgang Streeck and Philippe C. Schmitter, eds., *Private Interest Government: Beyond Market and State* (Los Angeles, 1985). See the Introduction, note 12, on historical institutionalism and the organizational synthesis, schools of scholarship that provide means of studying the patterns of connection between the federal government and various societal groups.

2 Jacob S. Hacker, *The Divided Welfare State: The Battle over Public and Private Social Benefits in the United States* (New York, 2002), chapters 4 and 5; Colin Gordon, *Dead on Arrival: The Politics of Health Care in Twentieth-Century America* (Princeton, 2003), chapter 2; Jennifer Klein, *For All These Rights: Business, Labor, and the Shaping of America's Public-Private Welfare State* (Princeton, 2003); Marie Gottschalk, *The Shadow Welfare State: Labor, Business, and the Politics of Health Care in the United States* (Ithaca, NY, 2000).

3 Much of the following discussion is based on works that examine the postwar liberal consensus: Alan Brinkley, *The End of Reform: New Deal Liberalism in Recession and War* (New York, 1995); Collins, *Business Response to Keynes*; Alan Matusow, *The Unraveling of America: A History of Liberalism in the 1960s* (Athens, GA, 1986), 1–13; Louis Galambos and Joseph Pratt, *The Rise of the Corporate Commonwealth: United States Business and Public Policy in the Twentieth Century* (New York, 1989), 127–54; Olivier Zunz, *Why the American Century?* (Chicago, 1998), chapter 4. In recent years, scholars have paid greater attention to the antecedents of the New Right, tracing vigorous conservative and libertarian critiques to businessmen and scholars during the postwar era. See for example, Kim Phillips-Fein, *Invisible Hands: The Businessmen's Crusade against the New Deal* (New York, 2010); Angus Burgin, *The Great Persuasion: Reinventing Free Markets since the Depression* (Cambridge, MA, 2012). However, at least in the health care arena, I found little evidence that these views seriously challenged the bipartisan consensus in federal policymaking circles, which was premised upon the need to either eradicate or reform the insurance company model.

4 William M. McClenahan, Jr., and William H. Becker, *Eisenhower and the Cold War Economy* (Baltimore, 2011), 67–70.

5 Quoted in Griffith, "Dwight D. Eisenhower and the Corporate Commonwealth," 90.

6 David Stebenne, *Modern Republican: Arthur Larson and the Eisenhower Years* (Bloomington, IN, 2006); Griffith, "Dwight D. Eisenhower and the Corporate Commonwealth," 87–122; David Blumenthal and James A. Morone, *The Heart of Power: Health and Politics in the Oval Office* (Berkeley, 2009), 101–3; McClenahan and Becker, *Eisenhower and the Cold War Economy*, chapter 2; Dwight D. Eisenhower, "Annual Message of the Congress on the State of the Union," January 6, 1955, Gerhard Peters and John T. Woolley, *The American Presidency Project*, www.presidency.ucsb.edu/ws/?pid=10416 (accessed July 11, 2013); W. H. Lawrence, "Eisenhower Charts 'The Middle Road' to Domestic Goals," *New York Times*, August 21, 1952, 1–2.

7 Arthur M. Schlesinger, Jr., *The Vital Center: The Politics of Freedom* (Boston, 1949).

8 For an examination of the flexibility of Keynesian doctrine and its ability to shrink or expand to fit the conceptions of various political groups, see Daniel

Ritschel, *The Politics of Planning: The Debate on Economic Planning in Britain in the 1930's* (New York, 1997).

9 Although these policies were inaugurated during the 1930s, liberalizing the terms of Federal Housing Administration and Veterans Administration mortgages continued to animate housing politics throughout the postwar period.

10 Lizabeth Cohen, *A Consumer's Republic: The Politics of Mass Consumption in the Postwar Era* (New York, 2003), 114–29; Meg Jacobs, *Pocketbook Politics: Economic Citizenship in Twentieth-Century America* (Princeton, 2007); Robert M. Collins, *More: The Politics of Economic Growth in Postwar America* (New York, 2000).

11 *Source Book of Health Insurance Data* (New York, 1962), 10–11.

12 *Source Book of Health Insurance Data* (New York, 1959), 16.

13 For example, "What the Doctor Ordered," *Time*, August 18, 1952, 40–47; John E. McKeen, "Wonder Drugs' Wonder," *Time*, October 1, 1951, 93; "Hope of Victory over Cancer Is Held in Sight," *Chicago Daily Tribune*, January 7, 1950, A10; "New Techniques Save 98 Pct of Korea Wounded," *Chicago Daily Tribune*, February 4, 1951, 8; "100-Year Life Span Foreseen Average," *New York Times*, January 27, 1953, 27.

14 *National Health Program*, S.1606, 79th Cong., 1st sess., *Congressional Record* 91 (November 19, 1945): 10790–91; *Should America Have Compulsory Health Insurance? Altmeyer Says: Yes, Mannix Says: No* (Chicago, 1946), 72; Arthur Altmeyer, "How Can We Assure Adequate Health Service for All the People?" First Annual Conference of Presidents and Other Officers of State Medical Societies, Chicago, December 2, 1945, www.ssa.gov/policy/docs/ssb/v8n12/v8n12p12.pdf#nameddest=article (accessed July 9, 2012). Federal officials promised Blue Cross and Blue Shield leaders a role in "simplifying administration" and "promoting desirable professional relations." Although reformers aimed to move the system toward prepaid groups, doing so using existing nonprofit plans would have been possible by requiring Blues plans to use capitation payments and grant incentives to physicians for practicing together.

15 *National Health Program*, 10794.

16 On the enduring preference of health care reformers for prepaid groups, which lasted from the early twentieth century through the 1940s, see J. Dennis Chasse, "The American Association for Labor Legislation and the Institutionalist Tradition in National Health Insurance," *Journal of Economic Issues* 28 (December 1994): 1063–90. See also C. Rufus Rorem, "Economic Aspects of Medical Group Practice," in *Benefits of Group Practice*, ed. Alan Gregg (New York, 1949), 37–40; "Group Health Insurance Plans Encouraged by Recent Court Decisions," *Committee for the Nation's Health Bulletin* (October 1952), Reel 1, Microfilm Reels of the Committee for the Nation's Health Records, Michael M. Davis Collection, in the New York Academy of Medicine, U.S. National Library of Medicine, Bethesda, MD (hereafter Michael M. Davis Collection); *National Health Program*, 10794; Hubert H. Humphrey, "The Case for National Health Insurance," *New York Times*, May 8, 1949, SM15.

17 For more on this case, see Chapter 1.

18 Edward D. Berkowitz, *Mr. Social Security: The Life of Wilbur J. Cohen* (Lawrence, KS, 1995), 53–55, 230–31, 309; Edward D. Berkowtiz and Wendy Wolff, *Group Health Association: A Portrait of a Health Maintenance Organization* (Philadelphia, 1988), 48; Martha Derthick, *Policymaking for Social Security* (Washington, D.C., 1979), 115–16, 121–24.

19 Altmeyer, "How Can We Assure Adequate Health Service," 15–16; *National Health Program*, 10794; "Text of the President's Health Message Calling for Compulsory Medical Insurance," *New York Times*, November 20, 1945, 13. Certainly, physicians who opted out of the system (which would have been increasingly difficult to do as citizens purchased their insurance through the federal program) would have been permitted to continue practicing individually.

20 Altmeyer, "How Can We Assure Adequate Health Service," 15.

21 Policymakers also pledged that fee-for-service compensation would continue. However, fee-for-service payments represented only one among several planned reimbursement methods and officials clearly favored fixed salaries and capitation fees. It is therefore highly likely that they planned to gradually eliminate fee-for-service compensation, which many analysts deemed responsible for high health care costs. Altmeyer, "How Can We Assure Adequate Health Service," 15–16; *National Health Program*, 10790–91.

22 For narratives of the Truman health care debates that highlight Cold War overtones and accusations of "communism," see Monte M. Poen, *Harry S. Truman versus the Medical Lobby: The Genesis of Medicare* (Columbia, MO, 1979); Jill Quadagno, *One Nation Uninsured: Why the U.S. Has No National Health Insurance* (New York, 2005), chapter 1.

23 Harry S. Truman, "Special Message to the Congress Recommending a Comprehensive Health Program," November 19, 1945, *Public Papers of the Presidents, Harry S. Truman*, www.trumanlibrary.org/publicpapers/index. php?pid=483&st=&sti= (accessed January 8, 2013). See also "What Is 'Socialized Medicine'?" *New York Times*, February 24, 1946, 75; "Britain's Medicine Rejected by Ewing: State Control Is a Russian Idea," *New York Times*, June 12, 1950, 20; Douglas Dales, "Lehman Assailed: Dulles Charges His Opponent Attempts to Give Socialized Plan a New Label," *New York Times*, October 18, 1949, 30.

24 Truman, "Special Message to the Congress."

25 Federal Security Agency, *The National Health, A Ten-Year Program: A Report to the President*, by Oscar Ewing (Washington, D.C., 1948), 7.

26 Truman, "Special Message to the Congress"; *National Health Program*, 10790; Altmeyer, "How Can We Assure Adequate Health Service," 12; Claude Pepper, "Should Congress Approve National Compulsory Medical Insurance? Pro," *Congressional Digest* (March 1949): 92–94.

27 Margaret McKiever to Margaret C. Klem, "Statements on Voluntary Health Insurance Made at Hearings on S. 1606," May 31, 1946, Box 3, Division of Research and Statistics, Records of the Social Security Administration (hereafter SSA), RG 47, National Archives, College Park, MD (hereafter NARA); Frank W. Bishop to Barkey S. Sanders, "Dr. Sensenich's Testimony," July 10, 1946, Box 3, Division of Research and Statistics, SSA,

RG 47, NARA; Margaret C. Klem, "Voluntary Medical Care Insurance," *Annals of the American Academy of Political and Social Science* 273 (January 1951): 101–2; "A&H Council Protests S.S. Data on Health Insurance," *Eastern Underwriter* 54 (January 9, 1953): 9; "Health Insurers Blast Altmeyer's Critical Statement," *National Underwriter* 57 (January 9, 1953): 3.

28 Jerry Voorhis, "Money Spent Unwisely," *Committee for the Nation's Health Bulletin* (March 1955), Reel 1 (microfilm), Michael M. Davis Collection. Similarly, James Howard Means, "The Doctor's Lobby," *The Atlantic Monthly*, October 1950 (Chicago: Reprinted by the Committee for the Nation's Health, 1950), Reel 1 (microfilm), Michael M. Davis Collection. See also Gordon, *Dead on Arrival*, 264–66.

29 Truman, "Special Message to the Congress"; "Senate Body Backs Health Insurance," *New York Times*, July 22, 1946, 16.

30 Quoted in Hacker, *Divided Welfare State*, 226–27. See also "With Firm and Regular Step," *Journal of the Michigan State Medical Society* 50 (June 1951): 632–61.

31 Klein, *For All These Rights*, 219–20; Gordon, *Dead on Arrival*, 60–63; National Physicians' Committee for the Extension of Medical Service, *Opportunity for Private Enterprise* (1944), Reel 6 (microfilm), Michael M. Davis Collection. On the Chamber's Health Advisory Council, see Nathan Sinai, Odin W. Anderson, and Melvin L. Dollar, *Health Insurance in the United States* (New York, 1946), 39–40.

32 Chamber of Commerce, *You and Socialized Medicine* (Washington, D.C., 1948), 17.

33 *Source Book of Health Insurance Data* (1962), 60–61. Between the late 1940s and the early 1960s, health care costs climbed 61 percent. During the same period, transportation costs rose 48 percent and housing prices escalated 33 percent. Food and apparel rose 21 percent and 10 percent, respectively. See also Odin W. Anderson, Patricia Collette, and Jacob J. Feldman, *Changes in Family Medical Care Expenditures and Voluntary Insurance: A Five-Year Resurvey* (Cambridge, MA, 1963), 100–101; Anne R. Somers and Herman M. Somers, "Coverage, Costs, and Controls in Voluntary Health Insurance," *Public Health Reports* 76 (January 1961): 4–5.

34 *Source Book of Health Insurance Data* (1962), 10–11.

35 Wallace Croatman, "Are Health Plans Giving People What They Want?" *Medical Economics* 34 (August 1957): 298.

36 In 1948, the National Labor Relations Board ruled that unions had the right to negotiate over fringe benefits as "conditions of employment." Klein, *For All These Rights*, 231–32. Although this arrangement left most insurance plans under employer management, in some industries, unions gained control of health care funds. For more on these funds, also known as Taft-Hartley plans, see Gottschalk, *Shadow Welfare State*, 44–53.

37 Edith Evans Asbury, "Hospitals Urged to Expand Roles," *New York Times*, September 21, 1955, 21 for quote; A. J. Hayes, "What's Wrong with Health Insurance Today," *Medical Economics* 32 (December 1955): 170–72.

38 Klein, *For All These Rights*, 213–18, 221–28; Raymond Munts, *Bargaining for Health: Labor Unions, Health Insurance, and Medical Care* (Madison, WI, 1967), chapter 9.

39 Unidentified Milwaukee Blue Cross administrator, interview by Odin W. Anderson, transcript, August 9, 1972, Cunningham Papers.

40 E. A. Van Steenwyk, "Recent Developments in the Use of Blue Cross and Blue Shield Plans," *American Journal of Public Health* 41 (February 1951): 147; Robert Cunningham III and Robert M. Cunningham, Jr., *The Blues: A History of the Blue Cross and Blue Shield System* (DeKalb, IL, 1997), 12.

41 "Expansion is Aim of Hospital Plans," *New York Times*, May 20, 1953, 47; Cunningham, *The Blues*, 30–32.

42 "Message from Dr. Walter B. Martin on Comprehensive Medical Care," *JAMA* 158 (July 2, 1955): 734. See also David B. Allman, "Medicine's Role in Financing Health Care Costs" (*Health Insurance Association of America Annual Meeting*, Washington, D.C., May 7, 1959).

43 "Misinterpretation of 'Needs' for Medical Care," *JAMA* 148 (March 8, 1952): 848–49; "Message from Dr. Walter B. Martin on Comprehensive Medical Care," 734; "Committee on Prepayment of Medical and Hospital Services," *JAMA* 159 (October 29, 1955): 942; F. J. L. Blasingame, "Things of Good Report," Meeting of the Texas Medical Association, Dallas, TX, April 29, 1957, Box 20, F. J. L. Blasingame Papers, Truman G. Blocker Jr. History of Medicine Collections, University of Texas Medical Branch, Galveston, TX (hereafter Blasingame Papers).

44 David B. Allman, "The President's Page," *JAMA* 164 (August 31, 1957): 2053; David B. Allman, "Medicine's Role in Financing Health Care Costs," *JAMA* 165 (November 23, 1957): 1573.

45 Frank G. Dickinson, "Building Health by Commission," *JAMA* 151 (March 21, 1953): 1035.

46 John H. Miller, *Basic Principles of Health Insurance* (Washington, D.C., 1954), 49–57; Edwin J. Faulkner, *Health Insurance* (New York, 1960), 73, 153–54; "Terms Catastrophe the Only True Insurance in Medical Field," *National Underwriter* 55 (February 9, 1951): 17; "Insurance Really Fulfilling Function," *National Underwriter* 57 (May 8, 1953): 23, 27; "Hansen Survey of A.&H. Evolution," *Eastern Underwriter* 54 (October 16, 1953): 44.

47 Health Insurance Council, *Health Insurance Story* (New York, n.d.), 24–25, Box 42A, RG4, Equitable Archives.

48 Alvin B. Dalager to Agency Managers and General Agents, May 18, 1954, Box 42A, RG 4, Equitable Archives (emphasis in original).

49 Joseph F. Follmann, Jr., "Major Medical Expense Insurance – Its Development and Problems," *JAMA* 165 (November 23, 1957): 1585. Follman was an insurance industry leader writing for a physician audience.

50 John A. Appleman, "Health and Accident Insurance Policies – How Much Can You Rely on Them?" *Reader's Digest*, September 1953, 23–26. See also "Reader's Digest Article on A&H Causes Headaches," *National Underwriter* 57 (August 28, 1953): 7; Blake Clark, "Be Sure You Know What's in Your Health and Accident Policy," *Reader's Digest*, July 1954, 115–19; Milton Silverman, "Is This the Pattern of the Future?"

The Saturday Evening Post, June 21, 1958, 30, 100–102; Andrew J. Biemiller, "The Need for Health Insurance," *Consumer Reports*, April 1949, 174; "How Good Are the 'Blue' Plans?" *Consumer Reports*, October 1950, 456–57; "Why It Costs More to Insure against Illness," *U.S. News and World Report*, January 31, 1958, 83–85; Russell Baker, "Health Insurance Poses a National Problem," *New York Times*, February 6, 1955, E6; Robert K. Plumb, "U.S. Studies Gaps in Medical Plans," *New York Times*, January 11, 1957, 14.

51 Croatman, "Are Health Plans Giving People What They Want?" 291–304.
52 Bess Furman, "Mrs. Hobby to Set Health Policies," *New York Times*, May 10, 1953, 1, 61.
53 Senate Committee on Labor and Public Welfare, *President's Health Recommendations and Related Measures*, 83rd Cong., 2nd sess., March 17, 1954 (Dwight D. Eisenhower, "Message from the President of the United States Transmitting Recommendations to Improve the Health of the American People"), 19.
54 *Source Book of Health Insurance Data* (1962), 12–17.
55 Although the 1956 Health Research Facilities Act was the first legislation to explicitly fund medical schools, the federal government began subsidizing medical university research during World War II.
56 Odin W. Anderson, *Health Services as a Growth Enterprise in the United States since 1875* (Ann Arbor, MI, 1990), 139–43; "For the Nation's Health," *Time*, December 29, 1952, 34–35.
57 "'Dues' Health Plan Is Urged by Kaiser," *New York Times*, January 12, 1954, 11.
58 "Creeping Socialism by Commission," *JAMA* 151 (March 21, 1953): 1003; "Statement of Board of Trustees on Report of the Truman Commission," *JAMA* 151 (January 24, 1953): 302–3.
59 To Members of the Texas Medical Association, "Fact Sheet on the Wolverton Bill," 1954, Box 7, Blasingame Papers (emphasis in original).
60 Francis T. Hodges, "Supermarket Medicine," Annual Conference of Blue Shield Plans, New York, April 4–8, 1954, Cunningham Papers.
61 James G. Burrow, *AMA: Voice of American Medicine* (Baltimore, 1963), 347–51.
62 Hacker, *Divided Welfare State*, 226–27, 400–401 n. 30, 32; Poen, *Truman versus the Medical Lobby*, 166.
63 Arthur Altmeyer, *The Formative Years of Social Security* (Madison, WI, 1966), 261–62.
64 "Two Senators Urge US Health Insurance Aid," *Washington Post*, March 2, 1953, 5; "3 Senators Offer Health Plan," *Washington Post*, January 15, 1955, 2; "Health Aid Bill Offered," *New York Times*, January 15, 1955, 9. In 1950, a group of liberal Republicans circulated a declaration of principles that designated the Flanders-Ives approach as their preferred model for health care reform. Marquis Childs, "Liberal Republicans: How to Finance Progressive Views?" *Washington Post*, April 5, 1950, 15.
65 Hacker, *Divided Welfare State*, 226–27, 400 n. 30; Poen, *Truman versus the Medical Lobby*, 165–67, 228–29.

66 Reminiscences of Roswell Perkins, part I (April 2, 1966), 38, Social Security Project, Columbia Center of Oral History Collection, Columbia University, New York, NY (hereafter CCOHC).

67 Bess Furman, "Health Plan Asks Insurance Subsidy," *New York Times*, February 23, 1953, 39. See also "Health Commission Hears Proposals for Both Compulsory, Subsidized Programs," *National Underwriter* 56 (October 17, 1952): 7; C. Rufus Rorem, interview, transcript, n.d., Cunningham Papers; Cunningham, *The Blues*, 19–21, 77–79; Van Steenwyk, "Recent Developments in the Use of Blue Cross and Blue Shield Plans," 150. At this time, Philadelphia Blue Cross was formally called Associated Hospital Service of Philadelphia.

68 "Magnuson Report Urges Wide Federal Entry in A&H Field," *National Underwriter* 56 (December 19, 1952): 5.

69 Cunningham, *The Blues*, 122–24.

70 Roswell Perkins, Reminiscences, 39–40.

71 Burrow, *AMA*, 347–51; Council on Legislation, "Blue Print for 1950," April 6, 1950, Box 20, Blasingame Papers; "Three Challenges of the Future," *JAMA* 151 (January 17, 1953): 212–13; Gordon B. Leitch, "Summary of Remarks Delivered before Regional Legislative Conference of the American Medical Association at San Francisco," January 23, 1954, Box 7, Blasingame Papers.

72 Arthur R. Abbey to W. R. McBee, August 27, 1956, Box 19, Blasingame Papers.

73 Health Insurance Association of America, "Meeting of Board of Directors," November 20, 1956, Box 25, Orville Francis Grahame Papers, University of Iowa Special Collections, Iowa City, IA (hereafter Grahame Papers); "Minutes of the 1953 IESA Annual Meeting," October 6, 1953, Box 28, Grahame Papers; "Eddy Speaks His Mind on Group A&H Trends," *Eastern Underwriter* 54 (October 16, 1953): 45, 48.

74 Senate Committee on Labor and Public Welfare, *President's Health Recommendations and Related Measures*, 18–19.

75 "Statement by Oveta Culp Hobby," March 11, 1954, Box 7, Blasingame Papers; "Mrs. Hobby Explains Details of Re. Measure," *Eastern Underwriter* 56 (February 11, 1955): 37; U.S. Department of Health, Education, and Welfare, "Fact Sheet Issued in Connection with Legislative Proposals of 1954," March 11, 1954, Box 7, Blasingame Papers. The idea of federal reinsurance for health care policies appears to have originated with Harold Stassen, perennial contender for the Republican presidential nomination. In 1949, he floated the idea of government reinsurance, but only for nonprofit policies. In 1950, Representative Charles A. Wolverton (R, NJ) put forth a reinsurance proposal in H.R. 8746. The Wolverton version would have allowed government underwriting for both nonprofit and commercial policies but would have required insurers to include certain benefits. The reinsurance proposal surfaced during the Eisenhower administration when Nelson Rockefeller, as assistant secretary of HEW, presented the idea to Secretary Hobby. Given the government's activities in underwriting home mortgages, it is unsurprising that politicians attempted to apply the same logic to health care. "What's in the Wolverton Health Bill," *Medical Economics* 27 (September 1950): 109–10.

76 House Committee on Interstate and Foreign Commerce, *Hearings on Health Reinsurance Legislation, H.R. 8356*, 83rd Cong., 2nd sess., March 31, 1954 (Statement of Henry S. Beers), 207–37; Edwin J. Faulkner, "Why Reinsurance Can't Work," *Medical Economics* 31 (July 1954): 147–48; E. J. Faulkner, "Review of Accident and Sickness Insurance," *Journal of the American Association of University Teachers of Insurance* 22 (March 1955): 78–82. Fearing that federal authority would encroach on state regulatory jurisdiction, the National Association of Insurance Commissioners also opposed reinsurance legislation. Roswell Perkins, Reminiscences, 44–45; "Address by Oveta Culp Hobby," National Association of State Insurance Commissioners Meeting, Detroit, MI, June 19, 1954, Box 7, Blasingame Papers.

77 Roswell Perkins, Reminiscences, 43–45, 66–67.

78 Frank E. Wilson to F. J. L. Blasingame, "Legislative Action, Health Reinsurance Bill," August 17, 1954, Box 7, Blasingame Papers; Blumenthal and Morone, *The Heart of Power*, 111–12.

79 James E. Bryan, "Blue Shield's Role in the Future of Medicine," *Medical Economics* 31 (July 1954): 161–85; James E. Bryan, "The Role of Blue Shield in the Future of Medical Practice," Annual Conference of Blue Shield Plans, New York, April 4–8, 1954, Cunningham Papers.

80 Reminiscences of Roswell Perkins, part II (July 11, 1966), 91–92, CCOHC; House Committee on Interstate and Foreign Commerce, *Hearings on Health Reinsurance Legislation, H.R. 8356*, 83rd Cong., 2nd sess., March 26, 1954 (Statement of William S. McNary), 151–53.

81 Reminiscences of Marion B. Folsom, part II, (October 13, 1965), 172–74, CCOHC; Roswell Perkins, Reminiscences (April 2 and July 11, 1966), 34–50, 46–47, 66–81, 91–92.

82 Roswell Perkins, Reminiscences (April 2, 1966), 42. Nor were Social Security Administration officials eager to cede their authority over health care to a new federal agency.

83 "Address by Oveta Culp Hobby."

84 Eisenhower, "Annual Message of the Congress."

85 "Address of Congressman Oren Harris," *JAMA* 164 (June 22, 1957): 885.

86 "Folsom Exhorts Insurance Group," *New York Times*, December 15, 1955, 59.

87 "Keen Interest in Doctor-Hospital Panel Talks," *Eastern Underwriter* 54 (January 30, 1953): 32.

88 A. M. Wilson, "Where Do We Go from Here?" (*The Bureau-Conference Group Accident and Health Insurance Meeting*, Chicago, February 7–9, 1955), 89.

89 House Committee on Interstate and Foreign Commerce, *Hearings on Health Reinsurance Legislation, H.R. 8356*, 83rd Cong., 2nd sess., April 5, 1954 (Statement of David B. Allman), 295–98.

90 Ibid., May 5, 1954 (Statement of Frank E. Smith), 388–401.

91 Ibid., May 5, 1954 (Statement of Henry S. Beers), 216.

92 Hacker, *Divided Welfare State*; Klein, *For All These Rights*.

93 Hacker, *Divided Welfare State*, 217–18, 239–42; Klein, *For All These Rights*, 183–84; Blumenthal and Morone, *The Heart of Power*, 112–13.

94 "Summary of Meeting with Advisory Group on Fringe Benefits in Mr. Folsom's Office," April 20, 1954; "Summary of Meeting of the Advisory Group on Fringe

Benefits," May 5, 1954; "Report of Meeting of the Advisory Group," June 9, 1953; all in Box 59, Office of Tax Policy, General Records of the Department of Treasury, RG 56, NARA. House Democrats attempted to tie the tax break to regulations compelling businesses to either cover low-wage employees or a stipulated percentage of their workforce. Following the administration's recommendations, senators stripped these "nondiscrimination requirements" from the final legislation.

95 On union bargaining over "private welfare benefits," see Klein, *For All These Rights*; Gordon, *Dead on Arrival*, 60–67; Gottschalk, *Shadow Welfare State*, chapter 3; Sanford Jacoby, *Modern Manors: Welfare Capitalism since the New Deal* (Princeton, 1997); Nelson Lichtenstein, "From Corporatism to Collective Bargaining: Organized Labor and the Eclipse of Social Democracy in the Postwar Era," in *The Rise and Fall of the New Deal Order, 1930–1980*, ed. Steve Fraser and Gary Gerstle (Princeton, 1989), 122–52; Rick Mayes, *Universal Coverage: The Elusive Quest for National Health Insurance* (Ann Arbor, MI, 2001), chapter 4; Munts, *Bargaining for Health*.

96 Quoted in Hacker, *Divided Welfare State*, 240.

97 Gottschalk, *Shadow Welfare State*, 48.

98 Munts, *Bargaining for Health*, 124.

99 Ibid., 87.

100 Robert Cunningham, letter to the editor, "Refuting the 'Accidental System,'" *Health Affairs* 19 (May/June 2000): 285; Herbert Klarman, "Changing Costs of Medical Care and Voluntary Health Insurance" (*Meeting of the American Economic Association and American Association of University Teachers of Insurance*, Cleveland, OH, December 28, 1956), 14–15. This figure may somewhat underrepresent the average costs borne by employers because, at the time, businesses usually had closer relationships with commercial insurance companies than with nonprofit plans.

101 Klarman, "Changing Costs of Medical Care," 16.

102 Munts, *Bargaining for Health*, 86.

103 Although the United States has an employer-provided insurance system, businesses have not actually shouldered the expense of employee medical coverage. Companies have traditionally based hiring decisions on the total annual cost to employ a worker, not on salary alone. Thus, employers have been paying workers less in the form of salary and more in the form of health insurance and benefits administration expenditures. See Mark V. Pauly, *Health Benefits at Work* (Ann Arbor, MI, 1997) for a discussion of how insurance costs are passed on to employees. Richard V. Burkhauser and Kosali I. Simon attribute stagnating middle-class wages to the spiraling cost of employer-purchased medical coverage. Burkhauser and Simon, "Measuring the Impact of Health Insurance on Levels and Trends in Inequality," National Bureau of Economic Research, Working Paper Series, no. 15811 (March 2010): 1–39. For an alternative view that claims employees do not bear the full cost of health insurance, see Lewin-VHI, Inc., *The Financial Impact of the Health Security Act* (Fairfax, VA, 1993).

104 Klein, *For All These Rights*, 228–30; Gordon, *Dead on Arrival*, 10; Nancy S. Jecker, "Can an Employer-Based Health Insurance System Be Just?" in *The*

Politics of Health Care Reform, ed. James A. Morone and Gary S. Belkin (Durham, NC, 1994), 259–75; Joni Hersch and Shelly White Means, "Employer Sponsored Health and Pension Benefits and the Gender/Race Wage Gap," *Social Science Quarterly* 74 (December 1993): 851–66.

105 Survey results in James E. Bryan, "Blue Shield Faces Its Hour of Decision," *Medical Economics* 32 (May 1955): 197–224.

106 James E. Stuart, "The Blue Cross Story," unpublished manuscript, n.d., 267, Cunningham Papers.

107 T. H. Kirkpatrick, "Task Force No. 3 Meeting," October 1954, Box 17, Grahame Papers; "General Manager's Report to the Board of Directors on the Affairs of the Health Insurance Association of America," 1956, Box 25, Grahame Papers.

108 "Report of the Group Insurance Committee to the Board of Directors of the Health Insurance Association of America," November 30, 1956, Box 25, Grahame Papers.

109 Barron K. Grier to John W. Castellucci, September 17, 1956, Blue Cross and Blue Shield Archives, Washington, D.C. (hereafter BCBS D.C. Archives); *25 Years of Service* (Washington, D.C., 1974), BCBS D.C. Archives. Because the commercial industry's plan appeared to have a good chance of passage, Washington, D.C. Blue Cross and Blue Shield plan leaders, despite years of criticizing such coverage, created their own major medical policy.

110 Blue Cross Commission, "News Release," June 22, 1956, BCBS D.C. Archives.

111 Subcommittee on Insurance of the Committee on Post Office and Civil Service, *Hearings on the Health Insurance Program for Federal Employees,* S.94, 86th Cong., 1st sess., April 30, 1959 (Statement of Manton Eddy), 289–90.

112 "Federal Employee Health Insurance Program," September 28, 1956; Grier to Castellucci; Jerry Kluttz, "The Federal Diary," *Washington Post,* July 6, 1956, 33; all in BCBS D.C. Archives.

113 J. D. Colman, interview by Odin W. Anderson, transcript, January 9, 1971, Cunningham Papers; Stuart, *The Blue Cross Story,* 268.

114 "Federal Workers Select Health Care Insurers," *Insurance Economics Surveys* 17 (September 1960), Box 28, Grahame Papers; Andrew E. Ruddock, "Federal Employees Health Benefits Program," *American Journal of Public Health* 56 (January 1966): 52. In 1960, Congress passed legislation to provide retired federal workers with health insurance.

3 Sclerotic Institution: The Declining Power of Organized Physicians and the AMA

1 David Wilsford, *Doctors and the State: The Politics of Health Care in France and the United States* (Durham, NC, 1991), chapter 4. Wilsford compares the relatively unified and large AMA to smaller, competing doctor organizations in France.

2 Monte M. Poen, *Harry S. Truman versus the Medical Lobby: The Genesis of Medicare* (Columbia, MO, 1979), 177–82; Elton Rayack, *Professional Power*

and American Medicine: The Economics of the American Medical Association (Cleveland, OH, 1967), 10–12; Paul Starr, *The Social Transformation of American Medicine: The Rise of a Sovereign Profession and the Making of a Vast Industry* (New York, 1982), 287–88; Colin Gordon, *Dead on Arrival: The Politics of Health Care in Twentieth-Century America* (Princeton, 2003), 261–69.

3 Theda Skocpol, *Protecting Soldiers and Mothers: The Political Origins of Social Policy in the United States* (Cambridge, MA, 1992), 55; Jill Quadagno, "Why the United States Has No National Health Insurance: Stakeholder Mobilization against the Welfare State, 1945–1996," *Journal of Health and Social Behavior* 45 (extra issue, 2004): 25–44; Harry Eckstein, *The English Health Service: Its Origins, Structure, and Achievements* (Cambridge, MA, 1958), 20–22; Oliver Garceau, *The Political Life of the American Medical Association* (Cambridge, MA, 1941), 118.

4 Interestingly, the book that goes farthest down the road of revisionist history, challenging the concept of an all-powerful association and revealing much of the internal dysfunction and conflict among organized physicians, is Frank D. Campion's AMA-authorized book, *The AMA and U.S. Health Policy since 1940* (Chicago, 1984).

5 James G. Burrow, *AMA: Voice of American Medicine* (Baltimore, 1963), 41–44.

6 Ibid., 21–26.

7 Skocpol, *Protecting Soldiers and Mothers*, 515–17; Sheila Rothman, "Women's Clinics or Doctors' Offices: The Sheppard-Towner Act and the Promotion of Preventative Health Care," in *Social History and Social Policy*, ed. David J. Rothman and Stanton Wheeler (New York, 1981), 176; Burrow, *AMA*, 157–64.

8 Campion, *AMA and U.S. Health Policy*, 7–9.

9 Morris Fishbein, *Morris Fishbein, M.D., An Autobiography* (New York, 1969), 204–5.

10 Odin W. Anderson, "Compulsory Medical Care Insurance, 1910–1950," *Annals of the American Academy of Political and Social Sciences* 273 (January 1951): 110; Fishbein, *Morris Fishbein*, 203–8. For an example of scholarship that exemplifies the traditional narrative of "astute" and "sophisticated" AMA political lobbying – in this case, during the 1930s and early 1940s – see Daniel S. Hirschfield, *The Lost Reform: The Campaign for Compulsory Health Insurance in the United States from 1932–1943* (Cambridge, MA, 1970).

11 Campion, *AMA and U.S. Health Policy*, 8.

12 Quoted in Starr, *Social Transformation of American Medicine*, 279. See also Gordon, *Dead on Arrival*, 215–17.

13 Campion, *AMA and U.S. Health Policy*, 127.

14 C. Joseph Stetler, "Legislative Outlook for Medicine in 1954," Annual Meeting of the Toledo, Ohio Academy of Medicine, January 13, 1954, Box 7, Blasingame Papers; Campion, *AMA and U.S. Health Policy*, 134–37

15 "Medicine at the Crossroads," *Medical Annals of the District of Columbia* 11 (May 1943): 193–94.

16 John M. Pratt, National Physicians' Committee for the Extension of Medical Care, *Abolishing Medical Practice* (Chicago, 1943), 21.

17 The letter referencing the antichrist created a rift between national AMA leaders and the Medical Society of the State of New York that took years to mend. "Race Bias Denied by Medical Group," *New York Times*, March 2, 1949, 8; Campion, *AMA and U.S. Health Policy*, 136–37, 144–45; Poen, *Truman versus the Medical Lobby*, 46–48, 143–44; David B. Truman, *The Governmental Process*, 2nd ed. (Berkeley, 1993), 174–75.

18 *National Physicians' Committee Bulletin* (October 1, 1942), Reel 6 (microfilm), Michael M. Davis Collection.

19 Because his responsibility for approving *JAMA* advertisements gave him close ties to the pharmaceutical industry, AMA critics contended that Fishbein was responsible for securing much of the NPC's funding. Moreover, the founder of the NPC, John M. Pratt, was known to be a Fishbein ally. Greer Williams, "Medicine's India-Rubber Man," *The Saturday Evening Post*, October 19, 1946, 92; "The Press: Medicine's Journal," *Time*, April 13, 1936, http://content.time.com/time/subscriber/article/0,33009,755993,00.html (accessed December 28, 2013).

20 Williams, "Medicine's India-Rubber Man," 26.

21 For example, "Should This Nation Adopt the National Health Insurance Program?" *American Druggist* 119 (January 1949): 78–81, 102–8. See also Campion, *AMA and U.S. Health Policy*, 124–25.

22 "Medicine: Nationalized Doctors?" *Time*, June 21, 1937, http://content.time.com/time/magazine/article/0,9171,757971,00.html (accessed December 28, 2013).

23 Williams, "Medicine's India-Rubber Man," 26–27, 91–94; Fishbein, *Morris Fishbein*; "Medicine: Nationalized Doctors?"; Morris Fishbein, interview by Charles O. Jackson, transcript, March 12, 1968, www.fda.gov/downloads/AboutFDA/WhatWeDo/History/OralHistories/SelectedOralHistory Transcripts/UCM264166.pdf (accessed December 28, 2013).

24 Williams, "Medicine's India-Rubber Man," 26.

25 For example, "The Committee on the Costs of Medical Care," *JAMA* 99 (December 3, 1932): 1950; "The Wagner-Murray-Dingell Bill," *JAMA* 128 (June 2, 1945): 364.

26 Fishbein, *Morris Fishbein*, 265; "Remedy for Fishbein," *Time*, July 15, 1946, www.time.com/time/magazine/article/0,9171,803878,00.html (accessed March 11, 2010).

27 "Health Insurance Legislation in California," *JAMA* 127 (February 17, 1945): 398. See also "Cutting the Doctor's Bill to Fit," *JAMA* 116 (February 1, 1941): 417.

28 Fishbein, *Morris Fishbein*, 257–60, 264–67; James Rorty, *American Medicine Mobilizes* (New York, 1939), 208–24; Williams, "Medicine's India-Rubber Man," 26–27. On the California Medical Association and Blue Shield, see Chapter 1. The "California Revolt" first began in 1938 when the state's delegation requested that Fishbein's activities be confined to editing *JAMA*. As they attempted to unseat Fishbein throughout the 1940s, California representatives received the most support from delegations of states where Blue

Shield was particularly strong – Michigan, New York, and New Jersey. For more on the Blue Shield-AMA divide, see Chapter 5.

29 Raymond Rich Associates, "Excerpts from Report on Public Relations to the Trustees of the American Medical Association," June 15, 1946, Reel 6 (microfilm), Michael M. Davis Collection.

30 Campion, *AMA and U.S. Health Policy*, 143–45.

31 William H. Halley, "An Open Letter to the Board of Trustees of the American Medical Association," *Rocky Mountain Medical Journal* (August 1947), Reel 6 (microfilm), Michael M. Davis Collection.

32 Quoted in Campion, *AMA and U.S. Health Policy*, 145.

33 Halley, "An Open Letter."

34 Campion, *AMA and U.S. Health Policy*, 143–45. The AMA created a more meager Department of Public Relations in 1947. The department provided canned articles to newspapers and magazines and sponsored traveling exhibits, radio ads, and pamphlets that touted the AMA's scientific and humanitarian accomplishments. However, department officials lacked prestige within the association and their activities seemed to have little influence on the public's perception of doctors. John W. Cline, "The President's Page: A Monthly Message," *JAMA* 148 (March 20, 1952): 1128–29; "Report of Assistant to the General Manager: Department of Public Relations," *JAMA* 153 (October 31, 1953); Tom Hendricks to F. J. L. Blasingame, "A.M.A. – 1958–1961," July 14, 1961, Box 11, Blasingame Papers.

35 Fishbein, *Morris Fishbein*, 305–12; William L. Laurence, "AMA to Retire Dr. Fishbein," *New York Times*, June 7, 1949, 1, 24; N.S. Haseltine, "AMA Imposes Gag on Dr. Fishbein," *Washington Post*, June 7, 1949, 2; "Medicine: Lightning Rod," *Time*, June 20, 1949, www.time.com/time/magazine/article/0,9171,800391-1,00.html (accessed January 13, 2010).

36 Thomas E. Mattingly, letter to the editor, *The Star*, June 29, 1949, Reel 7 (microfilm), Michael M. Davis Collection. On the rise and fall of Fishbein, see Campion, *AMA and U.S. Health Policy*, chapter 9.

37 Campion, *AMA and U.S. Health Policy*, 158–62; Adam Sheingate, "Building a Business of Politics," manuscript in preparation, chapter 5.

38 Clem Whitaker, "Professional Political Campaign Management," *Public Relations Journal* 6 (January 1950): 21.

39 Jacob S. Hacker, *The Divided Welfare State: The Battle over Public and Private Social Benefits in the United States* (New York, 2002), 227–28; Campion, *AMA and U.S. Health Policy*, 162–63.

40 Whitaker, "Professional Political Campaign Management," 19–23.

41 Carey McWilliams, "Government by Whitaker and Baxter," *The Nation*, April 14, April 21, and May 5, 1951, 346–48, 366–69, and 419–21; Whitaker, "Professional Political Campaign Management," 19–23; Gordon, *Dead on Arrival*, 222–24; "Inside the AMA's Lobby," *Committee for the Nation's Health Bulletin* (May 21, 1951), Reel 1 (microfilm), Michael M. Davis Collection.

42 Burrow, *AMA*, 361–64; Campion, *AMA and U.S. Health Policy*, 163.

43 "To Cooperating Organizations," *Committee for the Nation's Health Bulletin* (May 16, 1950), Reel 1 (microfilm), Michael M. Davis Collection; Campaigns

Inc., "Outline of Activity Field Organization: 'Socialized Medicine,'" n.d., Reel 7 (microfilm), Michael M. Davis Collection; "Legal Cues for Election Campaigns," *Medical Economics* 27 (April 1950): 64–65. Whitaker and Baxter hired a law firm to prepare a report about legally permissible activities for medical societies. The firm instructed physicians to record all contributions to "Healing Arts" funds, avoid soliciting corporations, and steer clear of promising candidates support based on specific issue positions.

44 "A Vital Message from Your Doctor" *Indiana Evening Gazette*, n.d., Reel 7 (microfilm), Michael M. Davis Collection; Jean Begeman, "The Doctors Needle Their Patients," *New Republic*, October 27, 1952, Reel 7 (microfilm), Michael M. Davis Collection.

45 Whitaker, "Professional Political Campaign Management," 19–23.

46 Burrow, *AMA*, 362.

47 Campion, *AMA and U.S. Health Policy*, 175.

48 Polling data from the 1940s indicate that public support for nationalized health care fell between 1945 and 1949. Moreover, when offered a choice between the two options, voters consistently favored private coverage over government-managed insurance. Hacker, *Divided Welfare State*, 234–35.

49 "Capital Stuff," *Medical Economics* 27 (June 1950): 38.

50 "Report of Washington Office," *JAMA* 153 (October 31, 1953): 842–44.

51 "Report of Committee on Legislation," *JAMA* 159 (October 29, 1955): 890.

52 "Report of Committee to Study Heller Report of Organization of the American Medical Association," 1957, Box 3, Blasingame Papers.

53 Ibid.

54 Campion, *AMA and U.S. Health Policy*, 133.

55 Martha Derthick, *Policymaking for Social Security* (Washington, D.C., 1979), 300–303; Edward D. Berkowitz, *Mr. Social Security: The Life of Wilbur J. Cohen* (Lawrence, KS, 1995), 74–76, 91. An AMA-sponsored telegram writing campaign had helped sink the disability freeze two years earlier.

56 F. E. Wilson to Dwight Murray, June 7, 1954, Box 7, Blasingame Papers. Doctors were brought into the Social Security pension program in 1965.

57 Mal Rumph to Elmer Hess, January 3, 1956, Box 8, Blasingame Papers; "Report of Washington Office," *JAMA* 159 (October 29, 1955): 888–90.

58 "Report of Washington Office," *JAMA* 162 (October 20, 1956): 764–65.

59 Reminiscences of Elliot L. Richardson, part I (May 4, 1967), 20–21, CCOHC.

60 Reminiscences of Roswell Perkins, part 2 (July 11, 1966), 58, 60, CCOHC.

61 Robert C. Albright, "Health Insurance Fight Pledged by Ike," *Washington Post*, July 15, 1954, Box 7, Blasingame Papers. The Senate refused to take up reinsurance legislation in 1954, and the bill was reintroduced the following year.

62 "Medical Care for the Indigent in 1958," *JAMA* 168 (December 20, 1958): 2151–54. Just how this increased funding affected doctors depended on the state. Some states disbursed money to municipalities, which hired dedicated physicians to provide indigent care. Other states paid any physician willing to serve the poor set fees in exchange for care.

63 "Disability Checks from Uncle Sam?" *Medical Economics* 27 (May 1950): 53–54.

64 "The Case against Disability Payments," *JAMA* 160 (March 24, 1956): 1058–71.
65 Berkowitz, Mr. *Social Security*, 114–18; Derthick, *Policymaking for Social Security*, 304–8, 319–20; Rick Mayes, *Universal Coverage: The Elusive Quest for National Health Insurance* (Ann Arbor, MI, 2004), 54–55. For a comprehensive examination of government policies for the disabled, see Edward D. Berkowitz, *Disabled Policy: America's Programs for the Handicapped* (New York, 1987).
66 "A.M.A. Attacks Aid to Disabled," *New York Times*, July 23, 1955, 19.
67 "Watch It, Doc," *Life*, June 22, 1953, 32; "Watch It, *Life*," *JAMA* 153 (July 18, 1953): 1142–43.
68 "The AMA Lobby Buys $1,110,000 Worth of Ads," *Consumer Reports*, October 1950, 454–55 for quote; "The Doctor in Politics," *Consumer Reports*, February 1950, 75–78.
69 George F. Lull, "Let's Keep the Door Open," *JAMA* 162 (October 27, 1956): 900–901; Burrow, *AMA*, 314–17, 383–84.
70 David R. Hyde and Payson Wolff, "The AMA: Power, Purpose and Politics in Organized Medicine," *Yale Law Journal* 63 (May 1954): 938–1022; "Yale vs. AMA," *Newsweek*, August 16, 1954, 78.
71 State society representatives held the majority of national House of Delegates seats. Following World War II and particularly during the 1970s, AMA leaders established special sections in the House of Delegates, creating seats for representatives of medical specialty societies, the federal health services, medical student governing bodies, physician residents, and medical school deans.
72 Starr, *Social Transformation of American Medicine*, 272–75; Rayack, *Professional Power and American Medicine*; Garceau, *Political Life of the American Medical Association*, chapter 1. Truman, *Governmental Process*, 128–29. Truman discusses how in American culture, democratic structure gives an association "respectability" and "legitimacy."
73 Truman, *Governmental Process*, 139–55. James Q. Wilson, *Political Organizations*, 2nd ed. (Princeton, 1995), chapter 11. Wilson argues that member preferences greatly constrain leadership actions. While this is generally true, during this period many physicians were compelled to join the AMA in order to purchase malpractice insurance or receive hospital privileges. Association leaders therefore had greater latitude to act against member wishes.
74 "Leadership Problem," *Medical Economics* 28 (April 1951): 47.
75 "Address of Speaker, Dr. F. F. Borzell," *JAMA* 149 (June 28, 1952): 851–52.
76 H. Sheridan Baketel, "The Referendum Idea," *Medical Economics* 28 (November 1950): 53.
77 "Address of Speaker, Dr. F. F. Borzell," 851–52; Garceau, *Political Life of the American Medical Association*, 24–28.
78 Truman, *Governmental Process*, 131–36.
79 Garceau, *Political Life of the American Medical Association*, 20, 68–77; Campion, *AMA and U.S. Health Policy*, 100–102; Elmer Hess, "The President's Page: A Monthly Message," *JAMA* 158 (July 30, 1955): 1174; Fishbein, *Morris Fishbein*, 181–82.

80 "Report of Reference Committee on Reports of Board of Trustees and Secretary," *JAMA* 159 (December 24, 1955): 1647.
81 F. J. L. Blasingame, "Upgrading the Role of the House of Delegates of the American Medical Association," n.d., Box 6, Blasingame Papers.
82 Ibid.
83 "Address of the President, Dr. John W. Cline," *JAMA* 149 (June 28, 1952): 854.
84 Campion, *AMA and U.S. Health Policy*, 195.
85 Ibid., 196.
86 Ibid., 195–97.
87 Robert L. Brenner, "Does the A.M.A. Need a Party Line?" *Medical Economics* 35 (January 6, 1958): 180.
88 "Report of Committee to Study Heller Report"; Campion, *AMA and U.S. Health Policy*, 196–97; F. J. L. Blasingame to Robert J. Needles, May 23, 1958, Box 27, Blasingame Papers. On the role of management consulting firms in spreading business models to nonprofit organizations, see Christopher D. McKenna, *The World's Newest Profession: Management Consulting in the Twentieth Century* (New York, 2006), chapter 5.
89 "Minutes: Committee to Study the Heller Report," October 25–26, 1957, Box 6, Blasingame Papers; "Highlights of A.M.A. Clinical Session," *JAMA* 165 (December 21, 1957): 2090–92; "AMA Objectives and Basic Programs," *JAMA* 167 (May 17, 1958): 342.
90 "Alesen Committee Report," *JAMA* 168 (December 20, 1958): 2149; Campion, *AMA and U.S. Health Policy*, 202–3.
91 Previously, the general manager also had responsibilities as the association's secretary. The House voted to separate those duties from those of the general manager and place them in an elected secretary-treasurer position. "Administrative Structure of the Association," *JAMA* 169 (February 7, 1959): 604.
92 F. J. L. Blasingame, "Report on National Legislation to Executive Council of Board of Trustees," 1950, Box 20, Blasingame Papers; John F. Pilcher to F. J. L. Blasingame, March 10, 1949, Box 20, Blasingame Papers.
93 "Dr. Blasingame Is Firm Champion of Medical Integrity," *Houston Post*, July 22, 1956; "Introduction of F. J. L. Blasingame, M.D.," n.d.; "Ashbel Smith Award, Francis J. L. Blasingame," 1966; "Dr. F. J. L. Blasingame," *Texas State Journal of Medicine* 50 (May 1954): 275–77; all in vertical files, Blasingame Papers.
94 Ernest E. Anthony to F. J. L. Blasingame, November 14, 1953, Box 14, Blasingame Papers; F. J. L. Blasingame to Ernest E. Anthony, November 15, 1953, Box 14, Blasingame Papers. See also F. J. L. Blasingame and Frank G. Dickinson, "A Physician and an Economist Look at Old-Age and Survivors Insurance," *JAMA* 153 (November 7, 1953): 921–24.
95 "Administrative Structure of the Association," 604; Campion, *AMA and U.S. Health Policy*, 203.
96 Mal Rumph and Ernest E. Anthony to F. J. L. Blasingame, August 4, 1955, Box 12, Blasingame Papers; Mal Rumph to Elmer Hess, January 3, 1956, Box 8, Blasingame Papers; Campion, *AMA and U.S. Health Policy*, 203.

97 Ernest B. Howard to F. J. L. Blasingame, August 20, 1958, Box 7, Blasingame Papers; Campion, *AMA and U.S. Health Policy*, 203; F. J. L. Blasingame to W. R. McBee, April 13, 1958, Box 19, Blasingame Papers.

98 Garceau, *Political Life of the American Medical Association*, 118; Truman, *Governmental Process*, chapters 5 and 6.

99 Gordon B. Leitch, "Summary of Remarks Delivered before Regional Legislative Conference of the American Medical Association at San Francisco," January 23, 1954, Box 7, Blasingame Papers; Gordon B. Leitch to George Lull, January 27, 1954, Box 7, Blasingame Papers.

100 Berkowitz, *Mr. Social Security*, 80–81. The Social Security Board was established in 1935 as a freestanding federal entity. In 1939, it was absorbed by the Federal Security Agency. It assumed the name of the Social Security Administration during the 1940s, and then moved to the newly created HEW when the Federal Security Agency was abolished in 1953.

101 "AMA Says Yes to Ike," *Medical Economics* 31 (April 1953): 6–7; "Introduction and Address of the President of the United States, Hon. Dwight D. Eisenhower," *JAMA* 151 (April 4, 1953): 1200–1201. Eisenhower sought physician favor by reminding delegates that he opposed government-managed medicine: "I have found in the past few years that I have certain philosophical bonds with doctors. I don't like the word 'compulsory.' I am against the word 'socialized.'"

102 Louis H. Bauer, "President's Page: A Monthly Message," *JAMA* 151 (March 28, 1953): 1109. In congressional hearings on executive reorganization, Democrats questioned AMA representatives about the deal they had made with administration officials over the appointment of a special assistant. Physician leaders admitted that they had been promised influence over the post. "Will AMA Control Medical Policies of U.S. Government?" *Committee for the Nation's Health Bulletin* (March 17, 1953), Reel 7 (microfilm), Michael M. Davis Collection; "AMA Meeting March 14th Needs Watching," *Committee for the Nation's Health Bulletin* (March 10, 1953), Reel 7 (microfilm), Michael M. Davis Collection.

103 "Address of the President, Dr. Louis H. Bauer," *JAMA* 152 (June 20, 1953): 722–23; "Report of the Reference Committee on Reports of Officers," *JAMA* 152 (June 20, 1953): 723–24.

104 Greer Williams, "Ewing to Hobby to Folsom," *Medical Economics* 33 (January 1956): 107–12, 252. In an interview he gave over a decade later, Roswell Perkins refuted the claim, made in some press accounts, that Secretary Hobby had declared that "this in an AMA administration." According to Perkins, Hobby was frequently disappointed with the failure of organized physicians to compromise, particularly on reinsurance legislation. Roswell Perkins, Reminiscences, 55–56.

105 "Should Medicine Oppose All Federal Aid?" *Medical Economics* 33 (September 1956): 243; John K. Glen to Bing Blasingame, September 28, 1956, Box 6, Blasingame Papers.

106 For a discussion of AMA support for federal subsidization of hospitals, medical schools, and scientific research, see Daniel Fox, *Health Policies, Health Politics: The British and American Experience, 1911–1965* (Princeton, 1986), especially chapter 11.

107 "Should Medicine Oppose All Federal Aid?" 240–63, especially 252.
108 George Baehr et al. to Morris Fishbein, "A Protest against the Present
Attitudes and Policies of the American Medical Association in Regard to
the Problem of Medical Care," January 31, 1949, Reel 6 (microfilm),
Michael M. Davis Collection; "What the 'Loyal Opposition' Wants,"
Medical Economics 27 (June 1950): 61–63, 150–55.
109 "RX for Doubletalk," *Medical Economics* 27 (June 1950): 42.
110 Derthick, *Policymaking for Social Security,* 198–205, 296–97, 300–304,
307, 312.
111 Although this number amounted to approximately one-third of all doctors, it
somewhat overstates the problem of nonmembers by including nonpracticing
physicians. During this period, AMA membership rates were at a historical
high. Roger Menges, "Why They're NOT in the A.M.A.," *Medical Economics* 31 (February 1954): 100–104.
112 In 1895, the National Medical Association was organized to accept black
physicians. The AMA first passed a resolution against racial discrimination
in 1939. Although the AMA passed similar resolutions in subsequent
decades, national leaders did not set up a system of enforcement, which
included the possibility of medical society expulsion, until 1968. On the
difficulties that African American doctors had acquiring medical licenses,
see Chapter 1, note 46. American Medical Association, "Race and the AMA:
A Chronology," www.ama-assn.org//ama/pub/about-ama/our-history/race-
ama-a-chronology.page (accessed January 10, 2013); Robert C. Toth,
"Doctors to Fight A.M.A. Race Stand," *New York Times,* June 19, 1963,
20; Richard D. Lyons, "A.M.A. Vote Ends Bars to Negroes," *New York
Times,* December 4, 1968, 31.
113 Menges, "Why They're NOT in the A.M.A.," 100–104.
114 Rosemary Stevens, *American Medicine and the Public Interest* (New Haven,
CT, 1971), chapters 6, 9–15; Paul M. Gross, "The Rise of Specialism in
Modern Society," *JAMA* 179 (May 16, 1959): 285–89. Truman, *Governmental Process,* 156–67. Truman discusses how overlapping associational
memberships undermine cohesion in the dominant group. See also Rayack,
Professional Power and American Medicine, chapter 6.
115 As of 2011, only about 15 percent of practicing doctors were AMA
members. Roger Collier, "American Medical Association Membership Woes
Continue," *Canadian Medical Association Journal* 183 (August 9, 2011):
E713–14.
116 "Report of the Committee to Study AMA Objectives and Basic Programs,"
JAMA 169 (March 7, 1959): 1077–83.
117 Dr. Lester, Messrs. Webb and Hawthorne to W. R. Mcbee, "What A.M.A.
Can Do to Stop the Drift toward Socialized Medicine," August 2, 1955,
Box 19, Blasingame Papers.
118 David B. Allman, "The President's Page," *JAMA* 166 (January 25, 1958):
376. See also Everett C. Fox, "The Physician's Responsibility to Medical
Organizations," *JAMA* 159 (October 8, 1955): 546; Dwight H. Murray,
"Replace Apathy with Active, United Profession," *JAMA* 162 (December 15,
1956): 1476–78; Elmer Hess, "The President's Page: A Monthly Message,"

JAMA 160 (January 28, 1956): 293; "Address of President Dwight H. Murray before the House of Delegates," *JAMA* 164 (June 22, 1957): 879–81.

119 Mal Rumph to Elmer Hess, January 3, 1956, Box 8, Blasingame Papers.

120 Campion, *AMA and U.S. Health Policy*, 204.

121 "Committee on Legislation," *JAMA* 168 (October 25, 1958): 1047.

122 F. J. L. Blasingame, "Things of Good Report," Meeting of the Texas Medical Association, Dallas, TX, April 29, 1957, Box 20, Blasingame Papers.

123 "Report of the Field Service Division," *JAMA* 171 (October 17, 1959): 967–68.

124 Blasingame to Needles.

125 Burrow, *AMA*, 335.

126 "Public Relations Forecast – 1956," *JAMA* 160 (May 5, 1956): 59–60.

127 To avoid running afoul of AMA proscriptions against physician advertising, doctors who hosted radio programs or wrote newspaper columns had to toe official AMA policy lines and discuss physicians and medicine as a whole rather than their own personal practices.

128 "Indigent Medical Care Study," *JAMA* 149 (May 10, 1952): 70; Report from Council on Medical Service, "Medical Care for the Indigent," *JAMA* 149 (May 10, 1952): 188–89; "Guides for Medical Societies in Developing Plans for Tax-Supported Personal Health Services for the Needy," *JAMA* 163 (January 19, 1957): 190–91; Council on Medical Service, "A Suggested Statement of Guides for Plans for Tax-Supported Personal Health Services for the Needy," October 8, 1955, Box 1, Blasingame Papers.

129 Louis H. Bauer, "The President's Page: A Monthly Message," *JAMA* 150 (September 27, 1952): 420 for quote. See also Louis H. Bauer, "Working Together in '52," *JAMA* 147 (December 15, 1951): 1509–10; Fox, "The Physician's Responsibility to Medical Organizations"; Gunnar Gundersen, "It Takes Two . . .," *JAMA* 166 (March 8, 1959): 1206–8.

130 "Message from Dr. Water B. Martin on Comprehensive Care," *JAMA* 158 (July 2, 1955): 734; David B. Allman, "Medicine's Role in Financing Health Care Costs," *JAMA* 165 (November 23, 1957): 1571–73; "Committee on Prepayment of Medical and Hospital Services," *JAMA* 159 (October 29, 1955): 942–44.

131 For example, "Address of President, Dr. John W. Cline," 854; "Address of President, Dr. Louis H. Bauer," *JAMA* 150 (December 27, 1952): 1679; "Address of the President, Dr. Walter B. Martin," *JAMA* 158 (June 25, 1955): 669–70; Elmer Hess, "The Physician's Obligation to Society," *JAMA* 163 (January 12, 1957): 121–23; F. J. L. Blasingame, "'Choosing Our Rut' in Voluntary Health Insurance," 1957, Box 20, Blasingame Papers.

132 "Resolution from Dr. C. G. Krupp," October 11, 1955, Box 1, Blasingame Papers.

133 Medical Expense Fund of New York, "Treason," n.d., Cunningham Papers.

134 American Medical Association, *Voluntary Prepayment Medical Benefit Plans* (Chicago, 1953), 12–13.

135 During the 1940s, large insurance companies and an industry trade group, the Health Insurance Council, worked with medical societies to ensure that

commercial policies were acceptable to physicians. However, these efforts could not possibly secure formal medical society approval for every commercial policy as dictated by physicians' 1938 resolution.

136 F. J. L. Blasingame, "Voluntary Health Insurance: Personal Reflections," 1957, Box 20, Blasingame Papers; Blasingame, "'Choosing Our Rut'"; Leitch, "Summary of Remarks Delivered before Regional Legislative Conference."

137 For example, "Committee on Prepayment of Medical and Hospital Services," 942–44; Leitch, "Summary of Remarks Delivered before Regional Legislative Conference"; "Report on Medical Prepayment Plans," *JAMA* 159 (December 3, 1955): 1368–69; Blasingame, "Voluntary Health Insurance."

138 John W. Cline, "The President's Page: A Monthly Message," *JAMA* 148 (February 23, 1952): 654; Campion, *AMA and U.S. Health Policy*, 131–34.

139 "Supplementary Report of Board of Trustees: Progress Report of Commission on Medical Care Plans," *JAMA* 159 (December 3, 1955): 1370–79. See also "Committee on Relations with Lay-Sponsored Voluntary Health Plans," *JAMA* 162 (October 20, 1956): 815.

140 "Report of Law Department," *JAMA* 159 (October 29, 1955): 896–98.

141 Brenner, "Does the A.M.A. Need a Party Line?" 186.

4 Organized for Profit: The Hidden Influence of Insurance Companies and the HIAA

1 The HIAA is known today as America's Health Insurance Plans (AHIP). Raymond A. Bauer, Ithiel de Sola Pool, and Lewis Anthony Dexter, *American Business and Public Policy: The Politics of Foreign Trade*, 2nd ed. (Piscataway, NJ, 2007). Bauer, Pool, and Dexter found that, during the 1950s, trade associations lacked the cohesion and resources necessary to lobby effectively for particular policy outcomes. In the case of the HIAA, the threat of federal intervention in the health insurance market allowed the association's leadership to unify the industry under clear policy positions, apply federal political pressure, and even shape the market actions of member firms. See also Louis Galambos, *Competition and Cooperation: The Emergence of a National Trade Association* (Baltimore, 1966).

2 Sharon Ann Murphy, *Investing in Life: Insurance in Antebellum America* (Baltimore, 2010), 2–5.

3 Ibid., 4–5.

4 Dan Bouk, *How Our Days Became Numbered: Risk and the Rise of the Statistical Individual* (Chicago, forthcoming); Murphy, *Investing in Life*, chapter 1.

5 Murphy, *Investing in Life*, chapters 5 and 6, 209–11. See also Viviana A. Zelizer, *Morals and Markets: The Development of Life Insurance in the United States* (Piscataway, NJ, 1983).

6 Murphy, *Investing in Life*, chapter 4. See also William J. Novak, *The People's Welfare: Law and Regulation in Nineteenth-Century America* (Chapel Hill, NC, 1996).

7 Murphy, *Investing in Life*, 286–87, 290–95; Richard Hooker, *Aetna Life Insurance Company: Its First Hundred Years* (Hartford, CT, 1956), 86–91; Marquis James, *The Metropolitan Life: A Study in Business Growth* (New York, 1947), 57–58; R. Carlyle Buley, *The American Life Convention, 1906–1952*, vol. 1 (New York, 1953), 90–92.

8 Morton Keller, *The Life Insurance Enterprise, 1885–1910: A Study in the Limits of Corporate Power* (Cambridge, MA, 1963), 10–11; Murphy, *Investing in Life*, 294–96.

9 The industry was also split between stock insurance companies and mutual firms. Mutual insurance companies granted ownership rights to policyholders, allowing them to vote for company officers and capture a portion of profits through either dividend payments or reduced premium prices. Particularly during the nineteenth century, policyholders exercised little real influence over the operation of mutual insurance firms. Murphy, *Investing in Life*, 167–76; Keller, *The Life Insurance Enterprise*, 40.

10 Maurice H. Robinson, "Government Regulation of Insurance Companies," *Publications of the American Economics Association* 8 (February 1909): 150; Phillip L. Merkel, "Going National: The Life Insurance Industry's Campaign for Federal Regulation after the Civil War," *Business History Review* 65 (autumn 1991): 528–53; Keller, *The Life Insurance Enterprise*, 235–40. For a discussion of how large corporations attempted to shape the legal environment to meet their needs, see Brian Balogh, *A Government Out of Sight: The Mystery of National Authority in Nineteenth-Century America* (New York, 2009), 339–44 and Charles W. McCurdy, "American Law and the Marketing Structure of the Large Corporation, 1875–1890," *Journal of Economic History* 38 (September 1978): 631–49.

11 Merkel, "Going National," 531–34; Keller, *The Life Insurance Enterprise*, 240.

12 Although not renamed the Life Insurance Association of America until 1944, I use this name throughout the narrative to avoid confusion.

13 Gabriel Kolko, *The Triumph of Conservatism: A Reinterpretation of American History, 1900–1916* (New York, 1963), 90–97.

14 Quoted in Ibid., 96; Buley, *American Life Convention*, vol. 1, chapter 5; Martha Derthick, *Policymaking for Social Security* (Washington, D.C., 1979), 137–39. Sharon Murphy examines collaboration among insurance companies during the nineteenth century; these efforts occurred through the similarly named American Life Underwriters' Convention. Murphy, *Investing in Life*, chapter 9.

15 Keller, *The Life Insurance Enterprise*, 245–69; "Life Insurance Reform in New York," *American Economic Association Quarterly* 10 (December 1909): 1–95; Robert F. Wesser, *Charles Evans Hughes: Politics and Reform in New York, 1905–1910* (Ithaca, NY, 1967), 33–48.

16 Robinson, "Government Regulation of Insurance Companies," 149; Albert Erlebacher, "The Wisconsin Life Insurance Reform of 1907," *Wisconsin Magazine of History* 55 (spring 1972): 213–30; Keller, *The Life Insurance Enterprise*, 254–59.

17 The Insurance Advertising Bureau, *Greater Efficiency in Insurance Advertising* (Indianapolis, IN, 1913); Haley Fiske, "Life Insurance as a Basis of Social

Economy," *Scientific Monthly* 4 (April 1917): 316–24; William A. Day, *Patriotism of the Life Insurance Business* (New York, 1916).
18 William G. Rothstein, *Public Health and the Risk Factor: A History of an Uneven Medical Revolution* (Rochester, NY, 2003), 150–51.
19 "Federal Control Hit in Insurance by Pink," *New York Times*, February 19, 1940, 32.
20 Rothstein, *Public Health and the Risk Factor*, 150–76; Fiske, "Life Insurance as a Basis of Social Economy," 322–23.
21 David T. Beito, *From Mutual Aid to the Welfare State: Fraternal Societies and Social Services, 1890–1967* (Chapel Hill, NC, 2000), 155–58; John E. Murray, *The Origins of American Health Insurance: A History of Industrial Sickness Funds* (New Haven, CT, 2007), chapters 2 and 3; Ronald L. Numbers, *Almost Persuaded: American Physicians and Compulsory Health Insurance, 1912–1920* (Baltimore, 1978); Beatrix Hoffman, *The Wages of Sickness: The Politics of Health Insurance in Progressive America* (Chapel Hill, NC, 2001); David A. Moss, *Socializing Security: Progressive-Era Economists and the Origins of American Social Policy* (Cambridge, MA, 1995), 139–39, 148–55; Frederick L. Hoffman, *Facts and Fallacies of Compulsory Health Insurance* (Newark, NJ, 1917).
22 "J. P. Hanna Report Cites Conference Staff Contributions during Past Year," *Eastern Underwriter* 56 (May 13, 1955): 44–46; Stewart M. La Mont, "Accident and Health Insurance," *Annals of the American Academy of Political and Social Science* 161 (May 1932): 128–33.
23 "Federal Activity in Loan Field Hit," *New York Times*, October 15, 1937, 35; Keller, *The Life Insurance Enterprise*, 286–87.
24 Quote from E. J. Faulkner, "Social Security and Insurance. Some Relationships in Perspective," *Journal of Insurance* 30 (June 1963): 198–201. See also Derthick, *Policymaking for Social Security*, 133, 136–42; Jacob S. Hacker, *The Divided Welfare State: The Battle over Public and Private Social Benefits in the United States* (New York, 2002), 104–5; Keller, *The Life Insurance Enterprise*, chapter 16.
25 Buley, *American Life Convention*, vol. II, 916–22; Derthick, *Policymaking for Social Security*, 138–39.
26 Thurman Arnold, "An Inquiry into the Monopoly Issue," *New York Times*, August 21, 1938, B1, B14–15.
27 Quoted in Charles Burton Robbins, "'State vs. Federal Regulation of Insurance': Discussion," *Journal of the American Association of University Teachers of Insurance* 8 (March 1941): 73. See also "O'Mahoney Denies Insurance Threat," *New York Times*, October 11, 1940, 37; "Parkinson Scores Government Moves," *New York Times*, April 24, 1940, 35; "'Prejudice' by SEC Seen in Insurance," *New York Times*, October 10, 1940, 39.
28 George W. Goble, "State vs. Federal Regulation of Insurance," *American Risk and Insurance Association* 8 (March 1941): 57–67; Robbins, "'State vs. Federal Regulation of Insurance,'" 72–77; Raymond Moley, "Business in the Woodshed," *The Saturday Evening Post*, April 6, 1940, 22–68; Buley, *American Life Convention*, vol. II, 838–62.
29 "Federal Regulation of Insurance Companies: The Disappearing McCarran Act Exemption," *Duke Law Journal* 1973 (January 1974): 1340–56;

Charles C. Moore, "Insurance: Federal Regulation," *Michigan Law Review*
57 (December 1958): 289–91.

30 Quoted in Derthick, *Policymaking for Social Security*, 139–42. See also
Jennifer Klein, *For All These Rights: Business, Labor, and the Shaping of
America's Public-Private Welfare State* (Princeton, 2003), 92–94, 207–8;
Hacker, *Divided Welfare State*, 112–13.

31 The term "socialized medicine" generally only appeared in trade association
periodicals and conferences that did not receive publicity beyond the industry. A 1951 *New York Times* article cited a Prudential executive stating that
the company's introduction of major medical was "intended to combat the
possibility of socialized medicine," but the quote stands out for its rarity.
Indeed, the fact that the newspaper clipping is in Equitable's archives may
indicate that industry leaders were unhappy about the political exposure.
"Prudential Plans Illness Coverage," *New York Times*, June 20, 1951,
Box 41C, RG4, Equitable Archives. IESA leaders stirred up the ire of their
colleagues for attempting to turn the Truman debates into a bloody ideological brawl. They accused pro-reform policymakers of promoting socialism and claimed that the proposal would "split the Constitution wide open."
These political tactics would later sink IESA's bid to become the health
insurance industry's primary associational representative. For example,
"War Seen as Screen for Socialist Ideas," *New York Times*, October 17,
1942, 17.

32 "60,995,000 Listed in Hospital Plans," *New York Times*, August 18, 1949,
23; Health Insurance Council, *Health Insurance Story*, n.d., Box 42A, RG4,
Equitable Archives; "Health Council Reports to Senate Subcommittee," *Eastern Underwriter* 52 (February 23, 1951): 43.

33 American Life Convention and Life Insurance Association of America, "Statement of Ray D. Murphy, Proposal for National Health Insurance," June
1949, Box 59A, RG 4, Equitable Archives.

34 "Medical Disaster Insurance," *Eastern Underwriter* 52 (January 5, 1951): 29.
See also "Prudential Plans Illness Coverage"; "Hipp Calls Experimentation
Spirit Greatest Bulwark against Socialism," *Eastern Underwriter* 52 (February 16,
1951): 36; Morton D. Miller, "Group Medical Expense Insurance," February 7,
1951, Box 32A, RG 4, Equitable Archives; "Shift to Offensive Will Put Stopper on
Government," *National Underwriter* 55 (September 14, 1951): 1, 20; "A.&H.
Companies Can't Operate in Vacuum," *National Underwriter* 56 (June 6,
1952): 6.

35 Reminiscences of Roswell Perkins, part I, (April 2, 1966), 38–39, 48–50,
CCOHC; James E. Stuart, "The Blue Cross Story," unpublished manuscript,
n.d., 261–62, Cunningham Papers; C. Joseph Stetler to F. J. L. Blasingame,
May 20, 1954, Box 7, Blasingame Papers.

36 Quoted in M. Allen Pond to Oveta Culp Hobby, 1954, Box 325, General
Classified Files, Records of the Department of Health, Education, and Welfare
(hereafter HEW), NARA.

37 Powell B. McHaney to Orville F. Grahame, April 12, 1955, Box 28, Grahame
Papers; Roswell B. Perkins to Mr. Celer, March 22, 1955, Box 28, Grahame
Papers.

38 Thomas P. Swift, "Life Insurance Companies Plan Part in U.S. Health Program," *New York Times*, May 16, 1954, F1.

39 House Committee on Interstate and Foreign Commerce, *Hearings on Health Reinsurance Legislation, H.R. 8356,* 83rd Cong., 2nd sess., March 31, 1954 (Paul F. Clark to the Hon. Charles A. Wolverton, June 10, 1954 and Frazar B. Wilde to the Hon. Charles A. Wolverton, June 18, 1954), 447–48.

40 For example, James E. Powell to Orville F. Grahame, December 10, 1954, Box 29; E. J. Faulkner to J. W. Scherr, Jr., and Alfred Perkins, March 31, 1955, Box 17; E. H. O'Connor to John W. Powell, May 1, 1956, Box 28; R. L. Paddock to Orville F. Grahame, November 29, 1954, Box 29; Orville F. Grahame to H. O. Fishback, December 7, 1954, Box 29; James E. Powell to Orville F. Grahame, January 13, 1955, Box 29; all in Grahame Papers.

41 Quote from "Remarks of E. H. O'Connor," Annual Meeting of Insurance Economics Society of America, Chicago, October 5, 1954, Box 28, Grahame Papers. See also Edwin J. Faulkner, "Why Reinsurance Can't Work," *Medical Economics* 31 (July 1954): 147–48; Powell B. McHaney, "An Address" (*Sixth Annual Accident and Health Spring Meeting*, Chicago, March 17, 1955); E. J. Faulkner, "Review of Accident and Sickness Insurance," *Journal of the American Association of University Teachers of Insurance* 22 (March 1955): 78–82.

42 House Committee on Interstate and Foreign Commerce, *Hearings on Health Reinsurance Legislation, H.R. 8356,* 83rd Cong., 2nd sess., March 26, 1954 (Statement of Edwin J. Faulkner), 106.

43 House Committee on Interstate and Foreign Commerce, *Hearings on Health Reinsurance Legislation, H.R. 8356,* 83rd Cong., 2nd sess., March 31, 1954 (Statement of Henry S. Beers), 207–10. In 1956, HEW Secretary Marion Folsom proposed a scaled-down reform plan to succeed federal reinsurance efforts. Legislation that enabled "pooling" would have permitted insurance companies to merge financial and administrative capacities without fear of antitrust prosecution. Folsom hoped that this organizational innovation would help insurers cover the elderly at reasonable costs. However, because insurers were actively fighting to maintain state regulatory jurisdiction, endorsing federal pooling legislation seemed too risky. But the idea was significant: commercial insurers pursued similar legislation at the state level in order to help them grow aged insurance coverage and thereby stymie Medicare proposals. Reminiscences of Marion B. Folsom, part II (October 13, 1965), 174–78, CCOHC; Reminiscences of Reinhard Hohaus, part I, (July 27, 1965), 29–32, 119–22, CCOHC; Reminiscences of Robert Neal, part I (1967), 15–16, 26–27, CCOHC.

44 "R. R. Neal Asks Sound Industry Program to Cure Problems Confronting A.&H.," *Eastern Underwriter* 56 (March 18, 1955): 46–47; "Conference Cos. Unanimously Approve Single A.&H. Trade Association," *Eastern Underwriter* 56 (May 13, 1955): 39, 46; "President J. W. Scherr in Keynote Address Features Task Force Studies," *Eastern Underwriter* 56 (May 13, 1955): 42, 45.

45 "R. R. Neal Asks Sound Industry Program," 46–47.

46 Faulkner, "Review of Accident and Sickness Insurance," 78.

47 See note 31. See also Boxes 28 and 29, Grahame Papers.

48 "Follmann Observes 10th Year with Bureau," _Eastern Underwriter_ 56 (May 20, 1955): 45–6.

49 "General Manager's Report to the Board of Directors," 1955, Box 25, Grahame Papers.

50 E. J. Faulkner, "Be Not Afraid of Greatness," WALCO President's Club, Mackinac Island, MI, August 20, 1964, Series 9, Box 72, Faulkner Papers.

51 Faulkner to Scherr and Perkins.

52 Additional trade groups included the Life Insurers Conference, American Mutual Alliance, and Association of Casualty and Surety Companies. Each association appointed one representative and one staff member to work for the Joint Committee, while the largest insurance companies sent fourteen of their own delegates.

53 Frank S. Vanderbrouk, "Report of the Executive Committee," May 4, 1955, Box 17, Grahame Papers.

54 "General Manager's Report to the Board of Directors." In its first year, the HIAA had a budget of $818,000 for operational expenses and public relations activities.

55 Edwin J. Faulkner, _Health Insurance_ (New York, 1960), 467–68; Robert Neal, Reminiscences, 4–6.

56 The standing committees were as follows: Public Relations, Membership & Ethical Standards, Nominations, Administrative, Actuarial & Statistical, Health Insurance Council, Group Insurance, Individual Insurance, Legislative & Regulatory, and Legal.

57 "3d Generation ... of Faulkners," unidentified newspaper clipping, n.d., Series 1, Box 1, Faulkner Papers; Woodmen Accident and Life Company, "July Is the Time for Our President," n.d., Series 1, Box 2, Faulkner Papers; Faulkner, "Be Not Afraid of Greatness."

58 Milton Silverman, "The Post Reports on Health Insurance," _The Saturday Evening Post_, June 7, 1958, 27, 127.

59 "Reader's Digest Article on A.&H. Causes Headaches," _National Underwriter_ 57 (August 28, 1953): 7; "Don't Fall for Phony Health Insurance," _Coronet_, June 1951, 14; Blake Clark, "Be Sure You Know What's in Your Health and Accident Policy," _Reader's Digest_, July 1954, 115–19; Milton Silverman, "Is This the Pattern of the Future?" _The Saturday Evening Post_, June 21, 1958, 30, 100–102; Andrew J. Biemiller, "The Need for Health Insurance," _Consumer Reports_, April 1949, 174; Gerald R. Gibbons and John D. Johnston, Jr., "Termination of Personal Health Insurance Contracts by Cancellations or Nonrenewal," _Duke Bar Journal_ 5 (1956): 74–76.

60 Faulkner, "Review of Accident and Sickness Insurance," 79–80; Jarvis Farley, "Recent Developments in Sickness and Accident Insurance," _Journal of the American Association of University Teachers of Insurance_ 23 (March 1956): 113–15.

61 "Remarks of E. H. O'Connor"; Reminiscences of Wilbur Cohen, part I (July 20, 1966), 30, CCOHC; Kenneth J. Meier, _The Political Economy of Regulation: The Case of Insurance_ (Albany, NY, 1988), 111–13. See _FTC v. National Casualty Company_, 1958 and _FTC v. Travelers Health Association_, 1960.

62 Even industry leaders who favored government reinsurance continually stressed the need to word the legislation in a manner that would unequivocally prohibit federal regulation of insurance.

63 Gallup Poll, "Politics/Finances/United Nations," no. 1947–0402 (August 8–13, 1947).

64 "General Manager's Report to the Board of Directors"; James R. Williams, "Strengthening Public Confidence – Through Advertising" (*Health Insurance Association of America Annual Meeting*, Washington, D.C., May 13, 1958); E. J. Faulkner to Roger Billings, March 11, 1957, Box 19, Grahame Papers.

65 Robert Neal, Reminiscences, 25.

66 E. J. Faulkner to Orville F. Grahame, October 25, 1955, Box 19, Grahame Papers.

67 Wilbur Cohen, Reminiscences, 27.

68 Robert Neal, Reminiscences, 42–45; E. J. Faulkner, "Presidential Address" (*Health Insurance Association of America Annual Meeting*, Washington, D.C., May 7, 1957).

69 Robert Neal, Reminiscences, 42–43.

70 Frank E. Wilson to F. J. L. Blasingame, "Legislative Action, Health Reinsurance Bill," August 17, 1954, Box 7, Blasingame Papers.

71 "Committee on Legislation Minutes, American Medical Association," March 30, 1957, Box 8, Blasingame Papers.

72 Bauer, Pool, and Dexter, *American Business and Public Policy*; Galambos, *Competition and Cooperation.*

73 Some examples include Faulkner, *Health Insurance*, 69; "H.&A. Conference Has Golden Jubilee," *National Underwriter* 55 (May 18, 1951): 1, 21; "Shift to Offensive Will Put Stopper on Government," 1, 20; "A.&H. Companies Can't Operate in Vacuum," 6; Bernard R. Stone, "Government Encroachment in Insurance," May 1, 1952, Series 2, Box 5, Faulkner Papers; "Keen Interest in Doctor-Hospital Panel Talks," *Eastern Underwriter* 54 (January 30, 1953), 32; Faulkner, "Presidential Address"; V. J. Skutt, "Keynote Address" (*Health Insurance Association of America Annual Meeting*, Dallas, TX, May 16, 1960); Paul B. Cullen, "No One but You" (*Health Insurance Association of America Annual Meeting*, Dallas, TX, May 17, 1960); E. J. Faulkner, "Potential Innovations in Health Insurance" (*Annual Meeting of the American Association of University Teachers of Insurance*, St. Louis, MO, December 28, 1960), Series 9, Box 72, Faulkner Papers.

74 Malcolm Ruddock to Orville F. Grahame, August 18, 1955, Box 19, Grahame Papers; Malcolm Ruddock to Orville F. Grahame, August 30, 1955, Box 19, Grahame Papers.

75 Millard Bartels to the Legal Committee of the proposed Health Insurance Association of America, September 9, 1955; Manuel M. Gorman to Millard Bartels, September 14, 1955; Manuel M. Gorman to Orville F. Grahame, September 19, 1955; all in Box 19, Grahame Papers.

76 Orville F. Grahame to Earl W. Kintner, August 10, 1955, Box 19, Grahame Papers. This idea recalls aspects of Herbert Hoover's "associative state," which conceived of government officials coordinating with large trade associations that, by establishing industry cooperation, would stabilize the economy. See Ellis W. Hawley, "Herbert Hoover, the Commerce Secretariat, and

the Vision of an 'Associative State,' 1921–1928," *Journal of American History* 61 (June 1974): 116–40.

77 HIAA officials were able to regulate industry practices without provoking antitrust suits by abstaining from coercive enforcement outside of membership exclusion and by avoiding discussions of premium prices (although close examination of archival records gives one the impression that these conversations occurred off the record). During the 1960s, the courts began employing a rule of reason that allowed industry standardization projects – outside of product pricing – as long as collaborating firms did not isolate or competitively harm nonparticipants through "refusals to deal" or group boycotts. See "Antitrust: Limitation on the Group Boycott Per Se Rule," *Duke Law Journal* 1961 (autumn 1961): 606–13; "Trade Association Exclusionary Practices: An Affirmative Role for the Rule of Reason," *Columbia Law Review* 66 (December 1966): 1486–1510.

78 By 1960, all states except one had adopted both laws. Faulkner, *Health Insurance*, 485–94.

79 "Proposal to Establish the Health Insurance Association of America," December 1955, Box 19, Grahame Papers.

80 Joint Committee on Health Insurance, "Major Steps in Development of Proposed Organization," n.d., Box 19, Grahame Papers; "Health Insurance Association of America Application, Data Sheet and Authorization," n.d., Box 19, Grahame Papers.

81 Quote from "Proposal to Establish the Health Insurance Association of America". See also "HIAA Bylaws," n.d., Box 19, Grahame Papers; "Watt Tells About First Year's Results under Conference Advertising Code," *Eastern Underwriter* 56 (May 13, 1955): 40, 55; "A.&H. Pamphlet on Fine Print," *Eastern Underwriter* 56 (March 11, 1955): 40; "Minutes of the Meeting of the Subcommittee on Advertising Rules," September 19, 1956, Box 25, Grahame Papers.

82 Faulkner, *Health Insurance*, 418–19; "Medical Underwriting – A Retrospective," *Record of the Society of Actuaries* 25 (January 1999), www.soa.org/library/proceedings/record-of-the-society-of-actuaries/1990-99/1999/january/rsa99v25n3100pd.pdf (accessed March 3, 2011); "Thaler, Hotson and Lembkey Tell about Steps Taken to Start Conversion Plans," *Eastern Underwriter* 56 (February 11, 1955): 41; "Bureau Releases Statistical Study on Personal Accident Experience," *Eastern Underwriter* 56 (October 21, 1955): 36.

83 Faulkner, "Presidential Address"; Robert Neal, "Report of the General Manager" (*Health Insurance Association of America Annual Meeting*, Washington, D.C., May 7, 1957); Robert Neal, "Annual Report of the General Manager" (*Health Insurance Association of America Annual Meeting*, Washington, D.C., May 12, 1958); Joseph W. Moran, "Comprehensive Major Medical Expense Insurance at New York Life Insurance Company," February 4, 1957, Box 19, Grahame Papers; "Cancellable Accident and Health Insurance: A Study and Recommendations," April 1956, Box 18, Grahame Papers; "Kern Describes Inter-Ocean's Program for Physically Impaired Risks," *Eastern Underwriter* 56 (October 28, 1955): 44.

84 V. J. Skutt, "The Follow Through," Health Insurance Association of America Individual Insurance Forum, November 16, 1959, Box 19, Grahame Papers.

85 *Source Book of Health Insurance Data* (New York, 1964), 17.

86 Moran, "Comprehensive Major Medical Expense Insurance."

87 "Proceedings of the National Congress on Prepaid Health Insurance," 1960, Box 20, John B. Carter Files, RG 2, Equitable Archives.

88 Reinhard Hohaus, Reminiscences, 40–41.

89 "Report to Board of Directors," February 1965, Box 25, Grahame Papers; "Report of the Committee on Economics of Financing Medical Care," May 11, 1964, Box 25, Grahame Papers.

90 E. J. Faulkner to John H. Miller, August 6, 1958, Box 18, Grahame Papers.

91 "Report of the Special Committee on Continuance of Coverage," June 1960, Box 18, Grahame Papers.

92 E. J. Faulkner, "All That Glitters," Agency Managers' Conference, December 18, 1963, Series 2, Box 5, Faulkner Papers.

93 The aged insurance market (a discussion of which follows later in this chapter) demonstrates this point. The data I have collected on coverage for the elderly are uneven and conflicting. It nevertheless appears that nonprofit plans and commercial companies each insured somewhere in the range of 40 and 60 percent of all aged policyholders. If the commercial industry carried more aged subscribers than nonprofits, as at least one source indicates, that burden would have roughly reflected its market share of approximately 60 percent of health insurance policies at the end of the 1950s. (See Chapter 5, especially note 98.) However, Blue Cross and Blue Shield may well have suffered higher losses from elderly subscribers than did commercial companies. This financial disadvantage would have occurred for at least two reasons. First, the Blues tended to employ looser and more flexible enrollment techniques than insurance companies. Those practices would have led them to accept the sickest among the insured elderly. Second, nonprofit plans, particularly Blue Cross, likely offered senior citizens more generous coverage than commercial firms. See Melissa A. Thomasson, "Did Blue Cross and Blue Shield Suffer from Adverse Selection? Evidence from the 1950s," National Bureau of Economic Research, Working Paper Series, no. 9167 (September 2002): 1–25. See also Robert Ball, "Staff Paper on the Limitations of Private Health Insurance for the Aged," October 15, 1963, Box 299, Office of Commissioner, SSA, RG 47, NARA; "The Extent of Insurance Company Coverage for the Medical Expenses of the Senior Citizen," December 1961, Box 22, Grahame Papers; House Committee on Ways and Means, *Hearings on Social Security Legislation*, 85th Cong., 2nd sess., June 24, 1958 (J. Douglas Colman, "Hospital Service for the Aged and Its Finance," June 23, 1958), 641.

94 *Source Book of Health Insurance Data*, 11, 14.

95 "Report of the Special Committee on Continuance of Coverage"; "Cancellable Accident and Health Insurance"; "Industry Achievements Testify to Its Reasonableness Toward Public," *Eastern Underwriter* 56 (September 30, 1955): 38, 42; "The Aged and Private Health Insurance," *Health Insurance Viewpoints* 4 (January 1964): 1–3.

96 "Report of the Special Committee on Continuance of Coverage". A 1958 survey found that out of approximately 300 group plans under union

bargaining, 68 percent had retiree health benefits. In 97 percent of the plans that offered retiree benefits, the employer paid at least a portion of the premium. Union leaders understood that these contributions reduced the amount of resources available for the wages and benefits of younger, working employees.

97 Ibid.

98 "The Aged and Private Health Insurance," 1–3; "The Extent of Insurance Company Coverage for the Medical Expenses of the Senior Citizen." Insurers estimated that approximately 14 percent of the uninsured elderly were eligible, due to their low incomes, for health coverage under Kerr-Mills programming. See Chapter 7.

99 Quoted in Ralph J. Walker, "The Challenge of Voluntary Health Insurance," *Medical Economics* 31 (February 1954): 222–24. See also "Eddy Speaks His Mind on Group A.&H. Trends," *Eastern Underwriter* 54 (October 15, 1953): 4. Francis R. Smith, who served as Pennsylvania's insurance commissioner between 1955 and 1963, criticized commercial insurance companies for offering medical coverage as a loss leader to obtain group accounts. The practice had dramatically intensified the competitive pressure on Blue Cross and Blue Shield and financially destabilized their plans. See Margaret C. Albert, *A Practical Vision: The Story of Blue Cross of Western Pennsylvania, 1937–1987* (Pittsburgh, 1987), 50.

100 E. J. Faulkner to Bernard R. Stone, July 14, 1952, Series 2, Box 5, Faulkner Papers.

101 "Board of Directors: Progress Surrounding Recommendations Contained in the Blueprint," February 1965, Box 25, Grahame Papers.

102 Quoted in John H. Miller to Travis T. Wallace, August 1, 1958, Box 18, Grahame Papers (emphasis in original). See also F. L. Harrington to O. F. Grahame, November 4, 1958, Box 18, Grahame Papers. Some HIAA leaders worried that the tone of this memo was overly harsh. However, explained an association official, "it was felt very strongly by Ed Faulkner and others that unless we included the strong language in the report, nothing would be accomplished toward stirring up the chief executive officers of the companies to the realization of the perils here."

103 "The Extent of Insurance Company Coverage for the Medical Expenses of the Senior Citizen."

104 Reinhard Hohaus, Reminiscences, 119–22.

105 *Insurance Economics Surveys* 17 (August 1960), Box 28, Grahame Papers; "Minutes of the Meeting of the ALC-LIAA Joint Committee on Social Security and Health Care," February 16, 1961, Box 20, Grahame Papers; Horace H. Wilson, J. Henry Smith, and Morton D. Miller, "Medicare and Private Benefit Plans," n.d., Box 10, Harrison Givens Files, RG 2, Equitable Archives; Robert M. Ball, "'The Potential of Private Health Insurance,'" June 5, 1963, Box 299, Office of Commissioner, SSA, RG 47, NARA; Orville F. Grahame to Eugene Thore, April 13, 1960, Box 20, Grahame Papers; "Joint Committee on Social Security and Health Care," March 26, 1961, Box 20, Grahame Papers; Reinhard Hohaus, Reminiscences, 121–23.

5 The Conflicted Construction of Blue Shield: Caught between Blue Cross and the AMA

1 Academic literature on nonprofit health insurance tends to focus on Blue Cross, primarily because, as a legacy of their community-oriented ideology, hospital nonprofit leaders have tended to make themselves as well as plan archival materials accessible to scholars. Blue Shield's story has been much more difficult to uncover. On Blue Cross, see Sylvia Law, *Blue Cross: What Went Wrong?* (New Haven, CT, 1976); Odin W. Anderson, *Blue Cross since 1929: Accountability and the Public Trust* (Cambridge, MA, 1975); Irwin Miller, *American Health Care Blues: Blue Cross, HMOs, and Pragmatic Reform since 1960* (New Brunswick, NJ, 1996); Robert Cunningham III and Robert M. Cunningham, Jr., *The Blues: A History of the Blue Cross and Blue Shield System* (DeKalb, IL, 1997). I am highly indebted to Robert M. Cunningham III who generously shared his father's, Robert M. Cunningham, Jr.'s, personal collection of historical documents with me.

2 For an illuminating discussion of the various stages of Blue Cross development, see Lawrence D. Brown, "Capture and Culture: Organizational Identity in New York Blue Cross," *JHPPL* 16 (winter 1991): 651–70. See also Daniel Fox, David Rosner, and Rosemary A. Stevens, "Introduction: Between Public and Private: Half a Century of Blue Cross and Blue Shield in New York," *JHPPL* 16 (winter 1991): 643–50.

3 Some states hosted more than one plan.

4 Frank E. Smith, "The Growth of Prepaid Medical Care Plans," *Minnesota Medicine* 35 (April 1952): 321–24, 349. Physicians occupied 750 out of 1,200 Blue Shield governing board positions.

5 John R. Mannix, interview by Robert M. Cunningham, Jr., transcript, February 26, 1974, Cunningham Papers.

6 Duncan M. MacIntyre, "Thirty Years of Blue Cross and Blue Shield," *Journal of the American Society of C.L.U.* (summer 1964): 195–96, Cunningham Papers; Cunningham, *The Blues*, 72. Several Blue Shield programs functioned completely independently of Blue Cross. In contrast, by the early 1960s, seven Blue Shield plans had merged with their Blue Cross counterparts to create unified organizations that operated under a single Board of Directors.

7 Louis S. Reed, *Blue Cross and Medical Service Plans* (Washington, D.C., 1947), 163.

8 Smith, "The Growth of Prepaid Medical Care Plans," 321–24, 349; James E. Bryan, "Blue Shield Faces Its Hour of Decision," *Medical Economics* 32 (May 1955): 197–224.

9 Robert D. Eilers, *The Regulation of Blue Cross and Blue Shield Plans* (Homewood, IL, 1963), 87.

10 Howard Hassard, "Fifty Years in Law and Medicine: An Oral History" (1985): 36–37, Cunningham Papers.

11 Cunningham, *The Blues*, 52.

12 F. E. Elliott to the House of Delegates of the Medical Society of New York, April 27, 1938, Cunningham Papers.

13 Joseph W. Garbarino, *Health Plans and Collective Bargaining* (Berkeley, 1960), 106–11.

14 John R. Mannix, interview by Lewis Weeks, transcript, 1984, Cunningham Papers; John Castellucci, interview by Robert Cunningham III, transcript, October 30, 1990, Cunningham Papers; Cunningham, *The Blues*, 47–49.

15 James E. Stuart, "The Blue Cross Story," unpublished manuscript, n.d., 128–29, Cunningham Papers.

16 Ed Werner, "Speech at 30th Anniversary of FEP" (October 1990), Cunningham Papers. See also W. R. McBee to F. J. L. Blasingame, April 19, 1957, Box 19, Blasingame Papers; Unidentified Milwaukee Blue Cross Administrator, interview by Odin W. Anderson, transcript, August 9, 1972, Cunningham Papers; Fritz Lattner, interview by Odin W. Anderson, transcript, December 6, 1972, Cunningham Papers.

17 Quoted in Cunningham, *The Blues*, 73–74.

18 Quoted in Frank E. Smith, "The Blue Shield Medical Care Plans: Early Developments" (1952): 2, Cunningham Papers.

19 Robert M. Cunningham, Jr., *The Story of Blue Shield* (Chicago, 1961), 16.

20 MacIntyre, "Thirty Years of Blue Cross and Blue Shield," 195.

21 F. L. Feierabend, interview by Odin W. Anderson, transcript, August 31, 1971, Cunningham Papers; Genevieve Dougan and Ned Parish, "History of the Role of the American Medical Association in Establishment of Associated Medical Care Plans," Internal Report for NABSP, August 15, 1960, 13, Cunningham Papers; Cunningham, *The Blues*, 73–74.

22 Smith, "The Growth of Prepaid Medical Care Plans," 321–24, 349.

23 Quoted in Dougan and Parish, "History of the Role of the American Medical Association," 2–3.

24 Quoted in Ibid., 4; Cunningham, *The Blues*, 73.

25 Quoted in Dougan and Parish, "History of the Role of the American Medical Association," 6 (emphasis in original).

26 Quoted in Ibid., 2; Cunningham, *The Blues*, 73–74.

27 Dougan and Parish, "History of the Role of the American Medical Association," 12–13. Some physician leaders argued that official ties between the AMA and AMCP might provoke another antitrust suit from federal authorities.

28 Ibid., 10–11, 13, 15.

29 Both the joint trade organization – to be called the Blue Cross and Blue Shield Association (BCBSA) – and member plans would have held stock in the corporation. The Blue Cross Commission and Blue Shield Commission would have merged to create the BCBSA's Board of Governors.

30 *Source Book of Health Insurance Data* (New York, 1965), 14–18.

31 Cunningham, *The Blues*, 83–86.

32 Paul R. Hawley, "The Challenge," Blue Cross-Blue Shield Annual Conference, French Lick, IN, October 25, 1948, Cunningham Papers.

33 Quoted in Cunningham, *The Blues*, 85. See also Dougan and Parish, "History of the Role of the American Medical Association," 4–5; Stuart, "The Blue Cross Story," 184–85, 217–18.

34 Quoted in Dougan and Parish, "History of the Role of the American Medical Association," 6.

35 Stuart, "The Blue Cross Story," 218.

36 Dougan and Parish, "History of the Role of the American Medical Association," 8–10.

37 The AMCP adopted the name Blue Shield Medical Care Plans in 1950. In 1960, it became the National Association of Blue Shield Plans (NABSP). I use NABSP throughout the narrative to avoid confusion.

38 Quoted in Dougan and Parish, "History of the Role of the American Medical Association," 6.

39 Gordon B. Leitch, "Summary of Remarks Delivered before Regional Legislative Conference of the American Medical Association at San Francisco," January 23, 1954, Box 7; W. R. McBee to Arthur R. Abbey, August 22, 1956, Box 19; W. R. McBee to Sam J. Barham, May 16, 1956, Box 19; F. J. L. Blasingame, "Voluntary Health Insurance: Personal Reflections," 1957, Box 20; all in Blasingame Papers.

40 John R. Lindsey, "New Push for Professional Independence," *Medical Economics* 37 (January 4, 1960): 188–219; "Controlling Staff Appointments," *Medical Economics* 42 (April 5, 1965): 78–87; Paul Starr, *The Social Transformation of American Medicine: The Rise of a Sovereign Profession and the Making of a Vast Industry* (New York, 1982), 166–69, 347–51, 360–62; Rosemary Stevens, *In Sickness and in Wealth: American Hospitals in the Twentieth Century* (Baltimore, 1989), chapter 9. The AMA insisted that, rather than accepting salaries or payments from hospitals, physicians bill hospitalized patients separately for their services. This directive applied to pathologists, radiologists, and anesthesiologists who conducted their practices entirely or almost entirely within hospitals.

41 C. Rufus Rorem, interview by Odin W. Anderson, transcript, December 17, 1970, Cunningham Papers.

42 Quoted in Smith, "The Growth of Prepaid Medical Care Plans," Cunningham Papers.

43 Eilers, *Regulation of Blue Cross and Blue Shield*, 82; Sam Barham, interview by Odin W. Anderson, transcript, April 22, 1973, Cunningham Papers; C. Rufus Rorem, interview by Lewis E. Weeks, transcript, 1983, Cunningham Papers.

44 J. D. Coleman, interview by Odin W. Anderson, transcript, January 9, 1971, Cunningham Papers; Cunningham, *The Blues*, 28–32; Brown, "Capture and Culture," 651–70; Fox, Rosner, and Stevens, "Introduction: Between Public and Private," 643–50.

45 E. Kammer and M. Walker, interview by Odin W. Anderson, transcript, November 1972, Cunningham Papers.

46 Ralph Bethel, interview by Odin W. Anderson, transcript, April 24, 1973, Cunningham Papers.

47 Harold Maybee, interview by Odin W. Anderson, transcript, November 14, 1972, Cunningham Papers.

48 Harold Pearce, interview by Odin W. Anderson, transcript, June 11, 1973, Cunningham Papers. Evidently this was a common quip among Blue Cross

leaders; it is also in George Heitler, interview by Odin W. Anderson, transcript, June 12, 1973, Cunningham Papers. See also Cunningham, *The Blues*, 30–32.

49 "Cutting the Doctor's Bill to Fit," *JAMA* 116 (January 18, 1941): 417. See also "Message from Dr. Walter B. Martin on Comprehensive Medical Care," *JAMA* 158 (July 2, 1955): 734; David B. Allman, "Medicine's Role in Financing Health Care Costs," *JAMA* 165 (November 23, 1957): 1573; Cunningham, *The Blues*, 60.

50 J. Albert Durgom, interview by Odin W. Anderson, transcript, January 3, 1973, Cunningham Papers. See also C. Rufus Rorem, December 17, 1970; Bruce Taylor, interview by Odin W. Anderson, transcript, June 11, 1973, Cunningham Papers.

51 Jennifer Klein, *For All These Rights: Business, Labor, and the Shaping of America's Public-Private Welfare State* (Princeton, 2003), 156–60; Raymond Munts, *Bargaining for Health: Labor Unions, Health Insurance, and Medical Care* (Madison, WI, 1967), 131–32. On Walter Reuther, see note 53.

52 Wallace Croatman, "Labor Demands Full Coverage at Doctors' Expense," *Medical Economics* 31 (August 1954): 124–31; William McNary, interview by Odin W. Anderson, transcript, July 30, 1971, Cunningham Papers.

53 William McNary; Munts, *Bargaining for Health*, 134–35; Gerald Markowitz and David Rosner, "Seeking Common Ground: A History of Labor and Blue Cross," *JHPPL* 16 (winter 1991): 695–718; Klein, *For All These Rights*, 226–27; Harry Becker, "Social Security Aims of the UAW-CIO" and Martin E. Segal, "Significance of Union Health and Welfare Funds," Blue Cross-Blue Shield Annual Conference, French Lick, IN, October 25–28, 1948, Cunningham Papers; Stuart, "The Blue Cross Story," 240. In general, Blue Cross leaders understood that the criticism they received from labor leaders was intended to pull them away from undue service provider control. For example, even after Walter Reuther made highly publicized, critical remarks about nonprofit plans and even started his own prepaid group to compete against Michigan Blues programs, BCA leaders still considered him an ally who was helping push them toward stronger cost containment measures. Walter J. McNerney, interview Odin W. Anderson, transcript, June 13, 1973, Cunningham Papers.

54 Munts, *Bargaining for Health*, 134.

55 For example, Dr. Alphin to Board of Trustees, "Pending Legislative Drive for Hospitalization at Age 65," July 17, 1957, Box 8, Blasingame Papers; F. J. L. Blasingame to W. R. McBee, November 1, 1957, Box 8, Blasingame Papers.

56 Nathan Sinai, Odin W. Anderson, and Melvin L. Dollar, *Health Insurance in the United States* (New York, 1946), 26–28. AMA leaders also eventually, though somewhat reluctantly, endorsed federal funding for hospital construction. They favored government subsidies for indigent health care but only at the local and county or municipal level.

57 Hugh C. Sherwood, "Doctors See Greater Control over Blue Shield Plans," *Medical Economics* 35 (February 3, 1958): 129.

58 William Alan Richardson, "Where Are We Going with Voluntary Prepayment?" *Medical Economics* 30 (August 1953): 131.

59 "Blue Shield Revolt," *Medical Economics* 32 (February 1955): 12–18; Hugh C. Sherwood, "What Physicians Want from Blue Shield," *Medical Economics* 35 (January 6, 1958): 94–100.

60 Leonard J. Raider, "How to Prevent a Blue Shield Crash," *Medical Economics* 34 (August 1957): 276.

61 Ibid., 274–88.

62 Blue Shield Medical Care Plans to Medical Journal Editors, March 8, 1957, Box 19, Blasingame Papers. See also Medical Journal Editorial Service of Blue Shield Medical Care Plans, "What Makes Blue Shield Different," February 8, 1957, Box 19, Blasingame Papers; J. W. T. Jordan, "Is Blue Shield Sealing Its Own Doom?" *Medical Economics* 33 (September 1956): 163–75; "Health Plans Are Warned: 'Work Together or Else,'" *Medical Economics* 34 (February 1957): 14–15; Frank L. Feierabend, "Blue Shield and the Challenge of Changing Times," *Nebraska State Medical Journal* 42 (May 1957), Box 19, Blasingame Papers.

63 James E. Bryan, "Blue Shield's Role in the Future of Medicine," *Medical Economics* 31 (July 1954): 173.

64 James E. Bryan, "The Role of Blue Shield in the Future of Medical Practice," Annual Conference of Blue Shield Plans, New York, April 4–8, 1954, Cunningham Papers.

65 Bryan, "Blue Shield's Role in the Future of Medicine," 165, 169.

66 Bryan, "The Role of Blue Shield in the Future of Medical Practice," 92–102; Feierabend, "Blue Shield and the Challenge of Changing Times," 246.

67 Reed, *Blue Cross and Medical Service Plans*, 163; Eilers, *Regulation of Blue Cross and Blue Shield*, 87.

68 Quoted in Margaret C. Albert, *A Practical Vision: The Story of Blue Cross of Western Pennsylvania, 1937–1987* (Pittsburgh, 1987), 77. See also David W. Stewart, interview by Lewis E. Weeks, transcript, 1987, Cunningham Papers.

69 Carl M. Metzger, "Extended Benefits," March 22, 1955, Cunningham Papers; Hugh C. Sherwood, "Is Blue Shield Losing Out to the Competition?" *Medical Economics* 34 (October 1957): 306–29.

70 Cunningham, *Story of Blue Shield*, 26–27.

71 Robert D. Eilers, "Blue Shield: Current Issues and Future Direction," *Journal of Risk and Insurance* 33 (December 1966): 541.

72 Cunningham, *The Blues*, 123. Melissa A. Thomasson, "Did Blue Cross and Blue Shield Suffer from Adverse Selection? Evidence from the 1950s," National Bureau of Economic Research, Working Paper Series, no. 9167 (September 2002): 1–25.

73 Walter Polner, "New Experiments to Provide Voluntary Health Insurance for Retired Persons," *JAMA* 158 (September 13, 1958): 194–96; "Highlights of 12th Clinical Meeting," *JAMA* 168 (December 20, 1958): 2148–49; "Abstract of Proceedings of the House of Delegates," *JAMA* 169 (February 14, 1959): 713; "Health Insurance for Persons over 65 Years of Age," *JAMA* 169 (March 14, 1959): 1210–11.

74 House Committee on Ways and Means, *Hospital, Nursing Home, and Surgical Benefits for OASI Beneficiaries: Hearings on H.R. 4700*, July 17, 1959, BCBS D.C. Archives.

75 MIA was also known as National Blue Shield Service Inc.

76 The Blue Shield Commission and member plans elected fifteen MIA board members, eight of whom had to be physicians.

77 "Blue Shield Unveils National Agency," *Medical Economics* 28 (March 1951): 62–65.

78 Stuart, "The Blue Cross Story," 182–83, 203–5.

79 The survey queried the leaders of fifty-eight Blue Cross plans and forty-seven Blue Shield plans. Carl S. Mundy, "Report of the Committee on Rating of the Joint Operating Committee," Annual Conference of Blue Cross and Blue Shield Plans, Chicago, March 21, 1955, Cunningham Papers; Stuart, "The Blue Cross Story," 205.

80 Mundy, "Report of the Committee on Rating," 41–42; "Blue Shield Unveils National Agency," 62–65.

81 James E. Bryan, "Local Blue Shield Plans Meet a National Challenge," *Medical Economics* 34 (May 1957): 220.

82 John Castellucci, interview by Odin W. Anderson, transcript, March 23, 1973, Cunningham Papers; John Castellucci, October 30, 1990; Cunningham, *The Blues*, 49–50.

83 John Castellucci, March 23, 1973; John Castellucci, October 30, 1990.

84 John W. Castellucci to W. R. McBee, September 27, 1956, Box 19, Blasingame Papers.

85 Bryan, "Local Blue Shield Plans Meet a National Challenge," 212.

86 "Conference of Blue Shield Plans," *JAMA* 167 (June 21, 1958): 1007.

87 James C. Brown, "Price," Annual Conference of Blue Cross and Blue Shield Plans, Chicago, March 21, 1955, Cunningham Papers.

88 Royal A. Schaaf to Robert L. Novy, September 6, 1956, Box 19, Blasingame Papers.

89 John W. Castellucci to Royal A. Schaaf, September 13, 1956, Box 19, Blasingame Papers.

90 Syndicate arrangements had the benefit of creating less expensive policies because tax-exempt plans underwrote the principal contract; whereas MIA and HSI, as insurance companies, had to price contracts to reflect their tax burden.

91 Bryan, "Local Blue Shield Plans Meet a National Challenge," 216.

92 The AMA opposed the construction of additional Veterans Administration hospitals because they would compete with private doctors; association leaders also feared that federal officials would institute a "physician draft" to staff such facilities. Thus, CHAMPUS represented the best alternative for organized physicians in regard to military health care. CHAMPUS was also known as "Medicare" before the 1965 program for aged health insurance assumed the same name.

93 Mutual of Omaha administered the commercial insurance industry's share of CHAMPUS by subcontracting with other for-profit companies. Commercial insurers believed it was important to participate in CHAMPUS because of the precedent it might set for future government health care programs.

94 Quoted in Cunningham, *The Blues*, 110–11.

95 "News Release from Blue Cross Commission," April 12, 1957, Box 19, Blasingame Papers.

96 Howard Brower to E. B. Howard, "'Big 12' Proposal in Blue Cross," May 24, 1956, Box 19, Blasingame Papers; W. R. McBee to Phillip R. Overton, July 26, 1956, Box 19, Blasingame Papers.

97 McBee to Barham; McBee to Abbey; Arthur R. Abbey to W. R. McBee, August 27, 1956, Box 19, Blasingame Papers; John Castellucci, March 23, 1973.

98 MacIntyre, "Thirty Years of Blue Cross and Blue Shield," 196–97. While Blue Shield underwrote more regular medical policies than commercial insurers during the 1940s and early 1950s, for-profit companies consistently controlled the larger surgical insurance market. Taking both coverage categories into account, commercial insurers had a small lead over Blue Shield in policies for physician services. This lead widened. By 1960, Blue Shield's market share for both surgical and medical coverage had fallen to between 35 and 38 percent.

Blue Cross ruled the field of hospital insurance during the 1930s and 1940s, with about 63 to 64 percent of total coverage during the mid-1940s. Blue Cross soon fell behind commercial insurers, accounting for approximately 46 percent of hospital expense policies sold in 1955 and about 40 percent in 1965. Blue Cross plans were much larger than Blue Shield programs, because customers usually purchased hospital insurance before considering surgical or regular medical coverage. *Source Book of Health Insurance Data*, 12–19; Raider, "How to Prevent a Blue Shield Crash," 276. Note that these figures discount the market share of alternative delivery plans, which represented less than 10 percent of all policies between the 1940s and 1960s. These data also disregard duplicate coverage as well as additional forms of insurance, such as major medical.

99 Jay C. Ketchum, "A Product for National Accounts," Annual Conference of Blue Shield Plans, San Francisco, CA, March 24–28, 1957, Cunningham Papers.

100 Bryan, "Local Blue Shield Plans Meet a National Challenge," 212–26.

101 David Dolnick, "Labor's Experience with Blue Shield," Annual Conference of Blue Shield Plans, New York, April 4–8, 1954, Cunningham Papers. Within a year, Dolnick would be serving the newly unified AFL-CIO.

102 Brown, "Price," 21.

103 Although Blues plans carried a greater percentage of high-risk subscribers than commercial companies, the difference between the two sets of insurers was not as significant as has sometimes been portrayed in scholarly narratives. For a fuller discussion of this theme, see Chapter 4. Moreover, the costs of carrying additional high-risk policyholders would have been magnified by the provision of service benefits, which made nonprofit plans responsible for a higher portion of the subscriber's total medical bill.

104 Charles Abbott, interview by Odin W. Anderson, transcript, April 25, 1973, Cunningham Papers. Cunningham, *The Blues*, 97–101, 118–19.

105 Frank Van Dyk, interview, transcript, September 23, 1954, Cunningham Papers.

106 James F. Coleman, "Some Principles of Rating and Their Effect on Blue Shield Product Development," Annual Conference of Blue Shield Plans, San Francisco, CA, March 24–28, 1957, Cunningham Papers.

107 Cunningham, *The Blues*, 48–50; John R. Mannix, February 26, 1974; Sam Barham; Reginald Cahalane, interview by Odin W. Anderson, transcript, August 5, 1971, Cunningham Papers; Eilers, "Blue Shield: Current Issues and Future Direction," 543; "Score of Blue Shield," *Medical Economics* 28 (October 1951): 126; Walter J. McNerney and Staff, *Hospital and Medical Economics: A Study of Population, Services, Costs, Methods of Payment, and Controls* (Chicago, 1962), 1298.

108 John S. Thompson, *Insurance against Costs of Hospital and Medical Services in the United States* (Cambridge, MA 1960), 27; Eilers, "Blue Shield: Current Issues and Future Direction," 541–43.

109 The few states that did tax Blue Shield usually applied lower rates to non-profit plans than to commercial companies. By the end of the 1950s, commercial insurers were mounting state political campaigns challenging the special tax and regulatory treatment of nonprofits, particularly since many Blues plans had dropped community rating and since the for-profit industry had begun shouldering a heavy load of high-risk policyholders such as the elderly. These efforts usually met with little success. Furthermore, before policymakers and the public, commercial insurers deliberately restrained their hostility toward nonprofits because their overriding political strategy – tailored to discourage federal health care reform – required them to argue that the entire voluntary insurance sector was robust and flourishing.

  Also differentiating their plans from the commercial industry, Blue Cross and Blue Shield had lower administration costs than insurance companies (at least among subscribers in the private market – this distinction did not apply to public programs). The variance most likely occurred because nonprofits had direct financing relationships with service providers. For example, doctors who participated in nonprofit programs routinely completed Blue Shield paperwork to receive reimbursements. Thus, physician offices established the administrative capacity to regularly manage nonprofit claims. In contrast, commercial firms paid indemnity fees to a disparate group of policyholders who were generally unaccustomed to filing bills and paperwork with their insurer. This situation made administrative tasks associated with paying claims more difficult and costly.

110 Bryan, "Blue Shield Faces Its Hour of Decision," 224.

111 Quoted in "Conference of Blue Shield Plans," 1006.

112 Eilers, *Regulation of Blue Cross and Blue Shield*, 147–56; Eilers, "Blue Shield: Current Issues and Future Direction," 547. The Cunninghams argue that Blue Cross plans were never as firmly under provider control as some scholars have assumed. Cunningham, *The Blues*, 63–64, 90. Indeed, Blue Cross plans had traditionally reserved a higher percentage of governing board seats for community representatives than had Blue Shield.

113 "Conference of Blue Shield Plans," 1006.

114 F. L. Feierabend.

115 F. L. Feierabend, "Philosophy of a Medical Service Plan," *JAMA* 136 (January 3, 1948): 57–58. See also Frank L. Feierabend, "Blue Shield and the Challenge of Changing Times," *Virginia Medical Monthly* 84 (September 1957): 508–10.

116 Cunningham, *The Blues*, 54–55.
117 Bryan, "Blue Shield Faces Its Hour of Decision," 197–224; Cunningham, *The Blues*, 96, 105.
118 Quoted in W. R. McBee to F. J. L. Blasingame, "H.R. 7225," May 17, 1954, Box 19, Blasingame Papers.
119 John Castellucci, March 23, 1973.
120 House Committee on Post Office and Civil Service, *Hearings on Legislation to Provide a Health and Medical Program for Federal Employees*, July 28, 1959, BCBS D.C. Archives.
121 Werner, "Speech at 30th Anniversary of FEP."
122 Ibid.; John Castellucci, March 23, 1973; Cunningham, *The Blues*, 112–15.
123 John Castellucci, March 23, 1973.
124 By the 1970s, the FEHBP accounted for approximately 8 percent of total premium income for nonprofit plans. Cunningham, *The Blues*, 111–14; Law, *Blue Cross: What Went Wrong?* 50–58.
125 Stuart, "The Blue Cross Story," 284–86.
126 Werner, "Speech at 30th Anniversary of FEP."
127 For a more complete account of how the BCA centralized authority, see Cunningham, *The Blues*.
128 Eilers, *Regulation of Blue Cross and Blue Shield*, 57–61; Cunningham, *The Blues*, 116–17.
129 Gibson et al. to E. A. Rowley, September 26, 1956, Box 19, Blasingame Papers.
130 Eilers, *Regulation of Blue Cross and Blue Shield*, 57–61; Cunningham, *The Blues*, 116–17, 194–99.

6 Corporate Health Care: From Cost Controls to Medical Decision Making

1 For discussions about the link between moral hazard and rising costs, see for example, Richard Zeckhauser, "Medical Insurance: A Case Study of the Trade-Off between Risk-Spreading and Appropriate Incentives," *Journal of Economic Theory* 2 (March 1970): 10–26; Mark V. Pauly, "The Economics of Moral Hazard: Comment," *American Economic Review* 58 (June 1968): 531–37; Roger Feldman and Brian Dowd, "A New Estimate of the Welfare Loss of Excess Health Insurance," *American Economic Review* 81 (March 1991): 297–301; Willard G. Manning and M. Susan Marquis, "Health Insurance: The Tradeoff between Risk Pooling and Moral Hazard," *Journal of Health Economics* 15 (October 1996): 609–40. In two influential articles among health care economists, Richard Zeckhauser (1970) and Mark V. Pauly (1968) asserted that generous health insurance drove up medical care pricing because consumers demanded more services and procedures. Over the last several decades this view has become less accepted among economists. In this narrative, I build upon moral hazard arguments while also emphasizing that service providers have oversupplied care. For discussions about how fee-for-service reimbursements have created "supplier-induced demand," see, for

example, Jonathan Gruber and Maria Owings, "Physician Financial Incentives and Cesarean Section Delivery," *RAND Journal of Economics* 27 (spring, 1996): 99–123; Thomas H. Rice and Roberta J. Labelle, "Do Physicians Induce Demand for Medical Services?" *JHPPL* 14 (fall 1989): 587–600; Eric M. Patashnik and Alan S. Gerber, "Sham Surgery: The Problem of Inadequate Medical Evidence," in *Promoting the General Welfare: New Perspectives on Government Performance,* ed. Eric M. Patashnik and Alan S. Gerber (Washington, D.C., 2006), 43–73.

A related strand of scholarship contends that in the health care sector, there is an "information problem," because patients lack the expertise to evaluate medical care or know when a service is necessary. This literature has its antecedents in Kenneth Arrow's work, which famously asserted that health care is a unique economic sector because of the information asymmetries between consumers or patients and service providers (in addition to the uncertainty, even among physicians, about how medical conditions will manifest and the most appropriate means of treatment). Kenneth Arrow, "Uncertainty and the Welfare Economics of Medical Care," *American Economic Review* 53 (December 1963): 941–73; H. E. Frech and J. Michael Woolley, "Consumer Information, Price and Nonprice Competition among Hospitals," *Developments in Health Economics and Public Policy* 1 (1992): 217–41; Mark V. Pauly and Mark Satterthwaite, "The Pricing of Primary Care Physicians' Services: A Test of the Role of Consumer Information," *Bell Journal of Economics* 12 (autumn 1981): 488–506; Victor R. Fuchs and Marcia J. Kramer, *Determinants of Expenditures for Physicians' Services in the United States* (Cambridge, MA, 1972); Eli Ginzberg with Miriam Ostow, *Men, Money, and Medicine* (New York, 1969); David Dranove, "Demand Inducement and the Physician/Patient Relationship," *Economic Inquiry* 26 (April 1988): 281–98. See also Deborah Haas-Wilson, "Arrow and the Information Market Failure in Health Care: The Changing Content and Sources of Health Care Information," *JHPPL* 26 (October 2001): 1031–44.

However, apart from the faulty insurance company model around which it has developed, the health care market is not as economically distinct as many scholars have argued. Viewing the market from a historical perspective demonstrates that the barriers that have prevented patients from accessing price and quality information were erected either by AMA policies or characteristics particular to the insurance company model, rather than by features inherent to health care economies more generally. For example, the AMA went to enormous lengths to prevent physicians from competing on the basis of either price or quality of care while insurance has discouraged patients from comparing prices or even ascertaining the costs of care. The problems associated with information asymmetries could have been mitigated under alternative delivery models and payment structures that provided physicians and hospitals with the incentive not only to constrain service utilization and costs, but also to supply patients with the best possible care as the primary path to augmenting revenues. Under such arrangements, practices such as listing prices and publicizing patient reviews would have been commonplace. Moreover, consumers have proven themselves capable of adapting to the sale of products that require high levels of expertise to evaluate. For example, in the automobile and computer markets, purchasers have myriad ways of appraising products, whether through rating agencies, consumer information bureaus, or customer reviews (which, before the internet, were primarily delivered via word of mouth). Certainly, services are often more difficult to evaluate than tangible goods and, moreover, health care services are broadly supplied from numerous locations. But these conditions only increase the value of consumer information. And when a product or service is valuable, organizations and enterprises tend to form to provide it. Indeed, technology has increased the availability of information for each set of health care participants, whether insurers, providers, or consumers.

2 Victor Fuchs, "Economics, Values, and Health Care Reform," *American Economic Review* 86 (March 1996): 8. In the mid-1990s, Fuchs surveyed health care economists; 81 percent of them agreed with the following statement: "The primary reason for the increase in the health care sector's share of GDP over the past 30 years is technological change in medicine." See also Joseph P. Newhouse, "Medical Care Costs: How Much Welfare Loss?" *Journal of Economic Perspectives* 6 (summer 1992): 3–21; Sherry Glied, "Health Care Costs: On the Rise Again," *Journal of Economic Perspectives* 17 (spring 2003): 125–48; David M. Cutler and Mark McClellan, "Is Technological Change in Medicine Worth It?" *Health Affairs* 20 (September/October 2001): 11–29.

   Historians have situated technology within its institutional context to demonstrate that it is derivative of cultural and social structures, rather than a causal force that independently drives societal development. For example, Thomas P. Hughes, *Networks of Power: Electrification in Western Society, 1880–1930* (Baltimore, 1983); Wiebe E. Bijker, Thomas P. Hughes, Trevor Pinch, and Deborah G. Douglas, eds., *The Social Construction of Technological Systems: New Directions in the Sociology and History of Technology* (Cambridge, MA, 1989); W. Bernard Carlson, *Innovation as a Social Process: Elihu Thompson and the Rise of General Electric, 1870–1900* (New York, 1991).

3 Some analysts have noted that the prices of services based on innovative technologies and procedures have fallen significantly in medical specialties that operate without insurance, for example, in the fields of plastic surgery and vision correction surgery. Scholars have pointed out that barriers still exist for consumers attempting to steward their resources wisely, including misleading advertisements, the difficulty of accessing price and quality information, and the need for urgent care. Again, similar obstacles to consumer purchasing exist in other market sectors as well. For a discussion of these issues, see Ha T. Tu and Jessica H. May, "Self-Pay Markets in Health Care: Consumer Nirvana or Caveat Emptor?" *Health Affairs* 26 (March 2007): 217–26.

4 For narratives that trace health care cost problems back to the passage of Medicare and Medicaid, see Rashi Fein, *Medical Care, Medical Costs: The Search for a Health Insurance Policy*, 2nd ed. (Cambridge, MA, 1989); Karen Davis, Gerard F. Anderson, Diane Rowland, and Earl P. Steinberg, *Health Care Cost Containment* (Baltimore, 1990); Jill Quadagno, *One Nation Uninsured: Why the U.S. Has No National Health Insurance* (New York, 2005), chapter 4. For scholarship finding that medical costs became a problem much

earlier, see Jennifer Klein, *For All These Rights: Business, Labor, and the Shaping of America's Public-Private Welfare State* (Princeton, 2003), 217–18, 242–43; David J. Rothman, "The Public Presentation of Blue Cross, 1935–1965," *JHPPL* 16 (winter 1991): 684–87.

5 Stephen L. Fielding, "Changing Medical Practice and Medical Malpractice Claims," *Social Problems* 42 (February 1995): 38–55; A. Dale Tussing and Martha A. Wojtowycz, "Malpractice, Defensive Medicine, and Obstetric Behavior," *Medical Care* 35 (February 1997): 172–91; Daniel P. Kessler and Mark B. McClellan, "The Effects of Malpractice Pressure and Liability Reforms on Physicians' Perceptions of Medical Care," *Law and Contemporary Problems* 60 (winter 1997): 81–106.

6 The insurance company model rewards doctors for providing as many billable services and procedures as possible, not for time spent time with individual patients or for more ambiguous obligations related to bedside manner, such as thoroughly explaining a diagnosis or offering moral support. John A. Robbins, Klea D. Bertakis, Azari R. Helms, Edward J. Callahan, and D. A. Creten, "The Influence of Physician Practice Behaviors on Patient Satisfaction," *Family Medicine* 25 (January 1993): 17–20.

7 On the corporate nature of health care, see David Dranove, *The Economic Evolution of American Health Care: From Marcus Welby to Managed Care* (Princeton, 2000); Paul Starr, *The Social Transformation of American Medicine: The Rise of a Sovereign Profession and the Making of a Vast Industry* (New York, 1982), 420–49. Under corporate arrangements, a principal-agent relationship was created between insurers and physicians. The literature on principal-agent relations examines how managers, whom Alfred Chandler found so important to the development of U.S. businesses, often have goals that differ from those of stockholders and financiers. Viewed through this framework, insurer-principals have differing objectives from physician-agents. Alfred Chandler, *The Visible Hand* (Cambridge, MA, 1977); Daniel Raff and Peter Temin, "Business History and Recent Economic Theory," in *Inside the Business Enterprise: The Use and Transformation of Information*, ed. Peter Temin (Chicago, 1991), 43–71; Roger Clarke and Tony McGuinness, eds., *The Economics of the Firm* (New York, 1987); John W. Pratt and Richard J. Zeckhauser, eds., *Principals and Agents: The Structure of Business* (Boston, 1985). See also Olivier Zunz, *Making America Corporate, 1870–1920* (Chicago, 1990).

8 Managed care practices – which received a good deal of political attention and publicity during the 1970s before taking a firm hold in health care during the 1980s – amplified an existing trend toward cost containment and, moreover, were made possible by the system's existing institutional framework.

9 "People Want What They've Paid for," *Medical Economics* 38 (June 19, 1961): 113–33.

10 Leonard Raider, "Let's Use – Not Abuse," Proceedings of the National Congress on Prepaid Health Insurance, Chicago, May 13–14, 1960, Box 20, John B. Carter Files, RG 2, Equitable Archives; Dr. Andrew Tessitore, interview with the author, transcript, January 21, 2010; "There's No Stopping 'Social Demand,'" *Medical Economics* 38 (June 19, 1961): 67–71; "Who's

Causing Those Higher Insurance Costs?" *Medical Economics* 35 (December 29, 1958): 30; J. Milo Anderson, "Increasing Demands versus Increasing Costs," Proceedings of the National Congress on Prepaid Health Insurance, Chicago, May 13–14, 1960, Box 20, John B. Carter Files, RG 2, Equitable Archives.

During this period, commercial insurance leaders intensively studied the problem of "overinsurance" – the term described individuals who held multiple health care policies. This situation sometimes occurred inadvertently when, for example, policyholders who purchased coverage individually were also insured through their spouses' work benefits. However, some consumers deliberately took out numerous policies to obtain indemnity payments from multiple sources over the course of an illness, whether real or feigned. This problem abated when insurance companies began creating direct financing linkages with physicians and hospitals.

11 "Why You're Being Blamed for It," *Medical Economics* 38 (June 19, 1961): 146; "Implies M.D.s Wreck Voluntary Insurance," *Medical Economics* 28 (August 1951): 218, 222.

12 O.D. Dickerson, "The Problem of Overutilization in Health Insurance," *Journal of Insurance* 26 (spring 1959): 65–72; E. J. Faulkner, "Meeting Health Care Costs through Insurance," *Journal of Insurance* 24 (September 1957): 13.

13 "'Is This Hysterectomy Really Necessary?'" *Medical Economics* 31 (October 1953): 267, 278; "Needless Surgery – Doctors, Good and Bad," *Reader's Digest*, May 1953, 53–57; Walter J. McNerney, "Utilization of Hospital and Physician Services," Proceedings of the First National Conference on Utilization, Chicago, March 2–3, 1962, Cunningham Papers; Robert Cunningham, Jr., interview by Lewis E. Weeks, transcript, March 25, 1980, Cunningham Papers. Some women welcomed an otherwise medically unnecessary hysterectomy as a form of birth control, particularly because some states still regulated the use of contraceptives. These restrictions were struck down in the landmark 1965 *Griswold v. Connecticut* case.

14 "Too Much Unnecessary Surgery: Interview with Dr. Paul Hawley," *U.S. News and World Report*, February 20, 1953, 48–55. Hawley's accusations so angered physicians that they sponsored more than eleven resolutions to censure him during the AMA's 1953 summer meeting. After considering the resolutions, Reference Committee members maintained that they too deplored Hawley's "ill-advised statement" but, fearing negative publicity, recommended that the House take no action. "Report of Reference Committee on Insurance and Medical Service," *JAMA* 152 (June 20, 1953): 839–42.

15 Monroe Lerner, "The Extent to Which Patients Use Hospital Plans," Proceedings of the First National Conference on Utilization, Chicago, March 2–3, 1962, Cunningham Papers.

16 "Cites Doctors' Abuses of Blue Cross Contracts," *Medical Economics* 29 (January 1952): 223, 225; Milton Silverman, "The Post Reports on Health Insurance," *The Saturday Evening Post*, June 7, 1958, 25–27; "Ill-Advised Practices May Take 'Voluntary' Out of Health Insurance," *National Underwriter* 57 (December 18, 1953): 22; Milton Silverman, "The High Cost of Chiseling," *The Saturday Evening Post*, June 14, 1958, 36, 124–26; Faulkner,

"Meeting Health Care Costs through Insurance," 13; "Why You're Being Blamed for It," 152; Robert Cunningham III and Robert M. Cunningham, Jr., *The Blues: A History of the Blue Cross and Blue Shield System* (DeKalb, IL, 1997), 104.

17 Black Clark, "Let's Stop Abusing Hospital Insurance," *Reader's Digest*, November 1954, 63.

18 Milton Silverman, "Sabotage of Our Health Insurance," *Reader's Digest*, September 1958, 64–67; Dickerson, "The Problem of Overutilization in Health Insurance," 68.

19 William H. Wandel, "Rising Medical Care Costs with Special Reference to Hospital Expenses," *Journal of Insurance* 27 (June 1960): 65. See also Lerner, "The Extent to Which Patients Use Hospital Plans"; Anne R. Somers and Herman M. Somers, "Coverage, Costs, and Controls in Voluntary Health Insurance," *Public Health Reports* 76 (January 1961): 3–6; Odin W. Anderson and Paul B. Sheatsley, *Hospital Use: A Survey of Patient and Physician Decisions* (Chicago, 1967).

20 Milton Roemer and Max Shain, *Hospital Utilization under Insurance* (Chicago, 1959); Milton Roemer and Max Shain, "Hospital Costs Relate to the Supply of Beds," *Modern Hospital* 92 (April 1959): 71–73; Milton Roemer, "Bed Supply and Hospital Utilization," *Hospitals* 35 (November 1961): 36–42.

21 Rosemary Stevens, *In Sickness and in Wealth: American Hospitals in the Twentieth Century* (Baltimore, 1989), 251–52, 257–67.

22 After the passage of Medicare, this phenomenon became widely known as "cost shifting." Today the term "cost shifting" is usually applied to situations in which service providers inflate charges for privately insured patients to cover perceived shortfalls in government payments. To little avail, commercial insurers continually battled the American Hospital Association over inequitable service pricing and what they viewed as unmerited favoritism, in terms of lower rates, for Blue Cross subscribers. "Experience and Trends in Group and Hospital and Surgical Insurance," *Eastern Underwriter* 52 (February 16, 1951): 39; "Relations between Private Insurance and Medical Profession Improved," *Eastern Underwriter* 60 (November 11, 1959): 40, 42; "Health Insurance Council in Action," *Eastern Underwriter* 61 (December 16, 1960): 122, 125; "They've Got the Craziest Pricing System!" *Medical Economics* 38 (June 19, 1961): 83–102.

23 "Do Doctors Hike Fees for Insured Patients?" *Medical Economics* 35 (May 1958): 34, 38; "Insurance Plan Leads 7 in 10 M.D.s to Raise Fees," *Medical Economics* 36 (May 11, 1959): 29; "Physicians May Scrap Service-Type Health Plan," *Medical Economics* 31 (April 1953): 112–13; Herbert E. Klarman, "Changing Costs of Medical Care and Voluntary Health Insurance" (*American Economic Association and American Association of University Teachers of Insurance*, Cleveland, OH, December 28, 1956, 30–34); A. T. Murphey, "Beware the Gimmick!" *Medical Economics* 28 (February 1951): 206, 209; "Says Money-Mad M.D.s Ruin Blue Shield," *Medical Economics* 30 (August 1953): 205, 207; C. Arthur Williams, Jr., "How They're Insuring Those Major Medical Expenses," *Medical Economics* 32

(November 1954): 97–109; "'Doctors Are Endangering Major Medical Plans,'" *Medical Economics* 33 (May 1956): 12; "Major Medical Hurt by High Fees," *Medical Economics* 35 (February 17, 1958): 30, 36; "Remarks of Moderator Everett" (*Health Insurance Association of America Annual Meeting*, Philadelphia, May 5, 1959); L. A. Orsini, "Report of the Health Insurance Council," 1965, Box 20, Grahame Papers.

24 Quoted in "Need for Cooperation in Health Care Field," *Eastern Underwriter* 48 (May 17, 1957): 65. Similarly, Ralph J. Walker, "The Challenge of Voluntary Health Insurance," *Medical Economics* 31 (February 1954): 222–24; Silverman, "Sabotage of Our Health Insurance," 64–67; "Transcript of Proceeding of Meeting between the Board of Trustees, AMA and the Health Insurance Council," July 19, 1957, Series 17, Box 193, Faulkner Papers.

25 *Source Book of Health Insurance Data* (New York, 1962), 60. During the same period, transportation costs rose 48 percent, personal care prices increased 34 percent, and housing prices escalated 33 percent. The categories with the least amount of inflation – food and apparel – rose 21 and 10 percent, respectively.

26 Somers, "Coverage, Costs, and Controls in Voluntary Health Insurance," 4–5.

27 "Prudential Raises Group Hospital, Surgical Rates," *National Underwriter* 56 (May 23, 1952): 1, 20.

28 "Why It Costs More to Insure against Illness," *U.S. News & World Report*, January 31, 1958, 83–85.

29 Walter Klem to the President, "New Premium Scales," June 13, 1962; William A. Feeney to R. P. Coates, December 26, 1961; R. P. Coates to Walter Klem, February 8, 1962; all in Box 42A, RG 4, Equitable Archives.

30 John Cline, "The President's Page: A Monthly Message," *JAMA* 148 (January 19, 1952): 208–9. See also Frank G. Dickinson, *Is Medical Care Expensive?* (Chicago, 1947); "Medical Debt," *JAMA* 151 (January 17, 1953) 215; "A New Look at Prices," *JAMA* 152 (August 1, 1953): 1341; Frank G. Dickinson, *Medical Care Expenditures, Prices, and Quantity, 1930–1950* (Chicago, 1951).

31 For example, "Money for Tobacco," *JAMA* 147 (October 13, 1951): 668; Dickinson, *Is Medical Care Expensive?* ; "Medical Care Expenditures," *JAMA* 147 (December 1, 1951): 1361.

32 Frank G. Dickinson, "The Magnum Opus of Michael Davis," *JAMA* 158 (August 27, 1955): 158. See also Frank G. Dickinson and James Raymond, "The Economic Position of Medical Care," *JAMA* 159 (September 3, 1955): 41–50.

33 In the 1940s, the AMA hired Dickinson away from the University of Illinois, where he was an economics professor. The Bureau of Medical Economic Research grew from six to sixty staff members during the 1950s. James G. Burrow, *AMA: Voice of American Medicine* (Baltimore, 1963), 335; Frank D. Campion, *The AMA and U.S. Health Policy since 1940* (Chicago, 1984), 195; Louis H. Bauer, "President's Page: A Monthly Message," *JAMA* 148 (April 26, 1952): 1510.

34 "Misinterpretation of 'Needs' for Medical Care," *JAMA* 148 (March 8, 1952): 848–49; "Message from Dr. Walter B. Martin on Comprehensive Medical Care," *JAMA* 158 (July 2, 1955): 734; "Committee on Prepayment of Medical

and Hospital Services," *JAMA* 159 (October 29, 1955): 942; Dickinson, *Medical Care Expenditures, Prices, and Quantity*; "Report of Bureau of Medical Economic Research," *JAMA* 159 (October 29, 1955): 910–15.

35 David B. Allman, "Medicine's Role in Financing Health Care Costs," *JAMA* 165 (November 23, 1957): 1573.

36 For example, "Needless Surgery," 53–57; Clark, "Let's Stop Abusing Hospital Insurance," 63–66; Silverman, "The Post Reports on Health Insurance," 25–27; Silverman, "The High Cost of Chiseling," 36, 124–26; Silverman, "Sabotage of Our Health Insurance," 64–67; "Doctor Bills Pile Up: How Can Families Pay?" *U.S. News & World Report*, October 17, 1952, 65–66, 70; "What It Costs to Be Sick," *U.S. News & World Report*, December 24, 1954, 63–64. See also William T. Fitts, Jr., and Barbara Fitts, "Ethical Standards of the Medical Profession," *Annals of the American Academy of Political and Social Science* 297 (January 1955): 17–36; William Michelfelder, *It's Cheaper to Die – Doctors, Drugs, and the AMA* (New York, 1960); "'It's Cheaper to Die,'" *Medical Economics* 38 (April 10, 1961): 91–97.

37 Ernest Havemann, "Challenge of Mounting Expenses," *Life*, November 2, 1959, 82–98.

38 James Fuller, "How to Get Known as a Dollar Chaser," *Medical Economics* 29 (June 1952): 108, 111. See also "Public Attitudes about Physicians and Medical Care," *JAMA* 159 (October 15, 1955): 686–87; John R. Lindsey, "Reasonable Fees Speak Louder than Words," *Medical Economics* 37 (February 1, 1960): 69–74, 266–72; "Why You're Being Blamed for It," 141–56.

39 The Gaffin survey queried four thousand respondents. "Public Opinion Survey about Doctors," *JAMA* 160 (February 11, 1956): 471–72; "Some Meanings of Medical and Public Opinion about the AMA," *JAMA* 161 (May 5, 1956): 68–69.

40 "Address of the President, Dr. John W. Cline," *JAMA* 149 (June 28, 1952): 854.

41 "Transcript of Proceeding of Meeting between the Board of Trustees, AMA and the Health Insurance Council."

42 "Committee on Prepayment Medical and Hospital Service," *JAMA* 162 (October 20, 1956): 814.

43 E. Vincent Askey, "Medicine Meets the Challenge – A 10-Point Program of Action," Maricopa County Medical Society Meeting, Phoenix, AZ, February 28, 1961, Box 21, Blasingame Papers; Arch O. Pitman, "Background for Congress," Proceedings of the National Congress on Prepaid Health Insurance, Chicago, IL, May 13–14, 1960, Box 20, John B. Carter Files, RG 2, Equitable Archives.

44 "Supplementary Reports of Council on Medical Service," *JAMA* 169 (February 14, 1959): 713.

45 "County Medical Society Grievance Committees," *JAMA* 153 (October 3, 1953): 510–11; Council on Medical Service, "Survey of County Medical Society Activities," *JAMA* 160 (February 18, 1956): 564–67; Milton Golin, "Guardians of the M.D. Oath," *JAMA* 166 (April 5, 1958): 1735–41. By 1952, grievance committees had been established in 562 state and county medical societies.

46 "Transcript of Proceeding of Meeting between the Board of Trustees, AMA and the Health Insurance Council."

47 "Medical Society of Virginia, the Council," *Virginia Medical Monthly* 76 (April 1949): 193; "Reports for 1956 Annual Meeting," *Virginia Medical Monthly* 83 (October 1956): 454.

48 "Self-Discipline Starts at the Top," *Medical Economics* 38 (April 14, 1961): 134; "Are Grievance Committees Too 'Bashful'?" *Medical Economics* 29 (June 1952): 201–02.

49 W. R. McBee to Ralph E. Webb, "What Can Be Done to Improve the AMA's Public Relations Program," August 2, 1955, Box 19, Blasingame Papers.

50 "Self-Discipline Starts at the Top," 125–48; F. J. L. Blasingame, "The AMA – Today and Tomorrow," 1961, Box 21, Blasingame Papers.

51 "Doctors Publicize Average Fees," *Medical Economics* 27 (April 1950): 54–55; "Fixed Fees Urged," *Medical Economics* 31 (August 1954): 6–7; "Physicians May Scrap Service-Type Health Plan," 112–13.

52 It appears that the Nebraska Medical Society was the first state association to adopt an RVS. However, the California RVS attracted more publicity and inaugurated a drive to adopt such scales nationwide. Hugh C. Sherwood, "New Value Scale Wins M.D.s' Approval," *Medical Economics* 35 (August 1958): 78–79, 82; Arthur Owens, "Value Scale Spurs Insurance Pay," *Medical Economics* 33 (July 1956): 129–36, 40; John G. Morrison, "Usual or Medical Fee Plan," Proceedings of the National Congress on Prepaid Health Insurance, Chicago, May 13–14, 1960, Box 20, John B. Carter Files, RG 2, Equitable Archives.

53 "Committee on Medical Practices, Supplementary Report," *JAMA* 166 (March 29, 1958): 1621; Hugh C. Sherwood, "National Value Scale May Help You Set Fees," *Medical Economics* 35 (January 6, 1958): 147–48, 152–54; Leonard W. Larson, "For the People" (*Health Insurance Association of America Annual Meeting*, Philadelphia, May 5, 1959).

54 Jean Pascoe, "Get Set for a National Relative-Value Scale," *Medical Economics* 38 (June 19, 1961): 179–82, 186–92, 200–201.

55 Quoted in Milton Silverman, "Is This the Pattern of the Future?" *The Saturday Evening Post*, June 21, 1958, 100. See Also Klein, *For All These Rights*, 217–18.

56 Quoted in "Do Doctors Hike Fees for Insured Patients?" 38.

57 Malcolm L. Denise, "Management Views on the Financing of Hospital and Medical Care" (*Open Forum on Prepayment Hospital and Medical Care Plans, 1959*).

58 "Why the Pressure's on You," *Medical Economics* 41 (July 13, 1964): 60–71.

59 "Business Community Supports Plan," *The Review* (September 1974): 2, Independence Blue Cross Archives, Philadelphia, PA (hereafter BCBS Philadelphia Archives); "Comments on Rising of Group Insurance Health Costs," *Eastern Underwriter* 61 (May 27, 1960): 39, 60.

60 "Attacks Plan to Set Up Uniform Medical Fees," *Medical Economics* 31 (July 1954): 222–24. See also "Carey Discusses What Companies Do about Rising Medical Costs Problems," *Eastern Underwriter* 54 (February 6, 1953): 37; Faulkner, "Meeting Health Care Costs through Insurance," 12–13.

61 The Health Insurance Council, *The Health Insurance Story*, n.d., Box 43A, RG 4, Equitable Archives. See also Alan M. Thaler, "Group Major-Medical Expense Insurance," *Transactions of Society of Actuaries* 2 (January 1951): 429–82; "Carey Discusses What Companies Do," 37.

62 "Coinsurance in Medical Care Plans Is Examined by S. Gwyn Dulaney," *Eastern Underwriter* 54 (October 16, 1953): 46; "Price Aspect of Group Hospital Insurance Thoroughly Explored," *Eastern Underwriter* 54 (February 13, 1953): 47; Charles P. Hall, "Deductibles in Health Insurance: An Evaluation," *Journal of Risk and Insurance* 33 (June 1966): 253–63. For a discussion of deductibles and coinsurance, which even nonprofit insurers (who had prided themselves on fully covering service costs) increasingly adopted because of rising medical prices, see Beatrix Hoffman, *Health Care for Some: Rights and Rationing in the United States since 1930* (Chicago, 2012), 105–13.

63 Memorandum, "1099 Reporting on Payments to Doctors," n.d., Box 24, Grahame Papers.

64 "Insurance Plan Leads 7 in 10 M.D.s to Raise Fees," 29. See also "'Doctors Are Endangering Major Medical Plans,'" 12; "What to Charge a Patient Who Has Major Medical," *Medical Economics* 35 (December 1958): 54; Williams, "How They're Insuring Those Major Medical Expenses," 97–109; "The Physician and Major Medical Insurance," *Health Insurance Trends* (September–October 1964), Box 42A, RG 4, Equitable Archives.

65 James T. Phillips, "Some Considerations in the Development of an Individual Accident and Sickness Program," *Transactions of Society of Actuaries* 6 (1954): 1–63; "Why the Pressure's on You," 60–71.

66 "Meeting the Problems of Decentralization," *National Underwriter* 57 (April 17, 1953): 2, 35.

67 "Individual Accident and Health Insurance," August 27, 1959, Box 41C, RG 4, Equitable Archives; Paul O'Rourke, "Reorganization," July 30, 1975, Box 57A, RG 4, Equitable Archives.

68 "Comments on Rising of Group Insurance Health Cost," 39, 60; "4-Year Experience with Comprehensive Medical," *Eastern Underwriter* 48 (February 8, 1959): 41.

69 John G. Morrison, "Let's Use, Not Abuse," Proceedings of the National Congress on Prepaid Health Insurance, Chicago, May 13–14, 1960, Box 20, John B. Carter Files, RG 2, Equitable Archives; S. Bruce Black, "Control of Losses in Accident and Health Insurance" (*Health Insurance Association of America Annual Meeting*, Dallas, TX, May 17, 1960).

70 "Minutes of a Meeting of the Committee on Economics of Financing Medical Care," October 15, 1956, Box 25, Grahame Papers; William J. McNamara, "The Role of the Medical Director in Major Medical Expense Insurance," *JAMA* 165 (November 23, 1957): 1586–91.

71 Dr. Joseph Altman, "Simpler A.&H. Forms Should Ease Many Difficulties," *National Underwriter* 56 (December 12, 1952): 27–28; Arnold B. Brown, "Health Insurance Council" (*Health Insurance Association of America Annual Meeting*, Philadelphia, May 5, 1959); "Hospital Admission Plan Now Up-to-Date," *Eastern Underwriter* 56 (June 17, 1955): 47; Orsini, "Report of the Health Insurance Council."

72 For example, Health Insurance Council, *Nature and Types of Health Insurance*, 1956, Box 6, Blasingame Papers.

73 Louis A. Orsini, "Health Insurance Council – State Committee Chairman" (*Health Insurance Association of America Annual Meeting, Philadelphia*, May 5, 1959); Orsini, "Report of the Health Insurance Council"; "Closing Remarks of Moderator Everett" (*Health Insurance Association of America Annual Meeting*, Philadelphia, May 5, 1959). By 1965, local HICs had more than eight hundred insurance company employees helping to manage their activities.

74 "Keeping Patient Aware of Medical Care Costs," *Eastern Underwriter* 48 (May 24, 1957): 46; Albert Pike, "The Insurance Companies' Approach to Health Insurance," Annual Meeting of the Alabama Society of Internal Medicine, May 2, 1962, Box 29, Grahame Papers.

75 "HIAA Hears Browning, Blasingame, Terrell," *Eastern Underwriter* 61 (May 27, 1960): 52; "Major Medical Hurt by High Fees," 30, 36; "Medical-Insurance Relations Discussed," *Eastern Underwriter* 61 (November 25, 1960): 38.

76 Charles D. Scott, "Health Insurance Council" (*Health Insurance Association of America Annual Meeting*, Philadelphia, May 5, 1959); "Insurance, Texas Story Are Topics for Discussion," *Texas State Journal of Medicine* 60 (February 1964): 173–76.

77 W. R. McBee to Tom B. Bond, February 6, 1957, Box 19, Blasingame Papers.

78 R. G. Baker to F. J. L. Blasingame, March 30, 1954, Box 15, Blasingame Papers; "Grievances," *Texas State Journal of Medicine* 59 (June 1963): 578.

79 Scott, "Health Insurance Council"; "Report of Appointees to Hospitals-Insurance-Physicians Joint Advisory Committee of Texas," *Texas State Journal of Medicine* 59 (June 1963): 612.

80 "Report of Committee on Health Insurance," *Texas State Journal of Medicine* 59 (June 1963): 610–11; "Physicians, Insurance Companies Need Mutual Understanding," *Texas State Journal of Medicine* 59 (September 1963): 973; Walter Walthall, "Medical Ethics: The Board of Censors," *Texas State Journal of Medicine* 61 (January 1965): 68.

81 Health Insurance Council, "New York County Medical Society Review Committee Experiment," June 29, 1963, Box 42A, RG 4, Equitable Archives.

82 Orsini, "Report of the Health Insurance Council."

83 Brown, "Health Insurance Council."

84 "Speech to AMA Conference," *Eastern Underwriter* 60 (August 7, 1959): 32; "New Group Major Medical," *Eastern Underwriter* 60 (December 25, 1959): 22.

85 Owens, "Value Scale Spurs Insurance Pay," 129–36, 40; "Health Insurance Terminology Studied," *The Underwriter* 60 (June 5, 1959): 40.

86 "Machines to the Rescue in Help Shortage," *National Underwriter* 57 (March 13, 1953): 16; "Electronics Division of Metropolitan Life," *Eastern Underwriter* 56 (April 29, 1955): 3; "Mut. of Omaha; United Ben. New Electronic Machines," *Eastern Underwriter* 56 (June 17, 1955): 47; "How John Hancock Uses Its IBM 650," *Eastern Underwriter* 56 (March 18, 1955): 3, 21; Orsini, "Report of the Health Insurance Council." See also JoAnne Yates,

"From Tabulators to Early Computers in the U.S. Life Insurance Industry: Co-evolution and Continuities" (October 1993), Sloan School, WP #3618–93; Joanne Yates, *Structuring the Information Age: Life Insurance and Technology in the Twentieth Century* (Baltimore, 2008).

87 Arthur Browning, "Let's Use, Not Abuse," Proceedings of the National Congress on Prepaid Health Insurance, Chicago, May 13–14, 1960, Box 20, John B. Carter Files, RG 2, Equitable Archives.

88 "Three Pilot Programs Now Underway Where HIAA Is Exerting Leadership," *Eastern Underwriter* 61 (May 27, 1960): 50; "HIAA's Information and Research Division Covered a Lot of Ground," *Eastern Underwriter* 61 (May 27, 1960): 46, 63.

89 Vergil N. Slee, "Uniform Methods of Measuring Utilization," Proceedings of the First National Conference on Utilization, Chicago, March 2–3, 1962, Cunningham Papers; "Who's Controlling It," *Medical Economics* 41 (July 13, 1964): 80

90 "Medical Care Insurance Rating and Medical Economics," *Transactions of Society of Actuaries* 17 (1965): D94–D99; G. Mason Connell, Jr., "You and the Health Insurance Council," *Virginia Medical Monthly* 83 (November 1956): 493–95. By 1956, the HIC had launched trial hospital admission programs in Richmond, Virginia; Columbus, Ohio; Birmingham, Alabama; New Hampshire; and Connecticut. Under these programs, doctors answered eight questions and, within hours, insurers granted a "Certification of Benefits" that outlined the insured services and number of hospital days available to the patient.

91 Bruce Stuart and Ronald Stockton, "Control over the Utilization of Medical Services," *Milbank Memorial Fund Quarterly* 51 (summer 1973): 359.

92 Black, "Control of Losses in Accident and Health Insurance."

93 "When We Were Very Young," *Cross Currents* (October 1963): 1, BCBS Philadelphia Archives.

94 "Your Service Report," *Blue Shield* 1 (January 1950): 1, BCBS Philadelphia Archives; "Your District Offices," *Blue Shield* 1 (February 1950): 1–2, BCBS Philadelphia Archives.

95 Margaret C. Albert, *A Practical Vision: The Story of Blue Cross of Western Pennsylvania, 1937–1987* (Pittsburgh, 1987), 50.

96 The Hospital Administrators' Review Board and the Physicians' Review Board, "Report No. 1," n.d., BCBS Philadelphia Archives; "Utilization Review Helps Cut Costs of Health Care," *The Review* (October 1975): 3, BCBS Philadelphia Archives. Blues plans also used computers to track physician charges under "prevailing fee" programs, which were modified types of usual, customary, and reasonable reimbursements, often employed as the nonprofits rolled out their own versions of major medical coverage. Under prevailing fee programs, physician charges could not surpass what 90 percent of participating area doctors charged, and plans instituted maximum charges for each service and procedure. Robert D. Eilers, "Blue Shield: Current Issues and Future Direction," *Journal of Risk Insurance* 33 (December 1966): 549; John R. Lindsey, "They Call It 'Blue Sky' Blue Shield," *Medical Economics* 33 (May 1956): 104–10; "Pilots New Fee Plan," *The Review* (November 1965): 1, BCBS Philadelphia Archives.

97 "Utilization Review Helps Cut Costs of Health Care," 3; Perry Hyde, "Looking over the Doctor's Shoulder," *Virginia Medical Monthly* 93 (February 1966): 95.

98 "Utilization Review and Control Activities in Blue Cross Plans," *Blue Cross Reports* 4 (January–March 1966): 3, BCBS Philadelphia Archives.

99 "Hospitals and Health Services" *Journal of Machine Accounting* (1962), BCBS Philadelphia Archives; "Introducing the 1410," *Cross Currents* (January 1962): 1, BCBS Philadelphia Archives; Catherine Falabella, "It Takes More than Money to Pay a Hospital Bill," *Cross Currents* (October–November 1962), BCBS Philadelphia Archives; The Hospital Administrators' Review Board, "Report No. 1."

100 "Know the Answers," *Blue Shield* 1 (September 1949): 2; "Your Service Report," 1; "Watch Your Words!" *Blue Shield* 2 (December 1950): 3; all in BCBS Philadelphia Archives. Medical Service Association of Pennsylvania was the official name of the state's Blue Shield plan. The plan was headquartered in Harrisburg and had district offices located throughout the state, including in Philadelphia. In 1964, the plan's name was changed to Pennsylvania Blue Shield.

101 "You Represent Your Profession," *Blue Shield* 1 (September 1949): 2; "Doctors' Cooperation Vital to Blue Shield," *Blue Shield* 1 (October 1949): 2; "Blue Shield Progress Reviewed at Meetings," *Blue Shield* 1 (October 1949): 2; all in BCBS Philadelphia Archives.

102 "He Serves You," *Blue Shield* 1 (September 1949): 2, BCBS Philadelphia Archives; "He Serves You," *Blue Shield* 1 (October 1949): 2; BCBS Philadelphia Archives.

103 "Implies M.D.'s Wreck Voluntary Insurance," 218, 222; William Alan Richardson, "Where Are We Going with Voluntary Prepayment?" *Medical Economics* 31 (July 1953): 131–38, 193, 197, 200; Eugene Luiartin to Social Security Administration, December 14, 1965, Box 297, Bureau of Health Insurance, Intermediary-Carrier Files, SSA, RG 47, NARA.

104 "Your District Offices," 1–2; "Professional Relations Program Expanded," *Blue Shield* 2 (November 1950): 3–4, BCBS Philadelphia Archives; "Medical Director for MSAP," *Pennsylvania Medical Journal* 66 (May 1963): 42; California Physicians' Service, *Voluntary Health Care*, 1950, Cunningham Papers.

105 W. R. McBee to F. J. L. Blasingame, July 14, 1954, Box 15, Blasingame Papers; H. M. Cardwell to W. R. McBee, August 26, 1954, Box 15, Blasingame Papers.

106 "'Doctors Are Endangering Major Medical Plans,'" 12.

107 W. R. McBee to Members of the Executive Committee and General Counsel, September 17, 1957, Box 19, Blasingame Papers; W. R. McBee to Members of Our Board of Directors and General Counsel, December 10, 1957, Box 19, Blasingame Papers.

108 W. R. McBee, "Report and Comments to Board of Directors Group Hospital Service, Inc.," n.d., Box 19, Blasingame Papers; W. R. McBee to Harley B. West, January 1, 1957, Box 19, Blasingame Papers.

109 Richardson, "Where Are We Going with Voluntary Prepayment?" 193; "Utilization Review and Control Activities in Blue Cross Plans," 3.

110 Wallace Croatman, "Blue Shield Didn't Pay Me Enough," _Medical Economics_ 32 (July 1955): 140–45, 212–16; Leonard Raider, "Let's Use, Not Abuse."

111 "Blue Cross Streamlines Medical Review Plan," _The Review_ (October 1965): 1–2, BCBS Philadelphia Archives; "Doctors' Board Advises Blue Shield on Cases to Reject," _The Review_ (summer 1965): 1, 3, BCBS Philadelphia Archives.

112 "Meet Dr. Harer, An Amiable Watchdog," _Cross Currents_ (November 1963): 1, BCBS Philadelphia Archives.

113 _Source Book of Health Insurance Data_, 46–47. Even though Blue Cross's share of hospital policies fell to about 45 percent of the market by the mid-1950s, nonprofits paid out more generous benefits than insurance companies and, thus, still usually represented either about half or more of total third-party reimbursements for each hospital. Additionally, in some areas, local governments purchased Blue Cross hospital policies for the poor.

114 Albert, _A Practical Vision_, 80, 82.

115 Orsini, "Report of the Health Insurance Council."

116 Carlton Smith, "Will They Kill Off This Hospital?" _Medical Economics_ 42 (May 17, 1965): 109–13, 117–21; Stevens, _In Sickness and in Wealth_, 275–77.

117 Henry V. Weinert and R. Brill, "Effectiveness of Hospital Tissue Committee in Raising Surgical Standards," _JAMA_ 150 (November 8, 1952): 992; "Needless Surgery," 53–57; "Hawley Cites Needless Surgery by Two M.D.s," _Medical Economics_ 30 (September 1953): 258–62; "'Is This Hysterectomy Really Necessary?'" 267, 278.

118 Weinert and Brill, "Effectiveness of Hospital Tissue Committee in Raising Surgical Standards," 992; R. S. Myers and G. W. Stephenson, "Evaluation Form for Tissue Committees," _JAMA_ 156 (December 25, 1954): 1577. Appendectomies and hysterectomies often required subjective medical decision making to determine their necessity. It was therefore acceptable for approximately 10 percent of cases to be found unnecessary, either during surgery or during postoperative testing for diseased organ tissue.

119 "Why the Pressure's on You," 60–71. In 1959, the Joint Commission on Accreditation of Hospitals also began recommending that hospitals establish UR Committees. "Hospital Accreditation Seen as Hopeful Step," _Eastern Underwriter_ 60 (May 15, 1959): 44, 52.

120 Anthony J. J. Rourke, "Hospital Accreditation: The Significance to Health Insurance" (_Health Insurance Association of America Annual Meeting_, Philadelphia, May 5, 1959).

121 "Action in Michigan Blue Cross-Shield Studies," _Eastern Underwriter_ 48 (July 12, 1957): 40; Clark, "Let's Stop Abusing Hospital Insurance," 63–66; Faulkner, "Meeting Health Care Costs through Insurance," 9–22; Dickerson, "The Problem of Overutilization in Health Insurance," 68.

122 Hugh C. Sherwood, "Is Reuther Bluffing Medicine?" _Medical Economics_ 34 (March 1957): 131; Damon Stetson, "Michigan Studies 2 Medical Plans," _New York Times_, September 29, 1957, 51; Damon Stetson, "New Health Plan Forms in Detroit," _New York Times_, December 23, 1956, 30.

123 Wallace Croatman, "Is Labor through with Private Medicine?" *Medical Economics* 34 (October 1957): 174–75; Sherwood, "Is Reuther Bluffing Medicine?" 130–333, 296–97, 305–6. By working with Detroit's Metropolitan Hospital and a group of physicians who agreed to accept fixed salaries instead of fee-for-service compensation, Reuther helped establish the Community Health Association (CHA) in 1960. UAW members could choose between the CHA plan and Blue Cross and Blue Shield coverage. During the 1970s, when Health Maintenance Organizations (HMOs, an offshoot of earlier prepaid groups) became more popular, Michigan Blue Cross and Blue Shield purchased the CHA and renamed it the group Metro Health Plan, Inc. At the end of the 1970s, the plan merged with other organizations to create the Health Alliance Plan, currently one of the largest HMOs in Michigan.

124 Quoted in "Broader Blue Shield Plan Gains Amid Sniping," *Medical Economics* 35 (September 1958): 50, 54.

125 "Digest of Proceedings of House of Delegates, Committee on Medical Socio-Economics," *Michigan Medicine* 63 (December 1964): 36–37; "Governor Considers Health Recommendations," *Michigan Medicine* 64 (December 1965): 931.

126 Robert P. Gerholz, "Toward Good Care at Reasonable Costs," *Michigan Medicine* 65 (February 1966): 125.

127 "Health Facilities Planning Council Well Underway," *Michigan Medicine* 65 (June 1966): 479.

128 William S. McNary, "The Case for Blue Cross Responsibility" (*Blue Cross Program Session*, April 15, 1959), BCBS Philadelphia Archives; "Why the Pressure's on You," 60–71.

129 Smith, "Will They Kill Off This Hospital?" 109–13, 117–21; "Utilization Review and Control Activities in Blue Cross Plans," 3. See also Daniel M. Fox, "Sharing Governmental Authority: Blue Cross and Hospital Planning in New York City," *JHPPL* 16 (winter 1991): 719–46; Theodore R. Marmor, "New York's Blue Cross and Blue Shield, 1934–1990: The Complicated Politics of Nonprofit Regulation," *JHPPL* 16 (winter 1991): 761–92.

130 "Points to Challenge Facing Blue Shield," *Michigan Medicine* 65 (November 1966): 998; "Digest of Proceedings of House of Delegates, Ad Hoc Committee to Study Proposed Utilization Committee," *Michigan Medicine* 63 (December 1964): 26–27.

131 "Digest of Proceedings of House of Delegates, Ad Hoc Committee," 26–27.

132 "Digest of Proceedings of House of Delegates, Resolutions," *Michigan Medicine* 63 (December 1964): 50.

133 "Digest of Proceedings of House of Delegates, President-Elect's Address, Oliver B. McGillicuddy," *Michigan Medicine* 63 (December 1964): 12.

134 Lindsey, "Reasonable Fees Speak Louder than Words," 270.

135 Croatman, "Is Labor through with Private Medicine?" 174–75; Lindsey, "Reasonable Fees Speak Louder than Words," 69–72.

136 Jean Pascoe, "Who Says Blue Shield Is the Doctors' Plan?" *Medical Economics* 38 (May 8, 1961): 95–99.

137 "The Hospital Cost Crisis: It Can Cost You Your Freedom," *Medical Economics* 38 (June 19, 1961): 60–61; "Why You're Being Blamed for It,"

154; "Why the Pressure's on You," 60–71; "Report of Individual Accident and Sickness Insurance," April 30, 1959, Box 41C, RG 4, Equitable Archives; Robert L. Brenner, "Why Blue Cross Is In Trouble," *Medical Economics* 35 (August 1958): 157–68.

138 Quoted in "Why You're Being Blamed for It," 146.

139 Brenner, "Why Blue Cross Is In Trouble," 157–68; Albert, *A Practical Vision*, 86–89; Pascoe, "Who Says Blue Shield Is the Doctors' Plan?" 95–99.

140 Jim Reed, "Medical Public Relations," *Pennsylvania Medical Journal* 66 (February 1963): 47–51; "Official Reports, Second Councilor District," *Pennsylvania Medical Journal* 66 (July 1963): 48; "Official Reports, Eighth Councilor District," *Pennsylvania Medical Journal* 66 (July 1963): 55.

141 Quoted in Lindsey, "Reasonable Fees Speak Louder than Words," 74.

142 Ibid., 72.

143 "Insurance Commissioner Is Setting Doctors' Fees," *Medical Economics* 37 (April 25, 1960): 36–37; "Reports of Administrative Councils, Council on Medical Services," *Pennsylvania Medical Journal* 66 (July 1963): 66; Ross V. Taylor, "Who Will Decide?" *Michigan Medicine* 64 (November 1965): 56–57; Sydney E. Sinclair, "Blue Shield Is the Doctors' Plan," *Pennsylvania Medical Journal* 67 (January 1964): 39–40.

144 "Excerpts from Minutes of Meetings of Board of Trustees and Councilors," *Pennsylvania Medical Journal* 66 (May 1963): 62.

145 "Report, Council on Medical Services," *Pennsylvania Medical Journal* 66 (March 1963): 82.

146 Lindsey, "Reasonable Fees Speak Louder than Words," 69–74, 266–67, 270–72; "Blue Shield, Questions and Answers," *Pennsylvania Medical Journal* 66 (June 1963): 64; J. Everett McClenahan, "Applying the Results of Utilization Measurement," Proceedings of the First National Conference on Utilization, Chicago, March 2–3, 1962, Cunningham Papers; "Health Care Financing Reviewed," *Pennsylvania Medical Journal* 66 (February 1963): 66–67.

147 John A. Nave and Morris London, "Utilization Committees: Threat or Challenge," *Pennsylvania Medical Journal* 66 (September 1963): 25; McClenahan, "Applying the Results of Utilization Measurement"; "The Tightest Controls to Date," *Medical Economics* 41 (July 13, 1964): 102.

148 Quoted in "The Tightest Controls to Date," 110. Nave and London, "Utilization Committees," 24–25; Albert, *A Practical Vision*, 90–92.

149 "The Tightest Controls to Date," 99.

150 Nave and London, "Utilization Committees," 25–26; "The Tightest Controls to Date," 103–10.

151 Quoted in "The Tightest Controls to Date," 100.

152 McClenahan, "Applying the Results of Utilization Measurement."

153 "Health Care Financing Reviewed," 66–67; McClenahan, "Applying the Results of Utilization Measurement"; "Blue Shield – Our Opportunity," *Pennsylvania Medical Journal* 66 (March 1963): 24; "Address of the President-Elect, Richard A. Kern," *Pennsylvania Medical Journal* 67 (November 1964): 33–34; Nave and London, "Utilization Committees," 23, 26; "Report of the Pennsylvania Medical Care Program," *Pennsylvania Medical Journal* 66 (September 1963): 71.

154 "The Tightest Controls to Date," 110.

155 "Reports of Administrative Councils, Council on Medical Service," 65.

156 Carlton Smith, *Medicine's New Policeman: Blue Cross* (Oradell, NJ, 1965), Cunningham Papers.

157 "The Tightest Controls to Date," 103–10.

158 "Utilization Review and Control Activities in Blue Cross Plans," 3.

159 Quoted in "Make National Study of Blue Cross," *Michigan Medicine* 64 (April 1965): 287. See also Brenner, "Why Blue Cross Is in Trouble," 168; "Why the Pressure's on You," 68–69.

160 Rosemary Stevens, *American Medicine and the Public Interest: A History of Specialization*, 2nd ed. (Berkeley, 1998); Starr, *Social Transformation of American Medicine*, 223–25, 355–59.

161 T. Swann Harding, "The High Cost of Doctoring," *North American Review* 226 (October 1928): 390–98.

162 Judith R. Lave and Lester B. Lave, "Medical Care and Its Delivery: An Economic Appraisal," *Law and Contemporary Problems* 35 (spring 1970): 252–66.

163 Pearl Barland, "Now It's Official: Specialists Outnumber G.P.s," *Medical Economics* 38 (April 24, 1961): 72–79. Starr, *Social Transformation of American Medicine*, 355–59. Starr observes that because most specialties were hospital-oriented and insurance covered hospital services before expanding to cover office visits and procedures, medical students seeking elevated incomes had additional incentive to specialize.

164 "Internists Are Winning Higher Fees," *Medical Economics* 37 (January 18, 1960): 192–96, 200–206.

165 Richardson, "Where Are We Going with Voluntary Prepayment?" 126–28.

166 Dr. Andrew Tessitore. Similarly, Dr. Robert G. Bullock, interview with the author, transcript, January 22, 2010.

167 "How to Avoid a Killing Practice Pace," *Medical Economics* 41 (October 5, 1964): 134, 138; Barland, "Now It's Official," 72–79; Dr. Andrew Tessitore. Between 1949 and 1960, "part-time specialists," or general practitioners who also practiced obstetrics or surgery, decreased 38 percent.

168 Deborah A. Stone, "The Doctor as Businessman: The Changing Politics of a Cultural Icon," *JHPPL* 22 (April 1997): 533–56. Stone argues that physicians increasingly assumed the role of businessmen during the 1980s and 1990s under managed care regimes, when, like insurers, they began to consider patient care according to how it would influence their incomes. I attempt to show how this process began during the 1950s.

169 John A. Pond, "The Office and Related Business Aspects," in *The Physician and His Practice*, ed. Joseph Garland (Boston, 1954), 167–75.

170 Dr. Robert K. Duley, interview with the author, transcript, January 4, 2010.

171 R. Cragin Lewis, "They Help Doctors Make Good," *Medical Economics* 28 (October 1951): 67.

172 Dr. Robert Bullock.

173 "How Not to Pick a Location," *Medical Economics* 28 (January 1951): 179–80; "Practice Management Q & A," *Medical Economics* 42 (April 19, 1965): 153; Charles Miller, "Good Taste and Common Sense in Building a

Practice," *Medical Economics* 30 (May 1953): 149–54, 226; Horace Cotton, *Medical Practice Management* (Oradell, NJ, 1967), 131–36; Dr. Robert K. Duley; Dr. Charles Williams, interview with the author, transcript, January 27, 2010.

174 Donald F. Gearing and Robert L. Brenner, "They're Moving to the Suburbs," *Medical Economics* 35 (June 23, 1958): 98–104, 160–76.

175 Dr. Andrew Tessitore.

176 "How to Avoid a Killing Practice Pace," 119–22, 126.

177 William G. Crook, "How I Boosted My Productive Time," *Medical Economics* 42 (April 19, 1965): 75–85.

178 "More Office Calls," *Medical Economics* 31 (August 1954): 28–29, 32; "House Calls," *Medical Economics* 37 (January 18, 1960): 176–90; "Common-Sense for House Calls," *Medical Economics* 41 (October 5, 1964): 76–82.

179 Theodore Wiprud, *The Business Side of Medical Practice* (Philadelphia, 1937), 35–42; Clayton L. Scroggins, "Bad Management – An Expensive Luxury," *Medical Economics* 28 (November 1950): 141–47; Paul Gitlin, "Accounting Practices – The Income Tax," in *The Physician and His Practice*, ed. Joseph Garland (Boston, 1954), 205–25.

180 Dr. Andrew Tessitore. See also Dr. Charles Williams.

181 "Practice Management Q & A," *Medical Economics* 42 (May 17, 1965): 175.

182 Examples of such terms found in "Insurance Forms," *Medical Economics* 37 (January 18, 1960): 142; "The Doctor's Aides," *Medical Economics* 33 (December 1956): 120–27; "Where to Find an Aide," *Medical Economics* 37 (February 15, 1960): 260; "Five Top Consultants Advise You on Fees," *Medical Economics* 42 (May 31, 1965): 97–148.

183 "The Doctor's Aides," 120–27.

184 Scroggins, "Bad Management," 146; Ulrich R. Bryner, "Auxiliary Services," in *The Physician and His Practice*, ed. Joseph Garland (Boston, 1954), 177–90.

185 John O'Connor, "How My Office Avoids Mix-Ups with Prepay Plans," *Medical Economics* 30 (May 1953): 202–12; Lewis, "They Help Doctors Make Good," 64–74; "Insurance Forms," 138–58; Horace Cotton, "How to Lick the Paper-Work Problem," *Medical Economics* 37 (March 28, 1960): 167–80.

186 Thomas Owens, "These New Insurance Forms Will Save You Time," *Medical Economics* 32 (April 1955): 140–42.

187 Lewis, "They Help Doctors Make Good," 67; Eli Eichelberger, "Office Hours? I've Had Enough!" *Medical Economics* 35 (March 17, 1958): 153–62; "How to Avoid a Killing Practice Pace," 119–48; Cotton, *Medical Practice Management*, 137–43.

188 Dr. Robert G. Bullock. See also Cotton, *Medical Practice Management*, 197–201.

189 O'Connor, "How My Office Avoids Mix-Ups with Prepay Plans," 202.

190 "Blue Shield, Questions and Answers," *Pennsylvania Medical Journal* 66 (November 1963): 76–77.

191 Interview with author, name withheld.
192 Interview with author, name withheld.
193 "L.A. Physicians Must Explain Charges," *Medical Economics* 27 (June 1950): 165; Orville S. Walters, "Show Them What They're Paying for," *Medical Economics* 28 (January 1951): 59, 203; "Are You Bashful about Discussing Fees?" *Medical Economics* 30 (August 1953): 201, 204; Wallace Croatman, "What Makes a Fee Fair?" *Medical Economics* 32 (June 1955): 157; "Unexplained Fees," *Medical Economics* 34 (August 1957): 80–81.
194 Lewis, "They Help Doctors Make Good," 66. See also "Setting My Fees Too Low," *Medical Economics* 37 (April 25, 1960): 147–48; "What to Charge a Patient Who Has Major Medical," 54.
195 John J. Coughlin, "How to Spell Fee Trouble: Usualcustomaryreasonable," *Medical Economics* 41 (August 24, 1964): 96–97; "Insurance Plan Leads 7 in 10 M.D.s to Raise Fees," 29.
196 Dr. Andrew Tessitore; Dr. Charles Williams. Both Drs. Tessitore and Williams, who practiced during the 1950s and 1960s, reported that they collected approximately 60 percent of their total patient bills. Tessitore practiced outside of Washington in Vienna, Virginia, and Williams practiced in Richmond, Virginia.
197 R. W. Tucker, "Assignment Form Pulls in the Payments," *Medical Economics* 33 (December 1956): 104–6.
198 "1099 Reporting on Payments to Doctors." Commercial companies paid approximately one-third of claims directly to service providers. Nonprofit plans almost always reimbursed physicians directly.
199 Interview with author, name withheld.

7 The Politics of Medicare, 1957–1965

1 Rashi Fein observes that behind the political wrangling over Medicare, there was an "emerging consensus" about the need to create a federal program of health care benefits for the aged. Rashi Fein, *Medical Care, Medical Costs: The Search for a Health Insurance Policy* (Cambridge, MA, 1989), 56. Other important accounts of Medicare include Theodore Marmor, *The Politics of Medicare*, 2nd ed. (New York, 2000); Paul Starr, *The Social Transformation of American Medicine: The Rise of a Sovereign Profession and the Making of a Vast Industry* (New York, 1982), 286–88, 367–70; Julian E. Zelizer, *Taxing America: Wilbur D. Mills, Congress, and the State, 1945–1975* (New York, 1998), chapter 7; Martha Derthick, *Policymaking for Social Security* (Washington, D.C., 1979), 320–34; Jonathan Oberlander, *The Political Life of Medicare* (Chicago, 2003).
2 See Kimberly J. Morgan and Andrea Louise Campbell, *The Delegated Welfare State: Medicare, Markets, and the Governance of Social Policy* (New York, 2011). While Morgan and Campbell focus on the Medicare Modernization Act of 2003, their book surveys Medicare since its inception to demonstrate that American welfare state responsibilities have traditionally been outsourced to private sector actors.

3 Jacob S. Hacker, *The Divided Welfare State: The Battle over Public and Private Social Benefits in the United States* (New York, 2002), 225–48.
4 Ibid.; Marmor, *Politics of Medicare*, 10–17, 23–24.
5 Derthick, *Policymaking for Social Security*, 320.
6 Marmor, *Politics of Medicare*, 24–25; Derthick, *Policymaking for Social Security*, 320–21.
7 On the high cost and limited benefits of aged voluntary insurance, see for example, American Public Welfare Association, "Why Private Insurance Is Not a Feasible Method for Providing Paid-Up Protection upon Retirement," 1961, Box 21, Grahame Papers; Alanson W. Willcox, "The Administration's View on Financing Health Care of the Aged," May 1, 1963, Box 299, Commissioner's Correspondence, 1939–69, SSA, RG 47, NARA; Harold R. Levy to Robert M. Ball, "Analysis of 'Medicare, The Cure That Could Cause a Setback,'" July 10, 1963, Box 299, Office of the Commissioner, SSA, RG 47, NARA. On the reduced earning power of seniors, see for example, Ivan A. Nestingen, "The Outlook for Medicare," Miami Beach Council of Senior Citizens and Golden Ring Clubs, February 24, 1964, Box 346, Secretary's Subject Correspondence, 1956–74, HEW, RG 235, NARA; Robert Ball, "Staff Paper on the Limitations of Private Health Insurance for the Aged," October 15, 1963, Box 299, Commissioner's Correspondence, 1939–69, SSA, RG 47, NARA.
8 Nestingen, "The Outlook for Medicare," 7.
9 For example, Wilbur J. Cohen to Cecil King, September 25, 1962, Box 19, Secretary's Subject Correspondence, 1956–74, HEW, RG 235, NARA; "Pain, Pressure & Politics Make Powerful Medicine," *Time*, May 9, 1960, http://content.time.com/time/subscriber/article/0,33009,897447,00.html (accessed June 7, 2012).
10 Quoted in "Pain, Pressure & Politics Make Powerful Medicine."
11 Quoted in "Pension Winds," *Time*, April 11, 1960, http://content.time.com/time/subscriber/article/0,33009,826196,00.html (accessed January 6, 2014).
12 Aime J. Forand, "Should the Forand Bill to Add Medical Assistance to OASDI Program be Enacted?" *Congressional Digest* 39 (March 1960): 76.
13 The subcommittee was established under the Committee on Labor and Public Welfare. Derthick, *Policymaking for Social Security*, 322; C. P. Trussell, "Senators Pursue Concerns of the Aged," *New York Times*, November 15, 1959, 63; Claude Sitton, "More Federal Aid for Aging Sought," *New York Times*, December 1, 1959, 22; Eve Edstrom, "Aged Fear Their Views Not Heeded," *Washington Post*, December 21, 1960, A11.
14 "Pain, Pressure & Politics Make Powerful Medicine."
15 "Statement by Arthur S. Flemming, Before the House Ways and Means Committee," May 4, 1960, Box 20, Grahame Papers.
16 Marmor, *Politics of Medicare*, 35–38; Robert Lieberman, *Shifting the Color Line: Race and the American Welfare State* (Cambridge, MA, 1998); Jill Quadagno, *The Color of Welfare: How Racism Undermined the War on Poverty* (New York, 1994). See also Jill Quadagno, "Promoting Civil Rights through the Welfare State: How Medicare Integrated Southern Hospitals," *Social Problems* 47 (February 2000): 68–89.

17 Zelizer, *Taxing America*, chapter 7; Edward D. Berkowitz, *Mr. Social Security: The Life of Wilbur J. Cohen* (Lawrence, KS, 1995), 122, 171–72.
18 Ten Republicans and seven Democrats voted against the legislation. Eight Democrats supported the measure.
19 Reminiscences of Marion B. Folsom, part I (1968), 11–12, CCOHC.
20 F. J. L. Blasingame, "Board of Trustees," n.d., Box 3, Blasingame Papers.
21 Dr. Alphin to the Board of Trustees, "Pending Legislative Drive for Hospital-ization at Age 65," July 17, 1957, Box 6, Blasingame Papers; Harold J. Peggs, "Doctors Can't Beat the Forand Bill," n.d., Box 9, Blasingame Papers. After Medicare passed, an AMA insider blamed the "Blasingame Bloc" for prevent-ing the AMA from campaigning for a scaled-down version of the program. Exactly when the AMA considered this plan and how it differed from the association's 1964 Eldercare proposal is unclear. "If we had put the plan before the public," claimed an association official, "Medicare would have been something we could more easily live with because we would have had a voice in writing the law." Dorsey Woodson, "Capital Rounds," *Medical World News*, October 11, 1968, Box 3, Blasingame Papers.
22 F. J. L. Blasingame, "Remarks," Mid-Atlantic Hospital Association Annual Meeting, Atlantic City, NJ, April 28, 1960, Box 21, Blasingame Papers.
23 Quoted in Peter A. Corning, "The Evolution of Medicare," Research Report no. 29, n.d., 89, Revolving Files, Social Security Archives, Baltimore, MD (hereafter SSA Archives).
24 Leonard W. Larson, "For the People" (*Health Insurance Association of America Annual Meeting*, Philadelphia, May 5, 1959).
25 "Minutes of Joint Meeting of ALC-LIAA Social Security Committee with HIAA Committee," February 15, 1960, Box 20, Grahame Papers; "Minutes of the Meeting of the Joint ALC-LIAA Social Security Committee," April 12, 1960, Box 20, Grahame Papers; Colin Gordon, *Dead on Arrival: The Politics of Health Care in Twentieth-Century America* (Princeton, 2003), 136–37.
26 Quoted in Dutton Stahl to Frank L. Harrington, January 26, 1959, Box 21, Grahame Papers.
27 E. J. Faulkner to John H. Miller, August 6, 1958, Box 18, Grahame Papers.
28 "The Aged and Private Health Insurance," *Health Insurance Viewpoints* (January 1964), Box 299, Commissioner's Correspondence, 1939–69, SSA, RG 47, NARA.
29 For example, Travis T. Wallace, "Address of the President" (*Health Insurance Association of America Annual Meeting*, Philadelphia, May 4, 1959); Health Insurance Association of America, "A Challenge to Private Health Insurers," 1962, Box 25, Grahame Papers; Gordon Farquhar, "Report and Action of the Comprehensive Coverage Subcommittee," May 1964, Box 25, Grahame Papers.
30 Quoted in F. L. Harrington to O.F. Grahame, November 4, 1958, Box 18, Grahame Papers.
31 Horace H. Wilson, J. Henry Smith, and Morton D. Miller, "Medicare and Private Benefit Plans," n.d., Box 10, Harrison Givens Files, RG 2, Equitable Archives; Robert M. Ball, "'The Potential of Private Health Insurance,'" June 5, 1963, Box 299, Commissioner's Correspondence, 1939–69, SSA, RG 47, NARA.

32 Ball, "Staff Paper on the Limitations of Private Health Insurance."
33 Orville F. Grahame to Eugene Thore, April 13, 1960, Box 20, Grahame Papers. Similarly, "Joint Committee on Social Security and Health Care," March 26, 1961, Box 20, Grahame Papers; Reminiscences of Reinhard Hohaus, part I (July 27, 1965), 121–23, CCOHC.
34 Eugene M. Thore to Orville F. Grahame, April 20, 1960, Box 20, Grahame Papers.
35 "Minutes of the Meeting of the ALC-LIAA Joint Committee on Social Security and Health Care," February 16, 1961, Box 20, Grahame Papers.
36 Thore to Grahame; Grahame to Thore; "Alternative Policy Positions Re Federal Legislative Proposals on Health Benefits for the Aged," March 20, 1961, Box 20, Grahame Papers.
37 Grahame to Thore.
38 House Ways and Means Committee, *Hearings on Social Security Legislation*, 85th Cong., 2nd sess., June 25, 1958 (Statement of Nelson H. Cruikshank), 763–64.
39 Blasingame, "Remarks," (emphasis in original). See also F. J. L. Blasingame to W. R. McBee, November 1, 1957, Box 6, Blasingame Papers.
40 House Ways and Means Committee, *Hearings on Social Security Legislation*, 85th Cong., 2nd sess., June 24, 1958 (Statement of J. Douglas Colman, filed with committee), 640–43.
41 House Ways and Means Committee, *Hearings on Social Security Legislation*, 85th Cong., 2nd sess., June 27, 1958 (Statement of Ray Amberg), 860–62.
42 Marv Reiter, interview, transcript, July 8, 1991, Cunningham Papers.
43 Quoted in W. R. McBee to F. J. L. Blasingame, November 6, 1957, Box 19, Blasingame Papers (emphasis in original though likely added to NABSP statement by McBee).
44 Ibid.
45 House Ways and Means Committee, *Hearings on Social Security Legislation*, 85th Cong., 2nd sess., June 25, 1958 (Statement of Dr. Donald Stubbs), 691–94; Donald Stubbs, "Hospital, Nursing Home, and Surgical Benefits for OASI Beneficiaries: Hearings," July 1959, BCBS D.C. Archives.
46 "Free Health Care for Aged Opposed," *New York Times*, June 28, 1958, 19.
47 Corning, "Evolution of Medicare," 83; "President Backs Plan to Open New Opportunities to the Aged," *New York Times*, November 13, 1959, 19; Bess Furman, "Nixon Is Pressing U.S. Medical Plan," *New York Times*, February 21, 1960, 48; Bess Furman, "Voluntary Plan for Aged Studied," *New York Times*, March 18, 1960, 9.
48 Quoted in Amos R. Koontz, "King-Anderson: 1963 Version of Socialized Medicine," *Maryland State Medical Journal* (January 1964), Box 346, Secretary's Subject Correspondence, 1956–74, HEW, RG 235, NARA. See also Robert M. Ball, "Perspectives on Medicare: What Medicare's Architects Had in Mind," *Health Affairs* 14 (winter 1995): 62–72; Derthick, *Policymaking for Social Security*, 334–35.
49 Congressman Robert N. Giaimo to Edward J. Delehanty, June 7, 1962, Box 29, Grahame Papers; Congressman Torbert H. Macdonald to Orville F. Grahame, July 11, 1962, Box 29, Grahame Papers; Willcox, "The Administration's View on Financing Health Care of the Aged."

50 Zelizer, *Taxing America*, 214; Marmor, *Politics of Medicare*, 14–17, 25–27; Derthick, *Policymaking for Social Security*, 228–32; Willcox, "The Administration's View on Financing Health Care of the Aged."

51 For example, "Another Approach to Meeting the Medical Care Needs of the Aged," September 21, 1959, Box 20, Grahame Papers; Eve Edstrom, "GOP Issues Its Plan for Medical Aid," *Washington Post*, April 6, 1960, A1, A12.

52 Quoted in Derthick, *Policymaking for Social Security*, 332–33.

53 Lawrence O'Brien to the President, January 27, 1964, Cohen Papers, SSA Archives; Zelizer, *Taxing America*, 232–37; Derthick, *Policymaking for Social Security*, 330–33; Eric M. Patashnik, *Putting Trust in the U.S. Budget: Federal Trust Funds and the Politics of Commitment* (New York, 2000), 97–100.

54 Quoted in Hacker, *Divided Welfare State*, 246. See also Wilbur J. Cohen "Analysis of Proposal for Optional Feature," February 15, 1961, Cohen Papers, SSA Archives; Morgan and Campbell, *Delegated Welfare State*, 71–74.

55 Eisenhower considered advancing a program financed through Social Security; however, he ultimately decided to support the position of congressional Republicans and oppose payroll tax increases. See David Blumenthal and James A. Morone, *The Heart of Power: Health and Politics in the Oval Office* (Berkeley, 2009), 119–26.

56 "Associated Press Dispatch," April 5, 1960, Box 20, Grahame Papers.

57 Quoted in Richard L. Lyons, "Health Plan Would Aid 12 Million," May 5, 1960, *Washington Post*, A1, A22. See also Edstrom, "GOP Issues Its Plan for Medical Aid," A1, A12.

58 "A.M.A. Lashes Federal Plan to Treat Aged," *Chicago Daily Tribune*, May 6, 1960, D8.

59 "Minutes of the Meeting of the Joint ALC-LIAA Social Security Committee," April 12, 1960.

60 Edstrom, "GOP Issues Its Plan for Medical Aid," A1, A12; Furman, "Voluntary Plan for Aged Studied," 9; Corning, "Evolution of Medicare," 83; Robert J. Donovan, "Republicans File Health Bill, Jump Gun on White House," *New York Herald Tribune*, April 8, 1960, A1, Box 20, Grahame Papers; John A. Goldsmith, "Nixon Splits with Ike on Medical Aid," *Washington Post*, August 21, 1960, A1, A17; Willian Theis, "3 GOP Senators Draft Own Proposal for Medical Care Program for Aged," *Washington Post*, March 27, 1960, A16. The legislation was also sponsored by Republicans George Aiken (VT), Clifford Case (NJ), Hiram Fong (HI), Kenneth Keating (NY), and Winston Prouty (VT). The press sometimes referred to the legislation as the "Javits-Flemming plan" because the HEW secretary, with encouragement from Vice President Richard Nixon, had devised a similar though less expensive proposal. Flemming's recommendations failed to obtain President Eisenhower's approval.

61 Reminiscences of Robert Neal, part I (1967), 11–12, 33–35, COHC.

62 "Alternative Policy Positions Re Federal Legislative Proposals"; Grahame to Thore.

63 Leo Egan, "Governor Blunt: Chides Vice President after Disclosing Plan to Eisenhower," *New York Times*, June 9, 1960, 1.

64 Wilbur Cohen to Myer Feldman, January 29, 1964, Cohen Papers, SSA Archives.

65 "Alternative Policy Positions Re Federal Legislative Proposals."

66 Cohen "Analysis of Proposal for Optional Feature."

67 For example, "Governors Back Aged-Care Plan," *New York Times*, June 30, 1960, 13.

68 Marmor, *Politics of Medicare*, 27–30; Zelizer, *Taxing America*, 215; Corning, "Evolution of Medicare," chapter 4.

69 Quoted in "Ask Aged Care Thru Social Security Plan," *Chicago Daily Tribune*, August 18, 1960, N5. See also "Kennedy Joins Anderson in Medical Plan for Aged under Social Security System," *Wall Street Journal*, August 18, 1960, 4.

70 "Senate Unit Votes New Kerr Plan on Medical Care," *Wall Street Journal*, August 15, 1960, 3; Walter Trohan, "Nixon Backing New Medical Aid Proposal," *Chicago Daily Tribune*, August 21, 1960, 11; John A. Goldsmith, "Nixon Splits with Ike on Medical Aid," *Washington Post*, August 21, 1960, A1, A17.

71 Corning, "Evolution of Medicare," 85–87; "Minutes of Joint Meeting of ALC-LIAA Social Security Committee," February 15, 1960; Benjamin B. Kendrick, "The Provisions on Medical Care for the Aged in the Proposed 1960 Social Security Amendments," June 21, 1960, Box 20, Grahame Papers; Frank D. Campion, *The AMA and U.S. Health Policy since 1940* (Chicago, 1984), 257.

72 Corning, "Evolution of Medicare," chapter 4.

73 Howard A. Rusk, "Candidates' Views on Federal Action for Aged Differ Mostly on Means," *New York Times*, October 30, 1960, 78.

74 Zelizer, *Taxing America*, 215–16.

75 Wilbur Cohen to Martin Thomas, May 19, 1964, Cohen Papers, SSA Archives.

76 Levy to Ball, "Analysis of 'Medicare, The Cure That Could Cause a Setback'"; Giaimo to Delehanty; Willcox, "The Administration's View on Financing Health Care of the Aged"; Ivan A. Nestingen, "Speech to Baltimore City Medical Society," February 7, 1964, Box 346, Secretary's Subject Correspondence, 1956–74, HEW, RG 235, NARA; "Major Amendments Relating to Hospital Insurance ... Reasons for Legislation," November 5, 1963, Revolving Files, SSA Archives.

77 Quoted in Odin Anderson, "The Politics of the Welfare State as Seen by Wilbur J. Cohen," unpublished manuscript, ed. Ronald Andersen, Arthur Kohrman, and Claire Kohrman (2012), 111, http://www2.asanet.org/medicalsociology/images/anderson.pdf (accessed January 11, 2014). See also Berkowitz, *Mr. Social Security*, 161, 166–67.

78 Anderson, "The Politics of the Welfare State," 111.

79 "Care for the Aged ... and This Nonsense about Socialized Medicine," *Good Housekeeping* (April 1962), Box 19, Secretary's Subject Correspondence, 1956–74, HEW, RG 235, NARA; Gerald W. Johnson, "Watch Out for Grandpap," *New Republic*, May 9, 1960, 8.

80 "President's Special Message to Congress," February 26, 1962, Box 21, Grahame Papers.

81 The National Council of Senior Citizens was established in 1961 with funding from the Democratic National Committee and AFL-CIO. Attempting to earn a reputation as nonpartisan, the leaders of the American Association of Retired Persons (AARP), which was founded in 1958, neither supported nor opposed Medicare. Henry J. Pratt, "Old Age Associations in National Politics," *Annals of the American Academy of Political and Social Science* 415 (September 1974): 106–19.

82 "Operation Negative," *National Council of Senior Citizens for Health Care through Social Security News Letter* (May 1962), Box 29, Grahame Papers.

83 "Kerr-Mills vs. King-Anderson," *Council for the Aging News Bulletin* (May–June 1962), Box 29, Grahame Papers; Zalmen J. Lichtenstein and Jack Di Nola to Anthony J. Celebrezze, October 5, 1962, Box 153, Secretary's Subject Correspondence, 1956–74, HEW, RG 235, NARA; "The Aged and Private Health Insurance."

84 Edith Evans Asbury, "4,000 Aged Attend Democrats' Rally," *New York Times*, November 4, 1960, 23; Philip Benjamin, "Elderly United as Lobby Force," *New York Times*, May 21, 1962, 22.

85 Hacker, *Divided Welfare State*, 245–46; Marmor, *Politics of Medicare*, 75–76; Gallup Poll, "Big Majority Favors Costlier Social Security," June 9, 1961, Box 21, Grahame Papers. See also Lawrence Jacobs, *The Health of Nations: Public Opinion and the Making of American and British Health Policy* (Ithaca, NY, 1993).

86 Colin Gordon, *Dead on Arrival*, 238; Corning, "Evolution of Medicare," 110–11.

87 "Folsom Backs Kennedy on Health Insurance," *Los Angeles Times*, January 10, 1961, 11; "Former Eisenhower Aide Folsom Backs Kennedy Plan on Medical Care for the Aged," *Wall Street Journal*, January 10, 1961, 12.

88 Corning, "Evolution of Medicare," 82–85, 87.

89 "Dr. Fishbein Says Conditions Change, He Is for Medicare," *New York Times*, October 30, 1965, 27.

90 "A.M.A. Lashes Federal Plan to Treat Aged."

91 Marmor, *Politics of Medicare*, 28–29.

92 Quoted in "Report on the UAW's Forand Bill Rally in Detroit," 1960, Box 9, Blasingame Papers. See also Eve Edstrom, "'Charity Medicine' Charge Leveled at AMA Stand on Aid for Aging," *Washington Post*, January 9, 1961, A1, A13.

93 For example, Koontz, "King-Anderson: 1963 Version of Socialized Medicine."

94 "TV: Medical-Care Issue," *New York Times*, February 3, 1961, Box 19, Grahame Papers.

95 Campion, *AMA and U.S. Health Policy*, 256.

96 Hospitals were segregated in other areas of the United States as well. However, in the South, the segregation of medical facilities was more widespread and often required by state law.

97 F. J. L. Blasingame, "The Socialized Medicine Fight in 1962," December 4, 1961, Box 21, Blasingame Papers. Similarly, American Medical Association, *Health Care for the Aged*, n.d., Box 29, Grahame Papers; Leonard W. Larson,

"Statement of the American Medical Association," Before Committee on Resolutions, 1960 Republican National Convention, July 21, 1960, Box 9, Blasingame Papers; E. Vincent Askey, "Helping Those Who Need Help," American Pharmaceutical Association Annual Meeting, 1960, Box 9, Blasingame Papers.

98 "Care for the Aged ... and This Nonsense about Socialized Medicine."

99 "Medicine: The A.M.A. & The U.S.A.," *Time*, July 7, 1961, http://content.time.com/time/subscriber/article/0,33009,872563,00.html (accessed January 9, 2014).

100 Wilbur J. Cohen to Cecil King, March 26, 1962, Box 19, Secretary's Subject Correspondence, 1956–74, HEW, RG 235, NARA.

101 Campion, *AMA and U.S. Health Policy*, 258–59, 262; Corning, "Evolution of Medicare," 89–90; "Medicine: The A.M.A. & The U.S.A."

102 "American Medical Political Action Committee: Origin and Activities," June 1961, Box 4, Blasingame Papers; Campion, *AMA and U.S. Health Policy*, 210–16.

103 Campion, *AMA and U.S. Health Policy*, 262–65; Blumenthal and Morone, *The Heart of Power*, 148–54; "Ed Annis Quits but Vows to Speak Out," *Medical World News*, June 20, 1969, Box 3, Blasingame Papers.

104 American Medical Association, "Refutation of AFL-CIO's Committee on Political Education in Its 'Political Memo,'" March 15, 1960, Box 9, Blasingame Papers.

105 "Transcript of Dr. Edward R. Annis and Walter P. Reuther on 'Face the Nation' Debate," n.d., Box 9, Blasingame Papers.

106 Quoted in E. Vincent Askey, "Medicine Meets the Challenge – A 10-Point Program of Action," Maricopa County Medical Society Meeting, February 28, 1961, Box 21, Blasingame Papers.

107 Dan Patrinos, "MU Dean, AMA Tiff Flares Again," *Milwaukee Sentinel*, May 15, 1964, Box 4, Blasingame Papers.

108 "Report of the Committee on Communications to AMA House of Delegates," June 1964, Box 10, Blasingame Papers.

109 Ronald Kotulak, "Bad Image Blamed for A.M.A. Shakeup," *Chicago Tribune*, September 11, 1968, Box 3, Blasingame Papers.

110 Jim Reed to F. J. L. Blasingame, October 7, 1966, Box 10, Blasingame Papers.

111 Campion, *AMA and U.S. Health Policy*, 261–62; F. J. L. Blasingame, "The Job Is Action," National Legislative Conference, Chicago, March 18, 1961, Box 21, Blasingame Papers; "Operation Hometown," *Pennsylvania Medical Journal* 66 (May 1963): 46–47; "Operation Hometown," *Texas State Journal of Medicine* 59 (October 1963): 997.

112 "Behind the AMA's Family Squabble," *Medical World News*, September 27, 1968, Box 3, Blasingame Papers; Campion, *AMA and U.S. Health Policy*, 269–70.

113 Robert M. Ball, "Medical Care: Its Social and Organizational Aspects," *New England Journal of Medicine* 270 (January 30, 1964), Box 300, Commissioner's Correspondence, 1939–69, SSA, RG 47, NARA.

114 Corning, "Evolution of Medicare," 91.

115 Donald Janson, "A.M.A. Reversal Urged," *New York Times*, June 29, 1962, Box 29, Grahame Papers.
116 Quoted in "Medicine: The A.M.A. & The U.S.A."
117 E. Vincent Askey, "Must Reason Be a Feeble Reed?" National Legislative Conference, Chicago, March 18, 1961, Box 21, Blasingame Papers. See also F. J. L. Blasingame, "Unity in Medicine," Twenty-First Clinical Convention of the American Medical Association, November 26, 1967, Box 24, Blasingame Papers.
118 F. J. L. Blasingame to Board of Trustees, "AMA Communications Program," September 19, 1967, Box 4, Blasingame Papers.
119 B. E. Montgomery to Frances A. Davis, September 30, 1968, Box 3, Blasingame Papers; Campion, *AMA and U.S. Health Policy*, 287–88.
120 F. J. L. Blasingame to Dr. Davis, November 8, 1968, Box 3, Blasingame Papers; "Resolution," n.d., Box 3, Blasingame Papers; Campion, *AMA and U.S. Health Policy*, 290–92.
121 "Report of the Committee on Communications to AMA House of Delegates," June 1964, Box 10, Blasingame Papers.
122 "Medical Care for the Aged," *New Republic*, March 7, 1960, 5.
123 Wilbur J. Cohen, "The Challenge of Aging to Insurance," *Journal of Insurance* 27 (December 1960): 16–17.
124 Elizabeth Wickenden to Wilbur Cohen, "R&I Advisory Committee," December 20, 1963, Box 301, Commissioner's Correspondence, 1939–69, SSA, RG 47, NARA; Ivan A. Nestingen, "Speech to Annual Delegates Meeting of Group Health Mutual, Inc.," March 13, 1965, Box 346, Secretary's Subject Correspondence, 1956–74, HEW, RG 235, NARA.
125 Nestingen, "The Outlook for Medicare."
126 Nestingen, "Speech to Annual Delegate Meeting of Group Health Mutual, Inc." Whereas aged hospital coverage was simply too costly for companies to provide, supplementary policies could be narrowly designed to insure less expensive services, such as physician care. So insurers could profit by selling such products, particularly if elderly citizens already had hospital coverage supplied by the government. Willcox, "The Administration's View on Financing Health Care of the Aged"; "Major Amendments Relating to Hospital Insurance"; Ball, "Medical Care: Its Social and Organizational Aspects."
127 Grahame to Thore.
128 "Minutes of the Meeting of the ALC-LIAA Joint Committee on Social Security and Health Care," March 29, 1961, Box 20, Grahame Papers.
129 Thore to Grahame; Grahame to Thore; "Alternative Policy Positions Re Federal Legislative Proposals."
130 "Minutes of the Meeting of the ALC-LIAA Joint Committee," March 29, 1961.
131 Quoted in "Alternative Policy Positions Re Federal Legislative Proposals."
132 "Minutes of the Meeting of the ALC-LIAA Joint Committee," March 29, 1961.
133 Corning, "Evolution of Medicare," 90; John S. Pillsbury, "Report of Public Relations Committee to the Board of Directors," October 27, 1964, Box 25, Grahame Papers; John D. Morris, "House Maneuver Planned to Pass Aged

Care Bill," *New York Times*, September 5, 1964, Box 301, Commissioner's Correspondence, 1939–69, SSA, RG 47, NARA.

134 "Some Significant MPA-PR Activity Highlights," July 21, 1965, Box 14, Grahame Papers; Robert Neal, Reminiscences, 31; Derthick, *Policymaking for Social Security*, 142.

135 "Minutes of the Meeting of the ALC-LIAA Joint Committee," March 29, 1961; "Financing Health Care for the Aged," May 31, 1961, Box 21, Grahame Papers; Orville F. Grahame to Benjamin B. Kendrick, June 13, 1961, Box 21, Grahame Papers; "Minutes of Meeting of the ALC-LIAA Joint Committee on Social Security and Health Care," April 26, 1962, Box 21, Grahame Papers; "Report of Joint Committee on Social Security and Health Care to the 1962 Annual Meeting of the American Life Convention," n.d., Box 21, Grahame Papers.

136 Frank T. Bow to All Interested Citizens, n.d., Box 29, Grahame Papers; Republican National Committee, *There Is a Better Way ... To Finance Medical Care for the Aged*, n.d., Box 29, Grahame Papers.

137 "Chairman Forand Comments on Republican Bow Bill," n.d., Box 29, Grahame Papers; "Minutes of Meeting of the ALC-LIAA Joint Committee," April 26, 1962; "Report of Joint Committee on Social Security and Health Care to the 1962 Annual Meeting."

138 Robert Neal, Reminiscences, 21.

139 Pillsbury, "Report of Public Relations Committee to the Board of Directors."

140 Health Insurance Association of America, *The King-Anderson Bill and What You Should Know About It*, n.d., Box 29, Grahame Papers. See also HIAA to Corresponding Officers, "Statement of Policy Approved by Board of Directors," May 12, 1959, Box 20, Grahame Papers.

141 H. Lewis Rietz to Frank L. Harrington, April 23, 1962, Box 29, Grahame Papers.

142 John A. Hill to Officers, April 23, 1965, Box 14, Grahame Papers; Orville Grahame, "Memo," May 17, 1965, Box 14, Grahame Papers.

143 John W. Spillane to Orville Grahame, May 25, 1962, Box 29, Grahame Papers. Similarly, Orville F. Grahame to the General Agents, May 15, 1962, Box 29, Grahame Papers; E. L. Carraway to Senator A. Willis Robertson, April 10, 1962, Box 29, Grahame Papers.

144 Grahame to Kendrick; "Minutes of the Meeting of the ALC-LIAA Joint Committee on Social Security and Health Care," June 8, 1961, Box 20, Grahame Papers; "Minutes of the Meeting of the ALC-LIAA Joint Committee," February 16, 1961.

145 Reinhard Hohaus, Reminiscences, 133; Peter Marstan, "'Social Security Is Insurance,'" *Chicago Tribune*, October 13, 1964, 18; Derthick, *Policymaking for Social Security*, 139–42. Conservative insurance leaders preferred a means-tested program funded through general tax revenues and resented that Social Security was labeled "insurance." However, other insurance executives, like Hohaus, viewed Social Security financing as a fiscally responsible way to provide elderly medical benefits. "Another Approach to Meeting the Medical Care Needs of the Aged"; "Minutes of the Meeting of the ALC-LIAA Joint Committee," March 29, 1961; "Minutes of the Meeting of the Joint ALC-LIAA Social Security Committee," April 12, 1960.

146 John W. Spillane to Orville Grahame, "Hearings Held before the House Ways and Means Committee on H.R. 4222," August 4, 1961, Box 21, Grahame Papers; Marjorie Hunter, "Showdown Nears on Aged-Care Bill," *New York Times*, January 26, 1964, 42; "Insurer Backs Medicare Plan," *Journal of Commerce* (May 28, 1962), Box 29, Grahame Papers.

147 Quoted in Nestingen, "Speech to Annual Delegate Meeting of Group Health Mutual, Inc."

148 Quoted in Ball, "Staff Paper on the Limitations of Private Health Insurance."

149 Wilson, Smith, and Miller, "Medicare and Private Benefit Plans"; S. Jerold Duran, "Memo," 1965, Box 10, Harrison Givens Files, RG 2, Equitable Archives.

150 Quoted in Cunningham, *The Blues*, 130.

151 Hacker, *Divided Welfare State*, 242; Sylvia Law, *Blue Cross: What Went Wrong?* (New Haven, CT, 1976), 50–58. By the 1970s, the federal account represented about 8 percent of total premium income for Blue Cross. Cunningham, *The Blues*, 111–14.

152 Nonprofit leaders who favored federal programming tended to hail from the Northeast, California, Michigan, and Minnesota or they held national positions with the BCA.

153 Blue Cross Association Annual Meeting, Chicago, April 20, 1961, Cunningham Papers.

154 Quoted in Ibid. See also Cunningham, *The Blues*, 133–35.

155 Cunningham, *The Blues*, 132–36; Walter J. McNerney, interview by Lewis E. Weeks, transcript, 1979, Cunningham Papers.

156 Walter J. McNerney, interview by Odin W. Anderson, transcript, June 13, 1973, Cunningham Papers.

157 Cunningham, *The Blues*, 135; Blue Cross Association Annual Meeting, 1961; "Official Policy Statement Adopted by the American Hospital Association," January 4, 1962, Box 21, Grahame Papers.

158 Quoted in Blue Cross Association Annual Meeting, 1961. See also Alvin M. David to Robert Ball, January 27, 1964, Box 299, Commissioner's Correspondence, 1939–69, SSA, RG 47, NARA; Arthur E. Hess to Robert M. Ball, February 3, 1964, Box 299, Commissioner's Correspondence, 1939–69, SSA, RG 47, NARA.

159 "Blue Cross Participation in Social Security Hospital Insurance," April 28, 1964, Cohen Papers, SSA Archives; O'Brien to the President; Wilbur Cohen to the Secretary, May 15, 1964, Cohen Papers, SSA Archives; Zelizer, *Taxing America*, 219, 225.

160 Robert Ball to the Secretary, "Alternative Arrangements for Administering a Program of Hospital Insurance for the Aged," August 16, 1963, Box 299, Commissioner's Correspondence, 1939–69, SSA, RG 47, NARA.

161 AFL-CIO Department of Social Security, *Eldersnare: Promise Them Anything – But Give Them Kerr-Mills*, n.d., Cohen Papers, SSA Archives; O'Brien to the President.

162 Ball to the Secretary, "Alternative Arrangements for Administering a Program"; Robert M. Ball to Ellen Winston, October 8, 1963, Box 299, Commissioner's Correspondence, 1939–69, SSA, RG 47, NARA; Cunningham,

The Blues, 141–42. Social Security Commissioner Robert Ball later reflected on the influence that Blue Cross and AHA leaders had over the final Medicare bill: "We kept working on the provisions and negotiating new points and modifying them for political reasons and for administrative reasons." National Academy of Social Insurance, "Reflections on Implementing Medicare," January 31, 1992, Revolving Files, SSA Archives.

163 Harold Maybee, interview by Odin W. Anderson, transcript, November 14, 1972, Cunningham Papers; John Castellucci, interview by Odin W. Anderson, transcript, March 23, 1973, Cunningham Papers.

164 John Castellucci.

165 Corning, "Evolution of Medicare," chapter 4; "Compromise on Medical Plan Urged by Javits," *Los Angeles Times*, March 5, 1962, 27; "Compromise on Medical Care," *New York Times*, July 1, 1962, 112; Blumenthal and Morone, *The Heart of Power*, 154–57. The Anderson-Javits amendment proposed including all senior citizens, regardless of Social Security beneficiary status, and designated nonprofit plans and insurance companies to administer the hospital benefits portion of the program.

166 Gallup Poll, "Hopes and Fears," no. 1964–637POS (October 1964); Corning, "Evolution of Medicare," 110–11.

167 "Alternative Policy Positions Re Federal Legislative Proposals"; Grahame to Thore; Robert M. Ball to Sidney A. Saperstein and Alvin M. David, May 5, 1964, Box 299, Commissioner's Correspondence, 1939–69, SSA, RG 47, NARA.

168 Hacker, *Divided Welfare State*, 246–47; Zelizer, *Taxing America*, 229–30; Cohen to Feldman; Robert Neal, "Supplement to Annual Report of the General Manager," January 1, 1964, Box 24, Grahame Papers.

169 Campion, *AMA and U.S. Health Policy*, 271; Jill Quadagno, "Why the United States Has No National Health Insurance: Stakeholder Mobilization against the Welfare State, 1945–1996," *Journal of Health and Social Behavior* 45 (extra issue, 2004): 25–44.

170 Marmor, *Politics of Medicare*, 48.

171 The AMA's House of Delegates passed a resolution stating that every citizen lacking sufficient resources, "regardless of age," should receive medical care. Campion, *AMA and U.S. Health Policy*, 272–73.

172 Campion, *AMA and U.S. Health Policy*, 272–74; "Organizations: Eldercare v. Medicare," *Time*, February 19, 1965, www.time.com/time/magazine/article/0,9171,940919,00.html (accessed January 11, 2014).

173 American Medical Association, *Why the Doctors' Eldercare Program Is the Best Answer to the Health Care Needs of the Elderly ... It Offers Better Care than "Medicare,"* n.d., Cohen Papers, SSA Archives (emphasis in original).

174 American Medical Association, *Why the Doctors' Eldercare Program Is the Best Answer.*

175 ALC-HIAA-LIAA Task Force, "Report on Medicare for the Aged," January 8, 1965, Box 25, Grahame Papers; James L. Moorefield to Mr. Grahame, April 1, 1965, Box 14, Grahame Papers.

176 "GOP in Spot on Medicare," *Evening Star*, March 24, 1965, Box 14, Grahame Papers.

177 Marmor, *Politics of Medicare*, 48; Wilbur J. Cohen to the President, "Health Insurance for the Aged Proposal by Representative John Byrnes," January 29, 1965, Cohen Papers, SSA Archives; Zelizer, *Taxing America*, 239–40.

178 American Life Convention and Life Insurance Association of America to Presidents of Member Companies, April 22, 1965, Box 14, Grahame Papers; Wilbur J. Cohen, "Hospital Insurance for the Aged through Social Security: Developments Today," March 2, 1965, Cohen Papers, SSA Archives.

179 Marmor, *Politics of Medicare*, 49–53; Zelizer, *Taxing America*, 241–43, 247–49; Patashnik, *Putting Trust in the U.S. Budget*, 97–100; National Academy of Social Insurance, "Reflections on Implementing Medicare"; Cohen, "Hospital Insurance for the Aged through Social Security." Title XIX built on state programs funded through Social Security provisions that, since 1950, had allowed welfare officials to directly purchase medical services in order to provide health care for the poor. Under Medicaid, federal officials established guidelines to regulate state programs, but state policymakers largely determined beneficiary qualification rules and available benefits. Through the 2010 Patient Protection and Affordable Care Act, federal policymakers raised and standardized both income eligibility levels and minimum benefits. A 2012 Supreme Court ruling rendered the expansion optional. Although choosing to enlarge Medicaid will require state governments to spend significantly more per year on indigent health care, many states will accept the modification because the federal government will cover a large portion of expansion costs. On Medicaid, see Laura Katz Olson, *The Politics of Medicaid* (New York, 2010); Robert Stevens and Rosemary Stevens, *Welfare Medicine in America: A Case Study of Medicaid*, 2nd ed. (Piscataway, NJ, 2003); Jonathan Engel, *Poor People's Medicine: Medicaid and American Charity Care since 1965* (Durham, NC, 2006).

180 Moorefield to Grahame.

181 Campion, *AMA and U.S. Health Policy*, 275; Zelizer, *Taxing America*, 247, 250–51; Marmor, *Politics of Medicare*, 54–55.

182 Cunningham, *The Blues*, 146–47; Edward D. Berkowitz, *Robert Ball and the Politics of Social Security* (Madison, WI, 2003), 139–40.

183 Campion, *AMA and U.S. Health Policy*, 278–80, 287; Blumenthal and Morone, *The Heart of Power*, 198–201.

184 Quoted in Health Insurance Institute Report, "A Summary of Senate Finance Committee Hearings," May 5, 1965, Box 14, Grahame Papers.

185 Wilbur Cohen to Larry O'Brien, March 11, 1965, Cohen Papers, SSA Archives.

186 Ball to the Secretary, "Alternative Arrangements for Administering a Program"; National Association of Blue Shield Plans, "Responses to Questions Posed by Senator Clinton P. Anderson," May 17, 1965, BCBS D.C. Archives.

187 Wilbur J. Cohen to Lawrence F. O'Brien, January 6, 1965, Cohen Papers, SSA Archives; Wilbur J. Cohen to Orville F. Grahame, May 5, 1965, Box 14, Grahame Papers. Insurers recognized that Part B would be more difficult to manage than Part A because each of the program's designated geographical areas hosted many more physicians than hospitals.

188 Orville F. Grahame to John W. Joanis, April 1, 1965, Box 14, Grahame Papers; Earl Clark to General Agents, May 6, 1965, Box 14, Grahame Papers.

189 Wilson, Smith, and Miller, "Medicare and Private Benefit Plans."

190 ALC-HIAA-LIAA Task Force, "Report on Medicare for the Aged"; Moorefield to Grahame.

191 V. J. Skutt to Robert R. Neal, May 25, 1965, Box 14, Grahame Papers.

192 American Life Convention and Life Insurance Association of America to Presidents of Member Companies; "GOP in Spot on Medicare." The AMA and insurers also supported Senator Russell Long's (D, LA) unsuccessful amendment to have Medicare employ means testing and cover only catastrophic costs.

193 Health Insurance Institute Report, "A Summary of Senate Finance Committee Hearings," May 10, 1965, Box 14, Grahame Papers.

194 "National Association of Blue Shield Plans Guiding Principles," June 23, 1965, BCBS D.C. Archives. See also "Draft Statement of National Association of Blue Shield Plans before Senate Finance Committee, H.R. 6675," 1965, BCBS D.C. Archives. In a move similar to commercial insurers' request that policymakers strip Part B from Medicare, Blue Shield leaders petitioned senators to modify that portion of the program to more closely resemble the FEHBP. Their proposal called for a federally managed exchange through which insurers could sell policies to supplement government-provided hospital benefits. National Association of Blue Shield Plans, "Responses to Questions Posed by Senator Clinton P. Anderson."

195 Lyndon B. Johnson, "Remarks with President Truman at the Signing in Independence of the Medicare Bill," July 30, 1965, Gerhard Peters and John T. Woolley, *The American Presidency Project*, www.presidency.ucsb.edu/ws/?pid=27123 (accessed January 2, 2014).

196 Wilbur J. Cohen to Lawrence F. O'Brien, "Summary of Social Security-Medicare Bill – Tentative," July 21, 1965, Cohen Papers, SSA Archives.

197 Berkowitz, *Robert Ball and the Politics of Social Security*, 149–53; Bernard Tresnowski, interview by Odin W. Anderson, transcript, September 7, 1973, Cunningham Papers; Don Cohodes, interview, transcript, July 21, 1992, Cunningham Papers. It appears that NABSP leaders' gambit to outwardly display allegiance to the AMA while only faintly opposing Medicare was not entirely successful. In some states, medical society leaders specifically requested that the local Blue Shield plan not act as their Medicare administrator. Physicians made this appeal not only because they were angry about the nonprofit's weak political resistance to Medicare but also because Blue Shield plans often had more rigorous cost containment methods than did commercial companies (though, ultimately, this difference would not count for much in Medicare's administration). Furthermore, while the BCA negotiated one master contract for all Blue Cross plans that participated in Part A, the Blue Shield plans that did perform Medicare administration sidestepped the NABSP to work individually with federal officials. This development partially unraveled some of the gains that NABSP leaders had obtained under the FEHBP. See Chapter 5. Many medical society leaders and some local Blue

Shield administrators continued to distrust NABSP officials – they suspected them of viewing Medicare as a means toward augmenting the national association's power over constituent plans and toward sharing additional interests and fostering closer relations with Blue Cross. Blue Shield plans, nevertheless, administered Medicare under standardized federal contracts that varied only slightly by region.

198 Beatrix Hoffman, *Health Care for Some: Rights and Rationing in the United States since 1930* (Chicago, 2012), 131–33.
199 Campion, *AMA and U.S. Health Policy*, 281–83; "A.M.A. Head Predicts Medicare Boycott," *New York Times*, August 18, 1965, 18. See also "A.M.A. Delegates Back a 'Boycott,'" *New York Times*, May 15, 1965, 15; "New A.M.A. Chief Warns against Medicare Boycott," *New York Times*, June 21, 1965, 1; "A.M.A. Split on Proposals for a Boycott of Medicare," *New York Times*, June 22, 1965, 1.
200 Kotulak, "Bad Image Blamed for A.M.A. Shakeup"; Reed to Blasingame.
201 Campion, *AMA and U.S. Health Policy*, 300; Starr, *Social Transformation of American Medicine*, 388–93; Naomi Rogers, "'Caution: The AMA May Be Dangerous to Your Health': The Student Health Organizations (SHO) and American Medicine, 1965–1970," *Radical History Review* 80 (spring 2001): 5–34; Richard D. Lyons, "Protestors Seize Stage at A.M.A. Convention," *New York Times*, June 17, 1968, 41; "AMA Seeks Initiative in Programs for Poor, but Young Demonstrators Disrupt Parley," *Wall Street Journal*, July 14, 1969, 10; Sandra Blakeslee, "Protest Disrupts Meeting of A.M.A," *New York Times*, July 14, 1969, 1, 20; Richard D. Lyons, "Protest Groups Force A.M.A. into Closed Session in Chicago," *New York Times*, June 22, 1970, 1, 29.

8 Epilogue: The Limits of "Comprehensive" Reform, 1965–2010

1 "Medicine: Debate Over National Health Insurance," *Time*, October 12, 1970, http://time.com/time/magazine/article/0,9171,942350,00.html (accessed June 17, 2010); Paul Starr, *The Social Transformation of American Medicine: The Rise of a Sovereign Profession and the Making of a Vast Industry* (New York, 1982), 384.
2 For example, Rudy Abramson, "Medical Cost Increase Highest in 18 Years," *Los Angeles Times*, June 28, 1967, 7; Edward Palmer, "Paying the Price for Health," *Chicago Tribune*, October 29, 1967, 28; Harold M. Schmeck, Jr., "Spiraling Medical Costs Reflect Deficiencies in U.S. Health Care," *New York Times*, April 28, 1968, 1, 79; Harold M. Schmeck, Jr., "President Warns of 'Massive Crisis' in Health Care," *New York Times*, July 11, 1969, 1, 40; "Holding Down Health Costs," *New York Times*, September 30, 1969, 46; John A. Hamilton, "Medicine; Grave Crisis over Rising Costs," *New York Times*, October 26, 1969, E6; Eve Edstrom, "Meany Blames Spiraling Health Costs on 'Profiteering,'" *Washington Post*, November 14, 1969, A2; Richard D. Lyons, "Dilemma in Health Care: Rising Costs and Demand," *New York Times*, September 13, 1971, 1, 28. For the discussion in this paragraph, see also Starr, *Social Transformation of American Medicine*, 381–84.

3 "The Doctor Shortage," *Washington Post*, June 26, 1971, A14.
4 "Infant Mortality: A U.S. Disgrace," *Los Angeles Times*, December 24, 1970, A2; Lynn Lilliston, "Minority Babies Chances Improved," *Los Angeles Times*, September 11, 1969, E1, 5–7, 9; Anthony Lewis, "Physician, Heal Thyself," *New York Times*, October 2, 1971, 31.
5 Quoted in Starr, *Social Transformation of American Medicine*, 381.
6 Harry Schwartz, "Health Insurance: A Fight for Survival," *New York Times*, October 30, 1977, 121.
7 Quoted in "Health Insurance at the Crossroads," *National Underwriter* 76 (January 8, 1972): 60. See also "Industry Critics – A Proper Response," *National Underwriter* 76 (October 28, 1972): 14; Robert Cunningham III and Robert M. Cunningham, Jr., *The Blues: A History of the Blue Cross and Blue Shield System* (DeKalb, IL, 1997), 178–79.
8 "The HMO – Time to Embrace a Fact of Life," *National Underwriter* 76 (June 3, 1972): 15.
9 Cunningham, *The Blues*, 195–99; Walter J. McNerney, interview by Lewis E. Weeks, transcript, 1979, Cunningham Papers; Walter J. McNerney, interview by Odin W. Anderson, transcript, June 13, 1973, Cunningham Papers.
10 Frank D. Campion, *The AMA and U.S. Health Policy since 1940* (Chicago, 1984), 291–96.
11 Ibid., 300–301, 306–11; Victor Cohn, "AMA Cautiously Looks to Future," *Washington Post*, June 23, 1968, A17; Richard D. Lyons, "A.M.A. Presents Its Plan for Health Insurance," *New York Times*, February 26, 1971, 18.
12 Campion, *AMA and U.S. Health Policy*, 300.
13 "AMA Seeks Initiative in Programs for Poor, but Young Demonstrators Disrupt Parley," *Wall Street Journal*, July 14, 1969, 10.
14 Starr, *Social Transformation of American Medicine*, 388–93; Naomi Rogers, "'Caution: The AMA May Be Dangerous to Your Health': The Student Health Organizations (SHO) and American Medicine, 1965–1970," *Radical History Review* 80 (spring 2001): 5–34.
15 "Report of the Committee to Study AMA Objectives and Basic Programs," *JAMA* 169 (March 7, 1959): 1077–83; Starr, *Social Transformation of American Medicine*, 398; Robert Pear, "Clinton's Health Plan; A.M.A. Rebels over Health Plan in Major Challenge to President," *New York Times*, September 30, 1993, http://nytimes.com/1993/03/30/us/clinton-s-health-plan-ama-rebels-over-health-plan-major-challenge-president.html (accessed July 12, 2010); Roger Collier, "American Medical Association Membership Woes Continue," *Canadian Medical Association Journal* 183 (August 9, 2011): E713–14. Today, approximately one-quarter of physicians belong to the AMA. Moreover, many AMA members do not pay their full membership dues, which are instead covered by the hospital or medical facility where they work.
16 Campion, *AMA and U.S. Health Policy*, 305–10, 312–17; "Medicine: Debate over National Health Insurance"; Mike Gorman, "The Impact of National Health Insurance on Delivery of Health Care," *American Journal of Public Health* 61 (May 1971): 962–71; Jill Quadagno, *Why the U.S. Has No National Health Insurance* (New York, 2005), 112–13; Starr, *Social Transformation of American Medicine*, 394.

17 Starr, *Social Transformation of American Medicine*, 394–95; Campion, *AMA and U.S. Health Policy*, 311; David Blumenthal and James A. Morone, *The Heart of Power: Health and Politics in the Oval Office* (Berkeley, 2009), 227–42. On business leaders' interest in social programs, including health care programs, as important for labor force development, see Cathie Jo Martin, *Stuck in Neutral: Business and the Politics of Human Capital Investment Policy* (Princeton, 2000), 79–87.

18 As insurance companies increasingly established direct financing relations with physicians (see Chapter 6), insurers had more latitude to create policyholder networks and restrict their availability to certain providers. The AMA no longer had the power to demand that insurance companies and plans include every doctor who wished to participate.

19 "Health Insurance at the Crossroads," 60–62; "Republican Task Force on National Health Care Hears HIA Spokesman," *National Underwriter* 76 (March 11, 1972): 14; Robert J. Cole, "Health Legislation: A Progress Report," *New York Times*, February 22, 1972, 53, 56. The HIAA now sometimes went by the acronym "HIA."

20 "Health Care Delivery in the 1970's," *Transactions of Society of Actuaries* 22 (January 1970): D55–308. One must speculate whether insurance company leaders, if they believe they are being pressed into unprofitability by Patient Protection and Affordable Care Act (ACA) mandates and regulations, will ultimately request a similar plan. See the discussion of the (ACA) below.

21 Cunningham, *The Blues*, 188–90.

22 "Blue Cross Plans and the Blue Cross Association," September 1975, BCBS Philadelphia Archives; "Blue Shield to Play 'Big Role' in NHI," *Pennsylvania Blue Shield Management Newsletter* 4 (April 1974): 1, BCBS Philadelphia Archives; "Statement of Walter J. McNerney, Presented before the Subcommittee on Health of the Committee on Ways and Means," April 15, 1975, BCBS Philadelphia Archives. Although nonprofit leaders were reluctant to officially endorse any one proposal, McNerney recommended that legislators consider universal coverage using the Federal Employees Health Benefits Program (FEHBP) as a model.

23 Quoted in Campion, *AMA and U.S. Health Policy*, 307.

24 Cohn, "AMA Cautiously Looks to Future," A17; Lyons, "A.M.A. Presents Its Plan for Health Insurance," 18; Campion, *AMA and U.S. Health Policy*, 306–11, 316–19, 322–24.

25 Blumenthal and Morone, *The Heart of Power*, 242–46; Campion, *AMA and U.S. Health Policy*, 320–24; Starr, *Social Transformation of American Medicine*, 404–5.

26 Marie Gottschalk, *The Shadow Welfare State: Labor, Business, and the Politics of Health Care in the United States* (Ithaca, NY, 2000), chapter 4; Starr, *Social Transformation of American Medicine*, 404–5, 412–13.

27 See Lawrence D. Brown, "Technocratic Corporatism and Administrative Reform in Medicare," *JHPPL* 10 (fall 1985): 579–99, for an overview of how federal officials, in their attempt to constrain aged insurance costs, have developed a pattern of structured negotiations with service providers.

28 Campion, *AMA and U.S. Health Policy*, 326.

29 Helen Smits, "PSROs: Origins, Directions, and Changing Assumptions," *Bulletin of the New York Academy of Medicine* 58 (January–February 1982): 11–18; Starr, *Social Transformation of American Medicine*, 400–403; Campion, *AMA and U.S. Health Policy*, 327–34; Lawrence D. Brown, "Political Conditions of Regulatory Effectiveness: The Case of PSROs and HSAs," *Bulletin of the New York Academy of Medicine* 58 (January–February 1982): 77–90.

30 In 1982, legislators replaced PSROs with Utilization and Quality Control Peer Review Organizations (PROs), which were consolidated groups that not only reviewed utilization necessity but also emphasized improving and standardizing the quality of care. Although the federal government reimbursed their services, physicians sponsored PROs. Renamed Quality Improvement Organizations in 2002, these associations were also tasked with gathering statistical data by institution and geographical location for comparison and assessment.

31 Lawrence D. Brown, *Politics and Health Care Organization: HMOs as Federal Policy* (Washington, D.C., 1983); Starr, *Social Transformation of American Medicine*, 400–403, 407–8; Quadagno, *Why the U.S. Has No National Health Insurance*, 114–18. On the Carter administration's attempt to breathe new life into HMO legislation, see Joseph L. Falkson, "The Rediscovery of HMOs," *JHPPL* 2 (spring 1977): 288–93. At some points during legislative debates, it was unclear whether policymakers would permit commercial insurance companies to participate in the program. They ultimately did. The 1973 act supplied loans and grants to HMOs while requiring businesses with more than twenty-five employees to offer HMO coverage if a qualifying group existed nearby and asked to be included. However, few organizations sought government subsidies because the legislation stipulated that federally funded HMOs had to charge uniform community rates while simultaneously offering expensive benefits, such as coverage for mental health and drug and alcohol abuse treatment.

32 "Death of the Blues and the Privates," *Medicare Report* (May 27, 1970), Cunningham Papers; "The HMO – Time to Embrace a Fact of Life," 14.

33 Walter J. McNerney, "Blue Cross and Group Practice Prepayment," Annual Meeting of Member Plans of the Blue Cross Association, April 1–2, 1970, Cunningham Papers; J. C. Woosley to Chief Plan Executives, "Alternative Delivery Systems Plan Status Report," May 1, 1973, BCBS Philadelphia Archives; Cunningham, *The Blues*, 180–83, 200–201; Irwin Miller, *American Health Care Blues: Blue Cross, HMOs, and Pragmatic Reform since 1960* (New Brunswick, NJ, 1996).

34 Starr, *Social Transformation of American Medicine*, 402; Theodore R. Marmor, "New York's Blue Cross and Blue Shield, 1934–1990: The Complicated Politics of Nonprofit Regulation," *JHPPL* 16 (winter 1991): 761–92; Brown, "Political Conditions of Regulatory Effectiveness," 77–90.

In 1974, Congress passed the Employee Retirement Income Security Act (ERISA) to regulate employer-provided pensions. Buried in the legislation was a measure exempting company-funded or self-insured health policies from state regulation. The provision encouraged increasing numbers of businesses to underwrite, or assume the financial risks of, their employee group's medical care in order to avoid state laws requiring that insurance policies offer certain expensive benefits, such as drug and alcohol addiction treatment or chiropractic care. Although increasing numbers of companies became, in effect, their own insurers, most of them continued to rely on insurance company administration and cost containment procedures. Gottschalk, *Shadow Welfare State*, 40–41, 54–57.

35 Schwartz, "Health Insurance: A Fight for Survival," 121.

36 Blue Shield Association, *The Health Care Maze: A Discussion of the Cost of Health Care* (Chicago, 1978), 19–21; "Blue Shield Starts Plan for 2d Opinion on Some Surgery," *New York Times*, December 3, 1975, Cunningham Papers; Linda C. Busek, "They Stopped Blue Shield from Pulling an Aetna," *Medical Economics* (April 16, 1973): 79, Cunningham Papers.

37 Schwartz, "Health Insurance: A Fight for Survival," 121.

38 A variety of financing and delivery types fall under the label of managed care; including Health Maintenance Organizations, Independent Practice Associations, Preferred Provider Organizations, and Point of Service Organizations.

39 Cunningham, *The Blues*, 183–85; Rick Mayes and Robert A. Berenson, *Medicare Prospective Payment and the Shaping of U.S. Health Care* (Baltimore, 2006). Similarly, many of the cost containment instruments used in private managed care arrangements were incorporated into Medicare Part C, which passed with the Balanced Budget Act of 1997. Rather than remunerating providers with fee-for-service payments, Medicare Part C, which supplied Medicare Advantage Plans, reimbursed doctors with per-capita fees and restricted beneficiaries to seeing physicians who participated in set networks. To convince beneficiaries to subscribe to the plans, Medicare Part C offered coverage for additional services beyond the traditional Medicare program.

40 Peter R. Kongstvedt, ed., *The Managed Health Care Handbook*, 4th ed. (Gaithersburg, MD, 2001); Theda Skocpol, *Boomerang: Health Care Reform and the Turn against Government* (New York, 1996), 168–71; Beatrix Hoffman, *Health Care for Some: Rights and Rationing in the United States since 1930* (Chicago, 2012), 190–95; Stephen Blakely, "The Backlash against Managed Care," *Nation's Business* (July 1998), http://findarticles.com/p/article/mi_m1154/is_n7_v86/ai_20797610/pg_2/ (accessed July 3, 2010).

41 Paul Starr, "What Happened to Health Care Reform?" *American Prospect* (winter 1995): 20–31; Pear, "Clinton's Health Plan"; "AMA to Seek 37 Changes to Clinton's Health Plan," *New York Times*, January 13, 1994, www.deseretnews.com/article/330875/AMA-TO-SEEK-37-CHANGES-IN-CLINTONS-HEALTH-PLAN.html (accessed June 10, 2010). See also Paul Starr, *Remedy and Reaction: The Peculiar American Struggle over Health Care Reform* (New Haven, CT, 2011), part II.

42 Skocpol, *Boomerang*, 134–39. See also Starr, *Remedy and Reaction*, 116.

43 The Patient Protection and Affordable Care Act was the Senate bill signed into law on March 23. The House sent an amended version of the bill, the Health Care and Education Reconciliation Act of 2010, to the president a week later.

44 Representative Anh "Joseph" Cao of Louisiana was the only Republican who voted for the November 2009 House-passed version of the bill. However,

Cao switched his vote and joined the rest of Republicans to oppose the final version of the legislation.

45 Starr, *Remedy and Reaction*, 187, 198, 218–19; Laura Meckler, "Insurers Offer to End Prices Tied to Illness," *Wall Street Journal*, March 25, 2009, 4; Robert Pear, "Health Insurers Ease Stance on Pre-existing Conditions," *New York Times*, March 25, 2009, B1; Reed Abelson, "Health Insurers Balk at Changes for Small Business," *New York Times*, June 3, 2009, B1; Reed Abelson, "Insurers' Cooperation on Reform Put to Test," *International Herald Tribune*, August 6, 2009, 4; J. James Rohack, "What AMA Wants," *Washington Times*, October 27, 2009, 18; Dave Michaels, "Doctors Seek Balance on Health Care Reform, Resolution Supports 'Public Option,'" *Dallas Morning News*, June 18, 2009, 1D.

46 McLean Robbins and Molly Bernhart, "AHIP Shoots for the Moon with New Health Insurance Proposal," *Employee Benefit News*, August 1, 2008. As health care legislation neared passage, private health interests expressed dissatisfaction with various aspects of the bills. For example, insurance leaders worried that the proposed tax penalties on individuals who failed to purchase coverage were far too low. AHIP officials protested that premiums would skyrocket if companies had to accept applicants with preexisting conditions while young, healthy subscribers could opt to pay a small tax penalty in lieu of purchasing insurance and then buy coverage if they got sick. John Fritze, "Message Evolves," *USA Today*, October 19, 2009, 5A; Ceci Connolly, "Health Insurers Emerge as Obama's Top Foe in Reform Effort," *Washington Post*, October 14, 2009, A06.

47 Amy Goldstein, "Influential AMA's Support for Reform Is Far from Certain," *Washington Post*, October 16, 2009, A4. Physicians sought a reprieve from Medicare payment cuts created by the sustainable growth rate formula enacted in the Balanced Budget Act of 1997. After the year 2000, the formula began generating cuts to physician reimbursements, which Congress often reversed with bipartisan legislation. The AMA wanted to reform the process so doctors would have more certainty about their compensation payments year to year.

Index